Walking Southern California

Other books in the *Walking the West* series:

Walking the East Mojave
Walking Los Angeles
Walking Santa Barbara
Walking the California Coast
Walking California's State Parks

Walking
Southern California

A Day Hiker's Guide

John McKinney

HarperCollins*West*

A Division of HarperCollinsPublishers

HarperCollins West and the author, in association with the Rainforest Action Network, will facilitate the planting of two trees for every one tree used in the manufacture of this book.

This book was previously published as *Day Hiker's Guide to Southern California* by Olympus Press in 1992.

FIRST HARPERCOLLINS EDITION

LIBRARY OF CONGRESS CATALOGING-IN-PUBLICATION DATA
McKinney, John
    Walking Southern California: a day hiker's guide / John
McKinney.
      p. cm. — (Walking the West)
      Rev. ed. of: Day hiker's guide to Southern California.
© 1992.
      ISBN 0-06-258511-8
      1. Hiking — California, Southern — Guidebooks. 2.
California, Southern — Description and travel.   I. McKinney,
John, 1952– , Day hiker's guide to Southern California. II.
Title. III. Series.
GV199.42.C22S685   1994 93-24210
917.94'9—dc20 CIP

 96 97 98 ❖/RRD H 10 9 8 7 6 5

Contents

Chapter 4: San Gabriel Mountains 121

A Foreword from the Field

No GUIDEBOOK has had such enthusiastic field-testers! By field-testers I mean the many readers of my weekly *Los Angeles Times* hiking column who took my words to the woods, deserts and coast, then wrote to me about their experiences on the trail.

By enthusiastic I mean the high you've felt high atop a mountain, that great aerobic workout you enjoyed, the fascination in the eyes of your children when you introduced them to nature's marvels.

I like to think I'm a rather enthusiastic field-tester myself. My job, as *Los Angeles Times* hiking columnist, is to take a hike and write about it. Every week I wander the world's trails looking for lonely beaches, desert dunes, dramatic summits, hills ablaze with wildflowers. (Yes, it's a dirty job, but somebody's got to do it.)

My enthusiasm increases every time I hear parents tell me how, with the help of one of my columns or books, they introduced their children to the wonders of nature. And my enthusiasm is boosted when I learn how fellow conservationists have managed to preserve another special place to walk and to give to future generations.

Although I've taken readers on journeys afoot around America, from the Olympic Rainforest to the Florida Everglades, and around the world from the mountains of Greece to the beaches of Tahiti, it's the hikes around Southern California that invariably prompt the most reader response. Let's face facts: it's easier, faster and a whole lot cheaper to enjoy the alpine air of Mount Baldy than to head off to Switzerland.

When you hike Southern California, you see the world—the Mediterranean in the Santa Monica Mountains, Santa Ynez Mountains and the Channel Islands; Little Switzerland atop Mt. San Jacinto and the San Gorgonio Wilderness; the Sahara Desert in the tall dunes of the East Mojave.

Included in this guide are many of my favorite Southern California mountain, coast and desert hikes. Experienced hikers will recognize some familiar terrain—Mts. Baldy, San Gorgonio and San Jacinto—but will find some new trails to travel. Newcomers to the Southland, and less-experienced hikers, will find helpful introductions to the land—the major mountain ranges, the forests, deserts, and the coastline.

This guide makes no attempt to cram every hike in Southern California between the covers of a book; I think it a rather silly exercise to catalog every hike in Los Angeles County or in the Coachella Valley as some guides have done. I want you to have a great day in the great outdoors so I left out many walkable but not-so-wonderful trails. You can imagine that a "professional" hiker like myself encounters a lot of turkey trails; that is to say, paths that start nowhere and go nowhere, trails battered by nature or neglected by park officials to the point where I decided they are too unsafe for you to use.

So with all this enthusiastic field-testing—mine, yours and that of park authorities—are you holding perfection in your hands?

Nope. Trails change over time. Like every hiker, I hate seeing a good trail go bad, but regrettably it happens. The ravages of fire and flood, rampant real estate development and bureaucratic neglect can ruin a favorite path. While out hiking, if you happen across a neglected, hazardous or overgrown trail, please report it to the relevant ranger or administrator. Only if you make your concerns known will conditions improve. It's up to all of us to preserve our trails—and the precious wild land they help us explore.

I hope that in some small way this book, in addition to suggesting some enjoyable hikes, contributes to a better understanding of the unique and fragile ecology of Southern California.

—J.M.

Author John McKinney in the field

Understanding Day Hiking in Southern California

THE LAND WE CALL Southern California is an island, ecologically isolated from the rest of the continent by a combination of geographic and climatic factors. Helen Hunt Jackson once said of Southern California: "It's an island on the land." Carey McWilliams popularized the phrase in his definitive history of the region, *Southern California: An Island on the Land*. The land's island nature is apparent when you enter it from the north or east. When you round Point Conception and the north-south orientation of California becomes east-west, it is obvious that you have entered a unique geographical province. If you come to Southern California from the east through Cajon Pass or San Gorgonio Pass, the change is immediately evident. The light is softer, the climate more temperate.

The land includes seven counties: Santa Barbara, Ventura, Los Angeles, Orange, Riverside, San Bernardino and San Diego. Usually, only those parts of San Bernardino, Riverside and San Diego Counties "west of the mountains" are considered to be part of Southern California, but a case can be made for including all of them and adding Imperial County as well. Some boosters insist Southern California's northern boundary is San Luis Obispo or even the Monterey County line, but geographically and ecologically it's at Point Conception. Southern California is the land south of the Transverse Range, which knifes across California toward the Pacific, just north of Santa Barbara.

Southern California is protected from the Mojave Desert by the San Bernardino and San Gabriel Mountain Ranges on the east and walled off from the San Joaquin Valley by other Transverse Ranges. The lowlands are covered with alluvial fans formed by earth washed down from the mountains. The coastal plain is "watered" by some of the driest rivers in the west: the Los Angeles, Mojave, San Gabriel and Santa Ana. Mark Twain may have been joking about them when he said he'd fallen into a California river and "come out all dusty."

Compass directions can be confusing to both newcomers and oldtimers. "Up the coast" in other parts of the world is usually taken to mean north, but it's not north in Southern California. To travel north from L.A., you head directly into the Mojave Desert, crossing east-west trending mountains in the process. If you traveled a straight line, as the crow flies, from San Bernardino to Santa Barbara, you would travel 137 miles west and only 27 miles north.

Carey McWilliams has suggested that "The analyst of California is like a navigator who is trying to chart a course in a storm: the instruments will not work; the landmarks are lost; and the maps make little sense." California may be geographically cockeyed and Southern California even more so, but we day hikers, before heading for the hills, ought to get our bearings. We need to find a few landmarks and consult a map. Orienting yourself to Southern California isn't that difficult. Try this:

Southern California Geography Made Easy

Get yourself an Auto Club map of California or one of those that gas stations used to give out free. Spread it on the floor. (This is hands-on learning, so if you have small hands, you might want to borrow a friend with larger ones.)

Put your thumb on Santa Barbara, your right pinkie on San Diego and spread your fingers in as wide a fan as you can manage. One of the first things you may notice is that your palm covers the L.A. Basin. Keep your palm firmly pressed down on L.A. to keep it from spreading into the wilderness. Look at your thumb. Above it is Point Conception, the northernmost point of Southern California. Above Santa Barbara are the Santa Ynez Mountains and beyond are those parts of the Los Padres National Forest we call the Santa Barbara Backcountry.

Along your index finger are the San Gabriel Mountains and the Angeles National Forest. (Careful! Don't get your finger pinched in the San Andreas Fault.) Your middle finger is in the San Bernardino Mountains. Near the eastern terminus of this range is Mount San Gorgonio, the highest peak in Southern California.

Between your middle and ring fingers, paralleling the coast in Orange Country are the Santa Ana Mountains, protected by the Cleveland National Forest. At the tip of your ring finger at the north end of Anza-Borrego Desert State Park lie the Santa Rosa Mountains. Take note of the Colorado Desert and farther to the north, the vast Mojave Desert.

Due east from your pinkie is the southern part of the the Cleveland National Forest, as well as the Palomar and Cuyamaca Mountain Ranges.

Now that you're oriented, raise that right hand of yours and pledge to preserve, protect and enjoy these places.

How to Use This Book

First decide where you want to hike. A palm oasis? An alpine meadow? A deserted beach? Consult our Southland map. Pick a trail number in your geographical area of interest. Once you've selected a number, turn to the corresponding hike description in the main body of the book.

Unsure of what to expect in the Santa Monica, San Bernardino or Cuyamaca Mountains? Read the appropriate chapter introductions.

There are 144 trails in this guide. Add the suggested options and you can design about 300 different hikes. Beneath the name of the trail is the trailhead and one or more destinations. Every day hike in this book has a soul and a goal. You provide the soul; this guide will provide the goals. We're a goal-oriented society and we hikers are no exception. We hike for majestic views or for the best fishing spot, not just to be out there. Some day hikers collect peaks the way motorhome drivers collect decals.

Mileage, expressed in round-trip figures, follows each destination. The hikes in this guide range from 2 to 20 miles, with the majority in the 5- to 10-mile range. Gain or loss in elevation follows the mileage. In matching a hike to your ability, you'll want to consider both mileage and elevation as well as condition of the trail, terrain, and season. Hot, exposed chaparral or miles of boulder-hopping can make a short hike seem long.

Use the following guideline: A hike suitable for beginners and children would be less than 5 miles with an elevation gain of less than 700 to 800 feet. A moderate hike is considered a hike in the 5- to 10-mile range, with under a 2,000 foot elevation gain. You should be reasonably fit for these. Preteens sometimes find the going difficult. Hikes over 10 miles, and those with more than a 2,000 foot gain are for experienced hikers in top form.

Season is the next item to consider. Although Southern California is one of the few places in the country that offers four-season hiking, some climactic restrictions must be heeded. You can hike some of the trails in this guide all of the time, all of the trails some of the time, but not all of the trails all of the time. Season recommendations are based partly on hiker comfort and partly on legal restrictions.

Those recommendations based on comfort can sometimes be disregarded by intrepid mountaineers. You can, if you so desire, hike to the top of Mount San Jacinto in the dead of winter, but you better bring snowshoes. It's possible to hike in the Mojave Desert in the middle of summer, but you'd better bring a water truck or a camel. Seasonal recommendations based on legal restrictions must not be disregarded. Closure for fire season is the chief restriction in certain state park and national forest areas. A few trails in this guide may be impassable in winter and spring due to high water. Relevant fire and flood information has been included in the hike description.

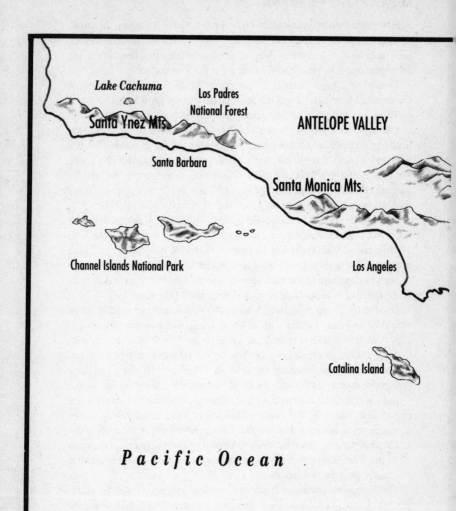

Lake Cachuma

Los Padres
National Forest

Santa Ynez Mts.

ANTELOPE VALLEY

Santa Barbara

Santa Monica Mts.

Channel Islands National Park

Los Angeles

Catalina Island

Pacific Ocean

Where would you like to hike?

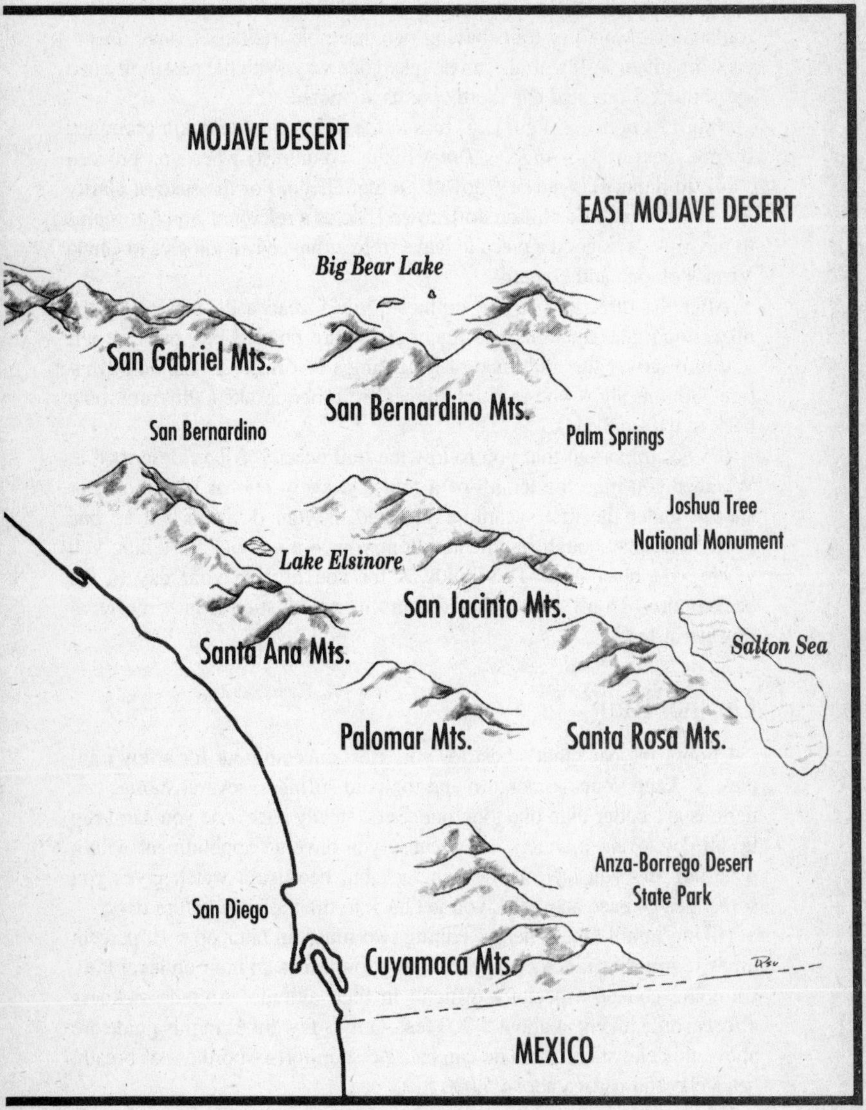

MOJAVE DESERT

EAST MOJAVE DESERT

Big Bear Lake

San Gabriel Mts.

San Bernardino Mts.

San Bernardino

Palm Springs

Joshua Tree
National Monument

Lake Elsinore

San Jacinto Mts.

Salton Sea

Santa Ana Mts.

Palomar Mts.

Santa Rosa Mts.

Anza-Borrego Desert
State Park

San Diego

Cuyamaca Mts.

MEXICO

A palm oasis? An alpine meadow? A deserted beach?

An introduction to each hike describes what you'll see along the trail: plants, animals, panoramic views. You'll also learn about the geologic and human history of the region.

Directions to trailhead take you from the nearest major highway to trailhead parking. For trails having two desirable trailheads, directions to each are given. A few trails can be hiked one way, with the possibility of a car shuttle. Suggested car shuttle points are noted.

You may notice a slight L.A. bias to the directions (no doubt prompted by my years as *Los Angeles Times* hiking columnist) when you proceed "up" to Santa Barbara or "down" to San Diego. For the sake of clarity and orientation, I've chosen downtown L.A. as a reference point. It seems to me, L.A. is as good a place to leave from as any. My apologies to Chula Vista, Pomona and Oxnard.

After the directions to the trailhead, you'll read a description of the hike. Important junctions and major sights are pointed out, but I've left you to discover the multitude of little things that make a hike an adventure. Options allow you to climb higher or farther or take a different route back to the trailhead.

It's not important that you follow the trail exactly as I've described it. Whether you hike the length of a trail and every one of its options, or snooze under the first sycamore you find, is your decision and no one else's. There's enough regimentation in your life without me telling you where you must hike. This guide is for you to plan your day in the backcountry. Don't stick your nose in this guide; stick it in some wildflowers instead.

On the Trail

Choose the pace that's best for you. Rest once an hour for a few minutes. To keep your momentum and to avoid stiffness, several shorter rest periods are better than one long one. Set a steady pace, one you can keep up all day. Wear a watch, not because you have an appointment with a waterfall and you have to be punctual, but because a watch gives you some idea of pace and helps you get back to the trailhead before dark.

Hiking uphill takes energy. Hiking two miles an hour up a 10 percent grade requires as much energy as hiking four miles an hour on level trail. Climbing can be especially difficult in high altitude. Altitude sickness affects some hikers at about 8,000 feet. Only a few hikes in this guide are above this elevation. Altitude can cause discomfort—shortness of breath, headache and nausea above 5,000 feet.

Hiking alone or with company is strictly a matter of personal preference. Most rangers warn you never to hike alone, primarily because they think most hikers are inexperienced, uncoordinated or both, and they hate to make rescues. Having two or three in your party is a definite advantage if something goes wrong; someone can go for help. Hiking with a group is a good idea for first-time hikers. Most inexperienced hikers are uncomfortable going solo.

Alas, backcountry travelers are not always immune from urban attitudes, stresses and crimes. While most of our Southland parks and preserves are far safer than our urban environment, hikers—particularly women hikers—must be aware that unsavory characters are not unknown on the trail. Your "street smarts" coupled with your trail sense are two keys to avoiding trouble.

Sometimes, after a few hikes, a craving for solitude develops—by which time you should be able to take care of yourself on the trail. There's a lot to be said for solitary hiking, as the writings of Thoreau, Whitman and Muir would seem to indicate.

Day Hiking Through the Seasons

Many have sung praises of Southern California's Mediterranean climate. Relentless sunshine, winter and summer, is how the climate is usually stereotyped. But the semi-tropical stereotype holds true only in coastal regions and only at certain times of the year. There is nothing Mediterranean about the climate of the Mojave Desert or the San Jacinto high country. In Southern California's backcountry, seasons arrive with clarity and distinction. Day hikers can find trails that are "in season" in every month of the year.

Winter brings snow to mountains in the Angeles, San Bernardino and Los Padres National Forests. Rain visits the coastal lowlands. Deciduous trees and shrubs lose their leaves. Some animals hibernate or become torpid.

But winter doesn't mean an end to all of nature's activities in Southern California, particularly in the lowland valleys and deserts. January is a fine time to take a beach hike, to visit shores laid bare by minus tides, or to see what treasure winter storms have cast ashore. In February, the desert begins to bloom. February and March, last of the winter months, are often looked upon by many Southern Californians as the first months of spring. Day hikers are guaranteed solitude in these months. High country trails are covered with snow and those on the lower slopes are muddy going.

Spring comes early to Southern California. Even the chaparral, so dull gray in other seasons, looks inviting. Ceanothus covers the lower slopes of the Santa Barbara Backcountry, the Santa Monica Mountains and San Gabriel Mountains with its dainty white and blue blossoms. In March, the giant coreopsis on Anacapa Island grows wild. As spring temperatures increase, flowers in the hotter Colorado Desert diminish, but those in the higher Mojave Desert arrive with a flourish. In June, the flower show moves to the high country of the Transverse Ranges. Lemon lilies appear streamside and lupine everywhere. Flocks of birds go about the business of building nests, laying eggs, raising young.

In summer, snowmelt-swollen creeks water emerald-green meadows. Scarlet-stemmed snow plant emerges in the pine forests. By August, even the highest peaks have lost their mantle of snow and day hikers can stand atop their summits and sign the hiker's register. A beach hike in the middle of summer is a pleasure. With the sun on your back, the surf at your feet and miles of beach in front of you, summer seems endless.

Autumn has its critics and its fans. Some say there's little use for a day that begins with frost, becomes hot enough to sunburn your nose by noon, and has you shivering by sunset. Wiser heads, those attached to day hikers no doubt, believe autumn is the best of all seasons. The high country is crisp, but still inviting, and desert washes have cooled. Autumn colors oaks, dogwoods, willows and sycamores in the Cuyamaca and Palomar Mountains with reds and golds. There's enough color change to satisfy even the most homesick New Englander.

Day Hiking Hints

Many day hikes require little more equipment than comfortable shoes, yet hikers often overburden themselves with such nonessentials as hunting knives, hatchets, and propane stoves. The idea with equipment is to take only what you need. You want to get so comfortable with your equipment that you don't think about it; what little you need is on your back and what you don't need is far away.

Footwear: Day hiking begins and ends with the feet. You've no doubt seen hikers wearing everything from old sneakers to World War II combat boots. For decades, lug-soled boots have been considered mandatory, but if you're carrying a day pack over easy terrain you don't need a heavy pair of boots. Running shoes can serve to get you started. But if you do much hiking over rough terrain, a good pair of boots is necessay and well worth the money. A lightweight pair with a Vibram sole will do nicely. Don't buy more boot than you need. Blisters can ruin any hike, so be sure to break-in your boots before you hit the trail. Walk around town and be sure your feet develop a callous indifference to your boots.

A number of fine walking shoes and running shoe/hiking boot combinations on the market will give you miles of comfortable walking.

Clothing: You have most of what you need lying around the house. A T-shirt layered with a cotton shirt that buttons gives you lots of temperature regulating possibilities. Add a wool shirt and a windbreaker with a hood and you'll be protected against sudden changes in temperatures.

Shorts are useful much of the year in Southern California. Test your shorts to make sure they're not too tight. Step up on a chair and if they pull around the groin, butt or thigh, they're too tight.

For cooler days or walking through brush, a sturdy pair of long pants is necessary.

Hats prevent the brain from frying and protect from heat loss when it is cold. Sunglasses are a big help when walking over snow or on hot, exposed slopes. Make sure you buy a pair that provides UV protection.

For protection from rain, cheap ponchos are okay unless you walk through brush; the Boy Scout ones aren't too bad. Some of the new breathable, high-tech fabric laminate jackets are superb, but expensive.

Food: On a day hike, weight is no problem, so you can pack whatever you wish. Remember to pack out what you pack in. The day you hike is not the day to diet. There's a lot of calorie burning on a hike and quite an energy cost. You'll need all your strength, particularly on steep grades. Gorp (trail mix with fruit, nuts, raisins, and M&M's) is good high-octane fuel. A sandwich, fruit and cookies make a good lunch. A more romantic repast—sourdough bread, a fine cheese and a bottle of chablis—is also nice. But avoid a big lunch. Exertion after a big lunch sets up a competition between your stomach and your legs and your legs lose, leading to weakness and indigestion.

Water: It's still possible to drink from some backcountry streams and springs without ill effect, but each individual water source should be carefully scrutinized. Reluctantly, I must advise you to do what I do: Don't drink untreated water in Southern California. Many hikers assume water is pure and 48 hours later have a queasy feeling that tells them that their assumption was wrong. Water may harbor the organism Giardia Lamblia, one of the causes of "traveler's diarrhea." When you approach that stream, Sierra cup in hand, think about what may be upstream. A campground? Cows? High rushing mountain streams are usually safer than stagnant ponds. Bring purification tablets or a portable filtering system and use them if you have the slightest doubt about water quality.

First Aid Kit: A standard kit supplement with an ace bandage in the event of hiker's knee or a sprained ankle. Take moleskin for blisters. Insect repellant won't stop mosquitos from buzzing around but it will inhibit their biting.

Day Pack or "Summit Pack": A day pack is a soft frameless pack that attaches to your shoulders and sometimes includes a hip band or waist belt for support. A good one will last a lifetime. Those thin cotton or nylon bike bags or book bags won't hold up well. Shoulder pads are a nice feature in a day pack. You'll only be carrying five or ten pounds, but the pads are comfortable on a long hike. Get one with a tough covered zipper. Double-O rings slip and aren't the greatest shoulder strap adjusters. Get tabler buckles; they don't slip and they adjust quickly.

Fanny packs have their fans among day hikers. Buy a good one with ample padding and storage, look for rugged, covered zippers and easy access to pouches. Be sure the pack you choose comfortably carries water bottles.

Precautions

We still react in instinctive ways when we feel threatened by some aspect of the natural world. Don't let the few biters, stingers, and hazards mentioned below make you apprehensive about going into the backcountry.

Blisters: There's nothing worse than walking on feet that burn like hot coals. To avoid blisters, make sure your boots fit properly. Keep pulling up your socks and see to it that they don't bunch up. Act quickly if you feel a blister develop. Cut a hole in moleskin a little larger than your red spot and stick it in place with the blister poking through the hole. The idea is to surround it so the boot can't get at it. (If you covered it you could irritate it further and you'd have to peel the tape off the blister. Ouch!) Some hikers put a double layer of tissue paper over the blister and tape the tissue in place with surgical tape. If you get a full-grown blister, pop it with a clean needle inserted under the edge and apply antiseptic, then put moleskin over the area.

Poison Oak: This infamous plant grows abundantly throughout Southern California mountains up to an elevation of 5,000 feet. It's a sneaky devil. It may lurk under other shrubs or take the form of a vine and climb up an oak tree. The leaves are one to four inches long and glossy, as if waxed.

All parts of the plant at all times of the year contain poisonous sap that can severely blister skin and mucous membranes. Its sap is most toxic during spring and summer. In fall, poison oak is particularly conspicuous; its leaves turn to flaming crimson or orange. However, its color change is more a response to heat and dryness than season; its "fall color" can occur

Poison Oak   *Effects of Poison Oak*

anytime in Southern California. Leaves on some plants can be turning yellow or red while plants in most spots are putting out green leaves. In winter, poison oak is naked, its stalks blending into the dull hue of the forest.

Contrary to popular belief, you can't catch it from someone else's rash, nor from oozing blisters, but petting an animal or handling a piece of clothing that carries it can make you a victim.

There are a multitude of remedies. Perhaps most common is the regular application of calamine lotion or cortisone cream. If you're particularly sensitive to poison oak, always wash down thoroughly immediately after a hike with cold water and a basic soap such as laundry detergent. Launder your hiking clothing separately as soon as possible. A dip in the ocean can help; a few tablespoons of baking soda added to a tub of lukewarm water calms the itchies as well. You organic types will probably want to pick some mugwort, an effective panacea. Its fresh juice applied directly to the pained area relieves itching.

Rattlesnakes: Like typical Southern Californians, rattlesnakes take to the trail to enjoy the sunshine, so keep an eye out. Despite the common fear of rattlers, few people see them and rarely is anyone bitten. An estimated 300 yearly snake envenomations occur in the Southland. Only a small percentage of these bites cause serious injury.

The red diamond rattlesnake is found in coastal, hill and desert regions, the sidewinder and Western Diamondback in the desert, and the Southern Pacific rattler lives in coastal regions between Malibu and San Juan Capistrano and in inland areas like remote sections of Griffith Park.

If you've been bitten, remain calm. Check to be sure you've actually been envenomated. Look for swelling around the wound within five minutes. If it doesn't swell, you've probably escaped and may not require hospital treatment. If swelling and other symptoms occur—numbness around the lips or hairline, a metallic taste in the mouth or twitching facial muscles, it got you and you need immediate treatment.

Getting to a hospital emergency room is more important than any other first aid. Keep the site of the wound as immobilized as possible and relax. Cutting and suction treatments are now medically out of vogue and advised only as a last resort if you're absolutely sure you can't get to a hospital within four hours.

Bees: More fatalities occur from allergic reaction to insect stings than from rattlesnake bites. People allergic to bee stings can get a desensitization shot and a specially equipped bee kit from an allergist.

Ticks: They're one-quarter to one-half inch long and about the same color as the ground, so they're hard to see. Ticks are usually picked up by brushing against low vegetation. When hiking in a tick area it's best to sit on rocks rather than fallen logs. Check your skin and clothing occasionally. If one is attached to the skin, it should be lifted off with a slow gentle pull. Before bathing, look for ticks on the body, particularly in the hair and pubic region.

Lyme disease, while rare in California, is the most common tick-carried disease. Symptoms usually include a red, ring-like rash on the skin where the tick attaches itself. The rash is often accompanied by flu-like symptoms of headaches, chills and fever, fatigue and aching muscles. If the disease goes untreated, second-stage symptoms are meningitis and abnormal heartbeat; third-stage symptoms (months or years later) can include arthritis. A blood test can determine if a person is infected. Antibiotics are a very effective treatment.

Getting Lost and Found

Even the experienced can get lost. Getting lost is usually the result of taking a "short cut" off an established trail. Danger is magnified if a hiker ventures out alone or fails to tell anyone locale and return time.

Try to avoid getting lost in the first place. Know your physical condition and don't overtax yourself. Check your boots and clothing. Be prepared for bad weather. Inquire about trail conditions. Allow plenty of time for your hike and allow even more for your return to the trailhead.

When you're on the trail, keep your eyes open. If you're hiking so fast that all you see is your boots, you're not attentive to passing terrain—its charms or its layout. STOP once in a while. Sniff wildflowers, splash your face in a spring. LISTEN. Maybe the trail is paralleling a stream. Listen to the sound of mountain water. On your left? On your right? Look up at that fire lookout on the nearby ridge. Are you heading toward it or away from it? LOOK AROUND. That's the best insurance against getting lost.

So you're really lost? Stay calm. Don't worry about food. It takes weeks to starve to death. Besides, you've got that candy bar in your day pack. You have a water bottle. And you have a jacket in case of rain.

You're in no immediate danger, so don't run around in circles like a mindless chicken.

LOOK AROUND some more. Is there any familiar landmark in sight? Have you been gaining elevation or losing it? Where has the sun been shining? On your right cheek? Your back? Retrace your steps, if you can. Look for other footprints. If you're totally disoriented, keep walking laterally. Don't go deeper into the brush or woods. Go up-slope to get a good view, but don't trek aimlessly here and there.

If it's near dark, get ready to spend the night. Don't try to find your way out in the dark. Don't worry. If you left your itinerary, your rescuers will begin looking for you in the morning. Try to stay warm by huddling against a tree or wrapping yourself in branches, pine needles or leaves. The universal distress signal is three visible or audible signals—three shouts or whistles, three shiny objects placed on a bare summit. Don't start a fire! You could start a major conflagration.

Relax and think of your next hike. Think of the most beautiful place you know—that creek of snowmelt gushing down from that stony mountain, a place where the fish bite and the mosquitos don't . . . You'll make it, don't worry.

Maps

Finding the trailhead—and staying on the trail—is far easier if you're in possession of a good map. Maps are invaluable aids to trip planning and provide relatively painless, hands-on geography lessons.

The Automobile Club of Southern California has seven county maps useful to the hiker, including Santa Barbara, Ventura, Los Angeles, Orange County, San Diego, Riverside and San Bernardino. Particularly useful is "Los Angeles County and Vicinity." Because many of the hikes in this guide begin at campgrounds, the Auto Club's "Southern California Camping" map is a good one to have.

The richly detailed Thomas Brothers maps will also help you get around Southern California.

Use care when you select a map off the rack. Many of the maps sold to tourists are okay for civic sightseeing, but don't show the backcountry.

About 40 percent of the hikes in this guide take place in one of the four Southern California national forests: Los Padres, Angeles, San Bernardino and Cleveland. Forest Service maps are available at ranger stations for a small fee. They're general maps, showing roads, rivers, trails and little else. You'll learn where the trailheads are located and where entry is restricted during the fire season. The Forest Service keeps its maps fairly up-to-date, so they're useful for checking out-of-date topographic maps.

Each route and trail in the national forest system has a route number. A route number might look like this: 2S21. Wooden signs, inscribed with the route number, are placed at some trailheads and at the intersection of trails to supplement other directional signs. The route numbers on your map usually correspond to the route numbers on the trail, but be careful because the Forest Service periodically changes the numbers.

Trails on Forest Service maps are drawn in red and black. Red trails are usually maintained and are in good shape. Black trails are infrequently maintained and their condition ranges from okay to faint.

Topographic maps show terrain in great detail and are the best way to prevent getting lost. Topos show trails, elevations, waterways, brush cover and improvements. Along with a compass they're indispensible for cross-country travel.

Backcountry Courtesy

- ◆ Leave your electronic music machines at home.
- ◆ Dogs, depending on the personality of the individual pooch, can be a disruption to hikers and native wildlife. Be warned, many state and county parks, as well as national forest wilderness areas, don't allow dogs, either on or off a leash.
- ◆ No smoking on trails
- ◆ Resist the urge to collect flowers, rocks or animals. It disrupts nature's balance and lessens the wilderness experience for future hikers.
- ◆ Litter detracts from even the most beautiful backcountry setting. If you packed it in, you can pack it out.
- ◆ You have a moral obligation to help a hiker in need. Give whatever first aid or comfort you can, and then hurry for help.
- ◆ Don't cut switchbacks.

Day Hiking to a New Land Ethic

Along Santiago Creek in the Santa Ana Mountains, 200-year-old oaks were uprooted to make room for a suburb. The toppled oaks, their roots drying in the sun, testify against a culture that is still searching for a meaningful land ethic. Santa Ynez Canyon in the Santa Monica Mountains suffered a similar fate. The canyon's sandstone walls were blasted away and terraced for hundreds of luxury homes. What was to be the jewel of Topanga State Park is now a tract of asphalt and stucco.

Environmentally unsound construction is evident all over Southern California. The forces of Cut & Fill and Grade & Pave each year engulf more and more open space. There are still places that remain inviolate from the earthmover and the cement mixer, but these places grow fewer each year. As the late Twentieth-Century version of the good life creeps into Southern California's backcounty, it may be time to ask ourselves, "What color is paradise?"

I think it's green.

A change in our land ethic begins with a change in perception and a change in perception begins with you. It's not a difficult change to make; in fact, day hiking can provoke it. The change I'm suggesting requires only that you open your eyes a little wider and see the natural world from a different perspective.

Perception is a funny thing. Did you ever notice the change in pitch of a train whistle as it goes away from you? A Nineteenth-Century Austrian physicist, Christian Doppler, figured that sound waves varied with the relative velocity of the source and the observer. He applied his Doppler effect to light waves, as well. He saw that as the position of observer and light source change, the colors of light will shift. Day hikers can notice a Doppler effect of their own. Looking up at Mount San Gorgonio from the L.A. Basin, the hiker sees a snowy peak rising above the smog. Atop the mountain, the hiker looks down on a thick brown inversion layer blanketing the Southland. Quite a difference in views between the bottom of the Basin and the top of the mountain!

To day hike is to alter your perceptions, to see things in a new light. You see where you are and what you left behind, and you realize that the two are closer together than you had imagined. The distinction between "out there" and "right here" blurs; when that happens, you've become a conservationist. As a conservationist, you'll perceive that our boulevards, our wilderness, and we ourselves, are part of a fragile island. The future of the island depends on your perceptions and your actions.

That anybody should undertake a jaunt of a hundred and fifty miles or so on foot for the pleasure of walking was unthinkable by the conventional Western mind; but I was already familiar with the strong points of tripping afoot and the lure of that splendid chain of mountains back of Santa Barbara. . . . To motor there seemed out of key with such a land, though thousands do it; and besides, motoring is expensive. No, for me "The footpath way" with kodak over my shoulder, a pocketful of dried figs, and freedom from care.

—Charles Francis Saunders
Under the Sky in California (1913)

1. Los Padres National Forest

Santa Barbara/Ojai Backcountry

WILDERNESS-BOUND travelers have a difficult task in deciding what to call the rugged mountain terrain arranged in a wide semi-circle around Santa Barbara. The padres left behind many names, but none of them fit. Elsewhere in Southern California, wilderness areas were named for the dominant mountain range in the vicinity. But there isn't a dominant mountain range behind Santa Barbara. Instead, there are a number of smaller ones with names like Pine and Topatopa, Sierra Madre and Santa Ynez.

So when we go, where do we say we're going?

Hikers sometimes say they're "going up to the Los Padres," an imprecise term at best, because Los Padres National Forest includes lands as far north as Big Sur. Geologists aren't much help either. They call the land the "Transverse Ranges Geomorphic Province."

Until popular use gives mapmakers new inspiration, the best names we have are the Santa Barbara Backcountry or the Ojai Backcountry. (Even the Mt. Pinos-Frazier Park Backcountry will do.) Anyway, whatever this land of great gorges, sandstone cliffs and wide blue sky is called, it's guaranteed to please.

Most of the backcountry is in Los Padres National Forest. Together, Santa Barbara and Ventura counties have more than a million acres of national forest land. The backcountry is under the jurisdiction of three forest districts. The Ojai District includes Sespe and Piru creeks as well as the Sespe Condor Sanctuary. The Santa Barbara District includes the Santa Ynez and San Rafael mountain ranges. Mount Pinos District protects high conifer forest and includes the backcountry's highest peak, Mount Pinos (8,831 feet).

Archeological work in the backcountry has been extensive and has contributed much to our understanding of Chumash Indian culture. Several thousand years before the arrival of the Spanish, an estimated 10,000 to 18,000 Chumash lived in the coastal mountains from Malibu Canyon north to San Luis Obispo. Early Spanish explorers admired Chumash craftsmen, their fine houses and wood plank canoes. But the padres and soldiers of Spain who followed the explorers forced the Chumash to give up their ancient ways. Mission life broke the spirit of the Chumash and destroyed their culture.

Gold and grass brought Americans to the backcountry. From the time of the early padres, rumors of the lost Los Padres Mine lured prospectors. Enough gold was discovered in the hills and streams to keep prospectors prospecting until well into the Twentieth Century, but no one ever found a big bonanza or the lost mine.

Lush grass on the San Joaquin side of the backcountry provided grazing for thousands of cattle. Cattle have grazed these hills since the era of the Spanish land grants, and the hiker will often surprise a few cows.

Wildfire was a major problem in the late nineteenth and early twentieth centuries. Within a twenty-year period, much of the backcountry burned, prompting the federal government to realize that the land needed protection. For fire prevention and and watershed management purposes, large backcountry sections were set aside in the Pine Mountain and Zaca Lake Forest Reserve and the Santa Ynez Forest Reserve by decree of President Theodore Roosevelt. Two years later, the area became known as the Santa Barbara National Forest. In later years, acreage was added and subtracted, with the backcountry finally coming under the jurisdiction of the Los Padres National Forest in 1938.

More than 1,600 miles of trail range through the various districts of Los Padres National Forest. Nearly half of this trail system winds through the area we call the Santa Barbara Backcountry. Many of these trails have been used for centuries. Follow a trail to its end and you might be surprised at what you find. Remains of Indian camps may be found in the farthest reaches of the forest, and in remote meadows are remnants of early homesteads.

Ranger Valentine on Santa Cruz Trail, 1926

1

McPherson Peak Trail

Aliso Park Campground to Hog Pen Spring Campground
  5 miles round trip; 900-foot gain

Aliso Park Campground to McPherson Peak
  10 mile loop; 2,900-foot gain

Season: Oct-June

The San Rafael Wilderness, heart of the Santa Barbara backcountry, inspired the late author/photographer Dick Smith and several naturalists before and after him to roam, explore, behold. This is, or was, and maybe someday again will be condor country, where these survivors from Pleistocene times were given their last sanctuary.

Smith spent fifteen years roaming the backcountry. He crouched behind improvised blinds for days at a time to observe the great, dark birds with their 10-foot wingspans. Through his book, *Condor Journal*, he alerted the public to the plight of this flying relic from the Stone Age.

This day hike takes you into Smith's favorite backcountry—preserved as the Dick Smith Wilderness—to the crest of the Sierra Madre, where dolphins swoop in the wind like dolphins of the sky. From McPherson Peak, you will have a commanding view of the San Rafael Wilderness to the south and the stark Cuyama badlands to the north. Get an early start. The trail is quite steep and exposed to the full effect of the sun.

Directions to trailhead: As the hawk flies, New Cuyama isn't all that far from Ventura, Santa Barbara or even Interstate 5, but by car it's quite a drive. There are a couple of long but scenic ways to reach New Cuyama:

You can exit Interstate 5 near Gorman on Frazier Mt. Park Road, then follow Mil Potrero Road to its intersection with California 33, which at this point is also California 166.

Second, you can exit U.S. 101 in Ventura and follow California 33 about 72 winding miles north to its junction with California 166.

From the junction of Highway 33 and Highway 166, proceed 13 miles northwest on the latter route to the signed turnoff for Aliso Park Campground (about 2½ miles past the hamlet of New Cuyama). Leaving the highway, you'll turn south on Aliso Canyon Road. Drive 1½ miles, bear right at the first fork, then continue 4½ miles to the Aliso Park Camp. The very rough road is not recommended for passenger cars, though trucks and four-wheel-drive vehicles can negotiate it.

The Hike: As you leave the campground on the Forest Service road, you'll notice an unsigned trail on your right leading south up a slope. This is the trail on which you'll return from McPherson Peak.

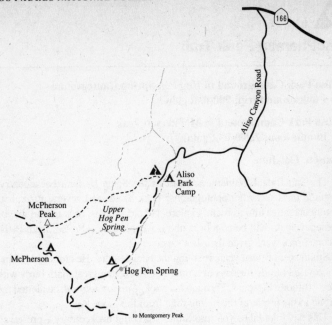

Follow the dirt road, which takes you from shaded Aliso Valley up through chaparral. A mile from the trailhead is a gate. Another 1½ miles brings you to Hog Pen Spring Campground. Hog Pen was named by the McPherson family, who once raised pigs in the area.

Now the real climbing begins as you follow many switchbacks on the ascent to Sierra Madre Road. The unsigned trail, which begins at the edge of the campground, follows the edge of a brushy canyon.

Turn west (right) on Sierra Madre Road and continue 2 miles to Mc-Pherson Peak. En route are magnificent views down into the Sisquoc River and the cliffs where condors nested and roosted over the centuries.

At McPherson Peak (5,749 feet) you have a commanding view in all directions. Watch the skies for condors; scientists began re-introducing zoo-bred birds into the backcountry in 1991.

Instead of retracing your steps back down to Aliso Park Campground, search the slope just east below the lookout for the old McPherson Trail. It takes you down through the chaparral along a rib of the peak. After a 2-mile descent, you reach an unsigned junction with an overgrown trail. Bear right and follow it downhill a bit more than 2 miles back to the campground. You might need to do a little bushwhacking, but the views of the Cuyama Valley and Cuyama Badlands make it all worthwhile.

2

Sulphur Spring Trail

Zaca Lake to Cedros Saddle
 4½ mile round trip; 1,000-foot gain

Return via Zaca Ridge Road
 6½ miles round trip; 1,500-foot gain

Season: All year

Long ago, the Chumash called the lake *Zaca* or "quiet place." The name still fits today. Zaca Lake, a private enclave within the boundaries of Los Padres National Forest, is a secluded spot offering canoeing, swimming and hiking.

Zaca is one of the very few natural lakes in Southern California. The lake is replenished by underground springs (a somewhat rare occurence).

Geologists speculate that Zaca Lake was formed about 10,000 years ago by a landslide. Before this slide, underground springs fed Zaca Creek, which meandered through Zaca Canyon. But loosened by fault activity and heavy rains, one of Zaca Canyon's walls collapsed, forming a dam across the canyon. This natural dam has contained rain run-off and underground sources within the boundaries of a small lake ever since.

Zaca Lake is owned by the Human Potential Foundation, "dedicated to the expansion of human awareness." The Foundation's facilities are rented out to New Age and community service groups, as well as to the traveling public. There's also a campground by the lake.

Several trails explore the Los Padres National Forest backcountry above Zaca Lake. Not all of them are in good shape, however, so it's best to ask at the lodge before you hit the trail.

Directions to trailhead: From Highway 101, some 50 miles up-coast from Santa Barbara, exit on Zaca Station Road. (This exit is the first one past 101's junction with Highway 154) You'll drive 3¼ miles, passing vineyards and the Firestone Winery to a junction with Foxen Canyon Road. Bear left, heading north 3½ miles to the poorly signed turnoff for Zaca Lake. Turn right onto the road leading to the lake. It's paved for the first mile or so, dirt for the next five. Take your time and watch for potholes. Sign in at the lodge and pay the day-use fee.

From the lodge, drive down the dirt road another half-mile to the picnic ground. Park in the shade.

Zaca Lake hours are 8 A.M. to 6 P.M. daily. Because the lake and lodge is occasionally rented to private parties, it's a good idea to call the Human Potential Foundation at Zaca Lake Lodge (805) 688-4891 before you set out for a hike.

The Hike: From the picnic ground, walk up the dirt road a half-mile to the signed beginning of Sulphur Spring Trail. Note another, unsigned trail, on your right; this very steep trail is your return route.

Sulphur Spring Trail ascends sometimes moderately, sometimes steeply a bit under 2 miles to Cedros Saddle and an intersection with dirt Zaca Ridge Road. Just below the saddle is a grove of incense cedar. The cedar, along with other varieties of pines were planted on the ridges around Zaca Lake during various forest service projects beginning about 1910. The incense cedar in these parts are doing well, but some trees—the Monterey pine for example—fared poorly in this part of the national forest.

(Sulphur Spring Trail resumes on the other side of Zaca Ridge Road and descends steeply to the northeast to Manzana Creek on the edge of the San Rafael Wilderness. For a grand view of the wilderness, the Sierra Madre Mountains and Hurricane Deck, walk a hundred yards down the trail.)

This hike heads right on Zaca Ridge Road, climbing moderately to a junction with Zaca Peak Road. You'll bear right (west on this dirt road and continue a mile to an orange flag, which marks the very steeply descending trail that will complete the loop back to the trailhead.

Ambitious hikers can continue west on Zaca Peak Road toward prominent Zaca Peak. Although the road passes below the peak (which is extremely difficult to reach because of the thick brush and bad trail), you can get a pretty good view right from the road. At the turn of the century, the first fire lookout station in what was to become Los Padres National Forest was established atop the peak. Every day during fire season, a patrolman rode his horse from Zaca Lake up to the lookout. The lookout itself resembled a modern-day lifeguard tower with a sun umbrella atop it.

Ultra-ambitious hikers can continue several more miles past Zaca Peak to well-named Lookout Mountain.

3

Manzana Creek Trail

NIRA to Lost Valley Camp
  2 miles round trip; 100-foot gain

To Fish Creek Camp
  6 miles round trip; 400-foot gain

To Manzana Camp
  6½ miles round trip; 1,100-foot gain

To Manzana Narrows
  14 miles round trip; 1,200-foot gain

Season: All year; caution during times of high water

San Rafael Wilderness was the first Wilderness Area set aside under the Federal Wilderness Act of 1964. "San Rafael is rocky, rugged, wooded and lonely," President Lyndon B. Johnson remarked when he signed the San Rafael Wilderness bill on March 21, 1968. "I believe it will enrich the spirit of America."

Manzana Creek Trail begins at NIRA, the major entry point for the San Rafael Wilderness. NIRA, an auto camp and popular day-use area, is an acronym for the National Industrial Recovery Act, a federal program launched during the Depression.

The trail passes tall thin alders and in spring, wildflowers. Four creek-side camps beckon the picnicker. In addition to a few stocked trout that

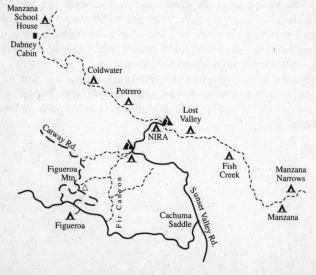

survive the legions of fishermen, you'll find frogs, crayfish and turtles in Manzana Creek. Rewarding the hiker after many stream crossings is Manzana Narrows, a narrow part of the canyon where there are some fine pools for fishing and cooling off.

Directions to trailhead: From U.S. 101 in Santa Barbara, exit on California 154 and follow the latter highway over San Marcos Pass. Beyond Lake Cachuma, turn right on Armour Ranch Road and proceed 2½ miles to Happy Canyon Road. Make another right and continue 17 miles (Happy Canyon Road becomes Sunset Valley Road after passing an intersection at Figueroa Mountain Road) to NIRA Camp. Parking space for hikers is provided at the south end of the campground.

The Hike: Leaving NIRA Camp the trail immediately crosses Manzana Creek and begins a gentle ascent along the north bank of the creek. The route switchbacks up a low ridge cloaked with digger pine and soon arrives at Lost Valley Camp, a small site tucked among oak and pine at the mouth of Lost Valley Canyon. This canyon reaches from Manzana Creek up to Hurricane Deck, heart of the San Rafael Wilderness. Lost Valley Trail departs from camp and climbs up to the magnificent deck.

Manzana Creek Trail meanders along the north bank of the creek for the next 2 miles. Look to your right across the creek and you'll spot Fish Creek Camp on the far side of the Manzana flood plain, where Fish Creek meets Manzana Creek. Fishermen like this camp because the creeks here usually support a large trout population.

Past Fish Creek, Manzana Creek Trail at first stays on the north wall of the canyon, passing through chaparral and dipping in and out of washes. Manzana Canyon narrows and the trail heads down toward the creek, which is lined by tall thin alders. The trail crosses the Manzana, and ½ mile later, crosses again. The canyon narrows even more and, after a few more creek crossings, the path brings you to Manzana Camp. Located beneath picturesque live oak, the camp offers a dependable water supply, fishing and swimming pools. The manzanita, which gave its name to half the geographical features around here, abounds.

Beyond this camp, the trail switchbacks up onto the east wall of the canyon, then soon descends to Manzana Narrows Camp. Wedged in the narrow canyon, the oak- and willow-shaded camp offers pools for fishing and cooling off.

4

Manzana Creek Trail

Davy Brown Camp to Potrero Canyon Camp
2½ miles round trip; 100-foot loss

Davy Brown Camp to Coldwater Camp
5 miles round trip; 200-foot loss

Davy Brown Camp to Dabney Cabin
14 miles round trip; 500-foot loss

Davy Brown Camp to Manzana School House Camp
17 miles round trip; 700-foot loss

The lower stretch of the Manzana Creek Trail begins near a camp and creek named for William S. (Davy) Brown who kept a cabin here during his retirement years, 1879 to 1895.

The trail ends at the confluence of Manzana Creek and the Sisquoc River, where Hiram Preserved Wheat and his cult of religious fundamentalists from Kansas settled. Wheat, it was said, had the power to heal with his hands. Hostile Indians were so impressed by the spiritual power of this white man that they inscribed his wagon with a sign indicating he was to be granted protection. Wheat and his followers stayed until almost two decades, but a number of drought years and restrictions on homesteading brought about by the creation of the Santa Barbara National Forest combined to end the settlement.

As you hike Manzana Creek Trail, don't be surprised to come across stone foundations and chimneys, or perhaps an old bottle or bit of barbed wire, all that remain of a rough life in a rough land.

Manzana means "apple" in Spanish, and it's guessed that apple orchards once grew in the area. On second guess, it takes its name from manzanita, "little apple" in Spanish.

A mellow day hike would be a journey down-creek to Potrero Canyon Camp or Coldwater Camp. Intrepid hikers in good condition will enjoy the much longer treks to the Dabney Cabin or historic Manzana School House; this would be a lot of ground to cover in one day but there's little elevation loss or gain to slow you down. Use caution at the many creek crossings and expect to get your feet wet if the creek is high.

Directions to trailhead: From U.S. 101 in Santa Barbara, exit on California 154 and follow the latter highway over San Marcos Pass. Beyond Lake Cachuma, turn right on Armour Road and proceed 2½ miles to Happy Canyon Road. Make another right and continue 16 miles (Happy Canyon Road becomes Sunset Valley Road after passing an intersection at

Figeroa Mountain Road). Just past the turnoff to Davy Brown Campground, the road crosses Davy Brown Creek; park just after the crossing.
The Hike: A San Rafael Wilderness sign marks the beginning of the Manzana Creek Trail. The path heads down-creek. Keep the creek on your right. A bit more than a mile's easy travel brings you to Potrero Canyon Camp in an oak woodland near the creek.

From the camp, you can push down-creek via either a high or low trail. The low trail crosses the creek many times as it winds to Coldwater Camp; the higher—and drier—high trail contours over digger pine- and chaparral-covered canyon walls. Coldwater Camp, set amongst pine and oak, is a fine place for a picnic. Even during dry years, water bubbles up from the creek bedrock, hence the camp's name.

Beyond the camp, the trail crosses Manzana Creek several more times before arriving at Dabney Cabin. The cabin, built by Charles Dabney in 1914, is leased by Santa Barbara's Sierra Club.

More creek crossings follow until you reach Manzana School House Camp, located near the confluence of Manzana Creek and the Sisquoc River. One-room Manzana School House, built at the turn of the century and now a County Historical Landmark, still stands.

Manzana Creek and the Sisquoc River have attracted anglers for years.

5

Davy Brown Trail

Davy Brown Camp to Harry Roberts Cabin
  3½ miles round trip; 900-foot gain

Davy Brown Camp to Figueroa Mt. Rd.
  6¼ miles round trip; 1,700-foot gain

Davy Brown Camp to Figueroa Mt. Lookout
  7½ miles round trip; 2,400-foot gain

Season: March-November

Figueroa Mountain, located in Los Padres National Forest 25 air miles behind Santa Barbara, is one of the most botanically intriguing areas in Southern California. The mountain's upper slopes are forested with Coulter pine, yellow pine and big cone spruce. Spring wildflower displays on the lower slopes are often exceptional. Among the more common roadside and trailside flowers are fiddleneck, Johnny jump-ups, shooting stars, lupine and cream cups.

Tree-lovers will find a variety of arboreal companions, including large specimens of California bay laurel and big leaf maple, and picturesque coastal, valley and blue oaks. At lower elevations are abundant digger pine. Its distinguishing features are long needles in bunches of three and the forking broom-like appearance of its trunk. The pines are named for a tribe of Indians in California's gold country, who were disparagingly called "diggers" by the Forty-Niners.

On higher slopes grows another three-needled pine—the yellow pine. It's a tall, regal tree with a reddish bark that looks fashioned of rectangular mosaic tiles. And yet another three-needled pine is the Coulter, which produces huge cones, the largest and heaviest of any native conifer.

One good way to explore the mountain's flora and colorful history is to take a hike on Davy Brown Trail, which ascends cool, moist Fir Canyon, climbs to the headwaters of Davy Brown Creek and visits the Forest Service fire lookout atop 4,528-foot Figueroa Mountain. The mountain honors José Figueroa, Mexican governor of California from 1833 to 1835. Anyone who climbs to the mountain's lookout, where there are grand views of the San Rafael Wilderness, Santa Ynez Valley, Point Conception and the Channel Islands, will agree that having such a mountain take your name is indeed an honor.

The trail, as well as a camp and a creek, is named for William S. (Davy) Brown who kept a cabin here during his retirement years, 1880 to 1895. Born in Ireland in 1800, Brown was eighty years old by the time he

Among the ruins of Harry Roberts's cabin

arrived in the Santa Barbara Backcountry with his two white mules, Jinks and Tommy. If even half of the accounts of his early years are true, he certainly had an adventurous life. He was reportedly an African slave trader, Indian fighter, hunter with Kit Carson and meat supplier for California '49ers. Though he was considered a recluse, many said that he welcomed visitors into his humble cabin. Davy Brown died in the sleepy Santa Barbara County town of Guadalupe in 1898, having fully experienced the 19th Century. His 16-by-20-foot cabin burned in a 1930 fire and is now the site of Davy Brown Camp.

Directions to trailhead: From Highway 101 in Santa Barbara, exit on Highway 154 and proceed 14 miles over Cachuma Pass and past Lake Cachuma to Armour Ranch Road. Turn right and drive 1.3 miles to Happy Canyon Road. Make a right and wind 14 pleasant miles to Cachuma Saddle Station. To reach the lower Davy Brown trailhead, you'll bear right at the saddle onto Sunset Valley Road and proceed 5 miles to Davy Brown Campground. To reach upper Davy Brown trailhead, bear left at Cachuma Saddle Station onto Figueroa Mountain Road and drive 5 miles to a turnout and signed Davy Brown Trail on your right.

You can also gain access to both trailheads by exiting Highway 101 north of the Buellton turnoff on Highway 154, turning left on Figueroa Mountain Road and driving 15 miles to the upper trailhead. During wildflower season consider a drive up Figueroa Mountain Road and down Happy Canyon Road—or vice-versa—to make a scenic loop through the Santa Barbara Backcountry.

The Hike: From the northwest end of Davy Brown Camp, you'll pass a green gate and a vehicle barrier and join the unsigned trail. You'll head west through forested Munch Canyon, cross Davy Brown Creek a couple of times, then begin angling southwest up Fir Canyon. Actually, no firs grow in Fir Canyon but its southern cousin, the big cone spruce, is plentiful here.

About 1¾ miles from the trailhead, you'll descend into a blue oak-shaded draw and arrive at the ruins of chrome miner Harry Roberts's cabin, built in the 1920s. A large big leaf maple shades the cabin, which is a good lunch stop or turnaround point if you're not feeling too energetic.

Beyond the cabin, maple-shaded Davy Brown Trail crosses and recrosses the creek. Keep a sharp lookout right for the unsigned side trail leading to Figueroa Mountain Lookout. (If you see signed Munch Canyon Spur Trail on your left, you overshot the trail; double back a hundred yards.)

Those wishing to follow Davy Brown Trail to its end will continue ascending along Davy Brown Creek through a wet world of mushrooms and banana slugs under the shade of oaks and laurel. A half-mile from the top of the trail you'll step carefully over a splintered white Monterey shale outcropping at a point where the canyon makes a sharp turn. Old-timers called this bend the Devil's Elbow.

Davy Brown Trail climbs to the headwaters of Davy Brown Creek, then out onto a grassy slope dotted with digger pine and buttercups. You might encounter a herd of bovine forest users on this grassy slope. Trail's end is Figueroa Mountain Road.

Figueroa Mountain Lookout-bound hikers will head right at the above-mentioned junction. The path gains elevation rapidly as it climbs out onto a drier slope cloaked in chaparral—toyon, ceanothus, black sage, scrub oak and mountain mahogany.

The trail descends for a short distance to a tiny meadow then immediately climbs steeply again. As the trail nears the top, notice the progression of pines from digger to Coulter to yellow.

The trail intersects a road to Figueroa Peak. Bear left on the road a half-mile to the lookout. Enjoy the far-reaching views of the major peaks of Los Padres National Forest and of the coast and Channel Islands.

6

Santa Cruz Trail

Upper Oso Camp to Nineteen Oaks Camp
 5½ miles round trip; 600-foot gain

Upper Oso Camp to Little Pine Saddle
 10 miles round trip; 3,300-foot gain

Upper Oso Camp to Happy Hollow Camp
 13 miles round trip; 3,300-foot gain

Season: All year

Santa Cruz Trail presents a lengthy climb, but rewards the hiker with a superb view of the Channel Islands and the Pacific. The trail tops Little Pine Mountain, an ecological island of conifers that one might expect to find only in the High Sierra. Another of this day hike's destinations, ponderosa pine-shaded Happy Hollow Camp, tucked between Little Pine Mountain and a sister peak, is appropriately named.

Hikers can work up quite a sweat while ascending the hot, exposed slope of Little Pine Mountain. Start trekking in the cool of the morning when the trail is shadowed and enjoy your lunch at the top beneath the boughs of a big cone spruce. An ocean breeze ususally keeps the mountaintop cool.

Families with young children may enjoy the easy part of Santa Cruz Trail—the first stretch leading to the quiet pools of Oso Creek and to picnicking at Nineteen Oaks Camp. Hikers in good condition or those looking for a good conditioning hike will relish the challenge of the climb to the top of Little Pine Mountain.

Directions to trailhead: From U.S. 101 in Santa Barbara, exit on California 154 and proceed northwest 11 miles over San Marcos Pass. Turn right onto Paradise Road and follow it east for 6 miles along the Santa Ynez River. Just after crossing the river and passing through a parking area, turn left on Oso Road and follow it a mile to Upper Oso Campground. Hiker parking is provided at the eastern end of the camp at the trailhead.

The Hike: The trek begins at a locked gate beyond the campground and for the first mile follows Camuesa Fire Road which unfortunately is a Forest Service designated "motorcycle route." The road stays just to the east of Oso Creek, where there are several fine swimming pools. When the road takes a sharp hairpin turn, hikers leave the two- and three-wheeled locusts behind by continuing straight ahead at a signed junction and joining the Santa Cruz Trail.

For the next mile the trail is relatively flat, although it drops in and out of washes on the east side of Oso Creek. Soon the hiker sees a signed spur trail on the right, which leads $1/10$ of a mile to Nineteen Oaks Camp. Oaks shade this camp, but not 19 of them. A few tables suggest a picnic. Geologically minded hikers will note the scars in the nearby hills where mercury, also known as cinnabar or quicksilver, was mined.

Santa Cruz Trail heads north, crosses Oso Creek, and begins switchbacking through grassy meadows. Dipping in and out of brush-smothered canyons, you ascend a hill to a saddle between the ridge you're traveling and Little Pine Mountain.

The trail soon switchbacks north, then west across the south face of Little Pine Mountain. You'll cross two large mountains, called "Mellow Meadows" by laid-back Santa Barbarans. The tall dry grass is the habitat of deer and even an occasional mountain lion. The trail climbs around the heads of half a dozen canyons before reaching Alexander Saddle. To the left a bulldozed road goes to 4,107-foot Alexander Peak. Santa Cruz Trail continues straight. You bear right on the connector trail that leads to Happy Hollow Camp.

From Alexander Saddle, the connector trail climbs steeply at first up the dramatic Little Pine Mountain ridgeline. Weatherworn pines on the ridge offer shade and you'll catch fabulous views of the Channel Islands, Santa Ynez Valley, and Lake Cachuma. Large sugar pines and a few live oaks cling to the north face of Little Pine peak. Farther along the trail you will be among yellow pine, spruce, and Douglas fir. The top of Little Pine Mountain is a great place to unpack your lunch or take a snooze.

From the peak, the trail descends a short way to Happy Hollow Camp, nestled among ponderosa pine, fir, and oak. The camp has a few tables and stoves. During the 1930s, this camp was a recreation site for Civilian Conservation Corps workmen. A handsome field station, resembling a chalet, stood here until razed in the mid-1970s. The name Happy Hollow is apt; the camp is indeed in a hollow, and hikers are no doubt happy after a 3,300-foot elevation gain in six miles.

7

Mesa Spring Trail

Mt. Cerro Noroeste to Quatal Canyon Road
  10 miles one-way; 2,400-foot loss

Season: April-November

A small portion of the Chumash's ancestral land is now a wilderness area—about 36,000 acres of pine forest and juniper woodland, grasslands and badlands.

"It's time we honor the Chumash," states Sally Reid, a Sierra Club activist who has been leading the charge for wilderness designation. "This land, highest in Los Padres National Forest, center of the Chumash universe, is very special."

The wilderness area has much diversity. A cool pine and fir forest covers Mt. Pinos and a couple of its over-8,000 foot neighbors. Mt. Pinos is a great place to cross-country ski during winter, and to hike during the other three seasons.

Another highlight is Quatal Canyon, a kind of Bryce Canyon-in-miniature, complete with dramatic pinnacles and weird eroded rock formations. Scientists are fascinated by the canyon because it is rich in vertebrate fossils, particularly from the Miocene Epoch (12 million to 16 million years ago). Quatal Canyon has been proposed as a "Natural National Landmark," a federal designation by the secretary of interior that recognizes outstanding examples of ecology or geology, and helps preserve them.

Of interest to scientists is San Emigdio Mesa, a large flat alluvial fan forested with pinyon pine and dwarf oak. The 1,200 acres of pinyon pine woodland is by far the most extensive of its kind in Southern California, and recalls some of the mesas of the Great Basin.

This trail begins in a high pine forest, but passes through other ecosystems—pinyon-juniper woodland, chaparral and grassland—as it descends from Mt. Abel to Toad Spring Camp. It's a great introduction to the lay of the land, a fine overview of the Chumash Wilderness.

One word of warning: the second half of this hike uses Toad Spring Trail, which the Forest Service in 1976, much to the consternation of conservationists, designated as a motorcycle route. Drought and fire dangers prompted the Forest Service to close Toad Spring Trail to motorcycles, but not to hikers. Wilderness status for this area would mean that Toad Spring Trail would be closed to motorcycles and revived as the footpath it was prior to 1976. Though it's not a particularly popular motorcycle trail and it's currently closed to such use, the concerned hiker may wish to contact the Mt. Pinos Ranger District and get the latest trail update.

Directions to trailhead: This trip requires a car shuttle—either two cars or a nonhiking friend. Hikers will want to depart from the Mt. Abel trailhead and arrive at the Toad Spring Campground trailhead.

From Interstate 5 in Frazier Park, exit on Frazier Mountain Park Road and head west. The road, which becomes Cuddy Valley Road, continues to a Y-junction. The left fork leads to Mt. Pinos, but you stay right and join Mil Potrero Road. Drive 8½ miles to Cerro Noroeste Road and turn left. Proceed 7 miles to the signed trailhead ½ mile below the summit of Mt. Cerro Noreoeste (Mt. Abel). Parking is not plentiful right at the trailhead, so park in a safe manner along the road.

From the Cerro Noroeste Road/Mil Potrero Road junction, continue right(west) on the latter road, which to make matters confusing takes on the name Cerro Noroeste Road. Travel a mile to the signed turnoff for Toad Spring Campground, turning left on (Forest Road 9N09), continuing $3/10$ mile to the camp, then another $4/10$ mile to the unsigned trailhead on the left (south) side of the road.

The Hike: Leaving signed Mt. Abel trailhead, the path descends very steeply for ½ mile down a draw into a forested hollow. Here there's a signed junction, with (incorrect) mileages for the trail leading left (southeast) to Mt. Pinos. You bear right on unsigned Mesa Spring Trail and descend past huge and widely spaced ponderosa pine. Scattered among the pines are silver fir, some of which are large enough and pretty enough to be the White House Christmas tree.

After a mile, you'll pass through a gate. (Cattle grazing used to be allowed on this land.) The path continues descending through a mixed transition forest of pine and oak. The area has unusual botany. Inhabitants of dry lands—coffee berry and manzanita and scrub oak—mingle with subalpine species—pine, fir and snowplant.

The path drops a couple more miles through pinyon pine country to Mesa Spring Camp, at about 6,000 feet in elevation. It's a simple trail camp with picnic tables and water. A hundred yards from camp is a huge watering trough.

Mesa Spring, Mesa Spring Camp and Mesa Spring Trail are named for San Emigdio Mesa, the pinyon pine-covered territory that you skirt as the path leaves camp. Stay right at an unsigned trail junction just below camp and continue walking for a couple miles on a flatland between the mesa on your left and the tall shoulder of Mt. Cerro Noroeste on your right.

At a (poorly) signed trail junction, you'll join Forest Service Trail 22W01, Toad Spring Trail, which leads northward 3¼ miles to Quatal Canyon Road. The trail climbs and dips over pinyon pine and juniper dotted slopes. You'll get grand views west and south over the proposed

Chumash Wilderness and of the Cuyama Badlands to the northwest. Best view of all is the view right below of Quatal Canyon. The pinnacle rock formations resemble those in Southwest Utah.

Toad Spring Trail, seriously eroded by motorcycles, but passable, skirts the rim of Quatal Canyon. The last mile of the trail marches steeply up and down some minor hills before reaching its terminus (or trailhead, depending on how you look at it) at Quatal Canyon Road.

Sierra Club activist Sally Reid proposed the Chumash Wilderness.

8

Mt. Pinos Trail

Mt. Abel to Sheep Camp
  5 miles round trip; 500-foot gain

Mt. Abel to Mt. Pinos
  10 miles round trip; 900-foot gain

Season: April-November

The five-mile Mt. Pinos Trail offers the peak-bagger four opportunities to climb an 8,000-foot peak. Between Mts. Abel and Pinos, there are easy cross-country climbs to Grouse and Sawmill mountains. The trail passes through dense pine and fir hollows, visits historic Sheep Camp, and ascends Mt. Pinos, a blustery peak that offers views of the San Joaquin Valley, the Mojave Desert and the sprawling Los Padres National Forest high country.

You can travel from Mt. Pinos to Mt. Abel or vice versa; the Mt. Abel trailhead is much less visited.

Directions to trailhead: Exit Interstate 5 at the Frazier Park turnoff and drive west on Frazier Mountain Park Road, then Cuddy Valley Road. Five miles past the hamlet of Lake of the Woods is a junction. To reach Mt. Pinos trailhead, bear left and continue 9 miles to the Chula Vista Picnic Area. One more mile on a dirt road (closed in winter) takes you to the Condor Observation Site near the top of Mt. Pinos and the beginning (or end) of the Mt. Pinos Trail.

To reach the Mt. Abel trailhead, bear right at the above-mentioned junction and proceed 8 miles on Mil Potrero Road to Cerro Noroeste Road. Turn left and go 7 miles to the signed trailhead, ½ mile below the summit of Mt. Abel. Parking is not plentiful right at the trailhead, so park in a safe manner along the road.

The Hike: Leaving the trailhead behind, you descend a draw into a forested hollow, ½ mile from the start. Bear left at the signed junction here. The trail begins ascending the side of Grouse Mountain, named no doubt for the resident blue grouse population. You might flush a number of these dark, ground-dwelling birds out of the bush.

Soon the trail levels and you'll come to a saddle on the east slope of Grouse Mountain. If you want to ascend to the summit, scramble a short distance up the slope to your right.

The trail continues following the saddle to a junction with North Fork Trail. To reach Sheep Camp, bear right on North Fork Trail and descend a pine-covered slope past a trickling little spring. Sheep Camp, ½ mile from the junction, was used as a base camp by San Joaquin Valley ranchers in the 19th Century. Today, Sheep Camp is one of the highest trail camps in Los Padres National Forest. For the day hiker, it's a pleasant picnic spot.

Return to the main trail, which soon passes close to the summit of Sawmill Mountain. It's an easy cross-country climb to bag the peak.

Continuing on the main trail, you will descend the pine-covered slopes of Sawmill Mountain, then ascend an open slope via switchbacks up balding Mt. Pinos. Every height ascended thus far has seemed the ultimate one, but they have been mere stepping-stones to 8,831-foot Mt. Pinos. Stand among the gnarled pine atop the summit and enjoy the view from the highest peak in Los Padres National Forest.

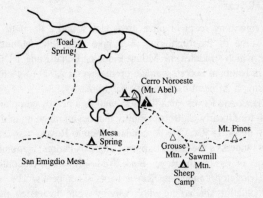

9

Reyes Peak Trail

Reyes Peak Roadhead to Potrero John Overlook
3½ miles round trip; 300-foot gain

To Haddock Peak
7½ miles round trip; 600-foot gain

To Haddock Trail Camp
11 miles round trip; 800-foot gain

Season: All year

The invigorating scent of pine, great views, and a dramatic ridgetop trail are some of the highlights of a hike atop Pine Mountain. The mountain, which straddles the Mount Pinos and Ojai Ranger Districts in Los Padres National Forest, is made up of several 7,000-foot-plus peaks, each offering a different backcountry panorama.

Reyes Peak and Reyes Peak Trail, as well as a nearby camp and creek, are named for an early California family that began ranching in the Cuyama Valley in the 1850s. One descendant, Jacinto Reyes, was among the first forest rangers of the Santa Barbara (later Los Padres) National Forest.

For most of its length, Reyes Peak Trail stays atop, or contours just below the ridgetop connecting Reyes to its sister peaks. The well-constructed footpath is shaded the whole way by white fir, Jeffrey, ponderosa and sugar pine. Inspiring views are offered from uninspiringly named Peaks 7091, 7114 and 7416, as well as from the saddles between the summits.

Directions to trailhead: From Highway 101 in Ventura, exit on Highway 33 and head north 47 miles (32 miles past Ojai) to the signed turnoff for Pine Mountain Recreation Area. Follow the narrow paved road past some campgrounds. After 6 miles the paved surface ends and you'll continue east one more mile on a dirt road (suitable for most passenger cars) to road's end, where there's a modest amount of parking.

The Hike: Follow the dirt road (closed to vehicles beyond the trailhead) about 150 yards. As the road curves southeast, join the unsigned eastbound trail that begins on the east side of the road. The trail descends slightly and soon passes below the pine- and boulder-covered summit of Reyes Peak (7,510 feet), high point of the Pine Mountain massif. Pine and fir shade the trail, which alternately follows the ridgeline and contours just below it.

You'll look down to the northwest at the farms and ranches of Cuyama Valley, and beyond to the stark sandstone Cuyama Badlands. Enjoy pine-framed views of Mount Pinos (8,831 feet), highest peak in Los Padres National Forest. From the ridgetop, you'll be able to peer southwest into the Sespe River gorge.

After about 1¾ miles of travel, you'll be treated to a view of the canyon cut by Potrero John Creek. The eroded cliffs at the head of the canyon recall Utah's Bryce Canyon National Park or Cedar Breaks National Monument.

Reyes Peak Trail continues east through pine and fir forest. After two more miles of travel, you'll spot an orange, triangular-shaped metal Forest Service marker, drop into and switchback out of a hollow, and arrive at signed Haddock Peak. The peak offers good views to the south and west of the Ojai backcountry.

From the peak, the trail descends in earnest. Almost two miles of travel brings you to Haddock (pronounced hay-dock) Trail Camp located on the banks of Piedra Blanca Creek.

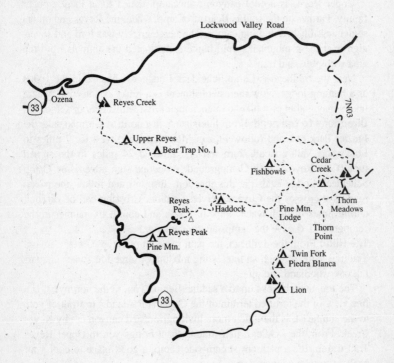

Beartrap Trail

Reyes Creek Camp to Upper Reyes Trail Camp
  6 miles round trip; 800-foot gain

Reyes Creek Camp to Beartrap #1 Trail Camp
  10 miles round trip; 1,100-foot gain

Season: All year

Reyes and Beartrap creeks are two of the many pretty watercourses that spill from the northern slopes of Pine Mountain in Los Padres National Forest. The creeks run full speed in spring, and even in dry years usually have water.

Upper Reyes is a cool canyon trail camp named for a local pioneer family. Farther up the trail is Beartrap Camp, where the Reyes and others settlers established hunting camps. The fierce grizzly was lord and sovereign over these mountains until hunters eliminated the animals from the area with guns and traps.

Near the trailhead is Camp Scheideck Lodge, established in the 1890s as a hunting lodge. Now the establishment is a funky country bar, where hikers may gather post hike to quench their thirst with a beer or soft drink.

Directions to trailhead: From Interstate 5, just north of Gorman, take the Frazier Park exit and follow Frazier Mountain Road west for 7 miles to Lockwood Valley Road. Turn left and proceed 24 miles to the signed turnoff for Reyes Creek Campground. A second sign advertising Camp Scheideck Lodge is also at this junction. Turn left and follow the paved road as it crosses the Cuyama River. Caution: Crossing can be difficult during times of high water. Park in a safe and courteous manner in the campground. (Leave the campsites for campers.)

The Hike: From the trailhead, the path rises out of Reyes Creek Canyon. The trail leads through an interesting mixture of three life zones: chaparral, oak woodland and pine.

The trail switchbacks up to a saddle. Behind you, to the northwest, is a fine view of the tortured terrain of the Cuyama Badlands. In front of you, to the southeast, is the much more inviting forested canyon cut by Reyes Creek. From the saddle, a half-mile descent brings you to Upper Reyes Trail Camp. It's a pleasant stream-side camp, a good place to cool your heels or to take a lunch stop.

Energetic hikers will assault the switchbacks above Upper Reyes Trail Camp and climb to the ridge separating Reyes Creek from Beartrap Creek. The trail descends to an oak- and pine-shaded camp on Beartrap Creek.

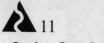 11

Cedar Creek Trail

Thorn Meadows to Cedar Camp
  4 miles round trip; 300-foot gain

To Fishbowls
  9 miles round trip; 1,000-foot gain

Return via Piru Creek
  12 miles round trip

Season: All year; caution during times of high water

The Fishbowls of Piru Creek are a deep series of potholes dredged out of the sedimentary rock creekbed by the erosive power of rushing water. You'll enjoy basking on nearby flat rocks and dreaming your life away. When you awake from your dreams, a plunge into the cold water of the Fishbowls will quickly clear your head.

This hike is one of the nicest in the Mt. Pinos area of Los Padres National Forest. The trail climbs through cedar and pine forest to the headwaters of Piru Creek. The creek springs from the slopes of Pine Mountain and bubbles through a maze of mountains. Piru Creek pools were the site of gold mining at the turn of the century. Even today, you can sometimes spot weekend prospectors looking for a flash in the pan.

Directions to trailhead: From Interstate 5 just north of Gorman, take the Frazier Park exit and follow Frazier Mountain Road west for 3 miles to Lake of the Woods Y intersection. Bear left here and continue 11 miles on Lockwood Valley Road (9N03), a dirt road suitable for most passenger cars. Proceed 7½ miles, then turn right on signed Thorn Meadows Road (7N03B) and drive ½ mile to the beginning of Cedar Creek Trail on the right. Parking is along the road near the trailhead.

The Hike: From the trailhead, head up a dirt road that is closed to vehicles. The road soon narrows to a trail, which stays near Piru Creek. It's pleasant hiking through oak woodland and scattered pines. Wallflowers, scarlet buglers and Johnny jump-ups brighten the path in places. Watch for the chia with its small blue flowers. A staple food of Southern California Indians, a single teaspoon of chia seed was reported to have been able to sustain a man on a 24-hour march.

After 2 miles of pleasant hiking, you arrive at peaceful Cedar Creek Camp on a south fork of Cedar Creek in a tiny basin ringed by cedar and big cone spruce. The camp is a wonderful place for a picnic and for soaking up some shade before the climb ahead.

The trail continues up forested slopes, along the backbone of a ridge

Cooling off in the Fishbowls.

and in a long mile reaches a signed junction. To the left, a trail leads to Pine Mountain Lodge Camp. Bear right, or north, to the Fishbowls on Fishbowls Trail (22W05). The trail swoops up and down two more ridges and offers great views of the sharp forested ridges of the Mt. Pinos high country. The trail then descends steeply to Fishbowls Trail Camp., 1½ miles from the trail junction.

The camp occupies a quiet, shady canyon cut by the headwaters of Piru Creek. From the camp, the Fishbowls area ¼ mile upstream.

Return the same way or take the long, lazy loop along Piru Creek back to the trailhead.

Return via Piru Creek: From Fishbowls Camp, Trail 21W05 winds lazily along Piru Creek. Piru flows sometimes gently, sometimes frothily, and a collects the contributions of lesser and more transitory creeks. Fishing is fair in some of the deep quiet pools of Piru. After 6 miles and many winding turns, you reach Grade Valley Road. Turn right and follow it ½ mile to the Thorn Meadows Road. Another ½ mile along this road brings you back to your car and the trailhead.

12

Piedra Blanca Trail

Lion Campground to Piedra Blanca
3 miles round trip; 200-foot gain

To Twin Forks Camp
6 miles round trip; 600-foot gain

To Pine Mountain Lodge Camp
11 miles round trip; 3,000-foot gain

Season: All year

Sparkling Piedra Blanca (White Rock) is the sort of place where Carlos Castaneda's Don Juan might lurk.

The sandstone formation extends for miles between the upper reaches of Sespe River and the mountains to the north. Most of the sandstone in the Sespe area, called the Sespe Formation, is distinguished by its red color. It's a land-laid formation, deposited in layers of mud and sand on land. Unlike the red rock that guards the mouth of Sespe Creek, Piedra Blanca's thick sequences of sedimentary rock are of marine origin. These marine deposits are particularly notable in the Santa Barbara Backcountry and are found in the Santa Ynez, Topatopa, Piru, and Pine Mountain ranges. Perhaps the most spectacular formations are found at Piedra Blanca.

Piedra Blanca Trail ascends chaparral-cloaked hillsides and visits mighty Piedra Blanca. The path then follows Piedra Blanca Creek and climbs for some distance to Pine Mountain Lodge Camp, the site of a hunting and fishing lodge that once stood on the slopes of Pine Mountain.

Directions to trailhead: From Ojai, take Highway 33 north 14 miles. Turn right on signed Rose Valley Road and continue 6 miles to Lion Campground. Park in the special day-use lot near the campground. The sometimes-signed trail begins across the creek.

The Hike: Cross Sespe Creek and join Piedra Blanca Trail. The trail cuts through chaparral and wastes no time heading for Piedra Blanca. These jumbo rocks are in your sight most of the way. Like clouds, the longer you gaze at the formations, the more they assume the shape of your imagination: dragons with missing teeth, white sand castles with spires and turrets, the Washington Monument . . .

From the rocks, the trail descends sharply to an unnamed tributary of Piedra Blanca Creek, finds the creek itself and follows it up the canyon. The trail dips in and out of the narrow oak woodland that lines the creek. You pass an attractive streamside trail camp named for the dominant

Piedra Blanca

sandstone, Piedra Blanca, and soon come to Twin Forks Trail Camp, named for its location near the North and Middle Forks of Piedra Blanca Creek. Either Piedra Blanca or Twin Forks are nice picnic spots.

From Twin Forks, the trail twists along with the north fork of Piedra Blanca Creek. It ascends steeply for about 2 miles, then leaves the creek and climbs chaparral- and pine-covered slopes toward the top of Pine Mountain. Pine Mountain Lodge Trail Camp, located at an elevation of 6,000 feet, is cool and green, a good place to take off your shoes and sit awhile.

13

Matilija Trail

Matilija Cyn. Rd. to Matilija Camp
  2 miles round trip; 200-foot gain

To Middle Matilija Camp
  7 miles round trip; 900-foot gain

To Forest Road 6N01
  15 miles round trip; 3,000-foot gain

Season: Oct-June

The meaning of Matilija is unknown, but it may have been the Chumash word to describe the showy Matilija poppy, prized by the Indians for its medicinal qualities. The poppy's botanical name, *Romneya coulteri*, honors two Irish scientists and longtime friends, astronomer Romney Robinson and botanist Thomas Coulter.

The Matilija poppy is found along many Ojai backcountry trails and often alongside the road into and out of Ojai—Highway 33. It blooms from May to July, stands 3 to 7 feet tall and is bushy at its base. The delicate flowers have six white crinkled petals and a golden center.

The Matilija Trail has the dubious distinction of being the flash point for some of the largest fires in Southern California history. In June of 1917 the Matilija-Wheeler Springs Fire burned for five days and nights and blackened more than 30,000 acres. The 1932 Matilija Fire burned nearly a quarter-million acres. One of the fire lines was Highway 33, then under construction. The 1985 Wheeler Fire scorched much of the Ojai backcountry, including the steep terrain watered by the many forks of Matilija Creek.

Matilija Trail, at its lower end, offers an ideal family outing alongside the Upper North Fork of Matilija Creek. More experienced hikers will enjoy pushing on to the canyon's upper reaches for fine ocean and mountain views. Many nice pools, cascades and flat sunny rocks offer pleasant picnic spots. Forest planners have recommended that 30,000 acres of Ojai backcountry be set aside as the Matilija Wilderness.

Directions to trailhead: Continue on Highway 33 about four miles past Ojai, and past the leftward turnoff to Matilija Hot Springs. A short mile past the hot springs, turn left on Matilija Canyon Road (Forest Service Road 5N13) and proceed 5 miles to a locked gate across the road. A parking area is located just before the gate.

The Hike: Pass the locked gate and hike along the dirt road through Matilija Canyon Ranch and a private wildlife reserve. Please stay on the

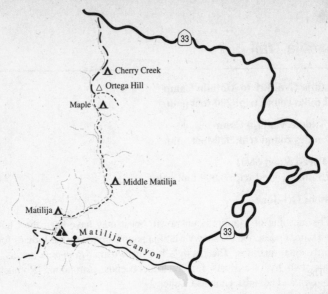

road and respect private property. After crossing two branches of Matilija Creek, the road turns left, but you will follow the unmarked spur that turns right and follows the creek. Within 50 yards, cross the creek twice more and begin hiking along the creek bank. A mile of nearly level walking brings you to Matilija Camp.

Matilija Camp is a nice picnic spot. Those geologically inclined will note how stream erosion in this area exposed areas of severe folding and faulting; past actions of the Santa Ynez Fault are very much in evidence.

Beyond the camp, the trail fords several small tributary creeks that feed the Upper North Fork of the Matilija, and crosses a wide meadow. The trail switchbacks above the creek for a while, then resumes again on the canyon bottom. Some level travel and few more crossings brings you to oak-shaded Middle Matilija Camp.

Beyond the camp, the trail crosses and re-crosses the creek half a dozen more times. The canyon floor is forested with big cone spruce, bay laurel and maple. You'll rise out of the canyon, then descend into the narrowing canyon and arrive at abandoned, but still serviceable, Upper Matilija Camp.

From this camp, the trail continues up-creek another mile, then rises steeply north out of the canyon. Switchbacks offer the hiker fine views of Old Man Mountain, the Santa Ynez range and the Pacific Ocean. The upper canyon slopes were severely burned in 1985. However, the maples at Maple Camp, the chokecherry, manzanita and scrub oak are recovering. A final steep climb brings you to the terminus of the trail at Forest Service Road 6N01 near Ortega Hill.

14

Gridley Trail

Gridley Road to Gridley Spring
  6 miles round trip; 1,400-foot gain

To Nordhoff Peak
  12 miles round trip; 3,500-foot gain

Season: All year

Prussian-born journalist Charles Nordhoff was one of the 19th Century's biggest boosters of California and the California way of life. Nordhoff, an editor with the *New York Evening Post*, traveled extensively throughout the Golden State in 1870–71, and wrote *California: for Health, Pleasure and Residence,* an enormously popular book that prompted much visitation and settlement.

The book had a profound effect on the nation's attitude toward California. No longer would California be regarded as the uncivilized far Western frontier, but as the perfect place in the sun—one that offered the chance to build a home or business, to raise crops or children in America's answer to the Mediterranean.

One of Nordhoff's favorite discoveries—quintessential Southern California as he saw it—was a beautiful valley located about 15 miles inland from Ventura. Nordhoff wrote about this valley for several Eastern magazines and newspapers, and as a result, the peaceful hamlet here quickly grew into a town. Grateful townspeople named it Nordhoff in 1874. Nordhoff it remained until 1916 when the anti-German sentiment of World War I prompted a change of name to Ojai.

Nordhoff's name remains on the 4,425-foot peak that forms a dramatic backdrop for the town of Nordhoff, er . . . Ojai. The summit offers splendid views of the Ojai Valley, the Ventura County coastline and the Channel Islands.

Ascending Nordhoff Peak is no picnic. Its slopes bear scars from the fury of the 1985 Wheeler Fire. The trail crosses steep, sun-baked slopes, but if you've picked a clear day for this trek, the views will reward your effort.

Directions to trailhead: From the intersection of Highways 33 and 150 in Ojai, proceed on the latter road, known as Ojai Avenue. You'll pass through town, and about 2 miles from the intersection, look for Los Padres National Forest Ojai Ranger Station on the left at 1190 Ojai Avenue. This is a good place to get the latest trail information. Proceed another half-mile and take the second left beyond the ranger station—Gridley Road. Follow Gridley 1.7 miles to its end. Signed Gridley Trail is on the left.

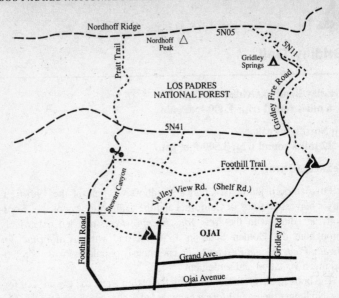

The Hike: Gridley Trail climbs a brushy draw, overhung with tall ceanothus. A half-mile's gentle ascent brings you to Gridley Fire Road (Forest Service road 5N11). Turn right and follow this crumbling dirt road as it ascends above avocado groves planted on steep slopes. Leaving behind the "Guacamole Wilderness," the route enters Gridley Canyon, climbing to the northwest (and thankfully a bit cooler) side of the canyon.

Not much remains of Gridley Spring Camp, incinerated along with thousands of acres of the Ojai backcountry in the Wheeler Fire. Still, the vegetation in the area has made an astonishing recovery, and the spring named for an early homesteader, still flows.

Past Gridley Spring, peak-bound hikers will continue along the dirt road into an east fork of Gridley Canyon and join a switchbacking trail for the rigorous ascent. Notice the superb succession of sedimentary rocks displayed by the Topatopa mountains above you. Far below is the Pacific Ocean.

Two miles from the springs, you'll meet Nordhoff Fire Road (5N05). Turn left and follow this road a mile to Nordhoff Peak.

To the south is Ojai Valley, with Lake Casitas and the Pacific beyond. To the west rise the higher peaks of the Topatopa range, including the 6,210-foot signature peak, Topatopa. Also to the west is Sespe Condor Sanctuary. To the north is the Pine Mountain range and many more Los Padres National Forest peaks.

15

Foothill Trail

Stewart Canyon to Gridley Road
Return via Shelf Road
  5½ miles round trip; 600-foot gain

Season: All year

Ojai, nestled in a little valley backed by the Topatopa and Sulphur Mountains, has meant tranquility to several generations of settlers and citrus growers, artists, musicians and mystics. Ojai Valley was the setting for Shangri-La in the 1937 movie *Lost Horizon*.

The 10-mile-long, 3-mile wide valley, surrounded by coastal mountain ranges has always had a sequestered feeling. Chumash Indians called this region *Ojai*, which means "nest." The meditative setting has spawned an artists colony, music festival and a number of health resorts. The environment has attracted the metaphysically minded too; the hiker can look down on the Krotona Institute of Theosophy on one side of town and the Krishnamurti Foundation on the other.

Ancient geologic forces shaped the Ojai Valley that modern-day visitors find so attractive. This part of Ventura County lies in a region geologists call the Transverse Range Province. Transverse means lying across; mountains and valleys in these parts have been moved, by seismic and other forces, out of California's usual north-south orientation into an east-west configuration.

This east-west positioning means a lot of sunshine, with early morning light and long, lingering sunsets. Southern California locales with a southern exposure—Ojai, Malibu, Santa Barbara—often seem bathed in a magical light that is most bewitching.

Foothill Trail offers the best view of the town and valley. From the path, hikers get great views of the harmonious Spanish architecture of Ojai, sweet-smelling citrus groves and the sometimes misty, sometimes mystical Ojai Valley.

Directions to trailhead: From the intersection of Highways 150 and 33, head east on the latter route one mile to North Signal Street in downtown Ojai. The post office and The Oaks resort are on this corner. Turn north on North Signal and drive¾ mile to a junction with an unsigned road on your left. A large water tower and a chain link fence are at this junction. Park along Signal.

The Hike: Take a look up North Signal, which ends in another hundred yards at its meeting with Shelf Road, the dirt fire road that will be your return route. Now turn west on the paved road below the water tank. The road soon turns to gravel and you'll march past a Ventura County flood control works, the Stewart Canyon Debris Basin. Two hundred yards from the trailhead, just as your road turns north toward some residences, you'll spot a white pipe fence and a Forest Service trail sign. Join the trail, which soon dips into brushy Stewart Canyon.

The trail zigzags under oaks and a tangled understory of native and non-native shrubs. You'll cross two dirt roads then wind through a eucalyptus grove, which marks the site of the elegant Foothill Hotel, a casualty of fire just after the turn of the century. Foothill Trail turns north and ascends along the west wall of Stewart Canyon. The trail nears some private homes, crosses a paved road, then joins a dirt one and passes a water tank on your left. Shortly thereafter is a signed trail on your left for Foothill Trail 22W09 and Pratt Trail 23W09. Continue another 100 yards on the dirt road to another signed junction with the Foothill Trail; this path you'll take east.

Foothill Trail ascends up fire-scarred slopes and over meadowland seasonally dotted with wildflowers. Keep an eye out for abundant poison oak. Just as you're beginning to wonder if this trail will ever deliver its promised views, it tops a rise and offers a first glimpse of Ojai Valley.

The trail soon descends to an unsigned junction. A connector trail leads north to Forest Road 5N11; this road heads east to Gridley Road but offers no valley views. Stay with Foothill Trail, which descends to a little seasonal creek then climbs eastward out onto open slopes for great views of Ojai. From some vantage points you can see almost the whole Ojai Valley, Shangri-La indeed.

About a half-mile from Gridley Road, you'll spot dirt Shelf Road 200 yards or so below Foothill Trail. Experienced bushwhackers can blaze a trail down to the road, but think twice; it's probably more trouble than the little time/distance saved.

Foothill Trail, near its end, descends more steeply, its route stabilized by railroad ties. The trail emerges at a crumbling asphalt road, which you'll follow 50 yards to Gridley Road. Turn right on Gridley Road. Walk a hundred yards, cross a one-lane bridge, then descend another hundred yards to Shelf Road on your right.

Shelf Road, closed to vehicle traffic by a white pipe gate, heads east and ascends moderately into the hills. Skirting orange trees and avocado groves, Shelf Road serves up views that are just a little less dramatic than those offered by higher Foothill Trail.

Just after the road bends south, you'll reach a gate and Signal Road, which you'll follow the short distance back to the trailhead.

16

Horn Canyon Trail

Thacher School to The Pines
  6 miles round trip; 1,800-foot gain

Season: Oct-June

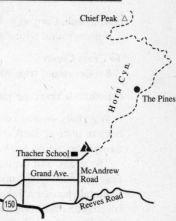

Horn Canyon was reportedly one of Krish-namurti's favorite walks. He sometimes told the tale of how in his younger days he befriended a mountain lion along this trail.

Horn Canyon today is still an inspiring walk—even if you don't talk to the animals. The canyon itself is a shady retreat watered by a seasonal stream. Climbing out of the can-yon, the trail offers fine views of the Ojai Valley. The Pines, the appropriately named goal of this hike, is a pine tree plantation, and a Forest Service trail camp that welcomes hikers with shade and a trickling spring.

Directions to trailhead: From downtown Ojai, head east on Highway 150 (Ojai Avenue). About a ¾ mile from the center of town, you'll see a national forest ranger station on your left (open Monday through Friday).

Continue a short distance past the station and turn left on Gridley Road. After ³/10 mile, turn right on Grand Avenue, continuing to McAndrew Road. Turn left. McAndrew Road bends left to join Thacher Road, but you continue straight into the Thacher school ground and park in an area assigned to visitors.

The Hike: From the school's visitors parking lot, walk toward the moun-tains along the asphalt road about 100 yards. At a signed fork directing you to "Gymkana Area and Jameson Field," angle right onto a dirt road, which leads another 100 yards through an orchard to a gated dirt road on your left. This dirt road, with a Forest Service trail sign, is the beginning of Horn Canyon Trail. The wide dirt path ascends up-canyon.

After a long mile, the road ends and Horn Canyon Trail becomes a narrow path that ascends the west wall of the canyon. The trail, stabilized by railroad ties, soon leaves the shade of the oaks and sycamores and climbs hot, exposed slopes.

The Pines, a green island floating atop a sea of gray chaparral, seems tantalizingly close when you first spot the stand from a bend in the trail. Actually, you'll have to climb steeply another half a mile before you reach the welcome shade of the conifers at an elevation of 3,260 feet.

17

Santa Paula Canyon Trail

Santa Paula Canyon to Big Cone Camp
 6 miles round trip; 800-foot gain

To Cross Camp
 8 miles round trip; 900-foot gain

Season: All Year; use caution at times of high water

Waterfalls, wading pools and swimmin' holes are some of the attractions of tranquil Santa Paula Canyon. A trail winds along the river bed through the canyon and visits some perfect-for-a-picnic trail camps.

The lovely trail begins at St. Thomas Aquinas College, and near a malodorous oil field once owned by infamous oilman and Southern California booster Edward Lawrence Doheny. Doheny's black-gold discoveries of 1892 made him an extremely wealthy man and began the first oil industry boom in Los Angeles. (Doheny's thirty-room mansion is located behind iron gates just off Highway 150.)

During the Harding administration, Doheny received drilling rights on federal land in Elk Hills without undergoing the inconvenience of competitive bidding. A 1923 Senate investigation of the Teapot Dome Scandal uncovered Doheny's $100,000 loan to Secretary of the Interior Fall and led to Fall's conviction for accepting a bribe; Doheny, however, was acquitted of offering one.

Floods periodically sweep Santa Paula Canyon and wash out the trail. And Los Padres National Forest administrators periodically take the trail off the forest map. Mapped or not, Santa Paula Canyon Trail is a great walk.

Directions to the trailhead: From the junction of Highways 33 and 150 in Ojai, head east from town on the latter road about 9½ miles to the bridge spanning Santa Paula Creek. The trailhead is located at the entrance to St. Thomas Aquinas/Ferndale Ranch on the north side of the road, but you continue on Highway 150 across the Santa Paula Creek bridge to a wide turnout on the south side of the highway. A sign informs you that the Santa Paula Canyon trail begins across the highway 500 feet away.

The Hike: From the often-guarded Ferndale Ranch/college entrance, you'll ignore a road leading to the oil fields and follow the asphalt drive onto the college grounds. The road curves around wide green lawns and handsome classrooms. At a few junctions, signs keep you "Hikers" away from the route taken by "Oil Field Traffic." A bit more than a half-mile from the trailhead, you pass an orchard and some cows, pass through

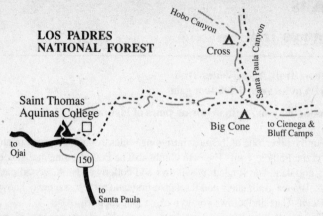

a pipe gate, and finally reach Santa Paula Creek and the true beginning of Santa Paula Canyon Trail.

The trail travels a short distance with Santa Paula Creek, crosses it, then joins a retiring dirt road—your route to Big Cone Camp. After crossing the creek again, the trail begins a moderate to stiff climb up a slope bearing the less-than-lyrical name of Hill 1989. The trail then descends to Big Cone Camp, perched on a terrace above Santa Paula Creek.

Just below the camp, the trail, now a narrow footpath, descends to the creek. As you descend, you'll look up-canyon and spot a waterfall and a swimming hole.

The trail crosses Santa Paula Creek and switchbacks up to an unsigned junction. A right at this junction leads above the east fork of Santa Paula Canyon 3½ miles on poor, unmaintained trail to Cienega Camp. Hardy hikers will enjoy bushwhacking along to this camp set in a meadowland shaded by oak and big cone spruce.

A left at the above-mentioned junction leads north up Santa Paula Canyon past some inviting pools. The path, sometimes called Last Chance Trail, climbs a mile to Cross, another big cone spruce-shaded camp. Here Santa Paula Creek offers some nice falls and great swimming holes. Caution: The creek current can be quite strong on occasion.

18

Pothole Trail

Pothole Trail, Agua Blanca Trail
   11½ miles loop; 2,200-foot gain

Season: All year, caution during times of high water

For the hiker, one of the most intriguing routes through Condor Country is via the Pothole Trail. The path climbs to The Pothole, a natural sink of lush grassland surrounded by willows and cottonwoods. A second path, Aqua Blanca Trail, takes you through a dramatic rock passageway known as Devils Gate and allows you to make a long loop trip.

The two trails add up to a long day hike, suitable for experienced hikers. Both trails are in rough to mediocre condition; they're passable but it's a good idea to wear long pants; lots of brush and poison oak crowd the way. Piru Creek is difficult, even dangerous to cross during times of high water.

Directions to trailhead: From Interstate 5 at Castaic Junction, head west on Highway 126 some 11 miles to the turnoff for Lake Piru. Head north on the road, which is called Main Street as it leads through citrus orchards and the hamlet of Piru. In seven miles you'll encounter an entrance kiosk for Lake Piru Recreation Area. Tell the attendant you're bound for Blue Point Campground and you'll receive a Forest Service day use permit.

Five more miles up the road, you'll see signed Pothole Trail on your left. Parking is scanty nearby. Instead, continue 1¼ miles past the trailhead to Blue Point Campground. Park in the campground if the water in Piru Creek is high, or across the creek in a day use lot. (The only problem with parking across the creek is that you must then wade the creek to begin the hike). Fill your canteen at the campground.

The Hike: From the campground, walk the shoulder of the paved road, enjoying good views of Lake Piru. A mile and a quarter of road walking brings you back to signed Pothole Trail on your right.

Pothole Trail takes you on a most strenuous ascent over an overgrazed hillside choked with mustard and thistle. Some reward for the pain and gain are memorable views of nearby sandstone outcroppings, and of the bluish rock called Blue Point. Also part of the panorama is a look down at Aqua Blanca Canyon and the Devil's Gateway.

The wicked ascent (1,800 feet in slightly more than 2 miles) brings you huffing and puffing toward a few isolated ridgetop walnut trees and to a hilltop crowned with a wildlife guzzler. Pause to catch your breath and to ready yourself for the final uphill assault.

Pothole Trail dips briefly then climbs along a ridgeline in earnest. Just

before cresting the hill, the path veers right (north), mercifully beginning several miles of descent. Stands of manzanita and thick chaparral crowd the trail, which zigzags down a steep slope.

After losing a thousand feet in elevation, you'll spot a wide potrero (grassland) to the west. The trail heads south, then west. Skirting Devil's Potrero, Pothole Trail turns north, but you want to look carefully for the thin, overgrown trail (marked by a single metal stake) leading a short quarter mile south to the Pothole. A natural depression or "sag pond" created by the nearby Agua Blanca earthquake fault, the grassy Pothole is bordered by cottonwoods and willows.

In 1890, William Whitaker homesteaded here. He had a small cattle operation and grew feed for his livestock on the potrero. Back on overgrown Pothole Trail, you plunge into a ravine, passing Whitaker's abandoned cabin with rusty farm implements out back.

Under the shade of oaks and big cone spruce, you'll cross and re-cross a fern lined creek, dodge a lot of poison oak, and finally descend to Agua Blanca Creek. Here you have a decision to make: If your spirit of adventure is high enough and the water in the creek low enough, you can wade down-creek through the Devils Gateway. The high rock walls of the Gateway squeeze the creek through a 20-foot wide passageway; water is likely to be waist-deep or higher during winter and spring months. You'll pick up the trail again on the other side of the Gateway.

The trail itself heads up-creek a short ways to a signed junction. Log Cabin Camp is 200 yards farther along the creekside trail. Your route, Agua Blanca Trail, detours a half-mile around Devils Gateway, first ascending then descending the canyon wall. Use caution on the descent along a couple eroded stretches of trail.

The trail descends moderately, mostly along the shaded south side of the canyon. Crossing Agua Blanca Creek a couple of times, the path brings you near tempting swimming holes.

The creek flow lessens near the mouth of the canyon. Aqua Blanca Trail gives way to a dirt road, you pass a few dilapidated buildings (private property), then reach a junction. The dirt road to the left leads north along Piru Creek. You continue more or less straight, contouring around a little hill and descending to Piru Creek. Cross the creek (usually about knee-deep) and follow the dirt road a mile to the Forest Service day-use area and Blue Point Campground.

Tunnel Trail, La Cumbre Peak

2. Santa Ynez Mountains

AFEW MILLION YEARS AGO, the Santa Ynez Mountains rose slowly from the sea. The mountains are not secretive about their origin and display their oceanic heritage in a number of ways. Tilted blocks of sedimentary rock, which aggregated tens of thousands of feet in thickness, provide the first clue to the mountains' former undersea life. Fossils of sea animals give further testimony that the mountains were once many leagues under the sea. Even the vegetation betrays the mountains' origin. The mineral-poor sandstone slopes formed in the ocean deep can support little more than dense brush, so it's the chaparral community—buckthorn, mountain lilac and scrub oak—that predominates.

The Santa Ynez Mountains are part of a series of east/west trending ranges known as the Transverse Ranges, which encircle Southern California from San Diego to Point Conception. The backbone of the Transverse Range are the San Bernardino and San Gabriel mountains; the Santa Ynez Mountains form the uppermost, westerly part of the Transverse Spine. The Santa Ynez extend almost fifty miles from Matilija Canyon on the east to Gaviota Canyon on the west. Compared to other ranges in the Transverse system, the Santa Ynez are quite small, ranging from 2,000 to 4,000 feet.

From the viewpoints, hikers can decipher Santa Barbara's sometimes confusing orientation; that is to say, the east-west direction of the coastline and the mountain ranges. Even many long-time Southern Californians are amused by looking south to the ocean. By all means, consider taking along a Santa Barbara county map to help with your orientation.

At first glance, the range seems smothered with a gray mass of tortured vegetation. On closer inspection, the Santa Ynez reveals more charm. Sycamores and bays line the canyons and a host of seasonal creeks wash the hillsides. In spring, the chaparral blooms and adds frosty whites and blues to the gray-green plants. The backcountry looks particularly inviting after the first winter rains. On upper peaks, rain sometimes turns to snow.

Santa Ynez Mountain trails mainly follow the canyons above Santa Barbara and Montecito. The network of trails generally follows streams to the top of the range. They start in lush canyon bottoms, zig zag up hot, dry canyon walls, and follow rock ledges to the crest. Many of the trails intersect El Camino Cielo (the sky road), which follows the mountain crest. From the top, enjoy sweeping views of the Pacific, Channel Island and coastal plain. Northward, row after row of sharp mountains spread toward the horizon. These mountains were born beneath the sea and may someday return to their birthplace. In the meantime, say for the next million years or so, the mountains will continue to provide splendid hiking.

19

Santa Ynez River Trail

Red Rock Trailhead to Gibraltar Dam Picnic Area
6 miles round trip; 400-foot gain

Our State Water Resources Control Board suggests that one of the most beneficial uses of the upper Santa Ynez River is for "water contact recreation." Translated from bureaucratic jargon: "Go jump in the river!" Great swimming holes await hikers who venture to the attractive Santa Ynez Recreation Area, located in the mountains behind Santa Barbara.

During dry years, the river's swimming holes are filled by periodic releases from Gibraltar Reservoir, up-river from the recreation area. Thanks to Santa Barbara's contribution of a small part of its municipal water supply, some of the pools maintain year-round depths of 6 to 18 feet.

Santa Ynez River Trail leads to several pleasant swimming holes and is an easy hike, suitable for the whole family. The most popular ol' swimmin' hole is Red Rock Pool, located only a short distance from the trailhead. The trail to the pools and to Gibraltar Dam Picnic Area follows the remains of an old mining road, built in the 1870s during a quicksilver mining boom. The road was later used by workers during the 1920 construction of Gibraltar Dam.

For more information about the Santa Ynez Recreation Area, stop by Los Padres National Forest Los Prietos Ranger Station, located midway between Highway 154 and Red Rock Trailhead on Paradise Road.

Directions to trailhead: From Highway 101 in Santa Barbara, take the "Lake Cachuma, Highway 154" exit. Proceed east on Highway 154. At the top of San Marcos Pass, you'll spot the historic Cielo Store, featured as "Papadakis Tavern," in the remake of the classic movie *The Postman Always Rings Twice*. A short distance over the pass, just past a Vista Point (about 10 miles from Santa Barbara if you're watching your odometer), turn right on Paradise Road and drive to the end of the road—10.7 miles. Leave your car in the large dirt parking lot adjacent to the trail, which begins at a locked gate.

If you're the kind of hiker who loves loop trips, note the presence of a second trail leading from the parking lot to Gibraltar Dam. The "high road," as its known by locals, makes a gentle traverse across the mountains above the river. Like the "low road"—Santa Ynez River Trail—it's about three miles long. It's a good trail to keep in mind for times of high water.

The Hike: Wide, flat Santa Ynez River Trail passes a "No Nudity Allowed" sign and after ¼ mile crosses the river. Near this crossing you

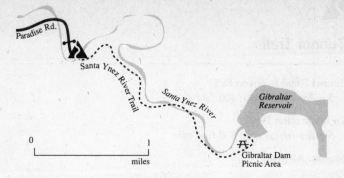

might observe some scattered bricks, all that remains of a turn-of-the-century quicksilver furnace. Quicksilver ore, mined in the nearby hills, was crushed and heated in the furnace. The ore became gaseous at a low temperature and the gas condensed into liquid mercury.

Soon after the first river crossing, you'll reach Red Rock, the most popular swimming hole. Geologically minded hikers will examine the red rock, metamorphosed volcanics of the Jurassic age. Other hikers will plunge into the river.

The trail passes through oak woodland and zigzags from bank to bank along the river. Alongside the river is a canopy of cottonwood, sycamore and willow.

Wildlife viewing opportunities, particularly during the early morning hours, are quite good near the Santa Ynez River because the area includes several different habitats: oak woodland, coastal sage scrub, grassland and freshwater marsh. You might spot a deer, gray fox, striped skunk, lizard, cottontail rabbit or raccoon. Watch for pond turtles basking on the rocks, logs and banks of large pools. The ecological diversity of the area also means a wide variety of bird-life. In the woodland areas, birders might sight a mourning dove, warbling vireo, northern oriole or a woodpecker. Cliff swallows, flycatchers and belted kingfishers swoop over the river.

Several more dry river crossings and a couple of wet ones, and some travel beneath the boughs of handsome coast live oaks, will bring you to Gibraltar Picnic Area, located a few hundred yards down-river from the dam. Oaks shade scattered picnic tables.

You may continue up the trail to Gibraltar Dam, named for the large rock here, which is said to resemble the great guardian rock of the Mediterranean. A second, shadeless picnic site is located at the southeast top edge of the dam. Observe the warning signs at the dam and stay out of restricted areas.

20

Tunnel Trail

Tunnel Road to Seven Falls
  3 miles round trip; 400-foot gain

To Inspiration Point
  5 miles round trip; 800-foot gain

Season: All year

A pleasant party spent yesterday up Mission Canyon visiting noted Seven Falls and afterward eating a tempting picnic dinner in a romantic spot on the creek's bank. To reach these falls requires some active climbing, able-bodied sliding and skillful swinging . . .

—Santa Barbara Daily Press, 1887

Seven Falls has been a popular destination of Santa Barbarans since before the turn of the century. The seven distinct little falls found in the bed of Mission Creek are still welcoming hikers.

Tunnel Trail was used by workers to gain access to a difficult city waterworks project launched by the city of Santa Barbara. Workers burrowed a tunnel through the Santa Ynez Mountains to connect the watershed on the backside of the mountains to the growing little city. Braving floods, cave-ins and dangerous hydrogen gas, a crew labored eight years and finished the project in 1912.

This easy family hike in the foothills follows Tunnel Trail, joins Jesusita Trail for an exploration of the Seven Falls along Mission Creek and ascends Inspiration Point for sweeping coastal views.

Mission Creek provided the water supply for Mission Santa Barbara. Near the mission, which you'll pass as you proceed to Tunnel trailhead, are some stone remains of the padres' waterworks system.

Mission Creek also flows through the Santa Barbara Botanic Garden, which is well worth visiting because of its fine displays of native California flora. Paths lead through chaparral, coastal sage and succulent environments to a Mission Creek dam built by the Spanish friars.

A ramble through the Santa Barbara foothills combined with a visit to the mission and botanic garden would add up to a very pleasant day's outing.

Directions to trailhead: From Highway 101 in Santa Barbara, exit on Mission Street. Turn east to Laguna Street, then left and drive past the historic Santa Barbara Mission. From the mission, drive up Mission Canyon Road, turning right for a block on Foothill Road, then imme-

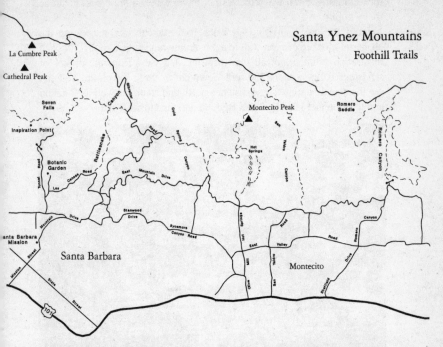

Santa Ynez Mountains
Foothill Trails

La Cumbre Peak

Cathedral Peak

Seven
Falls

Inspiration Point

Botanic
Garden

Montecito Peak

Romero
Saddle

Santa Barbara
Mission

Santa Barbara

Montecito

diately turning left back onto Mission Canyon Road. At a distinct V-inter-
section, veer left onto Tunnel Road and drive to its end. Park along the
road.

The Hike: From the end of Tunnel Road, hike past a locked gate onto a
paved road, which eventually turns to dirt as you leave the power lines
behind and get increasingly grander views of Santa Barbara. The road
makes a sharp left and crosses a bridge over the West Fork of Mission
Creek.

Beyond the bridge, you'll hike a short distance under some handsome
oaks to a junction. (Tunnel Trail angles northeast, uphill, leading three
miles to "the sky road," East Camino Cielo.) You join Jesusita Trail and
descend to Mission Creek.

At the canyon bottom, you can hike up creek into a steep gorge that was
cut from solid sandstone. Geologically inclined hikers will recognize
fossilized layers of oyster beds from the Oligocene Epoch, deposited some
35 million years ago. In more recent times, say for the last few thousands
of winters, rain water has rushed from the shoulder of La Cumbre Peak
and cut away at the sandstone layers, forming several deep pools. If you
decide to hike up Mission Creek, be careful; reaching the waterfalls—
particularly the higher ones—requires quite a bit of boulder-hopping and

rock-climbing. Even when there's not much water in the creek, it can be tricky going.

From the creek crossing, Jesusita Trail switchbacks steeply up the chaparral-cloaked canyon wall to a power line road atop a knoll. Although Inspiration Point is not all that inspiring, the view from the cluster of sandstone rocks at the 1,750-foot viewpoint is worth the climb. You can see the coastline quite some distance north and south, as well as Catalina and the Channel Islands, Santa Barbara and the Goleta Valley.

21

Rattlesnake Canyon Trail

Skofield Park to Tin Can Meadow
  4½ miles round trip; 1,000-foot gain

To Gibraltar Road
  6 miles round trip; 1,500-foot gain

Season: All year

Rattlesnake Canyon Trail is serpentine, but otherwise far more inviting than its name suggests.

The joys of the canyon were first promoted by none other than the Santa Barbara Chamber of Commerce. Many a turn-of-the-century visitor to Santa Barbara resorts enjoyed hiking and riding in the local mountains. Eager to keep the customers satisfied, in 1902 the chamber purchased easements from canyon homesteaders to develop a recreation trail.

"Chamber of Commerce Trail," as the chamber called it, was an immediate success with both tourists and locals. However, to the chamber's consternation, both the trail and the canyon itself continued to be called Rattlesnake. Chamber of Commerce Canyon sounded a bit self-serving, so the chamber tried to compromise with an earlier name, Las Canoas Canyon, and adopted a 1902 resolution to that effect. "The name of Rattlesnake Canyon is unpleasantly suggestive of a reptile," it argued, "which is found no more plentifully there than elsewhere along the mountain range and may deter some nervous persons from visiting that most delightful locality."

In the 1960s, the city of Santa Barbara purchased the canyon as parkland. A handsome wooden sign at the foot of the canyon proudly proclaims: Rattlesnake Canyon Wilderness.

This trail explores Santa Barbara's little wilderness canyon. Red-berried toyon, manzanita with its white urn-shaped flowers, and purple hummingbird sage cloak the slopes and offer a variety of smells and textures. In the early spring ceanothus blooms, adding frosty whites and blues to the gray-green thickets. Shooting stars, larkspur, and lupine also spread their color over the slopes and meadows.

Directions to trailhead: From downtown Santa Barbara, proceed uptown (toward the mountains) on State Street to Los Olivos Street. Turn right and proceed a half mile, passing by the Santa Barbara Mission and joining Mission Canyon Road. Follow this road past its intersection with Foothill Road and make a right on Las Canoas Road. Follow Las Canoas to Skofield Park. Leave your car on the shoulder of the road or in the large parking area near the picnic grounds. The trail begins on Las Canoas Road near the handsome stone bridge that crosses Rattlesnake Creek.

The Hike: From the sandstone bridge across from Skofield Park, hike up a brief stretch of trail and join a narrow dirt road that parallels the east side of the creek. For lovely picnicking, take any of the steep side trails down to the creek. In the early 19th Century the mission padres built a dam in the bottom of the canyon, which channeled water into a stone aqueduct and diverted it into the mission's waterworks system. Portions of the aqueduct still exist and can be seen by the careful observer.

The trail zigs and zags across the creek, finally continuing along the west bank to open, grassy Tin Can Meadow. The triangular-shaped meadow gets its name from a homesteader's cabin constructed of chaparral framing and kerosene can shingles and sidings. For the first quarter of this century, Tin Can Shack was an important canyon landmark and several guidebooks of that era mention it. It was a popular destination for picnickers who marveled at the inspired architecture and posed for pictures in front of it. In 1925, a brushfire destroyed the shack and it soon disintegrated into a pile of tin.

If you're feeling energetic, hike on toward the apex of the triangular meadow where you'll find a junction. The trail bearing left takes you mile and climbs 500 feet to its intersection with the Tunnel Trail—and incidentally to many points of interest in the Santa Barbara backcountry. To the right, Rattlesnake Canyon Trail climbs about ¾ of a mile and 500 feet to its intersection with Gibraltar Road. There you will be greeted by an unobstructed view of the South Coast. Watch for strangely patterned triangular aircraft overhead. A favorite hang glider's launching peak is almost within reach.

Mr. and Mrs. Lyman Pope at Tin Can Shack, Rattlesnake Canyon, 1916

22

Cold Springs Trail

Mountain Drive to Montecito Overlook
  3 miles round trip; 900-foot gain

To Montecito Peak
  7½ miles round trip; 2,500-foot gain

To Camino Cielo
  9 miles round trip; 2,700-foot gain

Season: All Year

Our favorite route to the main ridge was by a way called the Cold Springs Trail. We used to enjoy taking visitors up it, mainly because you come on the top suddenly, without warning. Then we collected remarks. Everybody, even the most stolid, said something.

—Stewart Edward White
The Mountains, 1906

After the Santa Ynez Forest Reserve was established in 1899, rangers recognized the desirability of a trail crossing the Reserve from coast to desert. In 1905, the Forest Service built a trail up the East Fork of Cold Springs Canyon.

And a lovely trail it is. It begins by the alder-shaded, year-round creek, then rises out of the canyon for fine coastal views.

Directions to trailhead: From Highway 101 in Montecito, a few miles south of Santa Barbara, exit on Hot Springs Road and proceed toward the foothills for 2½ miles to Mountain Drive. Turn left. A mile's travel on Mountain Drive brings you to the Cold Springs trailhead, which begins at a point where a creek flows over a cement drainage apron.

The Hike: The trail immediately crosses the creek to the east side of the canyon. It rises briefly through oak woodland, then returns to the creek. On your left, a quarter-mile from the trailhead, is the easily overlooked, unsigned West Fork Trail. This century-old trail ascends 1½ miles to Gibraltar Road.

Continuing past the West Fork trail junction, the East Fork Trail rises up the canyon wall and rejoins the creek a half-mile later. Look for a fine swimming hole below you to the right. The trail then switchbacks moderately out of the canyon to Montecito Overlook. Enjoy the view of the Santa Barbara coastline and the Channel Islands.

Past the overlook, you'll cross a fire road leading down to Hot Springs

Canyon, begin an uphill climb and soon encounter the Hot Springs connector trail.

(The one-mile-long connector trail leads down into Hot Springs Canyon. Along the trail thrives bamboo, huge agave, banana and palm trees—remnants of landscaped gardens that surrounded Hot Springs Resort during its glory days. Explore the ruins of Hot Springs Hotel, constructed during the early 1880s. Europeans and Americans from colder climes flocked here to "take the cure." A 1920 fire destroyed the hotel; it was rebuilt and burned again in 1964.

A trail leads down Hot Springs Canyon from the ruins of the old hotel to Mountain Drive. A mile's walk along one of Santa Barbara's more bucolic byways brings you back to the Cold Springs trailhead. As of this writing, paths leading into and through Hot Springs Canyon were closed, due to conflicts between trail users and private property interests.)

From the junction with the Hot Springs connector trail, Cold Springs Trail switchbacks up canyon and offers fine coastal views. A one-mile climb brings you to two eucalyptus trees (about the only shade en route!) and another ¾ mile of travel takes you to the unsigned junction with a side trail leading to Montecito Peak (3,214 feet). Enjoy the view and sign the summit register.

Cold Springs Trail continues a last mile to Camino Cielo. From the Sky Road, many trails lead into the far reaches of the Santa Barbara backcountry. Enjoy the grand views and return the same way.

San Ysidro Creek

San Ysidro Trail

East Mountain Drive to pools
  3 miles round trip; 70-foot gain

Mountain Drive to East Camino Cielo
  8 miles round trip; 2,900-foot gain

Season: All year

San Ysidro Trail is attractive and typical of Santa Barbara's foothill trails. It is suitable for several levels of hiking ability. Families with small children will enjoy sauntering along its lower creekside stretches. The more serious hiker will enjoy sweating up the switchbacks to Camino Cielo. Truly decadent hikers will make reservations for the sumptuous Sunday brunch at San Ysidro Ranch located very close to the trailhead.

Directions to trailhead: From Highway 101 in Montecito, take the San Ysidro Road offramp. Drive north on San Ysidro a mile to East Valley Road, turn right and drive a mile to Park Lane, which appears on the left just after crossing San Ysidro Creek. Turn left on Park Lane and in a half-mile veer left onto East Mountain Drive, which passes through a residential neighborhood to the trailhead. The signed trailhead is just opposite San Ysidro Stables. Parking is along East Mountain Drive.

The Hike: The trail, lined with sea fig, bougainvillea, and other exotic plants, parallels a driveway for a short time, passes a couple houses, then becomes a dirt road. Continue up the dirt road and look up occasionally at the handsome Coldwater sandstone formations above you. To your left across the creek is "The Gateway," a popular rock climbing area. After a half-mile's travel, you'll pass two signed connector trails, which lead to canyons on either side of San Ysidro. To the east is Old Pueblo Trail, to the west, Colonel McMenemy Trail.

San Ysidro Trail continues along the bottom of the narrow, snaky canyon. Along San Ysidro Creek you encounter beautiful oak woodlands. With mighty oaks in the foreground and impressive rock formations in the background, it is a striking scene. A number of quiet pools await in the creek. Hikers have stacked up rocks to make shallow swimming and wading pools.

Those hikers heading for the upper stretches of San Ysidro Canyon will leave the creek behind and follow the steep rocky trail. The trail continues along a rocky ledge, finds more solid ground, then crosses over to the west side of the canyon. You'll continue marching through the chaparral up long, steep switchbacks. When you reach East Camino Cielo you may return the way you came.

Romero Canyon Trail

6-mile loop through Romero Canyon
  1,400-foot gain

11-mile loop through Romero Canyon
  2,300-foot gain

Season: All year

Romero Canyon is the most easterly of the delightful Santa Ynez Mountains trails back of Santa Barbara. Oaks and sycamores shade a year-round creek and a tranquil path.

Romero Canyon was named for the Romero family, whose first members came to the Santa Barbara area more than two hundred years ago. Juan Romero was a soldier with Governor Felipe de Neve (first resident governor of California) and Captain José Francisco Ortega, who helped found El Presidio Real de Santa Bárbara in 1782.

Later Romeros living up in the canyon that took their name include Apolinario who reside near the mouth of the canyon, Mariano who settled way up the canyon, and Benito who lived in a rugged part of the canyon that some thought *ni servia para criar cachorra*—not fit even to raise lizards.

One meaning of *romero* in Spanish is "pilgrim" and pilgrims of several levels of hiking ability will enjoy a walk through Romero Canyon. Families with small children will enjoy sauntering along its lower creek-side stretches. More serious hikers will utilize fire roads to make a moderately graded loop through the canyon, while hikers in top form will trek all the way to El Camino Cielo (the sky road) which offers sweeping views from the crest of the Santa Ynez Mountains.

Directions to trailhead: From Highway 101 in Montecito, a few miles down-coast from Santa Barbara, exit on Sheffield Drive. Turn right on Sheffield Drive, which briefly parallels the freeway, then swings sharply left (north) toward the Santa Ynez Mountains. Drive 1½ miles to East Valley Road. Turn left, proceed 50 yards, then make an almost immediate right on Romero Canyon Road. A half-mile along, be sure to veer right at a fork in the road, and continue another mile farther to Bella Vista Road. Turn right and continue a quarter-mile to a red steel gate on the left side of the road. Park in a safe manner alongside Bella Vista Road.

The Hike: Walk around the red gate and head up canyon on the fire road. After a quarter-mile of travel, you'll cross a concrete bridge near Romero Creek. A half-mile from the trailhead, you'll cross the creek again. Just after the creek crossing, join unsigned Romero Canyon Trail on your left. Grasses and sedges, bay laurel and a tangle of vines line the creek.

Ascending moderately to steeply, the trail crosses the creek a couple more times, then climbs briskly via a quarter-mile of switchbacks to a signed four-way trail intersection.

Lower Loop: Turn right where the trail intersects the dirt road and begin your 4-mile descent. After 2 miles of walking, the road offers views of Montecito estates and the coastline, Anacapa and Santa Cruz Islands. The road intersects Romero Canyon Trail ½ mile from the trailhead.

Upper Loop: Follow signed Romero Trail, which climbs quite steeply over loose shale slopes to the head of the canyon. The trail crests at the top of the Santa Ynez Mountains, about 3,000 feet in elevation. Coastline views are good but the crest here has been scarred by off-road vehicles. From the crest, the trail descends through a brushy, narrow draw toward Camino Cielo. The trail parallels this dirt road for a short ways, then descends to it. Follow Camino Cielo ½ mile west to a water tank and the unsigned fire road leading into Romero Canyon. Follow this fire road, which makes a long loop south, then east, then north before dropping into Romero Canyon at the above-mentioned four-way trail intersection.

The copper-hued men who roamed these hills not so long ago were very likely better tenants than you and I will be. And when we are gone, as we will go, a few unnoticed centuries will wipe out our bravest scars, our most determined trails.

—John Russell McCarthy
Those Waiting Hills: The Santa Monicas, 1924

3. Santa Monica Mountains

THE SANTA MONICAS are the only relatively undeveloped mountain range in the U.S. that bisects a major metropolitan area. A near-wilderness within reach of sixteen million people, they stretch all the way from Griffith Park in the heart of Los Angeles to Point Mugu, 50 miles away. The mountains, which include the civilized Hollywood Hills and the oh-so-civilized Beverly Hills, extend westward to the steep wildlands above Malibu.

The range is 12 miles wide at its broadest point, and it reaches an elevation of a little over 3,000 feet. Large stretches are open and natural, covered with chaparral and oak trees, bright in spring with wildflowers. Water from winter rains runs down steep slopes and fosters a wide variety of life on the canyon floors. Oak woodland and fern glens shade gentle seasonal streams.

Ancestors of the Chumash Indians lived in the mountainsas early as 7,000 years ago. Abundant food sources helped the Chumash become the largest Indian tribal group in California at the time of Juan Cabrillo's arrival in 1542. The Chumash's highly developed culture included ocean-going plank canoes called tomols, and a system of astronomy that was both mystical and practical.

Spanish missionaries, soldiers and settlers displaced the Chumash. During the 19th Century, the Santa Monicas were controlled by a few large holdings—particularly including the Rancho Topanga-Malibu-Sequit and Rancho Guadalasca—and used primarily for cattle raising. As these holdings were broken up, ranchers supplemented their modest living by renting space to visiting horsemen and vacationers.

At the turn of the century, eccentric oilman Colonel Griffith J. Griffith gave 3,000 acres of his ostrich farm to Los Angeles on the condition that it be forever maintained as a park. Thus Griffith Park was formed on the eastern terminus of the Santa Monicas. Throughout the past three decades, conservationists have made inch-by-inch progress to secure park lands.

The largest areas of open space are in the western part of the mountains. Point Mugu State Park holds the finest native tall grass prairie and the best sycamore grove in the state. The gorge cut by Malibu Creek is an unforgettable sight.

In the eastern part of the mountains, open space is harder to find, but those little pockets that do exist are all the more valuable for being so close to the metropolis. Canyons such as Los Liones, Caballero, and Franklin are precious resources for the park-poor Los Angeles Basin.

Early auto touring, Topanga Canyon

Southern California nature lovers put on their hiking boots and jumped for joy in 1978 when the bill creating the Santa Monica Mountains National Recreation Area was approved by Congress. Eventually a larger park will be formed, to be overseen by the National Park Service. Allocations are slowly being made by the state and federal government to fund purchase of private land to supplement the four major holdings: Will Rogers, Topanga, Malibu Creek and Point Mugu State Parks. The Santa Monica Mountains Conservancy, a state agency, has been particularly effective in acquiring parkland.

The National Recreation Area is not one large area, but a patchwork of state parks, county parks, and private property still to be acquired. Currently, some 65,000 acres is the public domain.

The network of trails through the Santa Monicas is a rich pastiche of nature walks, scenic overlooks, fire roads and horse trails, leading through diverse ecosystems: meadowlands, savannas, yucca-covered slopes, handsome sandstone formations, and springs surrounded by lush ferns. The Backbone Trail, to run from Will Rogers State Historic Park to Point Mugu State Park, is slowly being completed and when finished, will literally and symbolically link the scattered beauties of the Santa Monicas.

25

La Jolla Valley Loop Trail

Ray Miller Trailhead to La Jolla Valley
  7 miles round trip; 700-foot gain

Return via Overlook Trail, Ray Miller Trail
  7 miles round trip; 800-foot gain

Season: All Year

Ringed by ridges, the native grassland of La Jolla Valley welcomes the walker with its drifts of oak and a peaceful pond. This pastoral upland in the heart of Point Mugu State Park is unique: it has resisted the invasion of non-native vegetation. It's rare to find native grassland in Southern California because the Spanish introduced oats and a host of other foreign grasses for pasture for their cattle. In most cases, the imported grasses squeezed out the natives; but not in La Jolla Valley.

La Jolla Valley Loop Trail passes a small waterfall and tours the beautiful grasslands of the valley. This is a fine pathway to follow during the spring when wildflowers and numerous coastal shrubs are in bloom; this is a trail that smells as good as it looks.

Another way to loop through the park is to make use of Ray Miller Trail. Sometimes called La Jolla Ridge Trail, this new trail is the beginning (or the end, depending on how you view the mountains) of the Backbone Trail. The path offers terrific coastal views and nicely complements the park's interior trails.

The trailhead in 1986 was named the Ray Miller Trailhead, a tribute to volunteer ranger Ray Miller. The first official camp host in the state park system, Miller spent his retirement years, from 1972 until his death in 1989, welcoming visitors to Pt. Mugu State Park. The trail was named for Miller in 1989.

Directions to trailhead: Drive about 30 miles up the coast on Pacific Coast Highway from Santa Monica (21 miles up from Malibu Canyon Road if you're coming from the Ventura Freeway and the San Fernando Valley). The turnoff is 1.5 miles up-coast from Big Sycamore Canyon Trailhead, which is also part of Point Mugu State Park. From the turnoff, turn inland to the parking area. The signed trailhead, near an interpretive display, is at a fire road that leads into the canyon. La Jolla Ridge Trail begins on the right (east) side of the parking lot.

The Hike: The fire road leads north up the canyon along the stream bed. As the canyon narrows, some tiny (seasonal) waterfalls come into view.

Past the falls, the trail passes some giant coreopsis plants. In early spring the coreopsis, also known as the tree sunflower, sprouts large blossoms.

At the first trail junction, bear right on the La Jolla Valley Loop Trail. In a little less than a half-mile, you'll arrive at another junction. Leave the main trail and you will descend the short distance to a lovely cattail pond. The pond is a nesting place for a variety of birds including the redwing blackbird. Ducks and coots paddle the perimeter.

Returning to the main trail, you'll skirt the east end of La Jolla Valley, enjoy an overview of waving grasses and intersect a T junction. To the right, .7 mile away, is Deer Camp Junction, which provides access to trails leading to Sycamore Canyon and numerous other destinations in the state park.

(To return via Overlook and Ray Miller Trails, bear right toward Deer Camp Junction. See instructions below.)

To continue with La Jolla Valley Loop Trail, bear left and in half a mile you'll arrive at La Jolla Valley Camp. The camp, sheltered by oaks and equipped with piped water and tables, is an ideal picnic spot. The valley is a nice place to spend a day. You can snooze in the sun, watch for deer, or perhaps stalk the rare and elusive chocolate lily, known as the Cleopatra of the lily family—the darkest and the loveliest.

After leaving the camp, you could turn left on a short connector trail that skirts the pond and takes you back to La Jolla Valley Loop Trail, where you retrace your steps on that trail and La Jolla Canyon Trail.

To complete the circle on La Jolla Valley Loop Trail, however, continue a half mile past the campground to the signed junction where you'll bear left and follow a connector trail back to La Jolla Canyon Trail.

Those returning via Overlook and Ray Miller Trails will find that bearing right (west) at the above described junction will soon bring you to Overlook Trail, a dirt road. Bear right (south) here, descending along the ridge that separates Big Sycamore Canyon to the east from La Jolla Canyon to the west.

At a fork, bear right, continuing your descent to a junction with Ray Miller Trail. Join this trail, which descends over some red rock, then parallels the coast and coast highway for a time.

Listen carefully and you can hear the distant booming of the surf. Enjoy the stunning ocean views. The Channel Islands—particularly Anacapa and Santa Cruz—are prominent to the northwest. Farther south is Catalina Island. During the winter months, you might catch sight of a migrating California gray whale on the horizon.

The path crosses slopes burned in an 1989 brushfire and works its way west, squeezing through a draw dotted with prickly pear cactus. The path marches down a brushy hill past a group camp and returns you to the trailhead.

26

Sycamore Canyon Trail

Big Sycamore Canyon to Deer Camp Junction
  6½ miles round trip; 200-foot gain

Return via Overlook Trail
  10 miles round trip; 700-foot gain

Season: All year

Every fall, millions of monarch butterflies migrate south to the forests of Mexico's Transvolcanic Range and to the damp coastal woodlands of Central and Southern California. The monarch's awe-inspiring migration and formation of what entomologists call over-wintering colonies are two of nature's most colorful autumn events.

All monarch butterflies west of the Rockies head for California in the fall; one of the best places in Southern California to observe the arriving monarchs is the campground in Big Sycamore Canyon at Point Mugu State Park.

The monarch's evolutionary success lies not only in its unique ability to migrate to warmer climes, but in its mastery of chemical warfare. The butterfly feeds on milkweed—the favored poison of assassins during the Roman Empire. This milkweed diet makes the monarch toxic to birds; after munching a monarch or two and becoming sick, they learn to leave the butterflies alone.

Monarch butterfly

The butterflies advertise their poisonous nature with their conspicuous coloring. They have brownish-red wings with black veins. The outer edge of the wings are dark brown with white and yellow spots. While one might assume the monarch's startling coloration would make them easy prey for predators, just the opposite is true; bright colors in nature are often a warning that a creature is toxic or distasteful.

Sycamore Canyon Trail takes you through a peaceful wooded canyon, where a multitude of monarchs dwell, and past some magnificent sycamores. The sycamores that shade the canyon bearing their name are incomparable. The lower branches, stout and crooked, are a delight for tree-climbers. Hawks and owls roost in the upper branches.

The trail follows the canyon on a gentle northern traverse across Point Mugu State Park, the largest preserved area in the Santa Monica Mountains. This trail, combined with Overlook Trail, gives the hiker quite a tour of the park. During October and November, Sycamore Canyon offers the twin delights of falling autumn leaves and fluttering butterflies. (Ask park rangers where the monarchs cluster in large numbers.)

Directions to trailhead: Drive up-coast on Highway 1, 32 miles from Santa Monica, to Big Sycamore Canyon Campground in Point Mugu State Park. Outside the campground entrance is an area where you may park. Walk past the campground entrance through the campground to a locked gate. The trail begins on the other side of the gate.

The Hike: Take the trail up-canyon, following the creek. Winter rains cause the creek to rise, and sometimes keeping your feet dry while crossing is difficult. Underground water keeps much of the creekside vegetation green year around—so this is fine hike in any season.

One half-mile from the campground you'll spot Overlook Trail, which switchbacks to the west up a ridge and then heads north toward the native tall grass prairie in La Jolla Valley. Make note of this trail, an optional return route.

A second half-mile of nearly level canyon walking brings you to another major hiking trail that branches right—the Serrano Canyon Trail. (See Serrano Canyon hike description.)

Another easy mile of walking beneath the sycamores brings you to a picnic table shaded by a grove of large oak trees. The oaks might be a good turnaround spot for a family with small children. The total round trip distance would be a little over 4 miles.

Continuing up the canyon you'll pass beneath more of the giant sycamores and soon arrive at Wood Canyon Junction, the hub of six trails which lead to all corners of the park. Bear left on signed Wood Canyon Trail and in a short while you'll reach Deer Camp Junction. Drinking water and picnic tables suggest a lunch stop. Oak trees predominate over the sycamores along Wood Canyon Creek; however, the romantic prefer

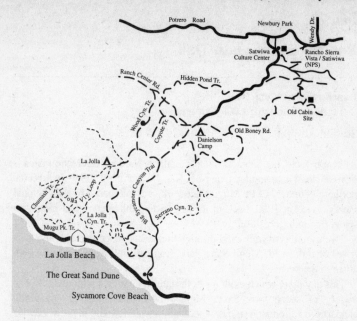

the sycamores, some of which have large clumps of mistletoe in the upper branches.

You can call it a day here and return the way you came. As you hike down the canyon back to the campground, the large and cranky bluejay population will scold you, but don't let them stop you from enjoying one of California's finest sycamore savannas.

To return via Overlook Trail: Continue past the junction with Wood Canyon Trail and Deer Camp Junction on the Wood Canyon Trail, which becomes Pumphouse Road. You'll climb over the divide between Sycamore Canyon and La Jolla Valley. Upon reaching a junction, you'll head south on the Overlook Trail, staying on the La Jolla Canyon side of the ridge. True to its name, Overlook Trail offers good views of grassy mountainsides, Boney Peak and Big Sycamore Canyon.

You'll pass an intersection with Scenic Trail, a rough path that hugs the ridge separating La Jolla and Big Sycamore Canyon, where you'll bear right and follow the fire road ½ mile back to the trailhead.

27

Rancho Sierra Vista Trail

Rancho Sierra Vista Trail
  8 miles round trip; 1,000-foot gain

Season: All year

Acre by acre, the Santa Monica Mountains National Recreation Area is ever-so-slowly expanding. One park, Rancho Sierra Vista/Satwiwa, on the northern boundary of Pt. Mugu State Park, was purchased by the National Park Service in 1980, back in the days when the agency had money to spend on land acquisition.

Twenty miles of trail wind through the park, connecting with about 70 miles of trail in Pt. Mugu State Park. You can trek from Rancho Sierra Vista to the ocean.

This day hike, which explores both state and national parkland, offers a variety of scenery—a Santa Monica Mountains sampler—including chaparral-covered slopes, oak woodland, a waterfall and giant woodwardia ferns.

The name of the park, Rancho Sierra Vista/Satwiwa reflects its history as both a 1940s horse ranch and as the longtime tribal land of the Chumash. Part of the park has been designated as the Satwiwa Native American Indian Natural Area. A short walk from the parking lot is the Native American Indian Cultural Center, which has exhibits of Chumash, Gabrielino and Hopi crafts and culture.

Directions to trailhead: From the Ventura Freeway (U.S. 101) in Newbury Park, exit on Wendy Drive. Head south for 4 miles, then turn west on Potrero Road for 2 miles. Follow the signs to Rancho Sierra Vista's parking lot on your left.

The Hike: From the parking lot, begin hiking on the dirt road. In a mile you reach an overlook perched above upper Sycamore Canyon. Turn left, heading east here, on the Fence Trail, which true to its name follows a barb wire fence.

The trail reaches Old Boney Road, which you'll follow to the right as you begin ascending the north slope of the canyon. After dropping down to a creek, the road leads beneath oaks and sycamores.

When you reach the first switchbacks to the right, enjoy a brief diversion by following a trail leftward. You'll soon intersect a creek, which can be followed a short distance to the waterfall. Woodwardia ferns thrive in the cool moist canyon. A series of a half-dozen tiny falls cascade from pool to pool.

After enjoying the falls, return to Old Boney Road and continue your ascent. On a clear day, the upper reaches of the road offer views of the wide Pacific and Channel Islands. The road forks and you'll continue straight ahead.

A little farther along, you'll spot a stone chimney standing amongst some oaks. The cabin that once stood here was used by ranch hands when cattle and sheep grazed these hills. When a 1956 fire burned from the valley side of the mountains to the ocean, the cabin was destroyed. Near the cabin, a year-round spring offers drinking water. If the bugs aren't biting, the area around the cabin makes a nice lunch stop.

You'll notice a trail that leads up Boney Mountain, but this day hike continues another mile on the road that brought you here. You'll intersect a steep one-mile connector trail branching right and take it a mile back to the paved park service road which returns you to the trailhead.

28

Serrano Canyon Trail

Serrano Canyon Trail
   8½ mile loop through Point Mugu State Park; 1,100-foot gain

Season: All year

*When the trail had climbed to a height of fifteen hundred feet, there opened
a still more striking landscape. Near by to the north rose the fine shape
of Boney Mountain, its highest crags hidden in dragging mists . . . More
to the west, blue with summer haze, the wide valley stretched away to the
pacific, and between lay the expanse of rough, brush hills through which
I had to find a way.*

—Joseph Smeaton Chase
California Coast Trails, 1913

Trail writer/rider Joseph Smeaton Chase had a tough time finding his
way through the west end of the Santa Monica Mountains. The tumbled-
up hills and valleys between Little Sycamore and Big Sycamore Canyons
were crisscrossed with cattle paths, which threw him off track. Though a
bit lost, the beauty of the land we now call Boney Mountain Wilderness
launched the British-born, Southern California-transplanted author into
paroxysms of purple prose.

Fortunately for Chase and Western literature, he spotted a small farm
belonging to old Jesus Serrano annd his son Francisco. The dirt-poor
Serranos offered Chase all they had—a bed in their tiny cabin, one of their
fine homemade Spanish cheeses and directions for getting back on the
right trail.

Families with small children will enjoy a stroll through nearly level Big
Sycamore Canyon. Experienced hikers will enjoy the climb through
Serrano Canyon, and the trek across Serrano Valley.

A warning: Autumn colors you might not be thrilled to see are the
oranges, reds and crimsons of the poison oak bushes that line Serrano
Canyon. As a precaution, wear long pants and a long-sleeved shirt when
you hike through the canyon.

Directions to trailhead: See previous hike.

The Hike: Walk through the campground and join the fire road (closed to
vehicular traffic) that leads into Big Sycamore Canyon. One half-mile
from the campground you'll spot signed Overlook Trail, which switchbacks to the west up a ridge, and then heads north toward the native tall
grass prairie in La Jolla Valley. Make a note of this fine trail for another
day's hike.

Another mile of nearly level canyon walking brings you to a signed junction with Serrano Canyon Trail. Join this trail, which soon enters its namesake canyon, a dramatic, water-cut, high-walled gorge. The trail is narrow and lightly-traveled; it's also off-limits to horses and mountain bicyclists.

The trail climbs moderately through a coastal sage community and eventually works its way down to the creek at the bottom of the oak- and sycamore-lined canyon. First a footbridge, then some railroad-tie-stair-steps on the creek banks help you across the creek. The creek is sprightly, with pretty pools in winter and spring, while in summer and autumn it flows with far less enthusiasm. The footbridge is as good a place as any to wiggle into those long pants for your upcoming meeting with the abundant poison oak that grows creekside.

The trail continues for more than a mile through the fern-filled canyon bottom. Finally, the trail emerges from the canyon. (You'll miss the shade and luxuriant vegetation, but not the poison oak.) The trail ascends a canyon wall, then comes to an unsigned junction in a shallow gully. Take the right fork, uphill, about 50 yards to an old fence line separating the chaparral community from the sweeping grasslands of Serrano Valley. The valley is a beauty, as quiet a place as you'll find in the Santa Monicas. A couple of Park Service trail markers keep you on the trail, which passes a solitary sumac and an abandoned aluminum and wood shed that houses an old pump.

The path cuts across the grasslands and reaches a signed junction. Serrano Valley Loop Trail veers right, but you contiue straight on the path signed "To Old Boney Trail" You'll reach an unsigned junction with Old Boney Trail, turn left and soon reach another unsigned trail that leads left. You can see Big Sycamore Canyon below. You'll join this trail, which plunges down the steep canyon wall.

The very steep trail drops to the floor of Big Sycamore Canyon. When you reach the fire road at the bottom of the canyon, you'll turn left. The fire road, Big Sycamore Canyon Trail, takes you a bit more than three miles down-canyon back to the trailhead.

29

Mishe Mokwa Trail

5-mile circle tour of Circle X Ranch
   1,100-foot gain

Season: All year

Sandstone Peak, highest peak in the Santa Monica Mountains, is one of the highlights of a visit to Circle X Ranch, a park located on the border of Los Angeles and Ventura counties. The park has more than 30 miles of trail and a much-needed public campground.

The State Coastal Conservancy awarded funds to the Santa Monica Mountains Conservancy to purchase the 1,655-acre Circle X Ranch from the Boy Scouts of America. The National Park Service now administers the park. Half a century ago, the land belonged to a number of gentlemen ranchers, including movie actor Donald Crisp, who starred in *How Green Was My Valley*. Members of the Exchange Club purchased the nucleus of the park in 1949 for $25,000 and gave it to the Boy Scouts. The emblem for the Exchange Club was a circled X—hence the name of the ranch.

About two decades ago, the Scouts, in an attempt to honor Circle X benefactor Herbert Allen, petitioned the U.S. Department of the Interior to rename Sandstone Peak. The request for "Mount Allen" was denied because of a long-standing policy that prohibited naming geographical features after living persons. Nevertheless, the Scouts held an "unofficial" dedication ceremony in 1969 to honor their leader.

Sandstone Peak—Mount Allen, if you prefer—offers outstanding views from its 3,111-foot summit. If the 5-mile up-and-back hike to the peak isn't sufficiently taxing, park rangers can suggest some terrific extensions.

Directions to trailhead: Drive up-coast on Pacific Coast Highway past the outer reaches of Malibu, a mile past the Los Angeles County line. Turn inland on Yerba Buena Road and proceed five miles to Circle X Ranch. You'll pass the park's tiny headquarters building and continue one more mile to the signed trailhead on your left. There's plenty of parking. What was once a small parking lot is now large enough to land a 747.

The Hike: From the signed trailhead, walk up the fire road. A short quarter-mile of travel brings you to a signed junction with Mishe Mokwa Trail. Leave the fire road here and join the trail, which climbs and contours over the brushy slopes of Boney Mountain. Late spring blooms include black sage, golden yarrow and wooly blue curls. Look for the orange-red, waxy petals of the rare lance-leaved dudleya.

Breaks in the brush offer good views to the right of historic Triunfo Pass, which was used by the Chumash to travel from inland to coastal

areas. The "drive-in movie screen" you
see atop Triunfo Peak is really an old
microwave relay station.

Mishe Mokwa Trail levels for a time
and tunnels beneath the boughs of handsome red shanks. Growing beneath the
drought-resistant chaparral plants found
along the trail are some ferns. The op-
portunistic ferns take advantage of the
shade offered by the chaparral and tap
what is for the Santa Monica Mountains
a relatively munificent water table located just below the surface. It's unlikely that the hiker will often find yuccas and ferns growing in close proximity on the same slope.

The trail descends into Carlisle Canyon. Across the canyon are some
striking red volcanic formations, among them well-named Balanced Rock.
The path, shaded by oak, and laurel, drops into the canyon at another aptly
named rock formation—Split Rock. Hikers have long had a tradition of
walking through the split in the rock.

Split Rock is the locale of a trail camp, shaded by oak and sycamore.
An all-year creek and a spring add to the camp's charm. It's a fine place
for a picnic.

From Split Rock bear right past an old outhouse—"the historic four-
holer" as it is known—and begin your ascent out of Carlisle Canyon on
an old ranch road. From the road's high point, you'll look straight ahead
up at a pyramid-like volcanic rock formation the Boy Scouts call Egyptian
Rock. To the northwest is Point Mugu State Park. You are walking on the
Backbone Trail, which when completed will stretch the length of the
mountains.

The fire road turns south and you'll pass a trail camp located amid some
cottonwoods. Past the camp, the fire road angles east. Look sharply to the
right for a short, unsigned trail that leads to Inspiration Point. Mount
Baldy and Catalina Island are among the inspiring sights pointed out by a
geographical locater monument.

Continue east on the fire road and you'll soon pass the signed intersection with Boney Peak Trail. This trail descends precipitously to park
headquarters. If for some reason you're in a hurry to get down, this bone-
jarring route is for you.

Continue ascending on the fire road. After a few switchbacks look for a
steep trail on the right. Follow this trail to the top of Sandstone Peak.
"Sandstone" is certainly a misnomer; the peak is one of the largest

Sandstone Peak, Circle X Ranch

masses of volcanic rock in the Santa Monica Mountains. Sign the summit register and enjoy the commanding, clear-day views: the Topatopa Mountains, the Oxnard Plain, the Channel Islands, and the wide blue Pacific.

After you've enjoyed the view, you'll descend a bit more than a mile on the fire road back to the trailhead.

30

Nicholas Flat Trail

Leo Carrillo State Beach to Nicholas Flat
  7 miles round trip; 1,600-foot gain

Season: All year

Leo Carrillo State Beach has always been a popular surfing spot. Surfers tackle the well-shaped south swell, while battling the submerged rocks and kelp beds. In recent years, the state added a large chunk of Santa Monica Mountains parkland to the state beach, and now Leo Carrillo is a pleasing place to take a hike.

Leo Carrillo's relatively remote location on the Los Angeles/ Ventura county line gives the park a mellow feeling that is lacking at other Southern California beaches. The park's shoreline is very popular with movie-makers, who roll some palm trees onto the strand and *voila*!—Leo Carrillo doubles for a Caribbean island.

Sequit Point bisects the beach, forming a bay to the south. Beach hikers will enjoy exploring the point's caves and coves, and beachcombing a mile up-coast to the county line.

The state beach is named after Angeline Leo Carrillo, famous for his TV role as Pancho, the Cisco Kid's sidekick. Carrillo, the son of Santa Monica's first mayor, was also quite active in recreation and civic affairs.

Nicholas Flat Trail departs from Pacific Coast Highway and climbs inland over steep, scrub-covered slopes to a wide meadow and a small pond. From its high points, the trail offers good views of the Malibu coast.

Nicholas Flat Trail can also be savored for one more reason: In Southern California, very few trails connect the mountains with the sea.

Get an early start. Until you arrive at oak-dotted Nicholas Flat itself, there's not much shade en route. In good wildflower-watching years, you might spot such fast-fading spring blooms as monkeyflowers, coyote brush, golden yarrow, bush sunflowers, hummingbird sage, and a lot of lupine along the trail.

Directions to trailhead: From the west end of the Santa Monica Freeway in Santa Monica, head up-coast on Pacific Coast Highway about 25 miles to Leo Carrillo State Beach. There's free parking along Coast Highway, and fee parking in the park's day use area. Signed Nicholas Flat trailhead is located a short distance past the park entry kiosk, opposite the day use parking area.

The Hike: If the state park hasn't mowed its "lawn" lately, the first fifty yards of Nicholas Flat Trail will be a bit indistinct. Immediately after its tentative beginning, the trail junctions. The right branch circles the hill,

climbs above Willow Creek, and after a mile, rejoins the main Nicholas Flat Trail. Enjoy this interesting option on your return from Nicholas Flat.

Take the left branch, which immediately begins a moderate to steep ascent of the grassy slopes above the park campground. The trail switchbacks through a coastal scrub community up to a saddle on the ridgeline. Here you'll meet the alternate branch of Nicholas Flat Trail. From the saddle, a short side trail leads south to a hilltop, where there's a fine coastal view. From the viewpoint, you can see Point Dume and the the Malibu coastline. During the winter, it's a good place to bring your binoculars and scout the Pacific horizon for migrating whales.

Following the ridgeline, Nicholas Flat Trail climbs inland over a chaparral-covered slope. Keep glancing over your right shoulder at the increasingly grand coastal views, and over your left at the open slopes browsed by the park's nimble deer. In the spring, the fast-fading wildflower population is dominated by that scrambling vine with the white trumpet-shaped flowers—the morning glory.

After a good deal of climbing, the trail levels atop the ridgeline and you get your first glimpse of grassy, inviting Nicholas Flat. The trail descends past a line of fire- blackened, but unbowed, old oaks and joins an old ranch road that skirts the Nicholas Flat meadows. Picnickers may unpack lunch beneath the shady oaks or out in the sunny meadow. The trail angles southeast across the meadow to a small pond. The man-made pond, used by cattle during the region's ranching days, is backed by some handsome boulders.

Return the way you came until you reach the junction located ¾ mile from the trailhead. Bear left at the fork and enjoy this alternate trail as it descends into the canyon cut by Willow Creek, contours around an ocean-facing slope, and returns you to the trailhead.

31

Ocean Vista Trail

3-mile loop through Charmlee Natural Area

Season: All year

Charmlee, a lovely park perched in the Santa Monica Mountains above Malibu, often has outstanding spring wildflower displays. Most of the park is a large open meadow; the flower display, given timely rainfall, can be quite good. Lupine, paintbrush, larkspur, mariposa lily, penstemon, and California peony bust out all over.

Stop at Charmlee's small nature center and inquire about what's blooming where. Also pick up a copy of a brochure that interprets the park's Fire Ecology Trail. This nature trail interprets the important role of fire in Southern California's chaparral communities.

Good views are another reason to visit Charmlee. The Santa Monica Mountains spread east to west, with the Simi Hills and Santa Susana Mountains rising to the north. Down-coast you can see Zuma Beach and Point Dume and up-coast Sequit Point in Leo Carrillo State Park. Off-shore, Catalina Island and two of the Channel Islands—Anacapa and Santa Cruz—can sometimes be seen.

Beginning in the early 1800s this Malibu meadowland was part of Rancho Topanga-Malibu-Sequit and was used to pasture cattle. For a century and a half, various ranchers held the property. The last of these private landholders—Charmain and Leonard Swartz—combined their first names to give Charmlee its euphonious name.

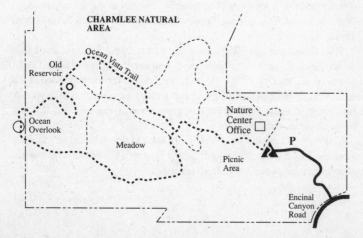

Golden Stars (Bloomeria crocea) are found throughout the Santa Monica Mountains from late May through June.

For the hiker, Charmlee is one of the few parks, perhaps even the only park, that actually seems to have a surplus of trails. Quite a few paths and old ranch roads wind through the park, which is shaped like a big grassy bowl. Because the park is mostly one big meadow fringed with oak trees, it's easy to see where you're going and improvise your own circle tour of Charmlee. Bring a kite and a picnic to this undiscovered park and enjoy.

Directions to trailhead: From Pacific Coast Highway, about 12 miles up-coast from the community of Malibu, head into the mountains on Encinal Canyon Road 4½ miles to Charmlee Natural Area.

The Hike: Walk through the park's picnic area on a dirt road, which travels under the shade of coast live oaks. The trail crests a low rise, offers a couple of side trails to the left to explore, and soon arrives at a more distinct junction with a fire road leading downhill along the eastern edge of the meadow. This is a good route to take because it leads to fine ocean views.

Follow the road as it skirts the eastern edge of the meadow and heads south. Several ocean overlooks are encountered but the official Ocean Overlook is a rocky outcropping positioned on the far southern edge of the park. Contemplate the coast, then head west to the old ranch reservoir. A few hundred yards away is an oak grove, one of the park's many picturesque picnic spots.

You may follow any of several trails back to the trailhead or join Fire Ecology Trail for a close-up look at how Southern California's Mediterranean flora rises phoenix-like from the ashes.

Solstice Canyon Trail

6-mile loop through Solstice Canyon Park; 600-foot gain

Season: All year

Solstice Canyon Park in the Santa
Monica Mountains is enjoyable
year-round, but winter is a particularly fine time to ramble through the
quiet canyon. From the park's upper
slopes, you might even sight gray
whales migrating past Point Dume.

Solstice, to we modern city
dwellers, may seem to be nothing
more than a scientific abstraction—
the time when the sun is farthest
south of the equator. To some of the
earliest occupants of Southern California, the Chumash, however, the
winter solstice was a very important
occasion. It was a time when the cosmic balance was very delicate. The
discovery of summer and winter solstice observation caves and rock art
sites, have convinced anthropologists that the Chumash possessed a system of astronomy that had both mystical meaning and practical application. To those of us who buy all our food in the supermarket, winter
solstice is just a date on the calendar, but to the Chumash, who needed to
know about when berries would ripen, when the steelhead would run up
Malibu Creek, when game would migrate, the day was an important one.

Solstice Canyon Park opened on summer solstice, 1988. The Santa
Monica Mountains Conservancy purchased the land from the Roberts
family. The park is administered by the Mountains Conservancy Foundation, the operations arm of the Conservancy. The Foundation transformed
the 550-acre Roberts Ranch into a park. Ranch roads became foot trails.
Milk thistle, castor bean and other non-native plants were eliminated.

Destroyed in a 1982 fire was the Roberts family home, an extraordinary
ranch-style residence that was highly praised by many home and architectural publications. The house incorporated Solstice Canyon's creek, waterfalls and trees into its unique design.

Another Solstice Canyon house—the Mathew Keller House—was built
in 1865 and is the oldest house in Malibu, perhaps in the Santa Monica

103

Mountains. When restoration is complete, the house will become a museum and visitor center.

Solstice Canyon's third structure of note is really a strange one. It resembles a kind of futuristic farmhouse with a silo attached and defies architectural categorization. Bauhaus, maybe. Or perhaps Grain Elevator Modern. From 1961 to 1973 Space Tech Labs, a subsidiary of TRW, used the building to conduct tests to determine the magnetic sensitivity of satellite instrumentation. The TRW buildings are now headquarters for the Santa Monica Mountains Conservancy.

Several trails explore Solstice Canyon. TRW Loop Trail leads to the canyon bottom, where the hiker can pick up Old Solstice Road (closed to vehicular traffic) and saunter through the canyon. Sostomo Trail climbs the park's east and south-facing ridges and offers fine coastal views.

Directions to trailhead: From Pacific Coast Highway, about 17 miles up-coast from Santa Monica and 3½ miles upcoast from Malibu Canyon Road, turn inland on Corral Canyon Road. At the first bend in the road, you'll leave the road and proceed straight to the very small Solstice Canyon parking lot. Beyond the parking lot, the park access road is usually closed; however, on weekends, visitors are permitted to drive in and park in a second, larger lot, located just up the road.

The Hike: Walk up the park road to a small house, which is headquarters for the Mountains Conservancy Foundation.

Near the house, join the signed TRW Trail, which switchbacks up toward the strange new home of the Santa Monica Mountains Conservancy.

TRW Trail crosses a paved road, ascends west, then drops south into Solstice Canyon. You'll turn right on Old Solstice Road. In a few minutes you'll pass the 1865 Mathew Keller House and in a few more minutes—Fern Grotto. The road travels under the shade of oak and sycamore to its end at the remains of the old Roberts Ranch House. Palms, agave, bamboo and bird of paradise and many more tropical plants thrive in the Roberts' garden gone wild. A waterfall, fountain and an old dam are some of the other special features found in this paradisiacal setting known as Tropical Terrace.

Just below Tropical Terrace is signed, Sostomo Trail, which ascends a chaparral-cloaked slope that still bears evidence of the 1982 fire. The trail dips in and out of a streambed, begins climbing, and offers a great view of Solstice Canyon all the way to the ocean. At a junction, the trail splits, with the right fork leading to Sostomo Overlook, while you head left toward Deer Valley. The trail crosses an open slope then tops a ridge for a great view of Point Dume. The trail briefly joins a dirt road, then resumes as a path and descends a coastal scrub-covered slope to the bottom of Solstice Canyon. A right turn on Old Solstice Road leads past El Alisar Picnic Area and returns you to the trailhead.

33

Backbone Trail

Castro Crest to Upper Solstice Canyon
  6-miles round trip; 1,000-foot elevation gain.

Season: All year

It's a humble enough plant, a low mass of woody stems and dull green herbage, clinging to life among the rocks. To most of us, the Santa Susana tarweed is a plant only a botanist could love—or even find.

From its discovery about 75 years ago until the late 1970s, the tarweed was believed to exist only atop isolated sandstone outcroppings in its namesake Santa Susana Mountains. In 1977, the Santa Susana tarweed was discovered high on the Castro Crest area of the Santa Monica Mountains, and later atop Calabasas Peak and in Charmlee Park.

Hemizonia minthornii may seem even more homely than it is because it comes from a beautiful botanic family—the Sunflower Family, in fact. Other members of the family—goldfields, golden yarrow, California everlasting and tidytips are real lookers and even such family members as shrubby butterweed and milk thistle have their moments in the sun.

Well, the Santa Susana tarweed isn't *that* ugly; in autumn it dons a cloak of yellow flowers. Its botanical name, *minthornii,* honors—perhaps a poor choice of words—botanist Theodore Wilson Minthorn and his sister Maud who collected in Southern California during the first two decades of this century. You can stalk the Santa Susana tarweed—and some genuinely pretty flowering plants—on a nice loop trail along the Castro Crest area of the Santa Monica Mountains.

.Author Milt McAuley reports that some defenders of the Santa Susana tarweed, concerned with its public image, have begun to refer to it as tar*plant*. "Some people say tarweed smells like fresh raspberries," explains McAuley, "but we tarweed boosters say raspberries smell like tarweed."

Geologically minded hikers will also enjoy tramping along Castro Crest. Towering above the parking area is gray sandstone/mudstone Sespe Formation, formed 40–25 million years ago. Down in Upper Solstice Canyon is the Coal Canyon Formation, of marine deposition, laid down 60–50 million years ago. Many a mollusk is visible in the long rock slabs.

Even those hikers without interest in botany or earth science will enjoy this hike. It samples both high and low segments of the Backbone Trail and provides great views and a good aerobic workout.

Directions to trailhead: From Pacific Coast Highway, about 2 miles upcoast from Malibu Canyon Road, turn inland on Corral Canyon Road. Proceed 5½ miles to road's end at a large dirt parking lot.

Castro Crest is the place to stalk the rare Santa Susan tarweed—or enjoy the terrific views.

The Hike: From the parking area, head past the locked gate up the wide dirt road, Castro Motorway. After a short climb, you'll be treated to a fine view of Mt. Baldy and the San Gabriel Mountains and of the Santa Susana Mountains—home of the elusive tarweed. Look for tarweed about ¾-mile from the trailhead on the north side of the dirt road near the junction of Castro Motorway with Bulldog Motorway.

Bulldog Motorway on your right leads to Malibu Creek State Park and its many miles of trail, but you continue climbing another mile to a junction with Newton Canyon Motorway, which you'll join by bearing left. (Castro Motorway continues west toward a forest of antennae atop Castro Peak) Newton Motorway descends to a junction at a saddle. You could go straight (south) here and drop into Upper Solstice Canyon; this would cut off about two miles from the six-mile distance of this hike.

Bear right on the stretch of Backbone Trail called Castro Trail and head west for a mile to paved Latigo Canyon Road. Walk along the road for a short while and join Newton Motorway on your left, which passes by a private residence then descends to the saddle discussed above and the connector trail leading back toward Castro Motorway.

Continue east, meandering along the monkey flower- and paintbrush-sprinked banks of Solstice Creek. Watch for a lovely meadow dotted with Johnny-jump-ups and California poppies. The trail turns north with the creekbed then climbs west for a time up a chaparral-covered slope back to the trailhead on Corral Canyon Road.

34

Backbone Trail

Tapia County Park to Castro Crest
  7 miles one way; 2,000 foot gain

**Return through Malibu Creek State Park via Bulldog Motorway,
Twentieth Century Road**
  14 miles round trip; 2,000 foot gain

Season: All year

The Backbone Trail route through Malibu Creek State Park has been
finished for quite some time and has proved very popular. Both a primary
and alternate route lead through the state park. The high "primary" route
follows a dramatic ridgetop toward Castro Crest while the "alternate"
route meanders along with Malibu Creek through the heart of the state
park.

This day hike connects the two branches of the Backbone Trail and
provides a grand tour of Malibu Creek State Park. Fine ocean and island
views are offered along the first half of the hike and a chance to explore
geologically and ecologically unique Malibu Creek Canyon on the second
half.

Directions to trailhead: From Pacific Coast Highway, turn inland on
Malibu Canyon Road and proceed 5 miles to Tapia County Park, located a
short mile south of Malibu Creek State Park.

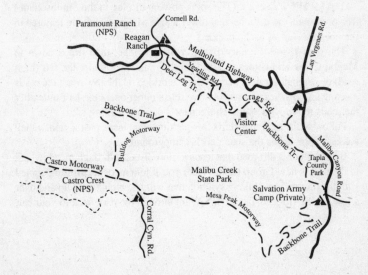

From the parking lot, return to Malibu Canyon Road and walk south. Using caution, cross the road and walk across the bridge spanning Malibu Creek. Recross the road and walk a few hundred feet to where the trail begins.

The Hike: Mesa Peak Motorway, as this dirt road is known, ascends steeply at first, gaining 1,500 feet in 2½ miles. With the elevation gain comes sweeping panoramic views of Point Dume, Santa Monica Bay, and Palos Verdes Peninsula. On clear days, Catalina, San Clemente, Anacapa and Santa Cruz Islands float upon the horizon.

The trail veers left toward Mesa Peak (1,844 feet) and continues climbing in a northwesterly direction through an area rich in fossilized shells. Hillside roadcuts betray the Santa Monica Mountains' oceanic heritage. As you hike the spine of the range, a good view to the north is yours: the volcanic rocks of Goat Butte tower above Malibu Creek gorge and the path of Triunfo Canyon can be traced.

The road passes through an area of interesting sandstone formations and intersects paved Corral Canyon Road, which is termed Castro Motorway from this point. Continue west on Castro Motorway for one mile, reaching the intersection with Bulldog Motorway.

Backbone Trail continues west toward the forest of antennas atop Castro Peak (2,824 feet) and hopefully, some day to Point Mugu.

Return via Bulldog Motorway: For a nice loop trip back through Malibu Creek State Park, bear right on Bulldog Motorway. Descend steeply under transmission lines, veering east and dropping into Triunfo Canyon. In 3½ miles, you reach Twentieth Century Road. Turn right and soon pass what was once the location of the exterior sets used by the "M*A*S*H" TV series. (The set is now on display in the Smithsonian.) The prominent Goat Buttes that tower above Malibu Creek are featured in the opening shot of each episode.

The road passes Century Lake, crosses a ridge, then drops down to Malibu Creek and comes to a fork in the road. Take either the left (high road) or continue straight ahead over the bridge on the low road; the roads meet again downstream, so you may select either one. One-half mile after the roads rejoin, you approach the park's day use parking area.

Follow a dirt road that skirts this parking area, leads past a giant valley oak and approaches the state park's campground.

Bear right on a dirt road that leads a short distance through meadowland to the park's new Group Camp. Here you'll join a connector trail, signed with the international hiking symbol, that will take you a mile up and over a low brushy ridge to Tapia Park. Walk through the park back to your car.

The gorge of Malibu Creek

35

Reagan Ranch Trail

4-mile loop through Malibu Creek State Park

Season: All year

Before Ronald Reagan purchased what was to become the most well-known ranch in the world—Rancho del Cielo in the Santa Ynez Mountains above Santa Barbara—he owned another spread in the Santa Monica Mountains. Reagan's Ranch, now part of Malibu Creek State Park, is a delight for hikers, who can enjoy the ranch's rolling meadowland and grand old oaks, and even probe the origins of the former president's conservative political philosophy.

During the 1950s when Reagan hosted television's *Death Valley Days,* he desired a more rural retreat than his home in Pacific Palisades. He bought the 305-acre ranch in the hills of Malibu as a place to raise thoroughbred horses. Land rose greatly in value, and taxes likewise; the tax increases really piqued Reagan and influenced his political philosophy. From this point on, he would be hostile toward government programs that required more and more tax dollars to fund.

Reagan's Ranch boosted his political career in another way: it was the locale of many a barbecue and gathering attended by the well-heeled politicos who supported his gubernatorial campaign. When Reagan was elected governor in 1966, he moved to Sacramento, and sold his ranch to a movie company. Today the ranch makes up the northwest corner of Malibu Creek State Park. When the property was acquired, the Reagan ranch house was in such grim condition that it had to be destroyed. The Reagan barn still stands and is now used for offices and storage by state park employees.

Trails loop through the Reagan Ranch and connect with the main part of the state park. One path, which I've dubbed Reagan Ranch Trail, uses a combination of trails—Yearling, Deer Leg, Lookout, Crag's Road and Cage Canyon—to explore Reagan country and the heart of the park.

Winter, after rains put a little green in the grassy meadows, and spring, when lupine, larkspur and poppies pop out all over, are the best seasons for a visit.

Directions to trailhead: From Santa Monica, take Pacific Coast Highway up-coast to Malibu Canyon Road, turn inland and proceed to Mulholland Highway. Turn left and drive 3 miles to the ranch entrance at the corner of Mulholland and Cornell Road. Or from the Ventura Freeway (101) in Agoura, exit on Kanan Road and head south. Make a left on Cornell Road and follow it to its intersection with Mulholland Highway.

The trailhead is on the southeast corner. Park carefully alongside Cornell Road.

The Hike: Walk into the park on Yearling Road. The dirt road leads a quarter-mile past a row of stately eucalyptus and soon arrives at the old Reagan barn. Continue on the road which passes a corral and heads across a meadow. Soon you'll pass the first of a couple of side trails leading rightward into a grove of oaks and linking up with Deer Leg Trail. Continue straight ahead on the meadow trail.

During spring, wildflowers color the field, a ¾ mile long grassy strip. At the east end of the meadow, the trail dips in and out of a canyon, tunnels through some high chaparral and ascends an oak-crowned ridge. Atop the ridge is a great view of Malibu Creek and the main features of the state park. Also on the ridgetop is an unsigned trail junction. You'll take the left-leading trail and begin descending southeast on well-named Lookout Trail. The trail drops to Crag's Road, the state park's major trail, near Century Lake.

Crag's Road leads east-west with Malibu Creek and connects to trails leading to the site of the old "M*A*S*H" set, the Backbone Trail and the park visitors center. More immediately, when you make a right on the road, you pass close to Century Lake. Near the lake are hills of porous lava and topsy-turvy sedimentary rock layers that tell of the violent geologic upheaval that formed Malibu Canyon. The man-made lake was scooped out by members of Crag's Country Club, a group of wealthy, turn-of-the-century businessmen who had a nearby lodge.

Walk up Crag's Road about 200 hundred yards and join unsigned Cage Canyon Trail on your right. The trail makes a short and rapid ascent of the oak- and sycamore-filled canyon and soon brings you to an unsigned intersection with Deer Leg Trail. Here you bear left and begin traveling under a canopy of oaks. You'll get occasional glimpses of the rolling grassland of the Reagan Ranch below.

One attractive oak grove shades a barbecue area where the Reagans once entertained. This grove is a good place for a picnic or rest stop.

Soon you'll bear leftward at a trail junction and begin ascending the cool north slope of a hillside above the ranch. Leaving the oaks behind, the trail climbs a brushy hillside to an overlook. Enjoy the view of Malibu Lake and Paramount Ranch. The trail intersects a fire road, which you take to the right on a steep descent to the meadow near park headquarters. The road vanishes here, so walk fifty yards across the meadow to Yearling Road, which leads back to the trailhead.

36

Malibu Creek Trail

Parking area to Rock Pool
3½ miles round trip; 150-foot elevation gain

Parking area to Century Lake
4½ miles round trip; 200-foot elevation gain

Season: All year

Before land for Malibu Creek State Park was acquired in 1974, it was divided into three parcels belonging to Bob Hope, Ronald Reagan and 20th Century-Fox. Although the park is still used for moviemaking, it's primarily a haven for day hikers and picnickers.

The trail along Malibu Creek explores the heart of the State Park. It's an easy, nearly level walk that visits a dramatic rock gorge and little Century Lake.

Directions to trailhead: From Pacific Coast Highway, turn inland on Malibu Canyon Road and proceed 6½ miles to the park entrance, one-fourth mile south of Mulholland Highway. If you're coming from the San Fernando Valley, exit the Ventura Freeway (101) on Las Virgenes Road and continue four miles to the park entrance. There is a state park day use fee.

The Hike: From the parking area, follow the wide fire road. You'll cross the all-but-dry creek. The road soon forks into a high road and a low road. Go right and walk along the oak-shaded high road, which makes a long, lazy left arc as it follows the north bank of Malibu Creek. You'll reach an intersection and turn left on a short road that crosses a bridge over Malibu Creek.

You'll spot the Gorge Trail and follow it upstream a short distance to the gorge, one of the most dramatic sights in the Santa Monica Mountains. Malibu Creek makes a hairpin turn through 400-foot volcanic rock cliffs and cascades into aptly named Rock Pool. The *Swiss Family Robinson* television series and some Tarzan movies were filmed here.

Return to the trailhead or retrace your steps back to the high road and bear left toward Century Lake. As the road ascends you'lll be treated to a fine view of Las Virgenes Valley. When you gain the crest of the hill, you'll look down on Century Lake. Near the lake are hills of porous lava and topsy-turvy sedimentary rock layers that tell of the violent geologic upheaval that formed Malibu Canyon. The man-made lake was scooped out by members of Crag's Country Club, a group of wealthy, turn-of-the-century businessmen who had a nearby lodge.

A trail for the whole family along Malibu Creek

You can call it a day here, or continue on the fire road past Century Lake. You'll pass the location of the now-removed set for the "M*A*S*H" television series. The prominent Goat Buttes that tower above Malibu Creek were featured in the opening shot of each episode.

37

Eagle Rock Trail (Loop Backbone Trail)

Topanga parking lot to Eagle Rock via Eagle Loop/Eagle Springs Rd.
  6½ miles round trip; 800-foot gain

To Will Rogers SHP via Eagle Rock, Fire Road 30, Rogers Rd.
  10½ miles one way; 1,800-foot loss

Season: All year

From Topanga State Park to Will Rogers State Historic Park, the Backbone Trail has been finished for quite some time and has proved very popular. The lower reaches of the trail offer a fine tour of the wild side of Topanga Canyon while the ridgetop sections offer far-reaching inland and ocean views.

The name Topanga is from the Shoshonean Indian dialect. These Indians and their ancestors occupied the canyon on and off for several thousand years B.C. until the Spanish evicted them and forced them to settle at the San Fernando Mission.

Until the 1880s, there was little permanent habitation in the Topanga area. Early settlers tended vineyards, orchards and cattle ranches. In the 1920s, the canyon became a popular weekend destination for Los Angeles residents. Summer cabins were built along Topanga Creek and in subdivisions in the surrounding hills. For $1 round trip fare, tourists could board a Packard Auto Stage in Santa Monica and be driven up Pacific Coast Highway and Topanga Canyon Road to the Topanga Post Office and other, more scenic, spots.

This hike departs from quiet and imperturable Topanga Canyon, surrounded by L.A. sprawl but retaining its rural character. Most of the trail is on good fire road. A longer one-way option takes you along brushy ridges to Will Rogers State Park. On a blustery winter day, city and canyon views are superb.

Directions to trailhead: From Topanga Canyon Boulevard, turn east on Entrada Road; that's to the right if you're coming from Pacific Coast Highway. Follow Entrada Road by turning left at every opportunity until you arrive at Topanga State Park. The trailhead is at the end of the parking lot. There is a park day use fee.

To Will Rogers State Historic Park trailhead: If you're taking the longer hike and want to be met (or leave your car) at Will Rogers State Historic Park, here are the directions to that destination: From Sunset Boulevard in Pacific Palisades, turn north at the park entrance. The road leads up to Rogers' estate, now a state historic park that interprets the cowboy/comedian/philosopher's life. Near Will Rogers' home, a signed trail climbs to Inspiration Point. Rogers Trail intersects it $^1/_{10}$ mile past the Inspiration Point Junction.

The Hike: From the Topanga State Park parking lot, follow the distinct trail eastward to a signed junction, where you'll begin hiking on Eagle Springs Road. You'll pass through an oak woodland and through chaparral country. The trail slowly and steadily gains about 800 feet in elevation on the way to Eagle Rock. When you reach a junction, bear left on the north loop of Eagle Springs Road to Eagle Rock. A short detour will bring you to the top of the rock.

To complete the loop, bear sharply right (southwest) at the next junction, following the fire road as it winds down to Eagle Spring. Past the spring, you return to Eagle Spring Road and retrace your steps back to the trailhead.

Three-mile long Musch Ranch Trail, which passes from hot chaparral to shady oak woodland, crosses a bridge and passes the park pond, is another fine way to return to the trailhead. Those hikers bound for Will Rogers State Historic Park will follow the loop trip directions to the northeast end of Eagle Rock/Eagle Spring Loop, then bear right on Fire Road 30. In ½ mile you reach the intersection with Rogers Road. Turn left and follow the dirt road (really a trail) for 3½ miles, where the road ends and meets Rogers Trail. Here a level area and solitary oak suggest a lunch stop. On clear days enjoy the spectacular views in every direction: To the left is Rustic Canyon and the crest of the mountains near Mulholland Drive. To the right, Rivas Canyon descends toward the sea.

Stay on Rogers Trail, which marches up and down several steep hills, for about two more miles, until is enters Will Rogers Park near Inspiration Point.

38

Santa Ynez Trail

Trippet Ranch to Santa Ynez Canyon
   6 miles round trip; 1,000-foot gain

Season: All year

   Ferns, falls, wildflowers and dramatic sandstone cliffs are some of the delights of a ramble through Santa Ynez Canyon in the Santa Monica Mountains. The canyon—and its waterfalls—can be reached from two trailheads; one is located at the edge of the tony Palisades Highlands development, the other is found in the heart of Topanga State Park.

   Santa Ynez Trail descends a ridge into Santa Ynez Canyon, then heads upstream to a 15-foot waterfall. Remember that the uphill part of this hike comes last; pace yourself accordingly.

Directions to trailhead: From Topanga Canyon Boulevard, turn east on Entrada Road; that's to the right if you're coming from Pacific Coast Highway and to the left if you're coming from the Ventura Freeway (101). Follow Entrada Road by turning left at every opportunity until you arrive at Topanga State Park. There is a State Park day use fee.

   If you're not feeling energetic, you can easily reach Santa Ynez Canyon via the Palisades Highland trailhead. From Sunset Boulevard in Pacific Palisades, a short distance inland from Pacific Coast Highway, turn north on Palisades Drive. As you enter the Palisades Highlands community, turn left on Verenda de la Montura. Park near the signed trailhead.

The Hike (From Topanga State Park): From the parking lot, you may proceed up the wide main trail or join the park's nature trail (a prettier way to go) and ascend past some oaks. Blue-eyed grass, owl's clover and lupine splash some springtime color on the grassy slopes. Both the nature trail and the main trail out of the parking lot lead a short quarter-mile to Fire Road 30A. Turn left on the dirt fire road and travel a short distance to signed Santa Ynez Trail. Start your descent into Santa Ynez Canyon.

   High on the canyon wall, you'll get good views of the canyon and the ocean beyond. A half-mile descent brings you to a reddish sandstone outcropping. The main route of Santa Ynez Trail stays atop a ridgeline, but you'll notice a few steep side trails that lead right down to the canyon floor.

   Soap plant, a spring bloomer with small, white, star-like flowers is abundant along the trail. This member of the lily family was a most useful plant to early residents of the Santa Monica Mountains. Indians cooked the bulbs to concoct a glue for their arrows. They also made a lather of the crushed bulbs and threw it into creeks to stun fish. White settlers stuffed mattresses with the plant's fiber.

Enjoy the views of tilted sandstone and the great bowl of Santa Ynez Canyon. As the trail nears the canyon floor it descends more precipitously. Once on the canyon bottom, turn left (down-canyon) and enter a lush environment shaded by oak and sycamore. The trail meanders with a seasonal creek to a signed junction. You'll turn left and head up-canyon on a path that crosses the creek several times. The fern-lined pools and the handsome sandstone ledges make an idyllic scene, marred only by the graffiti certain cretins have spray-painted on the boulders.

About ¾ mile of travel brings you to the base of the waterfall. Beyond the fall are some more cascades, but continuing farther is recommended only for experienced rock- climbers; most hikers make a U-turn here and head for home.

The Hike (From Palisades Highlands): This walk departs from what I call the Designer Trailhead. Here Santa Ynez Creek, lined by orange/beige artificial walls, spills over a cement creekbed. Creekside trees have been enclosed in planters, and stream-crossings are accomplished by means of cylindrical-shaped cement "stepping-stones." Once beyond this trail travesty, the path takes you into a canyon that's really quite lovely. Coast live oaks, sycamore and bay laurel line the trickling seasonal creek. Half a mile along the trail passes a pipe gate and forks. A sign points the way to Santa Ynez Falls, ¾ mile farther up the canyon.

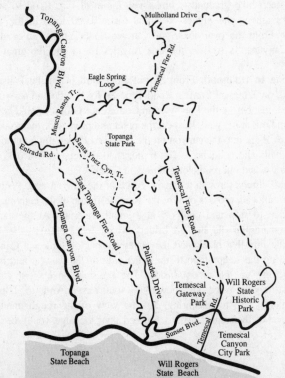

39

Temescal Canyon Trail

Canyon Floor to Ridge Overlook
  5½ miles round trip; 700-foot gain

To Rogers Road
  12½ miles round trip; 1600-foot gain

Season: All year

As you sweat it out crossing the exposed ridge above Temescal Canyon, you might be amused to learn that "temescal" is what the Chumash Indians called their village sweathouse. The Chumash took as many as two ceremonial sweat baths a day, in what anthropologists speculate might have been a religious ritual. A fire burned in the center of the sweathouse. When the Chumash began to perspire, they scraped the sweat off with special sticks, then rushed out and leaped into a cold stream. The mission fathers complained that the Chumash took too many baths and were a little too clean. More work at the mission and less relaxation in the sweathouse would be more productive, the padres thought.

This steep hike gradually climbs via Temescal Fire Road to scenic overlooks among the highest summits (over 2,000 feet) in the Santa Monicas. From the overlooks, you can see Santa Ynez, Temescal and Rustic Canyons, as well as the Los Angeles Basin and the great blue Pacific.

Directions to trailhead: From Sunset Boulevard in Pacific Palisades, turn north on Temescal Canyon Road. Proceed for ½ mile and park in the open area, just before the Presbyterian Conference Grounds. Hikers must sign in and out at the gate. Respect the quiet and privacy of the grounds.

The Hike: Walk into the canyon on the paved road, passing a number of meeting halls and residences. The route, shaded by coast live oak, next follows a washed out road along Temescal Creek.

The trail climbs through a narrow gorge of the canyon and, 1½ miles from the trailhead, crosses over to the west (left) side of the canyon. You might want to stop and cool off at a small waterfall. At the canyon crossing stands an old burned bridge, which fell victim to the 1978 Mandeville Fire that blackened the upper reaches of Temescal Canyon. Scramble up the steep slope to the other side of the canyon and begin switchbacking up the mountainside. The fire road levels out atop a northwest-trending ridge. The view to the southwest down at the housing developments isn't too inspiring, but the view of the rough unaltered northern part of Temescal Canyon is. Proceed along the ridge; you'll see some

Enjoy ocean views from viewpoints above Temescal Canyon.

rock outcroppings. A short side trip off the fire road will bring you to Skull Rock, where you can climb inside the wind-formed (aeolian) caves to cool off or picnic.

Return the same way or continue on the fire road.

Joining the fire road from the left are Split Rock Road and a mile farther north, Trailer Canyon Road. A microwave tower, atop what locals have dubbed "Radio Peak," stands halfway between the two points.

One and a half miles of mostly level walking beyond the Trailer Canyon intersection brings you to Rogers Road. Near the intersection is Temescal Peak (2,126 feet), highest peak in Topanga State Park. If you wish, scramble up a short and steep firebreak to the top for a fine view.

Rogers Road, a segment of the Backbone Trail, leads six miles rightward to Will Rogers State Historic Park and leftward to intersections with both loops of the Eagle Springs Trail, which in turn leads to Topanga State Park headquarters.

The above extensions suggest a car shuttle or a very long day of hiking. Otherwise, return the same way via Temescal Canyon Fire Road to the trailhead.

4. San Gabriel Mountains

THE SAN GABRIEL MOUNTAINS bless Los Angeles by keeping out desert winds, and curse it by keeping in the smog. Most of the range is included in the 700,000 acres of the Angeles National Forest, the most heavily used national forest in the United States.

The San Gabriels twist atop the San Andreas Fault. Geologists claim these mountains are the most fractured and shattered in California. The range consists of crystalline metamorphic and granitic blocks, sixty miles long and twenty miles wide, extending from Soledad Pass to Cajon Pass. Los Padres National Forest mountain ranges are to the west and the San Bernardino range is to the east.

The San Gabriels vary extensively in temperature. Along the northern rim at the edge of the Antelope Valley, the mountains seem an extension of the Mojave Desert. However, some alpine areas with peaks near 10,000 feet know snow from one winter to the next.

John Muir found it tough going in the San Gabriels: "The slopes are exceptionally steep and insecure to the foot and they are covered with thorny bushes from five to ten feet high." Muir was referring to the dominant plant community of the San Gabriels—the chaparral—that elfin forest of burrs and brambles which covers much of the sun-drenched lower slopes of the mountains. Higher elevations bring easier traveling and a wealth of taller trees: mountain laurel, oaks, pines, cedar. The arroyos are another special feature of the San Gabriels. These boulder-strewn washes seem dry and lifeless in the bottomland; however, as hikers follow their course upward, they'll soon find the arroyo's banks are verdant and graceful with a tangle of ferns and wildflowers.

As early as the 1880s, it became obvious to Southern Californians the mountains should be protected from the destruction of indiscriminate logging and other ventures. In 1892, the San Gabriel Timberland Reserve was proclaimed by President Harrison. It was the first forest reserve in California, and the second in the U.S. (The first was Yellowstone.)

On of the first trail construction projects in the San Gabriels began in 1864 when Benjamin Wilson revamped an old Indian path to his timbering venture on the mountain that now bears his name. Later, other Indian trails were improved. William Sturtevant, who came to California from Colorado in the early 1880s and became a premier packhorseman and trail guide, linked and improved several Indian trails and made it possible to cross the mountains from west to east. Until Sturtevant figured out a route, most people did not know that a network of Indian trails reached from the desert to the L.A. Basin.

More trails were built around the turn of the century when Southern California's "Great Hiking Era" began. With Rough Rider Teddy Roosevelt urging Americans to lead "the strenuous life," Southlanders challenged the nearby San Gabriels. Mountain farmers and ranchers, fighting against the odds of fire, flood and distance to market, began capitalizing on the prevailing interest in the great outdoors. As more and more hikers headed into the backcountry, the settlers began to offer food and accommodations. Soon every major canyon on the south side of the mountains had its resort or trail camp and many had several.

Most resorts were not big business, with the exception of the Mount Wilson and Echo Mountain complexes which featured luxury hotels and observatories. The majority were run by rugged entrepeneurs who offered rustic accomodations, hearty meals, and good fellowship. Visitors thronged to the resorts on weekends and holidays. Many stayed all summer.

The Depression brought about a golden age of public campground construction. These camps, tied to an ever-increasing network of highways, eventually doomed the private resorts and trail camps. Angeles Crest Highway, built between 1929 and 1956 by a motley assortment of Depression laborers, prison road gangs and various construction crews, linked many of the best high mountain picnic and camping areas.

Today, only a few stone foundations and scattered resort ruins remind the hiker of the "Great Hiking and Resort Era." Though the modern mountaineer will not be greeted with tea, lemonade or something stronger, or a hearty welcome from a trail camp proprietor, the mountains still beckon. That bygone era left us a superb network of trails—more than 500 miles of paths linking all major peaks, camps and streams.

Rising above the smog and din of the Big Basin, the San Gabriels still delight. When we manage to pry the fingers of our more mechanized citizens off their steering wheels and send them tramping through the San Gabriels, a second great hiking era may begin.

40

Placerita Canyon Trail

Nature Center to Walker Ranch Picnic Area
  4 miles round trip; 300-foot gain

Nature Center to Los Pinetos Ridge
  8 miles round trip; 1,600-foot gain

Return via Manzanita Mountain
  10 miles round trip; 1,600-foot gain

Season: All year

In 1842, seven years before the '49ers rushed to Sutter's Mill, California's first gold rush occurred in Placerita Canyon. Legend has it that herdsman Francisco Lopez awoke from his nap beneath a large shady oak tree, during which he had dreamed of gold and wealth. During the more mundane routine of fixing his evening meal, he dug up some onions to spice his supper and there, clinging to the roots, were small gold nuggets.

Miners from all over California, the San Fernando Placers, as they became known, poured into Placerita Canyon. The prospecting was good, though not exceptional, for several years. The spot where Lopez made his discovery is now called the Oak of the Golden Dream. A plaque marks his find.

The canyon has a gentleness that is rare in the steep, severely faulted San Gabriel Mountains. This hike through Placerita Canyon County Park takes you along the oak- and sycamore-shaded canyon floor by a creek, then climbs through chaparral and oak woodland to Los Pinetos Ridge for a view of the metropolis you've left behind. An optional return route via Manzanita Mountain and the Hillside Trail really gives you a grand tour of the park.

Be sure to visit the nature center.

Directions to trailhead: From Interstate Highway 5 go east on Highway 14 (Antelope Valley Freeway) to Newhall. Exit on Placerita Canyon Road and turn right (east) two miles to Placerita Canyon County Park. Park in the large lot near the Nature Center.

The Hike: From the parking lot, walk up-canyon, following the stream and enjoying the shade of oaks and sycamores. A 1979 fire scorched brush within a hundred feet of the nature center, but remarkably spared the oak woodland on the canyon bottom. Nature regenerates quickly in a chaparral community; many hikers looking up at the canyon walls don't realize that a severe fire took place. Some of the chamise on the slopes may be a hundred years old and veterans of dozens of fires.

The canyon narrows and after a mile the trail splits. Take your pick: the right branch stays on the south side of the canyon while the left branch joins the north side trail. The two intersect in a half-mile, a little short of Walker Ranch Group Campground, where you'll find a picnic ground with tables, water and restrooms.

Return the same way, or perhaps hike back to the nature center on the trail that follows the right (north) bank of the creek.

For a grand view of the surrounding area, from the nature center, head toward Los Pinetos Ridge. Skirt the edge of the campground and pick up the trail going up the right (south) slope. The trail climbs for two miles over the chaparral-covered slopes of Los Pinetos Canyon to Los Pinetos Spring, tucked in an oak and spruce glen. From the spring, ascend via the fire road or a steep trail to its right half a mile to a saddle on the main divide and an intersection with a fire road. Climb to any one of the nearby high points and enjoy the view. You can look northward over historic Placerita Canyon and Sand Canyon and southward over the San Fernando Valley sparkling below. Here on Los Pinetos Ridge, the 19th Century meets the 21st Century, and neither gives an inch.

To return via Manzanita Mountain, continue west on the fire road called Santa Clara Divide Road, until you reach a rough trail—sometimes referred to as a fuel break. Follow this trail northward until you reach a short ridge-top route that takes you to Manzanita Mountain. Follow the circuitous trail, which connects with the Hillside Trail and leads back to the nature center.

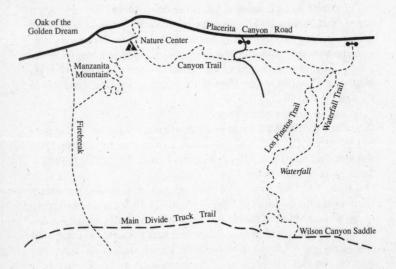

41

Trail Canyon Trail

Parking area to Trail Canyon Falls
  3 miles round trip with a 700-foot gain

To Tom Lucas Camp
  8 miles round trip with a 2,000-foot gain

Season: All year

Trail Canyon Trail isn't quite as redundant as it sounds. The "Trail" in Trail Canyon refers not to a footpath but to the "trail" left by tiny flakes of gold found in the gravel of the canyon's creekbed. Turn of the century placer miners worked the creek, but the "trail" didn't lead to any riches.

The real wealth of Trail Canyon is in its scenery: steep canyon walls that conceal a bubbling creek and a surprising waterfall. During dry months and drought years, the creek is a pokey watercourse, but swollen by rain and runoff it becomes lively, even raging. Because the path to the falls and to the trail camp crosses the creek numerous times, hikers should be careful at times of high water.

While not exactly back to its former verdant splendor, Trail Canyon has recovered nicely from the 1975 Big Santa Anita Fire that blackened this part of the forest.

Beyond the falls, the trail leads to shady Tom Lucas Camp, named for a grizzly bear hunter and one of the first forest rangers in that forerunner of the Angeles National Forest, the San Gabriel Timberland Reserve.

Directions to trailhead: From the Foothill Freeway (210) in Sunland, exit on Sunland Boulevard. Head east on Sunland, which soon merges with Foothill Boulevard. Continue to Mt. Gleason Avenue, turn north (left) and drive to its end at a T at Big Tujunga Canyon Road. Turn right and proceed 5 miles to a dirt road on the left, where a sign indicates parking for Trail Canyon. The road ascends a quarter-mile then forks; descend a quarter-mile to the right to an oak-shaded parking area.

The Hike: The trail, a closed fire road, passes some private cabins that date from the 1920s and 1930s and arrives at the creek. The road ends and the footpath begins ¾ mile from the trailhead at a creek crossing.

Trail Canyon Trail heads up-creek in the shade of sycamores, oak and alder. After a half-mile, the path switchbacks up the canyon's chaparral-covered west wall. After a couple of bends in the trail, look for Trail Canyon Falls below.

The side trail to the falls is a precipitous path, made by use, not design; proceed at your own risk. An alternative route to the falls is to simply

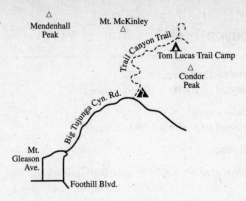

bushwhack up Trail Canyon from the point back where the trail leaves the canyon. The latter route is safer, except at times of high water.

Past the side trail to the falls, Trail Canyon Trail drops back into the canyon, crossing and re-crossing the creek for 2½ miles to Tom Lucas Trail Camp. This oak- and alder-shaded camp is perched on the edge of a meadow watered by the headwaters of Trail Canyon Creek. The meadowland is known as Big Cienega.

Energetic hikers will savor a late afternoon or early morning assault on 5,440-foot Condor Peak. Ascend Trail Canyon Trail another long steep mile to a firebreak, then climb another long steep mile to a point just below the peak. Clamber a hundred yards over fractured granite to the summit. Rewarding the peak-bagger are views of the San Fernando Valley, Santa Monica Bay and Catalina Island.

42

Stone Canyon Trail

Vogel Flats Campground to Mt. Lukens
  8 miles round trip; 3,200 foot gain

Season: All year. Caution during times of high water

Mt. Lukens, a gray whale of a mountain beached on the eastern boundary of Los Angeles, is the highest peak within the city limits. A hike up this mile-high mountain offers a great aerobic workout and terrific clear-day views of the metropolis.

Theodore P. Lukens, for whom the mountain is named, was a Pasadena civic and business leader, and an early supporter of the first scientific reforestation effort in California. A self-taught botanist, Lukens believed that burnt-over mountain sides could be successfully replanted. During 1899 alone, Lukens and fellow mountaineers planted some 65,000 seeds in the

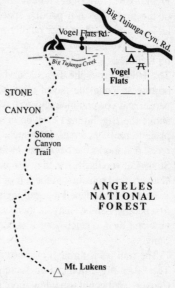

mountains above Pasadena. He started an experimental nursery atop Heninger Flats that grew thousands of knobcone pine, spruce and other trees for replanting in burnt-over areas in the San Gabriel and San Bernardino mountains. Today, this nursery furnishes a large percentage of the young trees planted in Southern California mountains.

After the death of Lukens in 1918, a 5,074-foot peak was named to honor the one time Angeles National Forest Supervisor and Southern California's "Father of Forestry."

Stone Canyon Trail is by far the nicest way to ascend Mt. Lukens. (Other routes are via long wearisome fire roads.) The trail climbs very steeply from Big Tujunga Canyon over the north slope of Lukens to the peak.

Carry plenty of water on this trail; none is available en route. A city map is fun to unfold on the summit to help you identify natural and man-made points of interest.

One warning: In order to reach the beginning of the Stone Canyon Trail, you must cross the creek flowing through Big Tujunga Canyon. During times of high water, this creek crossing can be difficult and dangerous—even impossible. Use care and your very best judgement when approaching this creek.

Directions to trailhead: From Foothill Boulevard in Sunland, turn north on Mount Gleason Avenue and drive 1½ miles to Big Tujunga Canyon Road. Turn right and proceed 6 miles to signed Vogel Flats Road. Turn right and drive into the Forest Service's Vogel Flats Campground and Picnic Area. Turn right on the Forest Service road. Leave your car in one of the many day use parking spaces, near water, restrooms and picnic tables; or proceed another quarter-mile through a private residential area to the end of the road where parking is limited to a few cars and there are no facilities.

The Hike: From the Forest Service parking area, walk a quarter-mile northwest along the paved road past some cabins. The road ends at a barrier and you continue on a trail which travels 150 yards or so along and above the Big Tujunga Canyon creekbed. Look leftward for (1) A good place to cross the creek (2) a metal trail registry on the other side of the creek that marks the beginning of the Stone Canyon Trail (3) well-named Stone Canyon itself, which resembles a waterfall of white boulders. Stone Canyon Trail runs just to the left of Stone Canyon.

After you've signed the trail registry, begin the vigorous ascent, which first parallels Stone Canyon, then switchbacks to the east above it. Pausing now and then to catch your breath, you'll enjoy the view of Big Tujunga Canyon.

The trail leads through chamise and ceanothus and the high chaparral. The 1975 Big Tujunga Fire scorched the slopes of Mt. Lukens. Stone Canyon Trail could use a few more shady big cone spruce and a little less brush. Theodore Lukens and his band of tree planters would today be most welcome on the mountain's north slopes!

Three and a half miles from the trailhead, you'll intersect an old fire road and bear left toward the summit. Atop the peak is a forest of radio antennae.

If you have the current Angeles National Forest map, you might notice the words "Sister Elsie" next to the peak. Before the peak was re-named for Lukens, Sister Elsie Peak honored a beloved Roman Catholic nun, who was in charge of an orphanage for Indian children located in the La Crescenta area.

Enjoy the sweeping panorama of the Santa Monica and Verdugo Mountains, Santa Monica Bay and the Palos Verdes Peninsula, and the huge city spreading from the San Gabriel Mountains to the sea.

43

Gabrielino National Recreation Trail

Switzer Picnic Area to Switzer Falls
   4 miles round trip with 600-foot loss; to Bear Canyon is 8 miles
   round trip with 1,000-foot gain; to Oakwilde is 9 miles round trip
   with 1,400-foot loss

Season: All year. Caution during times of high water.

Arroyo Seco is undoubtedly the best-known canyon in Southern California. It's the site of the Rose Bowl and has the dubious distinction of hosting California's first freeway, the Pasadena. But the ten miles of canyon dominated by the freeway bear little resemblance to the ten miles of wild and rugged arroyo spilling from the shoulder of Mount Wilson.

And the arroyo is rugged. A stream, lined with colonnades of alder and live oak, cascades over boulders of big gray granite. This hike is a journey through the wildest part of the Arroyo Seco and offers a visit to Swtizer Falls and a couple of peaceful trail camps.

Perry Switzer, a carpenter who regained his health in the invigorating San Gabriels, built a trail and a trail resort in the Arroyo Seco. He put up some rough log cabins, despite arguments that "no one would want to pay for a bed up among the grizzlies, mountain lions and bobcats." He earned the nickname "Commodore" because of his skill in navigating his squadron of burros as they forded the Arroyo Seco. His hospitality made Switzer's the most popular trail camp in the San Gabriels.

The resort passed into the hands of Lloyd Austin, who added a tennis court, chapel and dance floor. A sign across from the resort greeted visitors: "Leave your cars and animals this side of the stream." Switzerland was popular with hikers well into the 1930s, until Angeles Crest Highway rendered the peaceful camp "obsolete."

During the Great Hiking Era, a hiker could venture up the Arroyo Seco and within an hour lose all signs of civilization. Amazingly, you still can today. This hike takes you past the site of Switzer's retreat and visits Switzer Falls. Further exploration of the Arroyo Seco country is possible by taking one of the optional trails to Oakwilde and Bear Canyon.

Directions to trailhead: Take Angeles Crest Highway (2) north from La Canada for 10 miles. A short way past the junction of Angeles Crest and Angeles Forest (N3) Highways, you'll see the Angeles National Forest Clear Creek Information Station on your right. Inquire here about trails or road conditions.

A half-mile past the information station, turn right at the entrance to

Switzer's Chapel (1924–1959)

Switzer Picnic Area and continue one-quarter mile to the parking area. The trail begins across the bridge at the lower end of the picnic grounds.

The Hike: Cross the bridge and follow the trail into the canyon. The pathway meanders with the stream under oak, alder and spruce. You'll cross and recross the stream several times and do some easy boulder-hopping. Plan to get wet. In some places, stream crossing is quite difficult in the spring. In a mile, you'll reach Commodore Switzer Trail Camp. Perched on a bench just above the falls, it's an inviting place complete with picnic tables. The creek trail below the camp dead-ends above the falls.

From the camp, cross the stream and follow the trail on the west slope. You'll soon get a nice view of the falls. A signed junction soon appears. To the right (southwest) is the main trail down to Oakwilde and Pasadena. Bear left here and hike down into the gorge of the Arroyo Seco below the falls. When you reach the creek, turn upstream one-quarter mile to the falls. Heed the warning signs and don't try to climb the falls; it's very dangerous.

Return the same way.

To reach Bear Canyon Trail Camp, continue down the Arroyo gorge on a mediocre trail. This path was rescued from oblivion and is now maintained, thanks to the efforts of the Sierra Club, the Forest Service and the San Gabriel Mountain Trail Builders Club.

After three-quarters of a mile, the trail reaches Bear Canyon and heads east up the canyon, crossing and recrossing the creek. Along the way are many nice pools. In spring, the water is cold from snowmelt and little sun reaches the canyon floor. The trail, shaded by big cone spruce, closely parallels the creek.

When you look at an Angeles Forest map, you'll discover that Bear Canyon is surrounded on all sides by highways, dams and development. The canyon has no right to be so quiet, so pristine, but it is. As you boulder-hop from bank to bank, the only sound you'll hear is that of water cascading over granite and clear pools. Give thanks that there is at least one spot in the front range of the San Gabriels that is untouched wilderness, and continue to Bear Canyon Camp, two miles up the canyon.

If you're bound for Oakwilde: From the signed junction above Commodore Switzer Trail Camp, continue right on the Gabrielino National Recreation Trail. The trail leaves the main Arroyo Seco canyon, crosses a chaparral ridge, then drops into Long Canyon. It then descends to Arroyo Seco creek bottom and follows the creek an easy mile to Oakwilde Trail Camp. In this canyon, yuccas and a variety of wildflowers bloom seasonally.

"Oak Wylde," as it was known during the Great Hiking Era, was a jumping-off place for trips farther up the Arroyo Seco. Pack burro trains connected Oak Wylde with the stage station in Pasadena. The trail camp is located among the crumbling stone foundation of a resort. Alder and oak shade a pleasant campground and picnic area.

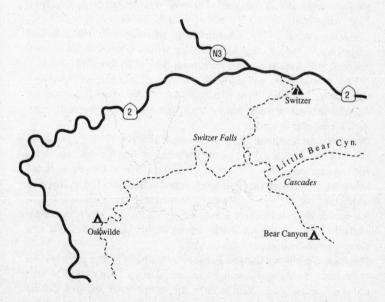

44

Millard Canyon Trail

To Millard Canyon Falls
   1 mile round trip

To Dawn Mine
   5 miles round trip; 800-foot gain

Season: All year

Hidden from the metropolis by Sunset Ridge, lush Millard Canyon is one of the more secluded spots in the front range of the San Gabriel Mountains. A cold stream tumbling over handsome boulders and a trail meandering beneath a canopy of alder, oak and sycamore, are a few of the many attractions of Millard Canyon.

The historical record is sketchy in regard to squatter Millard, who settled at the mouth of the canyon that now bears his name in about 1862. Millard eked out a living by keeping bees and by hauling firewood down to Los Angeles. He reportedly spent about a decade in the canyon, then left suddenly in 1872 after his wife and child died.

Millard Canyon is best known as the site of the Dawn Mine that produced more stories than gold. The mine was worked off and on from 1895, when gold was first discovered, until the 1950s.

You can explore Millard Canyon by two different routes, which lack an official name, but are often referred to as Millard Canyon Trail. An easy half-mile path meanders along the canyon floor to 50-foot Millard Falls.

Experienced hikers will enjoy the challenge of following an abandoned trail through Millard Canyon to the site of the Dawn Mine. Enough of the old trail remains to keep you on track, but it's slow going with many stream crossings en route.

Directions to trailhead: From the Foothill Freeway (210) in Pasadena, exit on Lake Avenue. Drive north four miles, at which point Lake veers left and becomes Loma Alta Drive. Continue a mile to Chaney Trail and turn right. Proceed another mile to a junction atop Sunset Ridge. If you're taking the hike to Dawn Mine, you'll bear right at this junction and park just outside the gate blocking Sunset Ridge Fire Road. If you're bound for Millard Canyon Falls, you'll stay left at the junction and descend to a parking lot at the bottom of the canyon.

The Hike: To Millard Canyon Falls. From the parking area at the bottom of Millard Canyon, you'll walk a hundred yards up a fire road to Millard Canyon Campground. Walk through the campground and pick up the signed trail leading to the falls. The trail heads east along the woodsy canyon bottom, crosses the stream a couple times, and arrives at the base of the waterfall. Don't try to climb up, over, or around the falls; people have been injured attempting this.

The Hike: To Dawn Mine. From the Sunset Ridge parking area, head up the fire road. Enjoy the clear-day ridgetop views of the metropolis. You'll soon pass a junction on your left with a trail leading down to Millard Canyon Campground.

A short quarter-mile from the trailhead, you'll spot the signed Sunset Ridge Trail, which you'll join and begin descending into Millard Canyon. A few minutes of walking down the well-graded path will reward you with an eagle's-eye-view of Millard Canyon Falls.

Near the canyon bottom, you'll meet a trail junction. Sunset Ridge Trail continues along the canyon wall, but you bear left and descend past a cabin to the canyon floor. As you begin hiking up-canyon, turn around and take a mental photograph of the trail that brought you down to the canyon; it's easy to miss on your return trip.

As you pick your way streamside amongst the boulders and fallen trees on the canyon floor, you'll follow vestiges of the old trail. Typically, you'll follow a fifty or one hundred yard stretch of trail, boulder-hop for a bit, cross the stream, then pick up another length of trail. The canyon floor is strewn with lengths of rusting pipe and assorted mining machinery. Several pools, cascades, and flat rocks suggest a streamside picnic.

After hiking a bit more than a mile up-canyon, you'll find that Millard Canyon turns north. From this turn, it's a bit less than a mile to the Dawn Mine site. Don't go in the mine shaft. Darkness and deep holes filled with water make it very dangerous.

Return the same way, and remember to keep a sharp lookout for the trail that leads out of the canyon back to the trailhead.

45

Mount Lowe Railway Trail

To Mount Lowe Trail Camp
  **10 miles round trip with 2,700-foot gain; to Inspiration Point is 11
  miles round trip.**

Season: All year

Professor Thaddeus Lowe, Civil War balloonist, man of fame and
fortune, was the quintessential California dreamer. His dream was to build
a railway into—and a resort complex atop—the San Gabriel Mountains
high above Pasadena. In the 1890s, his dream became a reality.

During the height of its popularity, millions took Professor Lowe's
"Railway to the Clouds" to fine hotels and spectacular views of Southern
California. Until it was abandoned in the 1930s, it was the Southland's
most popular tourist attraction.

From Pasadena, visitors rode a trolley up Rubio Canyon, where a
pavilion and hotel were located. After taking refreshments, they boarded
the "airships" of the great cable incline, where carried them 3,000 feet
(gaining 1,300 feet) straight up to the Echo Mountain Resort Area.
"Breathtaking" and "hair-raising" were the most frequent descriptions
of this thrilling ride.

Atop Echo Mountain was the White City, with a hotel, observatory, and
a magnificent searchlight purchased from the Chicago World's Fair. When
the searchlight swept the mountaintop, the white buildings of the resort
were visible from all over Los Angeles. From Echo Mountain, tourists
could board a trolley and ride another few miles to Mount Lowe Tavern at
the end of the line.

This historic hike follows the old railway bed, visits the ruins of the
White City and Mount Lowe Tavern, and concludes with some fine views
of Los Angeles from Inspiration Point. The old railway bed with its gentle
seven percent grade makes for easy walking.

An interpretive brochure is (sometimes) available from Angeles
National Forest headquarters in Arcadia.

Directions to trailhead: Exit the Foothill Freeway (210) at Lake Avenue
and follow it north to its end. Turn left on Loma Alta Drive. Go one mile
to Chaney Trail Road and turn right. At a Y in the road, take the right fork
to the Sunset Ridge parking area. The trailhead is located at the locked
gate, which bars vehicles from Sunset Ridge Fire Road.

The Hike: The trail begins just past the locked gate. Follow the paved
Sunset Ridge Fire Road. You may follow the fire road two miles to the

GRANITE
GATE
Ele.4072 ft

Mt. Lowe "Railway to the Clouds"—Granite Gate

135

junction with Echo Mountain Trail, but a more attractive alternative is described below.

Follow the road one-quarter mile to the signed Sunset Ridge Trail on your left. Join this trail, which for the most part parallels the fire road, and leads into peaceful Millard Canyon. Near the canyon bottom, the trail forks at a signed junction. Bear right and ascend back up to Sunset Ridge Fire Road. Follow the fire road about 75 yards, and on your right you'll spot the signed junction with Echo Mountain Trail.

Side trip to Echo Mountain: Bear right on Echo Mountain Trail, which leads one-half mile over the old railway bed to Echo Mountain. Echo Mountain takes its name from an echo that bounces around the semicircle of mountain walls. I've never managed to get very good feedback; perhaps even echoes fade with time.

On Echo Mountain are the foundations of Echo Mountain House and the chalet. The most prominent ruin is the large iron bull wheel that pulled the cars up the steep incline fromm Rubio Canyon. A fire swept Echo Mountain in 1900, leveling all of the White City except the observatory. Picnic tables suggest a lunch stop among the ruins.

Leave behind the ruins of the White City, return to Sunset Ridge Fire Road and bear right.

The paved road soon becomes dirt and an interpretive sign at "Cape of Good Hope" lets you know you've joined the Mount Lowe Railway tour. Continue along the railway bed, passing the tourist attractions that impressed an earlier generation of travelers: Granite Gate, Horseshoe Curve, and the site of the Great Circular Bridge.

Near the top, you'll come to the site of Mount Lowe Tavern, which burned in 1936. Almost all signs of the tavern are gone, but this peaceful spot under oaks and big cone spruce still extends its hospitality. On the old tavern site is Mount Lowe Trail Camp, which welcomes day hikers with its shade, water, restrooms and picnic tables.

Before heading down, follow the fire road east and then south for one-half mile to Inspiration Point. Where the fire road makes a hairpin left to Mount Wilson, go right. At Inspiration Point, you can gaze through several telescope-like sighting tubes aimed at Santa Monica, Hollywood and the Rose Bowl. After you've found a sight that inspires you, return the same way.

46

Mount Wilson Toll Road

Altadena to Henninger Flats
6 miles round trip; 1,400-foot gain

Season: All year

Consider the conifers. A wind-bowed limber pine clinging to a rocky summit. A sweet-smelling grove of incense cedar. The deep shade and primeval gloom of a spruce forest.

Where do trees come from?

I know, I know. "Only God can make a tree."

Keep your Joyce Kilmer. Hold the metaphysical questions. Our inquiry here is limited to what happens in the aftermath of a fire or flood, when great numbers of trees lie dead or dying.

Fortunately for California's cone-bearing tree population—and tree lovers—there is a place where trees, more than 120,000 a year, are grown to replace those lost to the capriciousness of nature and the carelessness of man. The place is Henninger Flats, home of the Los Angeles County Experimental Nursery.

Perched halfway between Altadena and Mount Wilson, Henninger Flats is the site of Southern California's finest tree plantation. On the flats you'll be able to view trees in all shapes and sizes, from seedlings to mature stands. A museum with reforestation exhibits, a nature trail, and the Los Angeles County foresters on duty will help you understand where trees come from.

The Flats have a colorful history. After careers as a gold miner, Indian fighter and first Sheriff of Santa Clara County, Captain William Henninger came to Los Angeles to retire in the early 1880s. While doing a little prospecting, Henninger discovered the little mesa that one day would bear his name. He constructed a trail over which he could lead his burros.

Atop the flats he built a cabin, planted fruit trees, raised hay and corn. His solitude ended in 1890 when the Mt. Wilson Toll Road was constructed for the purpose of carrying the great telescope up to the new observatory. Captain Henninger's Flats soon became a water and rest stop for hikers, riders and fishermen who trooped into the mountains.

After Henninger's death in 1895, the flats were used by the U.S. Forest Service as a tree nursery. Foresters emphasized the nurturing of fire-and-drought resistant varieties of conifers. Many thousands of seedlings were transplanted to fire- and flood-ravaged slopes all over the Southland. Since 1928, Los Angeles County foresters have continued the good work at Henninger Flats.

The Pasadena and Mt. Wilson Toll Road Company in 1891 fashioned a trail to the summit of Mt. Wilson. Fees were 50 cents per rider, 25 cents per hiker. A 12-foot-wide road followed two decades later. Senior Southland residents might recall a somewhat hair-raising Sunday drive up the steep grade. During the 1920s, the road was the scene of an annual auto race, similar to the Pikes Peak hill-climb. In 1936 the Angeles Crest Highway opened and rendered the toll road obsolete. Since then the toll road has been closed to public traffic and maintained as a fire road.

A moderate outing of just under six miles, on good fire road, the trail up to Henninger Flats is suitable for the whole family. The Flats offer a large picnic area and fine clear-day city views.

Directions to the trailhead: From the Foothill Freeway (210) in Pasadena, exit on Lake Avenue. Turn north and continue to Altadena Drive. Make a right, continue about ten blocks, and look closely to your left. Turn left on Pinecrest Drive and wind a few blocks through a residential area to the trailhead. The trailhead is found in the 2200 block of Pinecrest. You'll spot a locked gate across the fire road that leads down into Eaton Canyon.

The Hike: Proceed down the fire road to the bottom of Eaton Canyon. After crossing a bridge, the road begins a series of switchbacks up chaparral covered slopes. Occasional painted pipes mark your progress.

Henninger Flats welcomes the hiker with water, shade, and two campgrounds where you may enjoy a lunch stop. Growing on the flats are some of the more common cone-bearing trees of the California mountains including knobcone, Coulter, sugar, digger and Jeffrey pine, as well as such exotics as Japanese black pine and Himalayan white pine.

After your tree tour, return the same way.

Ultra-energetic hikers will continue up the old toll road to Mt. Wilson; the journey from Altadena to the summit is nine miles one-way with an elevation gain of 4,500 feet.

47

Mount Wilson Trail

Sierra Madre to Orchard Camp
  9 miles round trip; 2,000-foot gain

To Mount Wilson
  15 miles round trip; 4,500-foot gain

Season: All year; but may be closed by fire danger or winter snows

The Mount Wilson Trail up Little Santa Anita Canyon is the oldest trail into the San Gabriels. It was built in 1864 by Benjamin Wilson, who overhauled a Gabrielino Indian path in order to log the stands of incense cedar and sugar pine on the mountain that now bears his name.

The first telescope was carried up this trail to Mt. Wilson in 1904. During the "Great Hiking Era," thousands of hikers rode the Red Cars to Sierra Madre, disembarked, and hiked up this path to the popular trail resort to Orchard Camp. Forty thousand hikers and horseback riders passed over the trail in 1911, its peak year.

After the passing of the Great Hiking Era in the 1930s, the trail was all but abandoned until the late 1950s when rebuilding efforts began. Sierra Madre citizens, aided by Boy Scout troops, rebuilt the trail all the way up canyon to its junction with the old Mt. Wilson Toll Road.

Sierra Madre citizens also prevented county flood control engineers from bulldozing and check-damming Little Santa Anita Canyon. The aroused citizenry established Sierra Madre Historical Wilderness Area to preserve the canyon. This area is patterned after federal Wilderness Areas; that is, the land is to be preserved forever without development or mechanized use.

This hike takes you up Little Santa Anita Canyon, visits Orchard Camp, and climbs to the top of Mt. Wilson. It's a classic climb, one of the nicest all-day hikes in the Southland.

Directions to trailhead: From the Foothill Freeway (210) in Arcadia, exit on Baldwin Avenue and head north. Turn right on Miramonte Avenue near the junction of Mount Wilson Trail Road, which is on your left. The trail begins 150 yards up this road and is marked by a large wooden sign. After passing some homes, the trail shortly intersects the main trail.

The Hike: After trudging 1½ miles up Santa Anita Canyon you reach a junction with a side trail, which leads to the nearby canyon bottom. Here you can lean against an old oak, cool your heels in the rushing water, relax and watch the river flow.

Continue hiking on the ridge trail as it climbs higher and higher above the canyon floor onto sunny, exposed slopes. A hot 3 miles of walking brings you to Decker Spring and another ½ mile to Orchard Camp, a shady glen dotted with oak and spruce trees. When Wilson was building his trail, a construction camp called Halfway House was built here. Later homesteaders tried their hand planting apple and cherry trees—hence the name Orchard Camp.

During the Great Hiking Era, a succession of entrepreneurs utilized Orchard Camp as a trail resort and welcomed thousands of hikers. Hikers traveling through the canyon in the 1920s reported seeing "The Nature Man of Mt. Wilson," a tall bronzed hermit who looked like he stepped out of the pages of the Old Testament. The nature man carried a stone axe and worked on the trail for his keep. Some say he's still around, protecting the canyon—though he no longer springs out of the brush and greets every hiker who passes.

Orchard Camp is a nice place to picnic. You might want to call it a day here and return the same way. Otherwise, fill your canteen and plunge on.

The trail continues through thick chaparral up Santa Anita Canyon to its head. It contours on the shelf-like trail, heads east on a firebreak and crosses over a steep manzanita-covered ridge. At the intersection with Winter Creek Trail, turn left (west) and ascend steeply to Mt. Wilson Toll Road, 2 miles from Orchard Camp.

Turn right on the Toll Road and follow it a mile as it ascends through well-spaced spruce to Mount Wilson Road, just outside Skyline Park.

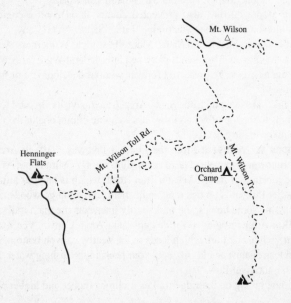

48

Gabrielino Trail

Chantry Flat to Sturtevant Falls
 3½ miles round trip; 500-foot gain

To Spruce Grove Camp
 8 miles round trip; 1,400-foot gain

To Mount Wilson
 8 miles one-way; 4,000-foot gain

Season: All year

Cascades, a waterfall and giant woodwardia ferns are a few of the many delights of historic Big Santa Anita Canyon. The bucolic canyon has been popular with Southern California hikers for nearly a hundred years.

William Sturtevant, known to his friends as "Sturde," pioneered many miles of San Gabriel Mountains trails. He traveled from California to Colorado in the early 1880s with forty burros. A packer *par excellence*, he soon found his services to be in great demand in the San Gabriels.

Sturtevant hewed out a trail over the ridge from Winter Creek to the top of the canyon and in 1898 opened Sturtevant Camp. The rustic resort consisted of a dining hall, tents, and a store and was a popular trail resort well into the 1930s.

In Santa Anita Canyon today some eighty-odd cabins are serviced by a burro train from Chantry Flats, named for another early packer, Charlie Chantry. One of the more colorful sights in the local mountains—and a look backward into a bygone era—is a glimpse at the pack animals plodding of the trail to Sturtevant Camp, now a Methodist Church retreat.

Sturtevant's trail is now a section of the 28-mile-long Gabrielino National Recreation Trail. The trail to Sturtevant Falls is very popular on weekends—but not as popular as it was on Fourth of July weekend 1919 when 5,000 people tramped into the canyon and signed the trail register! The ambitious hiker may continue past the falls to Spruce Grove Camp and even as far as the top of Mount Wilson.

Directions to trailhead: From the Foothill Freeway (210) in Arcadia, exit on Santa Anita Avenue and drive six miles north to its end at Chantry Flat. The trail begins across the road from the parking area. A tiny store at the edge of the parking lot sells maps and refreshments.

The Hike: Descend on the paved fire road, part of the Gabrielino Trail, into Big Santa Anita Canyon. At the bottom of the canyon you'll cross a footbridge near the confluence of Big Santa Anita and Winter Creeks. Here a small sign commemorates Roberts Camp, a resort camp founded in

1912. Owner Otto Roberts and other canyon boosters really "sold" the charms of the canyon to Southern Californians in need of a quiet weekend. As you follow the path up-canyon along the oak- and alder-shaded creek, you'll soon determine that the canyon "sells" itself.

The only blemish on the pristine scene is a series of check dams constructed of giant cement "Lincoln logs," by the Los Angeles County Flood Control District and the Forest Service in the early 1960s. In their zeal to tame Big Santa Anita Creek, engineers apparently forgot that fast-moving water is supposed to erode canyon bottoms; floods are what originally sculpted this beautiful canyon. Today, thanks to the check dams, the creek flows in well-organized fashion, lingering in tranquil pools, then spilling over the dams in fifteen foot cascades. Over the years, moss, ferns, alders and other creek-side flora have softened the appearance of the dams and they now fit much better into the lovely surroundings.

The trail passes some private cabins and reaches a three-way trail junction. To visit Sturtevant Falls, continue straight ahead. You'll cross Big Santa Anita Creek, then recross where the creek veers leftward. Pick your way along the boulder-strewn creek bank a final hundred yards to the falls. The falls drops in a silver stream fifty feet to a natural rock bowl. (Caution: Climbing the wet rocks near the falls is extremely hazardous to your health. Stay off.)

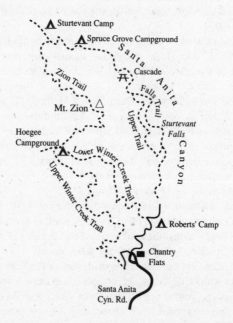

Sturtevant Falls

Return the same way, or hike onward and upward to Spruce Grove Trail Camp.

Two signed trails lead toward Spruce Grove. The leftward one zigzags high up on the canyon wall while the other passes above the falls. The left trail is easier hiking while the right trail heads through the heart of the canyon and is prettier. Either trail is good walking and they rejoin in a mile.

After the trails rejoin, you'll continue along the spruce-shaded path to Cascade Picnic Area. You can call it a day here or ascend another mile to Spruce Grove Trail Camp. Both locales have plenty of tables and shade.

Still feeling frisky? Hikers in top condition will charge up the trail to Mt. Wilson—an 8-mile (one-way) journey from Chantry Flat. Continue on the trail up-canyon a short distance, cross the creek and you'll find a trail junction. A left brings you to historic Sturtevant Camp, now owned by the Methodist Church. The trail to Mt. Wilson soon departs Big Santa Anita Canyon and travels many a switchback through the thick forest to Mr. Wilson Skyline Park.

143

49

Winter Creek Trail

Chantry Flat to Hoegees Camp
  6 miles roundtrip; 300-foot gain

Return via Mt. Zion Trail, Gabrielino Trails
  9 miles round trip; 1,500-foot gain

Season: All year

Before the turn of the century, packer/entrepeneur William Sturtevant set up a trail camp in one of the woodsy canyons on the south-facing slope of Mt. Wilson. This peaceful creekside refuge from city life was called Sturtevant's Winter Camp. In later years the name Winter was given to the creek whose headwaters arise from the shoulder of Mt. Wilson and tumble southeasterly into Big Santa Anita Canyon.

In 1908 Arie Hoegee and his family built a resort here that soon became a popular destination for Mt. Wilson-bound hikers and remained so until battered by the great flood of 1938. A trail camp named for the Hoegees now stands on the site of the old resort and offers the modern day hiker a tranquil picnic site or rest stop.

Another fine destination is Mount Zion, reached by Mt. Zion Trail, one of the paths constructed by turn-of-the-century pioneer packer/entrepreneur William Sturtevant. Sturtevant had constructed Sturtevant's Winter Camp on the banks of Winter Creek, and Camp Sturtevant, in upper Santa Anita Canyon. Obviously, he needed to connect his camps, so in 1896 he began constructing a three-mile link in the Sturtevant Trail that would later by known as Mt. Zion Trail. The first mile and a half of trail up Mount Zion from Winter Creek was a killer construct—a thousand-foot climb over the steep and rocky shoulder of Mt. Zion.

Mount Zion trail allows the modern mountaineer to make a grand loop by connecting the Winter Creek and Gabrielino Trails.

Directions to trailhead: From the Foothill Freeway (I-210) in Arcadia, exit on Santa Anita Ave. and drive six miles north to its end at Chantry Flat. The trail begins across the road from the parking area. A tiny store at the edge of the parking lot sells maps and refreshments.

The Hike: Descend ¾ mile on the paved fire road, part of the signed Gabrielino Trail, into Big Santa Anita Canyon. At the bottom of the canyon, you'll cross a footbridge near the confluence of Big Santa Anita and Winter Creeks

After crossing the bridge, look leftward for the signed Lower Winter Creek Trail. Following the bubbling creek, the trail tunnels beneath the boughs of oak and alder, willow and bay. You'll pass some cabins, built just after the turn of the century and reached only by trail.

After crossing Winter Creek, you'll arrive at Hoegees Camp. A dozen or so tables beneath the big cone spruce offer fine picnicking. Almost all signs of the original Hoegees Camp are gone, with the exception of patches of ivy. (In later years, Hoegees was renamed Camp Ivy).

Walk through the campground until you spot a tiny tombstone-shaped trail sign. Cross Winter Creek here and bear bear left on the trail. In a short while you'll pass a junction with Mt. Zion Trail [see description below], a steep trail that climbs over the mountain to Sturtevant Camp and Big Santa Anita Canyon.

After recrossing the creek, you'll pass a junction with a trail leading to Mt. Wilson and join the Upper Winter Creek Trail. This trail contours around a ridge onto open chaparral-covered slopes. This stretch of trail offers fine clear-day views of Sierra Madre and Arcadia. The trail joins a fire road just above Chantry Flat and you follow this road through the picnic area back to the parking lot where you left your car.

To Mt. Zion and beyond: Follow above directions as far as Hoegees Camp. Next walk through the camp until you spot a tiny tombstone-shaped trail sign. Cross Winter Creek here and bear left on the trail. After a short while, you'll arrive at a signed junction with Mount Zion Trail.

Mt. Zion Trail wastes little time in its steep ascent of the chaparral-cloaked mountain. You'll get good, over-the-shoulder views of the canyon cut by Winter Creek. About 1½ miles of climbing brings you to a signed junction. Here you'll find a small interpretive display that explains the history of the Mt. Zion segment of the Sturtevant Trail and the short side trail that leads to the peak. Follow the summit trail a hundred yards through manzanita to the 3,575-foot peak, where you can sign a summit register and enjoy clear-day views.

Mt. Zion Trail descends a bit more than a mile into Big Santa Anita Canyon. In the canyon bottom, you'll reach a junction. Here the Sturtevant Trail heads up canyon to Sturtevant Camp, now a Methodist Camp, and on to Mt. Wilson. You'll head down canyon to Spruce Grove Camp. Another mile of travel brings you to Cascade Picnic Area.

Below the picnic area, your trail, the Gabrielino Trail, forks. The left-ward, lower trail, which heads through the heart of Santa Anita Canyon, is prettier, while the upper trail, which zigzags along the canyon wall, is easier walking and offers good views. The trails rejoin in a mile and proceed down-canyon as one.

Once you reach the canyon bottom, you can detour on a short side trail to one more tribute to William Sturtevant—Sturtevant Falls.

After recrossing the Winter Creek footbridge, trudge up the paved fire road back to the trailhead.

Devil's Canyon Trail

Chilao to Devil's Canyon Trail Camp
   7 miles round trip; 1,500-foot loss

To Devil's Canyon Waterfall
   11 miles round trip; 2,300-foot loss

Season: All year

Los Angeles residents, while inching along on some crowded interchange, may be comforted by knowing that no other metropolis has a wilderness area so close. When you hike the primeval canyons of the San Gabriel Wilderness Area, you won't believe you're only eighteen as-the-crow-flies miles from downtown L.A.

The 36,137-acre wilderness is rough and rugged country, the bulk of which is contained in two canyons, Devil's and Bear. Chaparral coats the sunny canyon slopes while pine and fir reach from the ridges to the sky. In spring, this is color country: the laurels glow yellow with flowers, the willows fluff up, the ceanothus blossoms blue and white.

The wilderness area is surrounded on three sides by roads: on the north and west by Highway 2, on the east by Highway 39. Picnickers and campers crowd its edges, skiers peer down at it from nearby ridges. But despite its accessibility, most people only look at this wilderness. The view down from the brink of Devil's Canyon, the sharp descent, and the thought of the walk back up, scare off casual walkers.

Devil's Canyon Trail, from Chilao to the trail camp, is the most pleasant path in the wilderness. It takes you through the middle third of the canyon, past willow-shaded pools and dancing cascades, to spots that make the Big City seem hundreds of miles away.

Directions to the trailhead: From La Canada, drive 27 miles up the Angeles Crest Highway, a quarter-mile past the entrance to Upper Chilao Campground. Look for a parking lot on the left side of the highway. The signed trailhead, which is usually below snowline, is across the highway from the parking lot.

The Hike: Remind yourself, as you begin descending steeply into Devil's Canyon, that the tough part of this trip will come last. Pace yourself accordingly. The trail steps back and forth from pine and spruce on the shady slopes to thick chaparral on sunny slopes.

After two miles, the trail meets a pleasant little creek and descends with its bubbling waterway down into the canyon. At trail's end is Devil's Canyon Trail Camp, a primitive creekside retreat, where the only sounds you hear are the murmur of the creek and the rustling of alder leaves.

You can bushwhack and boulder-hop a mile upstream before the brush gets uncomfortably thick. From the trail camp, you can return the way you came or do some further exploring downstream.

Below the trail camp, a path follows Devil's Creek for a spell, but soon ends. You pick your way across rock islands in the creek. The walls of Dev-

ils Canyon close in and you find yourself in trackless boulder-hopping backcountry; pleasant, but slow-going. You continually cross the creek, decipher routes around deep pools and descend gingerly down misty boulders.

Blackened alder leaves cover the surface of still eddies, where pan-sized trout may lurk. The canyon narrows, its steep rock walls pinching Devil's Creek into a series of cascades. As the canyon narrows further, the cascades grow more spectacular and waterfalls occur. The first falls come from side creeks and ¼ mile farther down-creek you arrive at the first mainstream falls, which plunge 20 feet to a bubbling pool.

Expert mountaineers sometimes continue downstream from the falls, but it's a precarious route and is recommended only for the very skilled. Your return to Devil's Canyon Trail Camp may be faster than your descent, because it's easier to pick routes and climb up rocks, than down them. Your climb from the trail camp to the highway will, of course, be slower.

51

Silver Moccasin Trail

Chilao to Horse Flats Campground
  2 miles round trip; 200-foot gain

To Mt. Hillyer
  6 miles round trip; 1,000-foot gain

Season: All year

Even on the Angeles National Forest map, the trail looks intriguing: a red dashed line zigs and zags through the heart of the San Gabriel Mountains and connects Chantry Flat and Shortcut Station, Chilao, Cloudburst and Cooper Canyon. Designed by the Los Angeles Area Council of the Boy Scouts of America, the 53-mile long Silver Moccasin Trail, extends from Charlton Flat to the mountain named for the founder of the Boy Scouts, Lord Baden-Powell. Scouts who complete the week-long trek earn the prized Silver Moccasin award.

One pretty stretch of the Silver Moccasin Trail tours the Chilao country, a region of giant boulders and gentle, Jeffrey pine-covered slopes. Another path—Mt. Hillyer Trail—leads to the top of 6,162-foot Mt. Hillyer. From the top, you'll get great views to the north of the desert side of the San Gabriels.

Tiburcio Vasquez

During the early 1870s, stagecoach robber/horse and cattle thief Tiburcio Vasquez and his gang hid out in the Chilao country. The stolen horses were pastured in secluded grassland we now call Horse Flats. Vasquez, last of a generation of bandits to operate out of the Southern California backcountry, was captured in 1874. Many reporters visited Vasquez in his Los Angeles jail cell, and the highwayman soon found himself quite a celebrity. He was not an ordinary criminal, he told the press, but a patriotic Californio whose goal was to rid Southern California of the gringo influence. Southern Californians loved Vasquez's stories and knew that in a small way he represented the end of the Wild West; nevertheless, he was sent to the gallows in 1875.

One exhibit at the Chilao Visitor Center answers a trivia question that perplexes all day hikers who depart from Chilao area trailheads: What exactly does Chilao mean? As the story goes, one of Vasquez's men, José Gonzales, lived in a log cabin in the area where the visitor center now stands. Gonzales guarded the hideout and horses. His battle with a huge bear, which he killed using only a knife, earned him the name Chillia—roughly translated as "hot stuff." The name over the last century of use evolved into Chilao.

Located just off Angeles Crest Highway near the trailhead, the Angeles National Forest Chilao Visitor Center is well worth a visit. Exhibits interpret flora, fauna and forest history. Behind the station is a short nature trail.

Directions to trailhead: From the Foothill Freeway (210) in La Canada, exit on Angeles Crest Highway (2) and wind 27 miles up the mountain road to the signed turnoff for the Chilao Visitor Center. Turn left and follow the paved road past the visitor center a half-mile to signed Silver Moccasin Trail on your right. Parking at the trailhead is limited to a few cars, but there's a wide turnout located just up the road.

The Hike: The trail ascends a manzanita- and yucca-covered slope to the top of a minor ridge. A mile from the trailhead, the trail widens and you reach a signed junction. Here Silver Moccasin Trail swings southeast toward Angeles Crest Highway and Cooper Canyon, but you go right with a retiring dirt road one hundred yards to Horse Flat Campground. The Camp, with plenty of pine-shaded picnic tables, is a good rest stop.

Just as you reach the gravel campground road, you head left with the signed Mt. Hillyer Trail. The path switchbacks up pine, incense cedar- and scrub oak-covered slopes. Some big boulders suggest a perfect hideout, whether you're fleeing the sheriff or the stresses of modern life.

Up top, Mt. Hillyer may remind you of what Gertrude Stein said of Oakland: "There's no there there." The summit is not a commanding pinnacle, but a forested flat. With all those trees in the way, you'll have to walk a few hundred yards along the ridgeline to get your view of the green bandito country to the south and the brown, wrinkled desert side of the San Gabriels to the north.

52

Mount Williamson Trail

Islip Saddle to Mount Williamson
  5 miles round trip; 1,600-foot gain

Season: All year

Mt. Williamson stands head and shoulders above other crests along Angeles Crest Highway. The 8,214-foot peak offers grand views of earthquake country—the Devil's Punchbowl, San Andreas Fault and the fractured northern edges of the San Gabriel Mountains.

Desert views this peak may offer, but Mt. Williamson is anything but a desert peak. It's plenty green and bristling with pine and fir.

The summit of Mt. Williamson is the high point and culmination of well-named Pleasant View Ridge, a chain of peaks that rises from the desert floor to Angeles Crest Highway. It's quite a contrast to stand atop the piney peak, which is snow-covered in winter, and look down upon Joshua trees and the vast sandscape of the Mojave Desert.

Hot and cold, desert and alpine environments—these are the contrasts that make hiking in Southern California so very special.

The mountain's namesake is Major Robert Stockton Williamson, who first explored the desert side of the San Gabriels in 1853. Williamson, a U.S. Army mapmaker led an expedition in search of a railroad route over or through the mountains. Certainly Williamson found no passable route through the Mt. Williamson area or any other place in the San Gabriel Mountains high country, but the Major did find a way *around* the mountains, so his mission was definitely a success. Williamson's Pacific Railroad Survey report to Congress detailed two railroad routes: Cajon Pass on the east end of the San Gabriels and Soledad Canyon on northwest.

Two fine Forest Service trails ascend Mt. Williamson from Angeles Crest Highway. One trail leads from Islip Saddle, the other from another (unnamed) saddle 1½ miles farther west. Both are well-graded, well-maintained routes. Possibly, after a glance at a map, the idea of linking the east and west Mt. Williamson trails with a walk along Angles Crest Highway, in order to make a loop trip, will occur to you. Don't be tempted. The problem is that between the two trails, Angeles Crest Highway passes through a couple of tunnels—a definite no-no for pedestrians.

Both Mt. Williamson trails are winners; you can't go wrong. Mt. Williamson is a great place to beat the heat, and offers fine hiking in all seasons but winter, when snow covers the trail.

Directions to trailhead: From the Foothill Freeway (210) in La Canada, exit on Angeles Crest Highway (2) and drive about 38 miles, or 2½ miles

past (east of) the Krakta Ridge Ski Area. Look for the (sometimes) signed trail to Mt. Williamson on the left (north) side of the highway.

The Mt. Williamson east trail is easier to find. Continue 4 miles east of the Krakta Ridge Ski Area, and after you pass through the highway tunnels, you'll see the parking area at Islip Saddle on the left (north) side of the highway.

The Hike: At Islip Saddle, you'll spot South Fork Trail (remember this fine trail for another day) heading northeast down to South Fork Camp near Devil's Punchbowl County Park. But you'll join the trail to Mt. Williamson and begin ascending through a forest of Jeffrey and ponderosa pine.

Two miles of steep, but not brutal climbing brings you to a junction with the Mt. Williamson West trail. The two trails continue as one, passing scattered white fir (more numerous as you near 8,000 feet in elevation). You'll enjoy over-the shoulder views south of Bear Creek Canyon and the heart of the rugged San Gabriel Wilderness.

Keep hiking north on the trail, which gets a little fainter as it nears the summit of Mt. Williamson. From the peak, enjoy the dramatic views of the desert below. If you have a good map along, you can pick out the many playas (dry lake beds), buttes and mountain ridges of the dry lands below. At the base of Mt. Williamson is that greatest of earthquake faults—the San Andreas Rift Zone. Most striking of all is the view of Devil's Punchbowl and its jumbled sedimentary strata.

Remember that this isn't a loop hike; return the way you came.

53

Mount Islip Trail

Angeles Crest Hwy to Little Jimmy Trail Camp
3 miles round trip; 500-foot gain

To Mt. Islip
5 miles round trip; 1,100-foot gain

Season: April-November

Mt. Islip, (pronounced eye-slip) is not named, as you might guess, for a clumsy mountaineer, but for Canadian George Islip, who homesteaded in San Gabriel Canyon a century ago. The mountain is by no means one of the tallest San Gabriel Mountains peaks, but its relatively isolated position on the spine of the range makes its stand out. The summit offers the hiker fine views of the middle portion of the Angeles National Forest high country and of the metropolis.

Mt. Islip has long been a popular destination for hikers. The mountain was particularly popular with Occidental College students who in 1909 built a huge cairn (heap of boulders), dubbed the "Occidental Monument" atop the summit. The monument, which had the name Occidental on top, stood about two decades, until the Forest Service cleared the summit of Mt. Islip to make room for a fire lookout tower. Today, the monument and the fire lookout are long gone, but the stone foundation of the fire lookout's living quarters still remains.

One early visitor to the slopes of Mt. Islip was popular newspaper cartoonist Jimmy Swinnerton (1875–1974), well known in the early years of this century for his comic strip "Little Jimmy." By the time he was in his thirties, hard-working, hard-drinking Swinnerton was suffering from the effects of exhaustion, booze, and tuberculosis. His employer and benefactor William Randolph Hearst sent Swinnerton to the desert to dry out. Swinnerton, however, found the summer heat oppressive so, loading his paintbrushes onto a burro, he headed into the San Gabriel Mountains.

Swinnerton spent the summers of 1908 and 1909 at Camp Coldbrook on the banks of the north fork of the San Gabriel River. Often he would set up camp high on the shoulder of Mt. Islip near a place called Gooseberry Spring, which soon became known as Little Jimmy Spring. During the two summers Swinnerton was encamped in the San Gabriels, entertained passing hikers with sketches of his Little Jimmy character. His campsite, for many years known as Swinnerton Camp, now bears the name of Little Jimmy Trail Camp.

You can reach Mt. Islip from the south side of the mountains, the way

Jimmy Swinnerton did, or start from the north side from Angeles Crest Highway. This hike follows the latter route, which is a bit easier than coming up from Crystal Lake.

Directions to trailhead: From the Foothill Freeway (210) in La Canada, exit on Angeles Crest Highway (2) and proceed to signed Islip Saddle. (At the saddle, on the north side of the highway, is a large parking area. If you want, you can start your hike to Mt. Islip at the trailhead across the road from the parking area. An old trail heads west, paralleling the highway for a mile, then veers upward to meet the trail leading to Little Jimmy Trail Camp.)

From Islip Saddle, a mile-and-a-half drive east on Angeles Crest Highway brings you to the signed trailhead for Little Jimmy Trail Camp on the right (south) side of the road. There's parking on both sides of the highway.

The Hike: Your trail, at first, is a dirt road (closed to all but Forest Service vehicles). Jeffrey and sugar pine shade the route. A half-mile ascent brings you to a three-way junction. To your right is the old crest trail coming up from Islip Sadddle. The forest road you've been following continues to Little Jimmy Trail Camp.

Bear left on the signed trail to Little Jimmy. The trail stays just below and parallel to the road as it ascends a mile over forested slopes to Little Jimmy Trail Camp. The camp, popular with scout troops, has tables, stoves and restrooms. A side trail leads ¼-mile southeast to all-year Little Jimmy Spring.

At the west end of camp, pick up the signed trail to Mt. Islip. A half-mile of switchbacks through piney woods brings you up to a sharp ridgeline. From atop the ridge, you'll enjoy great views of Crystal Lake, the San Gabriel Wilderness, and the canyons cut by Bear Creek and the San Gabriel River. The trail turns east and follows the ridge for another half-mile to the 8,250-foot peak. Summit views include the ski areas of Krakta Ridge and Mt. Waterman to the west and Mt. Baden-Powell to the east.

54

Mount Baden-Powell Trail

Vincent Gap to summit
8 miles round trip; 2,800-foot gain

Season: May-November

This trail and peak honor Lord Baden-Powell, a British Army officer who founded the Boy Scout movement in 1907. The well-engineered trail, grooved into the side of the mountain by the Civillian Conservation Corps in the mid-1930s, switchbacks up the northeast ridge to the peak.

The peak was once known as North Baldy, before Southern California Boy Scouts lobbied the Forest Service for a name change. Mount Baden-Powell is the terminus of the scouts' 53-mile Silver Moccasin Trail, a rugged week-long backpack through the San Gabriels. Scouts who complete the long trail earn the Silver Moccasin Award.

The trail follows a moderate, steady grade to the top of the mountain, where there's a monument honoring Lord Baden-Powell. On the summit, you'll meet those ancient survivors, the limber pines, and be treated to superb views across the Mojave Desert and down into the Iron Fork of the San Gabriel River.

Directions to trailhead: Take the Angeles Crest Highway (2) for 53 miles from La Canada to the Vincent Gap Parking Area. The signed trailhead is at the northwest edge of the parking area.

If you're coming from the east, take Interstate 15 to the Wrightwood

exit, three miles south of Cajon Pass. Procceed 8 miles west on Highway 138 to its intersection with Highway 2. Turn left on Highway 2 and follow it for 14 miles to the trailhead.

The Hike: The trail immediately begins ascending from Vincent Gulch Divide, a gap which separates the upper tributaries of the San Gabriel River to the south from Big Rock Creek to the northwest. You begin switchbacking southwest through Jeffrey pine and fir. The trail numbers more than three dozen of these switchbacks, but so many beautiful attractions compete for the hiker's attention that it's hard to get an accurate count.

In 1½ miles, a side trail (unmarked) leads a hundred yards to Lamel Spring, an inviting resting place and the only dependable water en route.

With increased elevation, the switchbacks grow shorter and steeper and the vegetation changes from fir to lodgepole pine. Soon, even the altitude-loving lodgepoles give way to the heartiest of pines, the limber pine. A half-mile from the summit, around 9,000 feet in elevation, the first of these squat, thick-trunked limber pines come into view. Shortly, you'll intersect a side trail to the limber pine forest.

To Limber Pine Forest: A tiny sign points right (southwest) to the limber pine stand, ⅛ mile. These wind-loving, subalpine dwellers are one of the few living things that can cope with the rarefied atmosphere. *Pinus flexilis*, botanists call the species, for its long, droopy, flexible branches. They bow and scrape like hyperextended dancers and appear to gather all their nourishment from the wind.

Back on the main trail, a few more switchbacks bring you atop the ridge where Mount Baldy can be glimpsed. You walk along the barren crest and intersect the Pacific Crest Trail. PCT swoops off to Little Jimmy Spring.

You continue past the limber pines to the summit. A concrete monument pays homage to Lord Baden-Powell. Enjoy the superb view out across the Mojave to the southern Sierra and east to Baldy, San Gorgonio and San Jacinto.

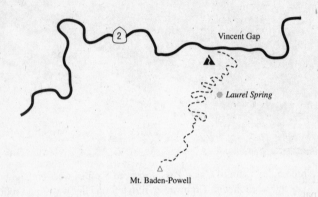

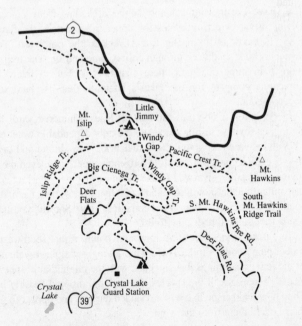

55

Islip Ridge Trail

Crystal Lake to Mt. Islip
 9 miles round trip; 2,200-foot elevation gain

Just below the crest of the Angeles Crest is a well-watered, cedar- and pine-forested basin. This basin has no outlet and thus gathers rainwater and snowmelt from the San Gabriel Mountains above. A happy result of this geographical happenstance is Crystal Lake, the only natural lake in the San Gabriel Mountains. During the 19th Century, the lake was known as Sycamore Lake; that is, until Pasadenan Judge Benjamin Eaton visited in 1887 and proclaimed: "The water is clear as a crystal and the party found it good to drink." Crystal Lake it has remained ever since.

Today, the Forest Service, along with dedicated volunteers, have made Crystal Lake Recreation Area an attractive destination, complete with nature trails, a pleasant campground and a visitors center.

The best hike in the Crystal Lake area is up Islip Ridge. Connoisseurs will appreciate the look—and feel—of hand-built Islip Ridge Trail. The moderate grade, well-engineered switchbacks, the rockwork and the way the path gently crosses the land are due to the skill and hard work of dedicated volunteers, particularly the San Gabriel Mountains Trail Builders.

This trail to Mt. Islip climbs the forested shoulder of the mountain, and intersects a summit trail which leads to the peak.

Directions to trailhead: From the Foothill Freeway (210) in Azusa, take the Highway 39/Azusa Ave. exit. Drive north on Highway 39 for 24 miles to the turnoff for Crystal Lake Recreation Area. After a mile you'll reach the Forest Service entry station.

Continue another mile to Crystal Lake Visitor Center, which is open on the weekends, then another ½ mile to a large dirt parking lot on your right and signed Windy Gap Trail on your left.

The Hike: Ascend moderately on Windy Gap Trail, which passes near a campground and heads into the cool of the forest. The trail crosses a forest service road leading to Deer Flat Campground, ascends some more and reaches the dirt South Mount Hawkins Truck Road. Cross the road and look left for the beginning of Islip Ridge Trail, which some of the trail builders like to call the Big Cienega Cut-off because it passes near Big Cienega Spring.

Enjoy the pleasant trail as it ascends moderately more or less west through pine, spruce and cedar forest. A bit more than a mile from the top, Islip Ridge Trail turns sharply north into a more sparse alpine forest.

The trail intersects the path coming from Windy Gap. Turn left and walk a short, but steep distance to the top of 8,250-foot Mt. Islip.

56

Blue Ridge Trail

Angeles Crest Highway to Blue Ridge Campground
4½ miles round trip; 1,000-foot gain

Here's a land for all seasons.

In winter, Big Pines is big on skiing. Downhillers take advantage of three popular slopes. In summer, Big Pines is big on camping—a place to beat the heat and sleep out under the stars. Eleven campgrounds are within a five miile radius of Big Pines Visitor Center.

For the hiker, mile-and-a-half-high Big Pines is an attractive destination in spring and autumn. The crisp alpine air, Sierra Nevada-like terrain, as well as the tall Jeffrey pines and white fir, add up to the Angeles National Forest at its most splendid.

Over the years, Big Pines has seen some big dreams materialize, then disappear. In the early 1930s, four ski jumps were constructed on the steep slopes below Blue Ridge. Thanks to local boosters, Big Pines was selected as the site for the 1932 Olympic Winter Games ski jump competition. Alas, poor Southland snow conditions that year prompted Olympic officials to move the competion to Lake Placid, New York.

Big Pines County Park, operated by L.A. County from 1923 to 1940, was a huge recreation complex: lodge, cabins, campgrounds, coffee shop, ice skating rink, swimming pool, tennis courts, groomed slopes for skiing and tobogganing. A beautifully crafted stone pedestrian overpass crossed Angeles Crest Highway and connected twin castle-like towers. The towers were more than mere architectural whimsy; they served as holding cells for drunks and troublemakers until the sheriff could transport the miscreants to jail in the flatlands below.

Unable to afford the cost of operating the facility, the County turned it over to the Forest Service in 1940, but not before removing everything from plumbing fixtures to picnic tables. Since taking over Big Pines, the Forest Service has maintained a more low key presence by emphasizing camping, hiking and nature study.

Today the former Swarthout Lodge is the Forest Service's Big Pines Visitor Center. Stop in Wednesday through Sunday to pick up pamphlets and inquire about campgrounds, trail conditions and interpretive programs.

Families—or anyone wanting to learn more about forest flora and fauna—will enjoy three Big Pines' nature trails:

Big Pine Nature Trail (½ mile), which begins back of the visitor center, winds through Jeffrey pines and assorted conifers. The path also interprets

chaparral shrubs and the various uses of these plants made by the Gabrielino people and other native peoples.

Table Mountain Nature Trail (1 mile), keyed to a pamphlet available at Big Pines Visitor Center, begins at the entrance to Table Mountain Campground. You'll get up-close looks at pine forest and oak woodland ecosystems.

Lightning Ridge Nature Trail (¾ mile) begins opposite Inspiration Point, just off Angeles Crest Highway, two miles west of the visitor center. The path switchbacks up a pine and fir blanketed slope to joint the Pacific Crest Trail. Near the junction of this trail and PCT is a panoramic view even more inspiring than that at Inspiration Point.

More challenging than the nature trails is Blue Ridge Trail, which switchbacks up a steep slope to meet the Pacific Crest Trail at Blue Ridge Campground. Plan a picnic under the pines at the campground. Reward for the climb is an eye-popping view of mounts Baldy and Baden-Powell.

You have a couple of options with this hike besides the usual out-and-back. You can walk over to Inspiration Point and arrange for a ride. You can also arrange to have a car waiting for you at Blue Ridge Campground, assuming the road is snow-free and open.

Directions to trailhead: From Interstate 15 at Cajon Junction, take the Highway 138 exit, heading west. After a bit more than a mile, the road forks and you leave 138, bearing left onto Lone Pine Road. Proceed 8½ miles to the Angeles Crest Highway (2). Turn west, passing the resort town of Wrightwood, and in five miles reaching Big Pines Visitor Center on your right. The trailhead and trailhead parking is across the highway from the visitor center.

The Hike: Begin your moderate ascent through well-spaced, mature stands of Jeffrey pine. To the north, you'll get over-the-shoulder and through-the-trees glimpses of two observatories atop Table Mountain.

A mile out, you cross an old road, then tackle some more switchbacks before intersecting Blue Ridge Road. Blue Ridge Campground with its viewful picnicking is just down the road. Up the road a short distance is a junction with the Pacific Crest Trail, which you can follow on a steep ascent near a ski run to a viewpoint offering a superb look at the snowy north shoulder of Mt. Baldy.

57

East Fork Trail

East Fork Station to the "Bridge to Nowhere,"
9 miles round trip; 1,000-foot gain

To Iron Fork
12 miles round trip; 1,400-foot gain

Season: All year. Use caution during times of high water.

Sometimes you'll see a weekend gold miner find a flash in the pan, but the real treasure of this section of the San Gabriel River lies in its beauty, its alders and tumbling waters. It's wet going; you'll be doing a lot of wading as well as walking, but you'll be well rewarded for all your boulder-hopping and stream crossings.

This day hike takes you through the monumental middle section of the East Fork of the San Gabriel River, into the Sheep Mountain Wilderness. The dizzy chasm of the Narrows is awesome, the steepest river gorge in Southern California.

Road builders of the 1930s envisioned a highway through the East Fork to connect the San Gabriel Valley with Wrightwood and the desert beyond. The great flood of 1938 interrupted these plans, leaving a handsome highway bridge stranded far up-river, the so-called "Bridge to Nowhere."

You'll pass the cracked asphalt remains of the old East Fork Road and gain access to the well-named Narrows. Expect to get wet at the numerous river crossings. High water during winter or spring means these crossings will likely be unsafe.

In the early years of this century, at the junction of Iron Fork with the main river, miner George Trogden had a home and angler's headquarters, where miners and intrepid fisher-men gathered to swap tales. Up-river from Iron Fork is Fish Fork, whose waters cascade from the shoulders of Mt. Baldy. It, too, has been a popular fishing spot for generations of anglers.

Directions to trailhead: From Interstate 10 (San Bernardino Freeway) exit on Azusa Avenue (Highway 39) and head north. You'll need to pick up a parking permit on weekends en route

161

"The Bridge to Nowhere"

from the ranger station on 39. Ten miles up Highway 39, turn right (east) on East Fork Road and continue eight more miles to the East Fork Ranger Station. You'll need a second permit—a wilderness permit—which you can fill out at the self-service dispenser at the base of the ranger station road.

Follow the service road above the east side of the river a half-mile to Heaton Flat Campground. The trail descends to the canyon floor and begins crossing and re-crossing the river. A bit more than two miles from the trailhead is Swan Rock, a mighty wall west of the river with the faint outline of a gargantuan swan.

As the canyon floor widens and twists northward, you'll climb up the right side of the canyon and continue up-river on the remains of East Fork Road, high above the rushing water. After ascending north a ways, you'll reach the "Bridge to Nowhere." No road meets this bridge at either end; the highway washed away in the flood of '38.

Cross the bridge and join a slim trail that soon drops you into The Narrows. A quarter-mile from the bridge is the site of former Narrows Trail Camp, now a fine place to picnic and view the handsome gorge. A rough trail—made by use not design—leads a bit more than a mile through The Narrows.

You, like the river, will squeeze your way between towering granite walls. Iron Fork joins the river from the left, six miles from the trailhead.

Yet another mile up-river is Fish Fork, where another abandoned camp offers good picnicking. You can slosh up Fish Fork for another mile before a falls and the sheer canyon walls halt your progress.

58

Icehouse Canyon Trail

Icehouse Canyon to Icehouse Saddle
 8 miles round trip; 2,600-foot gain

Season: May-October

Icehouse Canyon Trail, leading from Icehouse Canyon to several 8,000-foot peaks, is an ideal introduction to the high country delights of the Cucamonga Wilderness. The precipitous subalpine slopes of the wilderness, thickly forested with sugar pine, ponderosa pine and incense cedar, offer fresh mountain air and a network of good footpaths. The 4,400-acre wilderness, set aside by Congress in 1984, includes the Three T's—Timber Mountain, Telegraph Peak and Thunder Mountain—as well as 8,859-foot Cucamonga Peak, easternmost sentinel of the San Gabriel Mountains.

A wilderness permit is required for entry. Located at the far eastern end of the San Gabriel Mountains, the Cucamonga Wilderness sprawls across the boundaries of both the San Bernardino and Angeles National Forests, and a wilderness permit can be obtained from either agency.

Icehouse Canyon is the hiker's only easy entry into the Cucamonga high country. The saddle and nearby peaks offer fine views to the hiker. Sierra Club peak-baggers like this trail because several peaks are within "bagging distance" of Icehouse Saddle, an important trail junction.

Icehouse Canyon was for many years known as Cedar Canyon because, as the story goes, the great cedar beams for Mission San Gabriel were logged here. The name Icehouse originated in the 1860s when ice was cut in the lower canyon and shipped to San Gabriel Valley residents.

The Chapman Trail, constructed in 1980, was named for the family that built the Icehouse Canyon resort and numerous cabins in the 1920s. The well-constructed trail heads up Cedar Canyon to Cedar Glen. The cedars were severely scorched by the 1980 Thunder Mountain fire, but the canyon flora is slowly recovering. The trail climbs out of Cedar Canyon, then contours on a steady grade back over to Icehouse Canyon.

Another Chapman—no relation to the family whose name is found on the trail—figured in the history of Icehouse Canyon. Yankee Joseph Chapman arrived in Monterey in 1818, was accused of insurgency by the Spanish governor of California, and soon shipped to Los Angeles as a prisoner. Los Angeles, then a remote outpost, lacked lumber and when authorities learned that the New Englander was a master woodsman, they put him in charge of timber operations in the San Gabriel Mountains. The

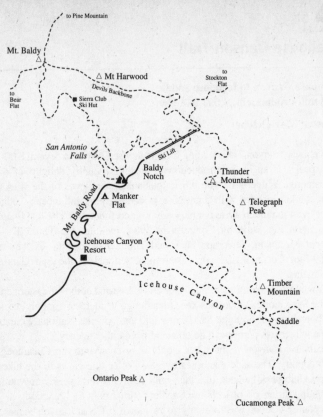

to Pine Mountain

Mt. Baldy
△

△ Mt Harwood
Devils Backbone

to
Stockton
Flat

to
Bear
Flat

■ Sierra Club
Ski Hut

San Antonio
Falls

Ski Lift

Baldy
Notch

Thunder
△ Mountain

▲ Manker
Flat

△ Telegraph
Peak

Mt. Baldy Road

Icehouse Canyon
Resort
■

I c e h o u s e   C a n y o n

△ Timber
Mountain

Saddle

Ontario Peak △

Cucamonga Peak △

Spaniards and their Indian helpers thought that Chapman's ability to chop a tree down—and make it fall whichever way he wanted—was nothing less than magical. Some of the more superstitious called him "Diablo Chapman."

The cedar beams, hewed square up in the mountains, were dragged out of the canyon by oxen. Chapman's logging operations here and in other parts of Southern California earned him amnesty from the governor. Some historians believe Chapman to be the third Anglo resident of California, and the first to reside in Los Angeles.

Directions to trailhead: From the San Bernardino Freeway (10) in Upland, exit on Mountain Avenue. Head north on Mountain, which joins Mount Baldy Road in San Antonio Canyon and winds its way to Mount Baldy Village. Go 1½ miles past the village to Icehouse Canyon Resort. Park in the dirt lot. The trail starts just to the right of the resort.

The Hike: The trail leads east along the floor of the canyon. The path stays close to the oak- and spruce-shaded creek and passes some cabins. Brick

Mount Baldy from upper Icehouse Canyon

chimneys and stone foundations are all that remain of other cabins, swept away during the great flood of 1938. After 1½ miles, the trail forks. You may take the "high route," the Chapman Trail, one mile to Cedar Flats and then three miles up to Icehouse Saddle, or continue straight ahead on the shorter and steeper Icehouse Canyon Trail directly up the canyon.

If you decided to continue on the Icehouse Canyon Trail, you'll pass a few more cabins. The trail climbs up the north slope of the canyon, before dropping down again and crossing the creek. The trail switchbacks steeply through pine and spruce. The tall trees frame a nice picture of Old Baldy. The Chapman Trail and the Icehouse Canyon Trail intersect and a single trail ascends a steep ¾ of a mile to the top of Icehouse Saddle.

You can enjoy the view and return the same way, or pick one of the fine trails that lead from Icehouse Saddle and add to your day hike. You can continue eastward and drop down the Middle Fork Trail to Lytle Creek. A right (southeast) turn puts you on a trail that climbs two miles to Cucamonga Peak. A sharp right southwest leads 2½ miles to Kelly's Camp and Ontario Peak. And a left on the Three T's Trail takes you past Timber Mountain, Telegraph Peak and Thunder Mountain, then drops to Baldy Notch.

59

Sunset Peak Trail

Glendora Ridge Road to Sunset Peak
5 miles round trip; 1,200-foot gain

Season: All year

When snow covers the San Gabriel high country, consider the short hike to Sunset Peak. For most of the winter and early spring, the 5,796-foot peak seems to be strategically positioned just below the snow line and just above the smog line. You'll get great clear-day views of Claremont and the San Gabriel Valley below and of Baldy and its neighboring peaks above. Sunset views are often glorious.

Directions to trailhead: From the San Bernardino Freeway (I-10) in Claremont, exit on Indian Hill Blvd. and head north. Drive 2 miles to Foothill Blvd. (old Route 66 for the nostalgic). Turn right and proceed ¾ mile to Mills Avenue, then turn left and follow Mills 2 miles to a stop sign, where the avenue becomes Mt. Baldy Road; continue another 8 miles to Glendora Ridge Road, which you'll spot on your left just short of the hamlet of Mt. Baldy. Turn left and follow Glendora Ridge Road a mile to a gravel parking lot on the right. The trailhead is on the opposite (left) side of the road.

The Hike: Sunset Peak Trail, a Forest Service fire road closed to vehicles, begins at a candy cane-striped barrier. The trail ascends moderately, but steadily up the pine and big cone spruce-shaded north side of Sunset Peak.

About halfway to the peak, you'll ascend out of the shade into chaparral country. A 1975 fire scorched these upper slopes and it will be a while before tall trees grow here again.

A very steep fire break offers a route to the summit, but it would be wise to ignore it and continue on the main trail. A half-mile from the top, at a wide bend in the road, the trail swings sharp left.

Just below the peak the fire road gives way to a steep footpath and you'll ascend a final hundred yards to the summit. Up top are a couple of cement pillars and other debris, remains of a Forest Service fire lookout tower that was abandoned because of several reasons: Smog hindered visibility and the Forest Service has for some years been replacing human lookouts with more automated surveillance. Also, a fire burned the peak!

The view of the metropolis below is notoriously undependable; however, the panorama of peaks above is always an inspiring sight.

60

Devil's Backbone Trail

Baldy Notch to Mount Baldy summit
7 miles round trip; 2,200-foot gain

Three saintly mountains—San Gorgonio, San Jacinto and San Antonio—tower over the City of the Angels. Lowest of the three, but by far the best-known is Mount San Antonio, more commonly known as Mount Baldy. The 10,064-foot peak, highest in the San Gabriel Mountains, is visible from much of the Southland. Its summit gleams white in winter and early spring, gray in summer and fall. Old Baldy is so big and bare that it seems to be snow-covered even when it's not.

Legend has it the padres of Mission San Gabriel, circa 1790, named the massive stone bulwark after Saint Anthony of Padua, Italy. The 13th-Century Franciscan friar was evidently a favorite of California missionaries; a number of geographical features, both in Monterey County and around Southern California, honor San Antonio. In the 1870s, San Antonio Canyon and the nearby high country swarmed with gold-seekers, who dubbed the massive peak a more earthly "Old Baldy."

Surely one of the most unique resorts in the San Gabriels was the Baldy Summit Inn, perched just below the summit of the great mountain. Gale-force winds battered the above-timberline camp, which consisted of two stone buildings and a cluster of tents. William Dewey, the owner/guide, and Mrs. Dewey, the chef, welcomed guests to their resort during the summers of 1910 through 1912. Advertised rates were $1 a meal, $1 a bed. The camp burned in 1913 and never reopened.

A moderate (compared to other routes up Baldy), but certainly not easy, ascent follows the Devil's Backbone Trail from Baldy Notch to the summit. This is a very popular trail and the one most hikers associate with Mount Baldy. A clear-day view from the top offers a panorama of desert and ocean, the sprawling Southland and the Southern high Sierras.

Baldy is a bit austere from afar, but up-close, the white granite shoulders of the mountain are softened by a forest of pine and fir. Dress warmly for this trip and keep an eye out for rapidly changing weather conditions.

Directions to trailhead: From the San Bernardino Freeway (10), exit on Mountain Avenue. Head north on Mountain, which joins Mount Baldy Road in San Antonio Canyon and winds 12 miles to road's end just beyond Manker Campground. Park in the ski lift parking area.

Purchase a ticket and ride the ski lift up to Baldy Notch. The lift is operated weekends and holidays all year.

167

"Old Baldy"

An alternative is to walk up a fire road to Baldy Notch. This option adds three miles each way and a 1,300-foot gain to the walk. The fire road switchbacks up the west side of the steep San Antonio Canyon, offers a good view of San Antonio Falls, then climbs northward to the top.

The Hike: From Baldy Notch, a wide gravel path leads to a commanding view of the desert. You then join a chair lift access/fire road, and ascend a broad slope forested in Jeffrey pine and incense cedar. The road ends in about 1¼ miles at the top of a ski lift, where a hiker's sign-in register beckons.

From the top of the ski lift, a trail leads out onto a sharp ridge known as the Devil's Backbone. To the north, you can look down into the deep gorge of Lytle Creek, and to the south into San Antonio Canyon. You'll then pass around the south side of Mount Harwood, "Little Baldy," and up through scattered stands of lodgepole pine.

The trail reaches a tempestuous saddle. (Hold onto your hat!) From the saddle, a steep rock-strewn pathway zigzags past a few wind-bowed limber pine to the summit.

Boulders are scattered atop Baldy's crown. A couple of rock wind-breaks offer some shelter. Enjoy the view of San Gabriel and San Bernardino mountain peaks, the Mojave and the metropolis, and return the same way.

61

Ski Hut Trail

To San Antonio Falls
2½ miles round trip; 200-foot gain

To San Antonio Canyon Overlook
6½ miles round trip; 2,600-foot gain

Manker Flat to Mt. Baldy summit
8½ miles round trip; 3,800-foot gain

Season: May-October

This day hike utilizes a pretty but not-so-well-known trail that leads up San Antonio Canyon to the top of Baldy. Locals call it the Ski Hut Trail because the Sierra Club maintains a hut halfway up the path. The trail doesn't have an official name and is not on the Angeles National Forest map.

Hikers of all ages and abilities will enjoy the half-mile walk to San Antonio Falls. After a little rain, the three-tiered, 60-foot waterfall is an impressive sight.

Beyond the falls the hiking is strenuous, definitely not for the in-experienced or out-of-shape. Hikers who want more than the "leg stretcher" walk to the falls but aren't quite up for an assault on the peak can choose two intermediate destinations: the Sierra Club ski hut, where there's a cool spring, or a high ridge overlooking San Antonio Canyon.

Hikers in top form, with good trail sense (the last mile of trail to the peak is rough and tentative), will relish the challenge of the summit climb. A clear-day view from the top offers a panorama of desert and ocean, the sprawling Southland and the southern High Sierra.

Directions to trailhead: Take the San Bernardino Freeway to Claremont, exit on Mountain Avenue and head north, joining Mt. Baldy Road in San Antonio Canyon and winding about 11 mile to Manker Campground. One-third mile past the campground entrance, look to the left for an unsigned paved road with a vehicle barrier across it. Park in the dirt lot just below the beginning of the road.

The Hike: Walk up the fire road, which is closed to all motor vehicles except those belonging to ski-lift maintenance workers. After a modest ascent, you will hear the sound of falling water and soon behold San Antonio Falls. If you decide to hike down to the base of the falls, watch for loose rock and use caution on the rough trail.

Resume walking along the road (unpaved beyond the falls). After about 10 minutes of walking at a moderate pace, look sharply left for an

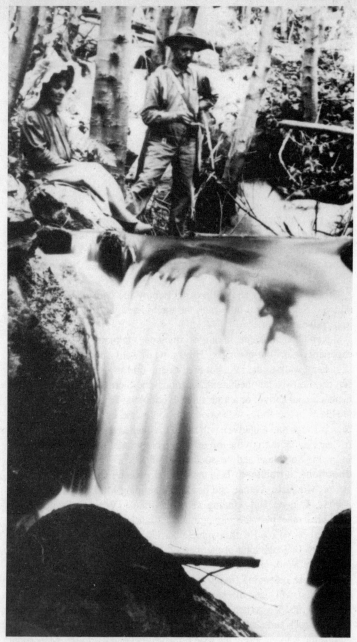

Early hikers admire San Antonio Canyon.

unsigned trail. Ducks (piles of rock) on both sides of the road herald the trail. (If you find yourself heading north up Manker Canyon and getting good views of the ski lift, you missed the turnoff.)

The no-nonsense trail ascends very steeply along the side of San Antonio Canyon. You'll get great over-the-shoulder views of the canyon bottom and of Mt. Baldy Village. Trail connoisseurs will appreciate this path, which, despite its steepness, has a hand-hewn, unobtrusive look and follows the natural contours of the land. Jeffrey pine, ponderosa pine and fir shade the well-constructed path, which is seasonally decorated with red Indian paintbrush and creamy yucca blossoms.

From the ski lift road it's 1¾ miles by trail to the Sierra Club ski hut. Near the hut, which was built in 1935, is a cool and refreshing spring.

Just past the ski hut the trail crosses a tiny creek, then snakes through a boulder field. Beyond the boulders the trail ascends via a half-mile series of steep switchbacks to a ridgetop overlooking the headwaters of San Antonio Canyon. There's a great view from the tree-shaded ridgetop, and it you aren't quite up for an assault on the peak, this is a good picnic spot or turnaround point.

Peak-baggers will continue up the extremely rugged trail for another mile to the summit. The trail is rough and tentative in some places, but rocks piled in cairns help you stay on course. You'll get good view of Devil's Backbone, the sharp ridge connecting Mt. Harwood to Mt. Baldy.

Boulders are scattered atop Baldy's crown. A couple of rock wind-breaks offer some shelter. Enjoy the view of San Gabriel and San Bernardino Mountain peaks, the Mojave and the metropolis.

Depending on your energy and inclination, you can either return the same way or take the Devil's Backbone Trail to Mt. Baldy Notch. From the Notch, you can follow the fire road down Manker Canyon back to the trailhead or ride down the ski lift.

5. Orange County

ORANGE COUNTY shares its coastline and coastal plain with neighboring Los Angeles County, but has a distinct geographical identity. This geography, which in the decades since World War II has been almost unbelievably altered by the hand of man, nevertheless still holds some intrigue for the lover of wild places.

The orchards that gave Orange County its name are nearly gone, but the hills and mountains occupying half the county still afford invigorating vistas. This guide seeks out what remains of the pastoral in the county's hills and canyons.

During the last decade of the 19th Century and the first few decades of the 20th, the county was known for its fruited plain watered by the Santa Ana River. (Although the Santa Ana for most of its length is now a cement-lined flood control channel, it was once a substantial river and even today is Southern California's leader in average annual runoff.) Citrus and other fruits, flowers and vegetables were successfully grown on the fertile coastal plain. Valencia orange groves, protected from the wind by long rows of eucalyptus, stretched across the plain to the foothills.

Today the coastal plain has been almost completely covered by residential and commercial development. Once huge farms and ranches such as Laguna Niguel, Moulton, Mission Viejo and Irvine are now suburbs. Although 782-square-mile Orange is not one of California's larger counties, it is the state's second most populous, right behind Los Angeles County.

In a county with more than two million residents and with most of its flatland developed, hikers must head for the hills to find untouched or less-touched places. In the backcountry, where level land and water are scant, there has been less settlement.

Protecting the last of Orange County's ecological heritage is Crystal Cove State Park and a half-dozen county parks. Oak woodland, chaparral slopes and grassy meadows are among the natural communities found in these parks.

Hiking this land is a good way to shed some stereotypes about Southern California in general, and Orange County in particular. One stereotype—that Orange County is nothing more than a monotonous urban-suburban sprawl—vanishes when you witness firsthand the ecological diversity of the backcountry. Another stereotype—that Orange County's history is all Anglo—disappears when you walk into the land's Spanish, Indian, German, Polish and Japanese heritage. The names on the land—from Flores to Modjeska to Anaheim—speak of this rich tapestry of cultures.

62

Carbon Canyon Nature Trail

Carbon Canyon Creek to Redwood Grove
  2 miles round trip

Season: All year

Carbon Canyon Regional Park offers some much-needed "breathing room" for fast-growing northeastern Orange County. The park has both a natural area with trails that connect to nearby Chino Hills State Park, and a more developed part with wide lawns, tennis courts, ball fields, picnic grounds and a lake.

The park spreads up-canyon behind Carbon Canyon dam. As Orange County grew, so did the need for flood control, and in 1959, a dam was built at the mouth of the canyon. If, as a result of winter storms, the Santa Ana River rises too high, the dam's floodgates will be closed, thus sparing communities downstream of the dam, but flooding the park.

A century ago, the arrival of the Santa Fe Railroad precipitated a minor land boom. Farmers and ranchers rushed to the area. Cattle and sheep were pastured in the canyon now called Carbon.

But it was another boom—an oil boom—that put Carbon Canyon on the map. E.L. Doheny, soon to become one of L.A.'s leading boosters, discovered oil in the area in 1896. His company and several others drilled the foothills of Orange County. The name Carbon was applied to the canyon because of the many dried-up oil seeps in evidence.

Santa Fe Railroad tracks were extended to the mouth of Carbon Canyon in order to haul out the oil. At the end of the tracks was the oil town of Olinda, boyhood home of the great baseball pitcher Walter Johnson. "Big Train," as the hurler was known, pitched for the Washington Senators, and led the American League in strikeouts each year from 1912 to 1919. Olinda boomed until the 1940s when the oil fields began to play out.

The undeveloped part of Carbon Canyon Regional Park is a narrow corridor along Carbon Canyon Creek. A one-mile nature trail leads creek-side through an interesting mixture of native and foreign flora. At the entrance station you can pick up an interpretive pamphlet, which is keyed to numbered posts along the nature trail, and details points and plants of interest.

During the summer months, early morning and late afternoon are the most comfortable times to hit the Carbon Canyon Nature Trail. Rewarding the hiker at trail's end is a small, shady redwood grove.

Directions to trailhead: From the Orange Freeway (57) in Brea, exit on Lambert Road. Drive 4 miles east on Lambert (which changes to Carbon Canyon Road east of Valencia Avenue) to the park entrance. There's a vehicle entry fee.

The Hike: From the parking area, walk back to the entrance station, and you'll spot the signed trail in a stand of pine, just east of the park entrance. On closer inspection, you'll discover that the pines are Monterey pines, native to California but not to this area. This stand is a holdover from a Christmas tree farm that was operated before the park opened in 1975.

Less-celebrated than the Monterey cypress but almost as rare, the Monterey pine is found growing naturally within Point Lobos State Reserve and at only two other areas along the California coast. This fog-loving three-needle pine has a very restricted natural range; however, it's cultivated for timber all over the world—particularly in the South Pacific.

From the pines, the nature trail descends to the Carbon Canyon creekbed. After crossing the creek, the trail forks. (The path to the left leads toward Telegraph Canyon and to a network of hiking trails that crisscross Chino Hills State Park. The 8-mile length of Telegraph Canyon, home of native walnut groves, is well worth exploring.) Carbon Canyon Nature Trail heads right with the creekbed. Creek-side vegetation is dominated by mustard, castor bean and hemlock. You'll also find two exotic imports— the California pepper tree, actually a native of Peru, and some giant reeds, bamboo-like plants that harm the native plant community because they take a great deal of the scarce water supply.

At the trail's mid-point, there's a distinct, but unmarked, side trail that angles across the creekbed to the developed part of the park. If for some reason you want to call it a day, here's your exit point.

As you near trail's end you'll get brush-framed glimpses of Carbon Canyon Dam. The trail ascends out of the creekbed to the park's redwood grove. The redwoods, planted in 1975, have a lot of growing to do before they rival their majestic cousins to the north.

63

Anaheim Hills Trail

Santiago Oaks Regional Park to Robber's Roost
 3½ miles round trip; 700-foot gain

Season: All year

Housing developments often take the name of the natural features around them, but in one Orange County suburb the naming process is reversed. Geologists and mapmakers have long referred to the long, low ridge extending west from the Santa Ana Mountains and rising above Santa Ana Canyon as the Peralta Hills, but almost no one uses that name anymore. Today the hills are known as the Anaheim Hills.

The hills honor, or did honor, Juan Pablo Peralta and his family, original owners of the huge Rancho Santiago de Santa Ana. Peralta is an excellent name, historic and euphonious. It recalls the Latin expression *Per Alta*, "through the high things." Sounds like a university motto, doesn't it?

Anaheim, which German settlers in 1858 named after the river Santa Ana plus the suffix *heim* (home), already names a city, a boulevard, a bay, a stadium and much more. Perhaps it's time for concerned day hikers and Orange Countians to rally to save the Peralta Hills. (Alas, it is not merely the name of the hills, but the hills themselves that are fast-disappearing beneath the suburban sprawl.)

Other names from the past still remain. Santiago Oaks Regional Park, Santiago Creek and Santiago Canyon are derived from the old Rancho Santiago de Santa Ana. One intriguing name for a rocky knob overlooking the regional park is Robber's Roost. From this lookout, such infamous 19th Century outlaws as Joaquín Murietta and Three-Finger Jack kept watch over rural Orange County. The outlaws would ride down from the hills to rob the Butterfield Stagecoach or ride into the hills to escape the sheriff's posse.

Santiago Oaks Regional Park preserves 125 acres of pastoral Orange County, including an oak woodland that attracts many species of birds. You can sample the park's ecosystem with Windes Nature Trail. A nature center, located near the trailhead, is well-worth a visit.

A network of fire roads and equestrian trails crisscross the park and extend into the Anaheim Hills. While the hills seem destined for suburban development, for now, at least, you can enjoy a ramble up to Robber's Roost and steal a last look at fast-vanishing rural Orange County.

Directions to trailhead: From the Newport Freeway (55) in Orange, exit on Katella. Turn east on Katella, which undergoes a name change in a

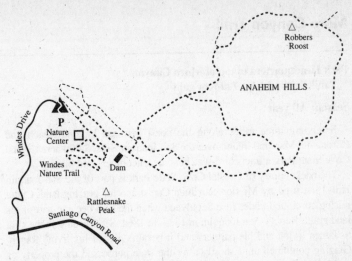

half-mile to Villa Park Road, then a second name change to Santiago Canyon Road. A bit more than two miles from the freeway, turn left on Windes Drive and drive a mile to Santiago Oaks Regional Park. An "Iron Ranger," a self-service entrance gate, collects your vehicle entry fee.

The Hike: From the end of the parking area, you'll spot Windes Nature Trail on your right, then swing left and cross Santiago Creek on some man-made stepping-stones. You'll pass a number of trails leading left into the woods, but for now stay with the main trail along the creek. Along with the native oaks, you might spot eucalyptus and pepper trees, and even a small grove of Valencia oranges.

Soon you'll see an old dam. With the aid of Chinese laborers, the Serrano and Carpenter Water Company built a clay dam here in 1879. This dam was destroyed by floods, and replaced in 1892 with a more substantial structure of river rock and cement. The dam looks particularly tiny when compared to the huge Villa Park Flood Control Dam a short distance upstream.

Bear left, and ascend a dirt road to the park's north boundary gate. Beyond the gate you'll ascend to an unsigned junction and bear left, then ascend a prickly pear cactus-dotted slope to a junction signed with an equestrian symbol and turn right. After passing under some transmission lines, the equestrian trail reaches Robber's Roost.

From the 1,152-foot peak, you can look over the Peralta Hills and trace the path of Santiago Creek. Not so long ago, the view would have taken in hundreds of cattle, orange groves, and barley fields. Nowadays the panorama is considerably less pastoral.

64

Moro Canyon Trail

Park Headquarters to top of Moro Canyon
  7 miles round trip; 700-foot gain

Season: All year

Extending three miles along the coast between Laguna Beach and Corona del Mar, and inland over the San Joaquin Hills, 3,000-acre Crystal Cove State Park attracts bird-watchers, beachcombers and hikers.

The backcountry of Crystal Cove State Park is part of the San Joaquin Hills, first used by Mission San Juan Capistrano for grazing land. Cattle raising continued under José Sepúlveda when the area became part of his land grant, Rancho San Joaquín, in 1837. In 1864, Sepúlveda sold the land to James Irvine and his partners and it became part of his Irvine Ranch. Grazing continued until shortly after the state purchased the property as parkland in 1979.

Former Irvine Ranch roads now form a network of hiking trails that loop through the state park. An especially nice trail travels the length of Moro Canyon, the main watershed of the park. An oak woodland, a seasonal stream and sandstone caves are some of the attractions of a walk through this canyon. Bird-watchers may spot the roadrunner, quail, Cooper's hawk, California thrasher, wrentit and many more species.

After exploring inland portions of the state park, allow some time to visit the park's coastline, highlighted by grassy bluffs, sandy beaches, tidepools and coves. The Pelican Point, Crystal Cove, Reef Point and Moro Beach areas of the park allow easy beach access.

Directions to trailhead: Crystal Cove State Park is located off Pacific Coast Highway, about two miles south of the town of Corona Del Mar or one mile north of Laguna Beach. Turn inland on the short park road, signed "El Moro Canyon." Drinking water, restrooms, interpretive displays and plenty of parking is available at the ranger station.

The Hike: Below the ranger station, near the park entry kiosk pick up the unsigned Moro Canyon Trail, which crosses the grassy slopes behind a school and trailer park down into Moro Canyon. At the canyon bottom, you meet a fire road and head left, up-canyon.

The hiker may observe such native plants as black sage, prickly pear cactus, monkeyflowers, golden bush, lemonade berry and deer weed. Long before Spanish missionaries and settlers arrived in Southern California, a native Indian population flourished in the coastal canyons of Orange County. The abundance of edible plants in the area, combined with the mild climate and easy access to the bounty of the sea, contributed to the success of these people, whom anthropologists believe lived off this land for more than four thousand years.

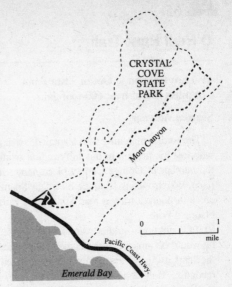

The canyon narrows, and you ignore fire roads joining Moro Canyon from the right and left. You stay in the canyon bottom and proceed through an oak woodland, which shades a trickling stream. You'll pass a shallow sandstone cave just off the trail to the right.

About 2½ miles from the trailhead, you'll reach the unsigned junction with a fire road. If you wish to make a loop trip out of this day hike, bear left on this road, which climbs steeply west, then northeast toward the ridgetop that forms a kind of inland wall for Muddy, Moro, Emerald and other coastal canyons.

When you reach the ridgetop, unpack your lunch and enjoy the far reaching views of the San Joaquin Hills and Orange County coast, Catalina and San Clemente Islands. You'll also have a raven's-eye-view of Moro Canyon and the route back to the trailhead. After catching your breath, you'll bear right (east) along the ridgetop and quickly descend back into Moro Canyon. A ¾-mile walk brings you back to the junction where you earlier ascended out of the canyon. This time you continue straight down-canyon, retracing your steps to the trailhead.

65

O'Neill Park Trail

Trabuco Canyon to Ocean Vista Point
  3 miles round trip; 600-foot gain

Season: All year

The soldier marching with Captain Gaspar de Portolá's 1769 expedition who lost his firearm in this hilly region would no doubt be astonished at the number of Orange County place-names inspired by his mistake. *Trabuco*, which means "blunderbuss" in Spanish, now names a canyon, a creek, a plain, a trail, a road and even a ranger district of the Cleveland National Forest.

If the unknown soldier who lost his blunderbuss trekked this way again he would be amazed at the names on the land, and even more amazed at the land itself, so drastically has it changed. Maybe though, he would recognize Trabuco Canyon, at least that part of it saved from suburbanization by O'Neill Regional Park. Here the modern trekker can explore a small slice of the pastoral Southern California of two centuries ago.

This land of grassy meadows, rolling hills and oak woodland was originally part of Rancho Trabuco, two leagues granted to Santiago Argüello in 1841 by Mexican Governor Alvarado. The rancho had various lessees and owners until it was purchased by James Flood, a wealthy businessman and his partner Richard O'Neill, a packing house owner. O'Neill built up quite a ranching empire here and elsewhere in California. O'Neill's Orange County property passed to various heirs who, in turn, gave 278 acres of Trabuco Canyon to Orange County for a park in 1948. Today, after various gifts and purchases, the park encompasses 1,700 acres of woodland and brushy hills, taking in Trabuco Canyon and neighboring Live Oak Canyon.

A good way to learn about the ecology of Trabuco Canyon is to walk the park's 1½-mile (round trip) nature trail. Trabuco Creek Trail, with stops keyed to a pamphlet available at the park's entry station, meanders through an oak/sycamore woodland and explores Plano Trabuco, or Trabuco Flat, a level alluvial surface deposited by runoff from the slopes of the Santa Ana Mountains.

Another way to explore a bit of rural Orange County is to hike the park's various fire roads and trails on a route I've dubbed O'Neill Park Trail. The trail ascends to Ocean Vista Point, which offers fine coast and canyon views.

Directions to trailhead: From the San Diego Freeway (5) in El Toro, exit on El Toro Road and drive 7½ miles to Santiago Canyon Road (S-18).

Turn right and proceed 3 miles to O'Neill Regional Park. There is a vehicle entry fee. Park in the day use lot near the entrance.

The Hike: From the entry station, walk north on a service road that parallels Live Oak Canyon Road. Soon you'll head left on another paved road that ascends toward some water tanks. After a quarter-mile's travel, leave the pavement and turn right on a dirt road. Two turns bring you to a junction with a dirt road on your right (an optional return route from the top).

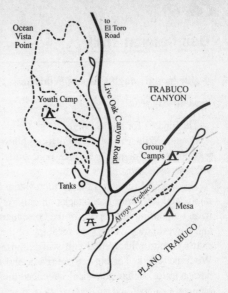

Continue your ascent along a ridge. Over your shoulder are two scenes typical of rural Orange County: Red-tailed hawks circling over classic Southland ranching country in one direction, and suburbs-in-the-making in the other.

Continue on a last steep ascent toward what appears to be a *Star Trek* movie set, but is actually Ocean Vista Point, sometimes known as "Cellular Hill." Up top, communications hardware helps car phoners complete their calls.

From the 1,492-foot summit, enjoy clear-day coastal views from Santa Monica Bay to San Clemente, with Catalina Island floating on the horizon.

For a different return route, head back two hundred yards and make a left at the first fork. Descend to an unused kid's camp, then follow the park's service road back to the trailhead.

66

Bell Canyon Trail

4-mile loop through Caspers Wilderness Park

Season: All year

This hike is for adults only.

Caspers Wilderness Park regulations allow only adults (18 and over), in groups of two or more, to hike park trails. Visitors must also obtain a wilderness permit.

The unusual rules and the permit system are a response to two highly publicized mountain lion attacks on children. The incidents also resulted in an outpouring of support for the beleaguered mountain lion population, and a questioning of the very meaning of the word "wilderness."

It's highly unlikely that you will glimpse a mountain lion in Caspers Wilderness Park. The big cats are scarce and elusive. Suburban sprawl and human intrusion have drastically reduced the number of mountain lions in Orange County, and in every other place in the Southern California backcountry.

Visitors to the 7,600-acre park in the Santa Ana Mountains near San Juan Capistrano will, however, have a good chance of sighting other wildlife: Deer, rabbits and coyote, as well as more furtive animals such as foxes and bobcats. Bird-watchers will want to consult the park's bird list and test their skill by identifying the many species found in the hills and canyons.

Crisscrossing Caspers Wilderness Park are thirty miles of trail, which explore grassy valleys, chaparral-cloaked ridges and native groves of coastal live oak and sycamore. In winter and spring the valleys are usually a deep green, sprinkled with lupine and blue-eyed grass. In dry years, the grassland quickly assumes its summer gold color.

Centerpiece of the park is oak-lined Bell Canyon. Acorns from the oaks were an important food source for the Juaneno Indians who lived in the canyon. As the legend goes, the Indians would strike a large granite boulder with a small rock to make it ring. The sound could be heard for a mile through what is now known as Bell Canyon. "Bell Rock" is now housed in Bowers Museum in Santa Ana.

Bell Canyon, San Juan Canyon, and surrounding ridges were once part of Starr-Viejo Ranch, which was purchased by Orange County in the early 1970s. The park honors Ronald W. Caspers, chairman of the Orange County Board of Supervisors, who was instrumental in preserving the old ranch as a park. Reminders of the park's ranching heritage include a windmill and a wooden corral where the branding and loading of cattle took place. The windmill still pumps a little water, which helps park wildlife make it through the long hot Santa Ana Mountains summers. During summer, the area around the windmill is the park's best bird-watching spot.

To learn more about the region's human and natural history, drop by the park's visitor center. Exhibits interpret Native American life, birds, mammals, geology, and much more. On weekends, park rangers lead nature walks.

The mostly level, Nature Trail-Oak Trail-Bell Canyon Trail-loop described below is only one of many possible day hikes you can fashion from the park's extensive trail network. The park's map is keyed to numbered posts located at trail junctions, so it's easy to design a hike that suits your time or energy level.

If you're an early riser and beat the heat, ascend one of the park's exposed ridges—via West Ridge Trail or East Ridge Trail. The latter trail connects to Bell Canyon Trail. From the higher ridges, a fine view is yours. To the north are the mile-high twin peaks of Saddleback Mountain, highest in Orange County. To the west and south you can see the town of San Juan Capistrano, the wide blue Pacific, and on an exceptionally clear day, San Clemente Island.

Directions to trailhead: From Interstate 5 in San Juan Capistrano, take the Highway 74 (Ortega Highway) exit. Drive eight miles inland to the entrance to Caspers Wilderness Park. There is a vehicle entrance fee. Each adult in your party must obtain a wilderness permit at the entry kiosk. Remember, no solo hiking, and no kids in the park.

From the entry kiosk, take the park road 1½ miles to its end at the corral and windmill. There's plenty of parking near the signed trailhead for Nature Trail.

The Hike: Nature Trail loops through a handsome grove of antiquarian oak. You might see woodpeckers checking their store of acorns, which the birds have stuffed in hidey-holes in the nearby sycamores. Beneath the oaks are some huge patches of poison oak, but the trail steers clear of them. You'll pass a junction with a left-branching trail that leads to Gunsight Pass and West Ridge Trail, and soon arrive at a second junction. (If you want a really short hike, keep right at this junction and you'll loop back to the trailhead via Nature Trail.)

183

Head north on signed Oak Trail, which meanders beneath the oak and sycamore that shade the west wall of Bell Canyon. The trail never strays far from Bell Creek, its streambed, or sandy washes. During drought years, it's difficult to imagine that in the last century, black bears used to catch spawning steelhead trout in Bell Creek.

Fragrant sages perfume the trail, which is also lined with lemonade berry and prickly pear cactus. Colorful, but fast-fading, spring blooms include blue dick, monkeyflower, thistle, Indian pink, lupine, and the humble pineapple weed.

Oak Trail reaches a junction at Post "12." You may take a short connector trail east to Bell Canyon or head north on another short trail, Star Rise, and join Bell Canyon Trail. A wide dirt road, Bell Canyon Trail travels the canyon floor. To return to the trailhead, you'll head south on Bell Canyon Trail, which passes through open oak-dotted meadows. Red-tailed hawks roost atop spreading sycamores. The trail returns you to the parking area, within sight of the beginning of Nature Trail, where you began your walk.

67

Harding Trail

Tucker Wildlife Sanctuary to Goat Shed Overlook
  3 miles round trip; 600-foot gain

To Laurel Spring
  10-miles round trip; 2,300-foot gain

Season: All year

The story of Modjeska Peak and Modjeska Canyon in Orange County began in Warsaw, Poland in the 1870s. Count Károl Bozenta Chlapowski edited a fiercely nationalistic patriotic journal that protested the cultural and political imperialism of czarist Russia and Germany. He and his wife, acclaimed actress Helena Modrzejewski, along with novelist Henryk Sienkiewicz (*Quo Vadis?*) and other Polish writers and artists, yearned for the freedom of America and the climate of Southern California.

The Count purchased an Orange County farm and the dreamy Polish aristocrats emigrated to the new world. While the setting and company was artistically inspiring, the immigrants had difficulties with some of the practical aspects of ranch life. No one, it seemed, knew how to milk a cow or care for citrus trees. Sienkiewicz preferred writing to working in the fields, Helena enjoyed singing and acting far more than cooking, and the Count lost a lot of money in a short time. Even utopian colonies have to pay their bills.

Mdm. Modjeska

Helena mastered English, shortened her name to Modjeska, and under the Count's management, began her tremendously popular stage career. In 1888, Madame Modjeska and the Count returned to Orange County; this time they bought a ranch in Santiago Canyon and hired professionals to run it. Madame called her ranch Arden after the enchanted forest in Shakespeare's *As You Like It*. Infamous New York architect Stanford White was commissioned to design a dream home, which looked out over a little lake, across which glided swans. The happy couple spent their mornings riding over

the ranch and inspecting the orange orchards and vineyards and their afternoons with friends in discussion of art, literature and the issues of the day. Evenings were given over to music recitals or Madame's performances of one of her favorite parts—Camille, Cleopatra or Lady MacBeth.

For two decades the Chlapowski/Modjeska household was a center of artistic and literary life in Southern California. Today, a state historical marker on Modjeska Canyon Road commemorates their home. A few years ago, the home was purchased by Orange County, which may some day restore the residence and open it to the public.

The natural history of Modjeska Canyon is as intriguing as its human history. In 1939, Dorothy May Tucker, a canyon resident, willed her land to the Audubon Society and the Tucker Bird Sanctuary was created. California State University Fullerton took over its operation in 1969.

The sanctuary is best known for its hummingbirds, which may be viewed from an observation porch. Because the sanctuary includes a mixture of coastal scrub, chaparral and oak woodland environments, it attracts a diversity of bird life. Nearly two hundred species have been spotted in the sanctuary.

Two short nature trails wind through the preserve. One trail interprets chaparral flora, and the other leads along the banks of Santiago Creek. Among the trailside exhibits is one interpreting the life of water bugs, and explaining the difference between a mayfly nymph and a dragonfly nymph. A small nature museum keeps the same hours as the sanctuary — 9 A.M. to 4 P.M. daily.

Tucker Wildlife Sanctuary is the trailhead for Harding Trail, a dirt road that ascends the western slopes of the Santa Ana Mountains. The trail, formerly known as Harding Truck Trail, is used by Cleveland National Forest fire crews and their trucks, but is closed to all other vehicles.

Old Saddleback, comprised of 5,687-foot Santiago Peak and 5,496-foot Modjeska Peak, forms the eastern boundary and highest portion of Orange County. You can reach the peaks via Harding Trail, but this would mean a 20-mile hike. A more reasonable destination, halfway up the mountain, is Laurel Spring, a tranquil rest stop tucked under the boughs of giant bay laurel. En route to the spring, you'll get great views of Madame Modjeska's peak and canyon, as well as much of rural Orange County.

Directions to Trailhead: From the San Diego Freeway (Interstate 5) in El Toro, exit on El Toro Road (S-18). Drive inland on the road, which after about 7 miles bends north and continues as Santiago Canyon Road. Eight and a half miles from the freeway, veer right onto Modjeska Grade Road, travel a bit more than a mile, then turn right and follow Modjeska Canyon Road a mile to its end at Tucker Wildlife Sanctuary. Park in the gravel lot by a tiny observatory. The trail, signed forest road 5S08, begins at a locked gate on the north side of the road.

The Hike: Harding Trail immediately begins a no-nonsense ascent above Modjeska Canyon, which, in all but its lower reaches, is officially known as Harding Canyon. To the northwest is Flores Peak, named for outlaw Juan Flores. Flores and his gang in 1857 robbed a San Juan Capistrano store, killed its owner, and then killed Sheriff John Barton. The gang fled to the Santa Ana Mountains, with General Don Andres Pico and his posse in hot pursuit. The gang was captured, but Flores escaped for a time; he was later caught and hanged in Los Angeles.

As you ascend, notice the lumpy, pudding-like clumps of conglomerate rock revealed by the road cuts. After a mile, the trail descends a short distance (the only elevation loss on the way to Laurel Spring), rounds the head of a canyon, and ascends to the remains of a funny-looking wood structure that locals call the Goat Shed. Enjoy the view of Modjeska Canyon. If you're feeling a bit leg-weary, this is a good turnaround point.

Chaparral-lined Harding Trail continues climbing east along a sharp ridgeline. To your left, far below, is deep and precipitous Harding Canyon, and to your right—Santiago Canyon. Four and a half miles from the trailhead, Harding Trail offers clear-day views of the southern end of the Los Angeles Basin, the San Joaquin Hills and the central Orange County coastal plain, the Pacific and Catalina Island. The view serves notice that you're nearing Laurel Spring. A narrow trail descends 50 yards from the right side of the road to the spring. The spring (unsafe drinking water), waters an oasis of toyon, ferns and wonderfully aromatic bay laurel.

6. Santa Ana Mountains

THE SANTA ANA MOUNTAINS may be the most overlooked and under-used recreation area in Southern California. Stretching the entire length of Orange County's eastern perimeter, the Santa Anas roughly parallel the coast. This coastal range is only about twenty miles inland and the western slopes are often blanketed with fog. By midmorning, the sun scatters the fog into long colorful banners that invite you to some far-off parade. The coast has a cooling influence on what is often a very hot range of mountains. Except for the dead of summer, most days offer pleasant hiking.

The Santa Anas offer no dramatic escarpment to compare with that of the San Jacintos, nor do they have the rugged tumbled look of the San Gabriels; these mountains are round, brushy, inviting. At first glance, they seem to be inundated by a monotonous sea of chaparral. But the chaparral teems wildlife, and even the most casual hiker will be amazed at the number of rabbit and quail who hop and flutter from the dense undergrowth. The range is covered with great masses of buckthorn, greasewood, sumac and scrub oak. Alternating with the chaparral are oak woodlands, wide potreros, and boulder-strewn creeks with superb swimming holes.

The range is a granite block, which has been uplifted and depressed below sea level several times. On top of the mountains, marine sediments occur in successive formations. The Santa Anas increase in altitude from north to south, culminating in the twin peaks of Old Saddleback—Mount Modjeska (5,440 feet) and Mount Santiago (5,860 feet). The crest of the range has been filed down and eroded by wind and weather exposing the hard granite at the surface.

The Santa Ana Mountains came under federal protection in 1893 when the Trabuco Canyon Forest Reserve was formed. The name was changed to the Trabuco National Forest in 1906; the forest later was enlarged and eventually assigned to the Cleveland National Forest in 1908. "Trabuco" is a name left behind by the 1769 Portolá expedition. It means "blunderbuss" and refers to the loss of such a weapon by one of Portolá's foot soldiers in these mountains. Today, 136,500 acres of the Santa Ana Mountains are included in the Trabuco District.

Many of the present hiking trails existed a hundred years ago. The San Juan and San Mateo trails are reworked Indian paths. Other trails were built by the CCC during the Depression. The Ortega Highway, which crossed the Santa Anas from San Juan Station to Lake Elsinore, opened up the mountains to camping and hiking, but not to the same extent the Rim

On patrol in the Trabuco District, 1921

of the World Highway opened up the San Bernardinos or the Angeles Crest Highway opened up the San Gabriels.

The Santa Anas see few people because off-highway access is a real pain in the axle, and many of the trailheads require traveling on dirt roads. Many Cleveland National Forest dirt roads are so washboarded that they are better-suited to foot travel. In past years, motorcycles ran rampant over the trails, but the Forest Service has, of late, done a much better job of controlling off-highway vehicles.

Highlight of the Santa Anas is the San Mateo Canyon Wilderness, set aside by Congress in 1984. The 40,000-acre preserve protects San Mateo Canyon, a relatively untouched land of 200-year-old oaks, potreros and quiet pools.

The Santa Ana Mountains can be a wonderful place to hike, particularly in the cooler months—October through May. Early morning is my favorite time here. A soft mist enshrouds the coastal range and chills the air. The wet dew glistens. As the sun slowly rises, the mist turns to haze and the brushy outlines of the ridges are silhouetted against the sky. The oak potreros glow golden, welcoming the new day.

Holy Jim Trail

Holy Jim Creek to Falls
  2½ miles round trip; 200-foot gain

To Bear Springs
  10 miles round trip; 2,200-foot gain

To Santiago Peak
  16 miles round trip; 4,000-foot gain

Season: All year

Holy Jim Trail, creek and canyon take their names from "Cussin'" Jim Smith, an early Santa Ana Mountains settler who, when displeased, unleashed a string of unholy epithets. Turn-of-the-century mapmakers were unwilling to geographically honor such a blasphemer, so they changed his name to "Holy."

The trail is one of the most popular in the Santa Anas, though many hikers go only as far as the falls. Holy Jim Trail is in fair-to-mediocre shape and is sometimes overgrown with brush. The trail is something of a Santa Ana Mountains sampler, giving the hiker a creek, a lush canyon, a water-fall, oak woodland and chaparral-covered slopes. All this and a view, too!

Directions to trailhead: Take Interstate Highway 5 to the El Toro Road exit (S-18); go east through Mission Viejo. Turn right on Live Oak Canyon Road (S-9). One mile after passing O'Neill Park, the road crosses Trabuco Wash. Turn left into the wash and head up rocky Trabuco Road. Don't be intimidated; the road gets better, not worse, as it heads up the wash, and it is suitable for most passenger cars. In 5 miles, you'll pass a volunteer fire department station and reach Holy Jim turnoff on your left. Park in the dirt area near the turnoff.

The Hike: Walk up Holy Jim Road, passing a number of summer homes. Beyond the last home, you'll reach a gate (locked during fire season). Holy Jim Trail (6W03) begins on the other side of the gate and heads up vine- and oak-filled lower Holy Jim Canyon. The trail stays near Holy Jim Creek for the first mile, crossing and recrossing the bubbling waters near some stone fish dams. A mile from the gate, the trail crosses the creek one last time. At this creek crossing, an unsigned, but well-used side trail heads upstream to Holy Jim Waterfall. It's a quarter-mile to the falls and well-worth a visit. Push your way through the wild grape, and boulder-hop up the creekbed to the cool grotto. The falls will seem even more spectacular if you engage in a little delayed gratification and save them for your return from Bear Springs.

To Bear Springs: At the creek crossing, Holy Jim Tail turns downstream for a few hundred yards. Enjoy good views of the northern Santa Ana Mountains. The trail begins a stiff climb up the west side of the canyon. After some hearty switchbacking through thick brush, the trail begins a long contour along the canyon wall. As the trail nears Bear Springs, it gets less brushy, and there is some flora you can look up to: shady oaks, big cone spruce or Coulter pine. Santiago Peak comes into view. The northern Santa Anas were once known as Sierra de Santiago for this dominant peak. You can't miss Santiago Peak; it's the only mountain around with a forest of antennae atop it.

Bear Springs is located at the intersection of the Holy Jim Trail and the Main Divide Truck Trail. An enclosed concrete water tank is at the intersection, but the tank does not dispense water to thirsty hikers. You can get plenty of water from the creek, but it should be purified. The shady area around the springs is cool and pleasant, an ideal lunch stop.

To Santiago Peak: Continue three miles (gaining 1,800 feet) on the Main Divide Truck Trail to Santiago Peak, highest summit in the Santa Anas. Clear-day views from the 5,687-foot peak are superb.

View from Holy Jim Trail

Bear Canyon Trail

Ortega Highway to Pigeon Springs
  5½ miles roundtrip; 700-foot gain

Ortega Highway to Sitton Peak
  10½ miles roundtrip; 1,300-foot gain

Season: All year

Bear Canyon Trail offers a pleasant introduction to the Santa Ana Mountains. The trail climbs through gentle brush and meadow country, visits Pigeon Springs, and arrives at Four Corners, the intersection of several major hiking trails through the southern Santa Anas. One of these trails takes you to Sitton Peak for a fine view. Along the trail, refreshing Pigeon Springs welcomes hot and dusty hikers to a handsome oak glen.

Directions to trailhead: Take the Ortega Highway (California 74) turnoff from the San Diego Freeway (Interstate 5) at San Juan Capistrano. Drive east 20 miles to the paved parking area across from the Ortega Oaks store. Bear Canyon Trail starts just west of the store on Ortega Highway. Departing from the parking lot is the 2-mile San Juan Loop Trail, another nice introduction to the Santa Ana Mountains. You can obtain trail information and purchase a Cleveland National Forest map at El Cariso Station, located a few miles up Highway 74.

The Hike: From the signed trailhead, the broad, well-graded trail climbs slowly up brushy hillsides. The trail crosses a seasonal creek, which runs through a tiny oak woodland.

A half mile from the trailhead, you'll enter the San Mateo Canyon Wilderness. After a mile, a deceptive fork appears on the left. Ignore it. The trail climbs on, skirts the periphery of a meadow and crests a chaparral-covered slope. Just before the trail joins the Verdugo Trail, there's a nice view down into San Juan Canyon. Turn right (south) on Verdugo Trail and proceed ¾ mile to Pigeon Springs.

Pigeon Springs includes a storage tank and horse trough. Forest rangers recommend that you purify the water before drinking. The springs are located among oaks on the left of the trail. If the bugs aren't biting this can be a nice place to picnic.

To continue on to Sitton Peak, hike down the Verdugo Trail another half mile and you'll arrive at Four Corners, a convergence of trails (fire roads). The Verdugo Trail pushes straight ahead to an intersection with the Blue Water Trail. To the left is Blue Water Fire Road leading down to Fisherman's Camp in San Mateo Canyon. To proceed to Sitton Peak, bear right on the Sitton Peak Trail.

Follow the trail as it begins to climb and contour around the peak. There are a few trees up on the ridge but little shade en route. In a mile you'll be at the high point of Sitton Peak Trail, a saddle perched over San Juan Canyon. The high point of the trail is approximately at Forest Service marker W-56. Follow the trail another mile until you reach the southeast face of the peak. Leave the trail here and wend your way up past the rocky outcroppings to Sitton Peak. On a clear day, there are superb views of the twin peaks of Old Saddleback (Mt. Modjeska and Mt. Santiago), Mt. San Gorgonio and Mt. San Jacinto, Catalina and the wide Pacific.

Mt. Modjeska

Chiquito Basin Trail

Ortega Highway to Lion Canyon
  11½ miles round trip; 1,100-foot gain

Season: All year

"Chiquito," which names a basin, a spring and the trail, is not named after a major brand of banana, as you might guess, but rather, was the name bestowed upon these features by a forest ranger in 1927 to honor his horse.

The trail will take you past a sparkling little waterfall, over brushy hillsides and oak-studded slopes to shady Lion Canyon Creek.

Directions to trailhead: Take the Ortega Highway 74 turnoff from the San Diego Freeway (5) at San Juan Capistrano, and drive east 19½ miles to the paved parking area across from Ortega Oaks store. The trailhead is the east end of the parking area and is signed as the San Juan Loop Trail.

The Hike: From the signed trailhead, you'll embark on the San Juan Loop Trail in a counterclockwise direction. Bear right at the first fork. The loop trail circles the base of a small peak, following a creek much of the way. Soon the trail arrives above San Juan Falls, a pleasant place for the return visit after you've completed this hot hike. The trail then drops down into a narrow, oak-lined canyon.

A mile from the trailhead, near the junction of Bear Creek and San Juan Creek, there's a flat area and the signed intersection with the Chiquito Basin Trail. You cross San Juan Creek, then follow an unnamed creek for a spell. All too soon, the trail leaves this peaceful creek and begins switchbacking up the west side of the canyon. Up, up, up the dry slopes you climb on this trail lined with toyon, buckwheat and chamise. The slopes are alive with lizards and horned toads. In spring and early summer, wildflowers abound along the trail. Views are excellent when you emerge in open areas and atop ridges. Just as you despair of ever finding any shade, an oak magically appears.

Five miles from the trailhead, the trail rounds a ridge and bears north toward Lion Canyon. Three-quarters of a mile after rounding the ridge, you'll arrive at a meadow watered by Lion Canyon Creek. There are a number of large oak groves in Lion Canyon. Any one of them makes a splendid picnic spot.

Return the same way. When you arrive at the junction with the San Juan Loop Trail, you may want to bear right and follow this trail through a campground back to your car. Or take the left fork and retrace your steps back to inviting San Juan Falls.

San Mateo Canyon Trail

Forest Road 7S01 to Fisherman's Camp
  3 miles round trip; 300-foot loss

To Lunch Rock
  8 miles round trip; 400-foot loss

To Clark Trail Junction
  14 miles round trip; 500-foot loss

Season: All year, except times of high water

Two-hundred-year-old oaks, tangles of ferns, nettles and wild grape, and the quiet pools of San Mateo Creek make the bottom of San Mateo Canyon a wild and delightful place. This section of the Santa Ana Mountains is steep canyon country, sculpted by seasonal, but vigorous streams. San Mateo Creek, a cascading waterway in winter, slows to a gurgle in summer and flows above ground only sporadically in the fall.

San Mateo Canyon Wilderness, set aside by Congress in 1984, protects 40,000 acres of the Cleveland National Forest, including the headwaters and watershed of San Mateo Creek.

San Mateo Canyon takes its name from one of the padres' favorite evangelists and holy men. It's the crown jewel of the Santa Ana Mountains, a relatively untouched wilderness of oaks, potreros and cattail-lined ponds. It's a haven for turtles and rabbits. Spring brings prolific wildflower displays. The canyon drops from 3,500 feet to the coastal plain at Camp Pendleton.

This day hike plunges through the southern part of San Mateo Canyon, easily the wildest place in the Santa Ana Mountains. The San Mateo Canyon Trail and other riding and hiking trails in the wilderness have been in use since the turn of the century. Orange County Sierra Club members work on the trail, but it's often in rough shape. Creek crossings are sometimes difficult to spot.

You can travel almost as far down the canyon as you like in one day. It's nine miles from Fisherman's Camp to the Marine base, with a hundred ideal picnic spots along the way.

Directions to the trailhead: Take either Highway 74 or Interstate 15 to Lake Elsinore, and from there drive southeast on I-15 to Wildomar and exit on Clinton Keith Road. Proceed seven miles southwest to the Tenaja turnoff, forking right on Tenaja Road (7S01). You'll pass Tenaja Fire Station and adjoining Tenaja Campground. Drive another three miles on 7S01 until it intersects Forest Road 7S02. Park here.

The Hike: Walk down the fire road, which is lined with wildflowers in spring. One-and-one-half miles of travel brings you to Fisherman's Camp, now abandoned. Once many "fisherman's camps" lay along San Mateo Creek. In the 1930s, anglers were attracted by superb fishing for steelhead and trout. San Mateo Canyon trail was the favorite route to the fishing holes. Steelhead ran these waters as late as 1969.

Cross the creek to the oak-shaded former campsite and begin hiking through ceanothus to a ridge offering a commanding view down San Mateo Canyon. The trail soon switchbacks down to the creek.

Along the creek, the trail may be indistinct; simply continue down-creek. About a mile after reaching the creek, you'll come to a small potrero dotted with oaks and sycamore. Here Bluewater Creek flows into San Mateo Creek and the Bluewater Trail leads off three miles to the Clark Trail and Oak Flat. You can picnic under the oaks near the trail junction and return, or continue down the canyon.

Continue down the creek on the San Mateo Canyon Trail, which follows the right side of the canyon, now and then dropping to wide sandy beaches along bends in the creek. The boulders get bigger, the swimming holes and sunning spots nicer. One flat rock, popular with hikers, has been nicknamed "Lunch Rock." A cluster of massive boulders form pools and cascades in the creek. It's a nice place to linger.

To Clark Trail Junction: The trail takes you under ancient oaks and sycamores, and along the cattail-lined creek. As you near the Clark Trail, San Mateo Canyon Trail utilizes part of an old mining road. Beyond the Clark Trail junction, San Mateo Canyon Trail soon peters out and the route down-canyon is trailless to Camp Pendleton, 9 miles from Fisherman's Camp. The Clark Trail, if you're game, ascends very steeply 1½ miles to Indian Potrero.

Santa Rosa Plateau Preserve

7. Riverside County

CROSSING Riverside County is a little like crossing the continent: You journey from suburbia to desert spas, from rich agricultural land to pine forests, from snow-capped mountains to sand dunes.

This ecological diversity is reflected in the many hiking adventures the county offers from alpine meadows high in the San Jacinto Mountains to the palm oases near Palm Springs.

In addition to the huge recreation areas found wholly or partly within county boundaries—Joshua Tree National Monument, Santa Rosa National Scenic Area, San Bernardino National Forest—Riverside also entices the hiker with parks and preserves close to population centers. The Bernasconi Hills near Lake Perris and the Box Springs Mountains behind Riverside are not well-known destinations, but they offer a pleasant time for the sojourner afoot.

Formed in 1893 from parts of San Bernardino and San Diego Counties, Riverside County's rich soil and benign climate made it an ideal location for growing navel oranges. By the turn of the century, residents of the "Orange Empire" around Riverside enjoyed one of the largest per capita incomes in the world.

In recent decades, the county has witnessed phenomenal Inland Empire-style growth; that is to say the construction of many highways and suburbs. The short hike to the top of 1,337-foot Mt. Rubidoux, located on the west side of Riverside, offers a superb 360-degree panorama of the county—one very different from the view of a century ago.

With such rapid development, the county's parks have a critical "breathing room" role to play. Riverside has an enthusiastic county parks department, which has ambitious plans to make recreation more user-friendly in its far-flung parks, and to improve its trail system.

Hills-for-People Trail

Ranch Road to McDermont Spring
  4 miles round trip; 400-foot gain

To Carbon Canyon Regional Park
  7½ miles one way; 800-foot loss from McDermont Spring

Season: All year

Chino Hills State Park, located in Orange, San Bernardino and Riverside Counties, preserves some much needed open space in this fast-growing area. Nearly three million people live within sight of the Chino Hills and more than nine million people live within a 40-mile radius of the park!

The park is the state's most expensive ever, with over $47 million spent by the time it opened for full time use in 1986. Right now, Chino Hills is a park-in-the-making. Few facilities have been installed. Development plans call for 35 miles of hiking trails.

The 10,000-acre park is located near the northern end of what geologists call the Peninsular Ranges Geomorphic Province. The Chino Hills are part of the group of hills that include the Puente Hills to the northwest. These hills form a roughly triangular area of approximately 35 square miles of valleys, canyons, hills, and steep slopes.

Extensive grasslands blanket the slopes. The hills are covered with wild oats, rye, black mustard and wild radish, On south-facing slopes is the soft-leaved shrub community, dominated by several varieties of sage.

High temperatures, often combined with heavy smog, suggest that a summer visit can be something of an ordeal. The park is much more pleasurable in the cooler months, and especially delightful in spring.

Hills-for-People Trail was named for the conservation group that was instrumental in establishing Chino Hills State Park. The trail follows a creek to the head of Telegraph Canyon. The creek is lined with oak, sycamore and the somewhat rare California walnut.

Directions to trailhead: Despite its location so close to the metropolis, Chino Hills State Park can be a bit tricky to find. The park is located east of Highway 71 between the Riverside Freeway (91) and the Pomona Freeway (60). Traveling south on 71 and 60, visitors should turn right on Los Serranos Road and then make a quick left onto Pomona-Rincon Road. (Visitors heading north on 71 from 91 will spot, before reaching Los Serranos Road, a left turn lane leading directly to Pomona-Rincon Road.) A half-mile of travel brings you to a brickyard with a mailbox marked "15838 Rolling M Ranch." Take the dirt road next to the brickyard for two miles to the park entrance. Continue on the main park road and follow signs to the park office and ranger station. The road forks just before the ranger station. To the right is the ranger station and visitors center. Bear left ½ mile on the dirt road to a vehicle barrier and trailhead parking. The signed trailhead is located a short distance past the vehicle barrier on the right of the road.

The Hike: Hills-for-People Trail descends to a small creek and follows the creek up canyon. Shading the trail—and shielding the hiker from a view of the many electrical transmission lines that cross the park—are oaks, sycamores and walnuts. Of particular interest is the walnut, a small tree, 15 to 30 feet tall. Often the tree has several dark brown trunks, which gives it a brushy appearance.

The trail, which can be quite slippery and muddy after a rain, passes a small (seasonal) waterfall. The slopes above the creekbed are carpeted with lush grasses and miners lettuce.

Along the trail is found evidence of the park's ranching heritage, including lengths of barbwire fence and old cattle troughs. For more than a century this land was used exclusively for cattle ranching.

Near its end, the trail ascends out of the creekbed to the head of Telegraph Canyon and intersects a dirt road. McDermont Spring is just down the road. One unique aspect of the state park is the livestock ponds, which were constructed during the area's ranching days. Some of these ponds still exist, and hold water year-round. McDermont Spring—along with Windmill and Panorama ponds—provide water for wildlife.

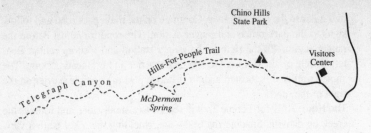

To Carbon Canyon Regional Park: Telegraph Canyon Trail (a dirt road closed to public vehicular traffic) stays close to the canyon bottom and its creek. It's a gentle descent under the shade of oak and walnut trees. The walnuts are particularly numerous along the first mile of travel and the hiker not inclined to hike the length of Telegraph Canyon might consider exploring this stretch before returning to the trailhead.

The route passes an old windmill and farther down the canyon, remains of a shepherd's camp. Near the bottom of the canyon the walnuts thin out. A lemon grove, owned by the state park but leased to a farmer, is at a point where the dirt road intersects Carbon Canyon Road. Walk along the broad shoulder of the latter road ½ mile to Carbon Canyon Regional Park.

California's most expensive state park.

73

Skyline Trail

Loop through Box Springs Mountain Park
4-6 mile round trip; 500-foot gain

Season: All year

Far too steep for suburban housing developments, the Box Springs Mountains in Riverside County remain a place to get away from it all. "It" in this instance is the hustle and bustle of the Inland Empire which surrounds this little known mountain range.

Little known the mountains may be, but remote they are not. Four freeways—the San Bernardino, Riverside, Pomona and Escondido—surround the Box Springs Mountains. Their location might remind football fans of a quarterback barking signals: "10-91-60-215-Hike!"

The peaks of the range rise sharply from the floor of the Moreno Valley to 3,000 feet and offer commanding clear-day views of the city of Riverside, the San Bernardino and San Jacinto Mountains, as well as a great portion of the Inland Empire.

The mountain's namesake peak, as well as 2,389 acres of native Southern California coastal sage terrain is preserved in Box Springs Mountain Park under the jurisdiction of Riverside County. The park is a natural island amidst one of the fastest growing urban and suburban areas in California.

Vegetation includes members of the coastal sage scrub community: chamise, lemonade berry, brittlebush, white sage, black sage and buckwheat. More than 30 types of wildflowers brighten the park's slopes in the spring.

Wildlife—coyotes, jackrabbits, skunks and kangaroo rats—is attracted by the tiny springs that trickle from the mountain. Wildlife biologists call Box Springs Mountain a "Habitat Island" because it provides a home for animals while being surrounded by development.

The mountains, along with "The Badlands" to the east of the range, were shaped in part by the San Jacinto Fault, a major branch of the San Andreas system. Some geologists believe that the granites of Box Springs were once attached to the granites of the San Jacinto Mountains but were moved to their present location, some 20 miles, by lateral displacement along the fault.

Perhaps the most eccentric resident of Box Springs Mountain was Helene Troy Arlington, who moved to the mountain in 1945. The self-styled hermit secluded herself in a mountain retreat she called *Noli Me Tangere*, a Latin phrase meaning "Do Not Touch Me."

Arlington was devoted to dogs, particularly Dalmatians, and kept many of them in her home. She wrote canine poems and magazine articles under the pen name "Dear Dog Lady." On a plot of land next to her home she established "Arlington Cemetery," a final resting place for her four-legged friends.

Dogs, in fact, were her only friends. She sold her land to the Riverside County Parks Department in 1974 and moved to Arlington, Virginia, to be near the grave of her long-dead husband Masefield. She wrote the parks department: "There was no reason to remain there any longer, as I still do not have one friend in California."

Park trails include 3-mile long Pigeon Pass Trail, which offers great views, and 1½ mile long Ridge Trail which travels over Box Spring Mountain. (Avoid Two Trees Trail, which climbs from Two Trees Road in Riverside to meet Box Springs Mountain Road inside the park. Trailhead access is poor, as is the trail itself.)

The park's premier path is Skyline Trail, which loops around Box Springs Mountain. If Riverside can be said to have a skyline, this is it; not tall office buildings but skyscraping granite and a top-of-the-world view.

Directions to trailhead: From the Pomona Freeway (60) in Moreno Valley, exit on Pigeon Pass Road. Proceed some 4½ miles north, then a short distance west. Pigeon Pass Road turns north again, but you continue west, joining a dirt road and following the signs into Box Springs Mountain Park. Signed Skyline Trail is on your right.

The Hike: From Box Springs Mountain Road, Skyline Trail heads west, soon serving up views of the city of Riverside. Next the trail contours north, passing rock outcroppings that are geologically and aesthetically similar to those found atop Mt. Rubidoux, Riverside landmark and site of a long-popular Easter service.

The path comes to an unsigned junction. Skyline Trail angles east and begins contouring around a hill back to the trailhead. Hardier hikers will join an extension of the trail known as "Second Loop" and make an even larger circle back to the trailhead.

74

Terri Peak Trail

Interpretive Center to Terri Peak
  3½ miles round trip; 800-foot gain

To Indian Museum, return via lakeshore
  6 miles round trip

Season: All year

Perris in the Spring. No need to battle the hordes of tourists flocking to that other similar-sounding place of romance across the Atlantic. No need to travel 6,000 miles and spend lots of money to have a good time.

For just a few francs you can visit a manmade wonder, *Lac de Paris*, otherwise known as Lake Perris State Recreation Area. So pack *du pain et du vin* and head for the most romantic Pomona Freeway offramp in all of Southern California.

Few nature lovers—or lovers of any kind—have discovered the romance of Perris. True, a million and a half visitors come to the lake each year, but the only nature most are interested in is that found wriggling on the end of a hook.

While *le parc* is oriented to *les autos et les bateaux*, there is a network of trails for those visitors who wish to explore Perris *à pied*. Perris pace-setters will enjoy the trek to Terri Peak, easily the most romantic spot in all of the Bernasconi Hills.

Springtime colors the hills with a host of wild *fleurs,* including gold-fields, California poppy, fiddleneck, baby blue eyes and blue decks. The view from Terri Peak on smog-free days is *très fantastique*.

Directions to Trailhead: From the Pomona Freeway (60), a few miles east of its intersection with I-215, exit on Moreno Beach Drive and proceed 4 miles to the park. Immediately after paying your state park day use fee at the entry kiosk, turn right on Lake Perris Drive. Look sharply right for the strange-looking international symbol indicating a campfire and an amphitheatre. Park in the campfire/Interpretive Center lot. The unsigned trail begins to the left of the campfire area.

The Hike: The trail ascends gradually west and occasionally intersects a horse trail. The unsigned path is tentative at first but an occasional wooden post helps keep you on the trail, which climbs boulder-strewn slopes.

The coastal scrub community—sage, buckwheat, chamise and toyon predominates. Also much in evidence are weedy-looking non-native species, as well as mustard, prickly pear cactus, morning glory and Russian thistle.

The trail climbs to a small flat meadow then turns southwest and climbs more earnestly to the peak. From atop Terri Peak, enjoy clear-day views of the San Bernardino Mountains to the northeast and the Santa Ana Mountains to the southwest. Below is fast-growing Moreno Valley, checkerboarded alternately with green fields and subdivisions. You can see all of Lake Perris, Alessandro Island, and thousands of boaters, anglers and swimmers.

The trail from Terri Peak down to the Indian Museum is in poor condition. Beginning hikers may want to retrace their steps to the trailhead. The more experienced will begin their descent. Expect to lose the trail a couple of times; however you won't get lost because it's easy to stay oriented with the lakeshore on your left and the Indian Museum ahead.

After a steep descent, the trail bends sharply east and deposits you at the Indian Museum's parking lot. The museum includes exhibits interpreting the Cahuilla, Chemehuevi, Serrano and other desert tribes and how they adapted to life in the Mojave Desert region.

From the museum, you follow the asphalt road down to Lake Perris Drive, cross this main park road and continue down to Perris Beach. Here, and at Moreno Beach one mile to the west, you may cool off with a swim.

Improvise a route along the lakeshore using the sidewalk and bicycle trail until you spot the main campground entrance on your left. Enter the campground, pass the kiosk, then pick up the intermittent footpath that winds through the campground. This path and some improvisation will bring you to Lake Perris Drive and back to the trailhead.

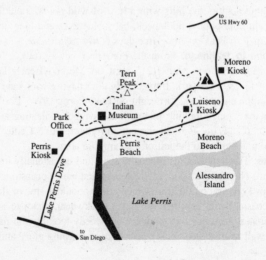

75

Trans-Preserve Trail

4-mile loop through Santa Rosa Plateau Preserve

Season: All year

Hard-riding Spanish vaqueros called the deep holes in creekbed *tenajas*. The holes held water year-around and provided crucial summer water sources for both cows and cowboys. Today the tenajas (Spanish for "tanks") offer habitat for such amphibians as the western pond turtle and red-legged frog. Tenajas, ancient Engelmann oaks, and more than 3,000 acres of rolling grassland are preserved in Santa Rosa Plateau Preserve, located at the southern end of the Santa Ana Mountains in Riverside County. The plateau is pastoral Southern California at its finest, that is to say the least changed since the days of the caballeros and gracious haciendas. Atop the plateau, time seems to have stopped at 1840.

Off the plateau, it's very much the 1990s; that is to say, huge housing developments have pushed up Clinton Keith Road and left the plateau something of an island on the land. The island was saved from Inland Empire-style development when, in 1991, a major plateau land owner agreed to sell 3,800 acres to the Nature Conservancy, greatly increasing the size of the preserve.

The preserve is more than a park or some much-needed breathing room in this fast-developing part of the Southland; it's an ecological treasure. Santa Rosa Plateau has been recognized by UNESCO as a biosphere reserve, one of only three such special places in all of California.

Now protected is one of the last healthy stands of Engelmann oaks; these trees were once widespread throughout the western U.S., but now range only between San Diego and Santa Barbara. For reasons researchers can't quite figure, most stands of Engelmann oaks contain just a few venerable specimens that are incapable of regeneration. The Engelmann oaks on Santa Rosa Plateau, however, are quite healthy.

The oaks were named for German-born physician/botanist Dr. George Engelmann, who explored and collected specimens in this country during the last century. Engelmann oaks are gnarled fellows, with a kind of checkered trunk and grayish leaves. When you visit the preserve you'll notice Engelmanns are noticeably different from their more common cousins, the coast live oaks. Coast live oaks are fuller, with smoother bark and leaves that are shiny green. Usually, the coast live oaks grow in lower, wetter locales, while the Engelmanns take higher and drier ground.

Directions to trailhead: From Interstate 15 in Riverside County, southeast of Lake Elsinore and northwest of Murrietta and the junction with

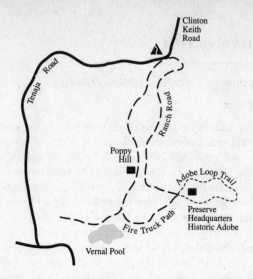

Interstate 215, exit on Clinton Keith Road. Follow the road about 5 miles south. Just as the road makes a sharp bend west and becomes Tenaja Road, you'll spot a turnout and the main gate of Santa Rosa Plateau Preserve. Park in a safe manner off the road.

The Hike: At the main gate, scan the bulletin boards, pick up a preserve map, then join the Trans-Preserve Trail.

The trail heads south across grassy slopes, dips into an oak-filled draw, then contours around Poppy Hill. To the west you'll see Ranch Road, your return route to the trailhead, and to the east, on private land, some cows grazing.

If you use your imagination, you can step back a century and a half in time, when Santa Rosa Plateau was part of 47,000-acre Rancho Santa Rosa given to cattle rancher Juan Moreno by Governor Pío Pico. The land was held by various ranching companies until 1984 when the Nature Conservancy acquired the land from the Kaiser Corporation and established the preserve.

Follow Trans-Preserve Trail and signs to Mesa de Colorado and Vernal Pools. Atop the mesa, you'll find (at least after winter rains) a couple vernal pools, some of the last in Southern California. The mesa is capped with basalt, which means it's an ideal rainwater collector. Depressions in the rock collect water into seasonal ponds called vernal pools. When winter and spring rains fill the ponds, the pools are visited by ducks, geese and other waterfowl. Wildflowers—particularly goldfields—are much in evidence when the water recedes.

After visiting the pools, decend to the main dirt road called Ranch Road

and head east toward a windmill. You'll soon come upon an old adobe and some ranch buildings, now used as preserve headquarters.

If you want to tour a little more of the preserve, continue east past preserve headquarters on Ranch Road, which becomes a footpath. On a clear day, you might be able to get a glimpse of Oceanside and the wide blue Pacific, about twenty miles away. Pick up signed Adobe Trail which meanders among old oaks, passes an olive grove, and loops back to headquarters.

Follow Ranch Road back to the trailhead.

8. San Bernardino Mountains

WHEN THAT RESTLESS breed of American—the trapper, the trader, the Army mapmaker—pushed westward, they had to reckon with arid country beyond the lower Colorado River. The Mojave Desert gave sustenance to few, and mercy to none. And if crossing the desert's uncharted sands wasn't enough of a problem, another formidable obstacle barred the way west—the San Bernardino Mountains: Sheer granite cliffs, thorny chaparral, snowbound passes.

The San Bernardino range is a vast fault block about sixty miles long and thirty miles wide, extending in a southwesterly direction across Southern California. The western portion is plateau-like with some rather broad uplands—unusual for Southern California mountains. At its western end, the mountains terminate abruptly at Cajon Pass, which separates the range from the San Gabriel Mountains. Geologists speculate that the two ranges may originally have been one. Rocks on both sides of the pass suggest the earth's convulsions wrenched the mountains fifteen to twenty-five miles apart. The earth is still shuddering in this area; the San Andreas Fault runs through the pass. It's an excellent place to observe fault features and view this Maker and Shaker of continents.

Although the two ranges look something alike at first glance, they aren't the same age. The San Gabriels are more sheer, more faulted. The San Bernardinos are younger, less fractured by earthquakes.

The southern slopes of the San Bernardinos consist of high ridges cut by many deep stream gorges. At the western end of the highest ridge is San Bernardino Peak. The ridge culminates toward the east in Mount San Gorgonio (Old Grayback, 11,502 feet), the highest peak in Southern California. To the south, San Gorgonio Pass separates the San Bernardinos from the San Jacinto Range. The discovery of the pass in 1853 enabled Los Angeles to be tied to the rest of the United States by railroad line.

By the mid-19th Century, industrious Mormons and other settlers arrived in the San Bernardinos. They drove the Serrano and Cahuilla Indians into the desert. Newcomers clear-cut miles of forest, dammed and channeled the wild rivers into irrigation ditches, and dynamited the mountains in search of gold.

But not all visitors blasted, mined and milled. Some came to relax in the alpine air and enjoy the good life. Summer tents and homes clustered around high-country lakes. To many people, the San Bernardinos no longer seemed so remote, so formidable.

A large portion of the San Bernardino Mountains was protected by the establishment of the San Bernardino Forest Reserve, created by President Benjamin Harrison in 1893. Subsequently, the name "Reserve" was changed to "National Forest." In 1908, the San Bernardino National Forest and Angeles National Forest were brought together and administered under the latter's name, but in 1925, President Coolidge divided them.

The San Bernardino National Forest is a huge parcel of land, bigger than the state of Rhode Island, the second-largest national forest in California (first is Los Padres). It's also one of the most heavily used national forests in the nation. One year, more than seven million people visited the San Bernardino Mountains. It was as if everyone in the L.A. Basin visited once.

The Rim of the World Highway, leading from San Bernardino to Lake Arrowhead and Big Bear Lake, opened up the mountains to recreation on a large scale. Chiseled into rock walls, the road takes many a switchback and hairpin turn, following the crest of the range and ascending to more than 7,000 feet. Even the highway's primitive forerunners—with their 41-percent grades—didn't stop thousands of guns and fishing rods from assaulting the wilderness. Big Bear and Arrowhead Lakes became one of Southern California's most popular resort areas. The rustic hotels, spas and lodges delighted Southern Californians in the same manner the Catskills and Berkshires served the needs of New Yorkers.

There are many quiet places in the 700,000-acre San Bernardino National Forest where the hiker can behold waterfalls, stunning fields of flowers, and golden eagles soaring above lofty crags. The San Gorgonio Wilderness contains all the delights of these mountains, and none of its "civilization." The San Gorgonio Wild Area was created by a law in 1931 as a place free of restaurants and roads, camps and resorts. In 1965, Congress declared it a Wilderness.

Seventy-one miles of hiking trails wind through the high-country wilderness. The 56,000-acre Wilderness is a lonely refuge from the glass and chrome world far below. On the high spine of the range, Mount San Gorgonio and other 10,000-plus foot peaks—Dobbs, Jepson, Charlton and San Bernardino—stand shoulder to shoulder. When you reach the summit of one of these peaks, you'll be only ninety miles from downtown Los Angeles and two miles high, but the city will seem more remote than the map indicates, and you'll feel much higher.

76

Deep Creek Trail

Highway 173 to Deep Creek Hot Springs
 12 miles round trip; 800-foot gain

Mojave River Forks Dam to Deep Creek Hot Springs
 8 miles round trip; 800-foot gain

Season: All year

Kick off your jeans and slip into the relaxing waters of Deep Creek, site of the only hot spring in the San Bernardino Mountains. Float awhile and gaze up at the sky. Feel your urban anxieties vaporize in one of nature's hot tubs.

Deep Creek is a study in contrasts. Upstream it contains pools of great size, flanked by sheer masses of stone. The water has scoured great basins and the creek bounds down the water-worn rocks from one pool to the other. The pools are home to rainbow trout, which attract the angler. Downstream Deep Creek is but a shadow of its former self. It ends ingloriously in the desert sands.

This is a fine hike on a well-built stretch of Pacific Crest Trail. The trailhead, formerly at Mojave River Forks Dam, has been relocated to Highway 173. The Army Corps of Engineers has closed the dam to the public. However, most day hikers still begin this trail at the dam. Call the San Bernardino National Forest, Arrowhead Ranger District, in Rimforest for the latest trail information.

A more popular route, because it's only a three-mile round trip to Deep Springs Hot Creek Springs, is along Goat Trail. Directions to this alternate trailhead are given below.

The trash situation sometimes gets out of hand in the vicinity of the hot springs. Please pack out what you packed in. Due to frequent injuries caused by broken glass, the Forest Service now prohibits the possession of glass containers in the Deep Creek area.

Directions to trailhead: From Interstate Highway 15, a few miles north of Cajon Pass, take the Hesperia turnoff. Go east through Hesperia on Main Street, following it as it curves south at the outskirts of town. Turn left (east) on Rock Springs Road. If the bed of the Mojave River is dry, you're in luck. Cross it and turn right (south) on Deep Creek Road. Follow this road to pavement's end. Bear left on a dirt road and drive straight up the spillway of the Mojave River Forks Flood Control Dam. Don't worry, you won't drive into a reservoir; the dam holds no water. The trail begins at the east (left) end of the parking lot.

To Highway 173 trailhead: Exit Interstate 15 on Highway 138. Go right (east) 9 miles and veer left on Highway 173, following the latter highway 8 miles to pavement's end. At the point where the dirt road begins, you'll find parking and a signed trailhead for the Pacific Crest Trail.

To Goat Trail trailhead: From Rock Springs Road, turn right (east) on Roundup Way. Follow it to Bowen Road and make a right (south) turn. When the road forks, bear right to the Bowen Ranch house, where you pay a toll. The road will then lead to a parking area at the beginning of Goat Trail. Note that Goat Trail ends on the north side of Deep Creek and you will have to cross Deep Creek to get to the hot pools. Crossing Deep Creek during spring, or at times of high water, can be difficult.

The Hike: (From Highway 173) The trail heads on a straight line for Deep Creek Canyon. It follows the roadbed of an asphalt road (broken-up, but not removed) through sagebrush down into the lower reaches of Deep Creek near its meeting with the Mojave River. Uncontrolled motorcycle and all terrain vehicle use has seriously eroded the creekbed. The noise echoing through the canyon is simply awful.

The trail proceeds on the right bank of the creek. You will have to cross the creek and pick up the trail on the other side. You can scramble around to the top of the dam and make your way over to the spillway where good trail resumes.

Past the spillway, you'll find another signed trailhead. Ascend five easy switchbacks to the north canyon wall. You stay high on the almost-barren wall for 2 miles until the trail descends to Deep Creek, then crosses it on an arched bridge. Now you follow the south slope for another mile and reach oak-shaded McKinley Creek. This is a good area for picnicking, cooling-off, or exploring. The last mile of trail contours along the south slope, then drops down close to the creek just before the hot springs.

The hot springs, enclosed by rocks bordering the creek, range from warm to hot. Pick your spot. You may be joined by the Hesperia locals, who usually take the Goat Trail.

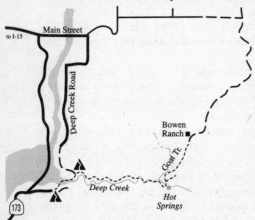

North Shore Trail

North Shore Campground to Little Bear Creek
  5 miles round trip; 600-foot gain

Season: All year

The Lake Arrowhead country is the prettiest alpine area in the San Bernardino Mountains. And the nicest place for a stroll when you're visiting Arrowhead is the tranquil canyon cut by Little Bear Creek. Shaded by sugar pines and Jeffrey pines, oaks, sycamores and incense cedars, the canyon is a woodsy retreat from metropolitan life.

The waters of Little Bear Creek feed Lake Arrrowhead. North Shore Trail is the name of the pathway that follows Little Bear Creek. This is an easy hike, suitable for the whole family, but keep in mind that it's an upside-down walk; the elevation gain occurs on the way back.

Directions to trailhead: From Interstate 10 in San Bernardino, take the Waterman Avenue/Highway 18 exit and wind 20 miles north into the San Bernardino Mountains. When Highway 18 junctions with 173, take the latter highway and proceed 3½ miles to Hospital Road and turn right.

Late in the year, the Forest Service closes the campground until spring. However, day hikers may park in the upper lot at Mountains Community Hospital and walk the short distance into the campground. The trailhead is just off the road between campsites 10 and 11.

The Hike: Head down-slope, continue straight at an unsigned four-way junction and drop to a dirt road. On the other side of the road you'll join signed Trail 3W12, pass by a seasonal creek and descend into the handsome canyon of Little Bear Creek.

Enjoy the sounds of the wind blowing through the pines, the murmuring creek. Norman-style Arrowhead Village and a shopping mall are just over the next ridge, but the resort might as well be a hundred miles away.

North Shore Trail sticks to the north bank of Little Bear Creek. The trail leaves the creek, humps over a knoll, then rejoins it after a quarter-mile.

Hang out along one of the bends in the creek before returning the way you came. If you want to walk every foot of North Shore Trail, continue to a creek crossing, boulder-hop over Little Bear Creek, and soon come to the trail's inglorious end at Hook Creek Road and an area popular with off-highway vehicles.

Heap's Peak Trail

¾-mile loop through Heap's Peak Arboretum

Season: April-November

San Bernardino National Forest is not only huge, it's botanically diverse; the forest hosts ecological communities ranging from sagebrush to subalpine, from Joshua tree to limber pine. One of the best places to learn about national forest flora is at Heap's Peak Arboretum, located near the tiny San Bernardino Mountains community of Running Springs. Most of the arboreteum is filled with mixed stands of pine and fir—the typical forest community of these parts. In addition, the arboretum grows trees and shrubs that are representative of other parts of the forest.

A walk through the arboretum is a relaxing—and quite educational—experience. Numbered stops along the trail are keyed to a pamphlet which can be picked up at the trailhead. The entertaining pamphlet, published by the Rim-of-the-World Interpretive Association, is a mini-botany course.

Nature lovers of all hiking abilities will learn something from the interpretive displays along Heap's Peak Trail. Did you know that the willow contains salicylic acid, the active ingredient in asprin? Did you know that the Coulter pine's eight-pound pine cones are the world's largest?

It's hard not to like a nature trail that begins with the forest philosophy of Buddha and ends with the natural history of the gooseberry.

After you've enjoyed Heap's Peak Trail, head down Highway 18 about 1½ miles to Switzer Park Picnic Area or drive over to nearby Lake Arrowhead.

Directions to trailhead: From Interstate 10 in Redlands, exit on Highway 30 and doggedly follow the highway signs through minor detours and suburbs-in-the-making. As Highway 30 begins to climb into the San Bernardino Mountains, it becomes Highway 330. Eighteen miles from Redlands, you'll reach a highway junction on the outskirts of Running Springs. You'll bear northwest on Highway 18 (following signs toward Lake Arrowhead). Four miles of driving along this winding mountain road brings you to Heap's Peak Arboretum. There's plenty of parking just off the road.

SAN BERNARDINO
NATIONAL FOREST

Heaps Peak
Arboretum Trail

to Hwy. 10   Switzer Park
Picnic Area

Rim of the World Dr.

to Hwy 330

79

Siberia Creek Trail

Forest Road 2N11 to Champion Lodgepole Pine
1 mile round trip; 100-foot loss

To The Gunsight
3 miles round trip; 600-foot loss

To Siberia Creek Trail Camp
8 miles round trip; 2,500-foot loss

California nurtures some superlative trees. The tallest tree on Earth is a coast redwood, the oldest tree a bristlecone pine. And in the San Bernardino Mountains gows the world champion lodgepole pine.

It's a pleasant stroll, suitable for the whole family, to the world champion. More ambitious hikers will enjoy tramping down Siberia Creek Trail to the appropriately named rock formation ''The Gunsight,'' and on to Siberia Creek Trail Camp for a picnic.

Siberia Creek, born atop the high mountains near Big Bear Lake, is a delightful watercourse. It flows southwest through a deep coniferous forest and lush meadowlands, then cascades down a steep rocky gorge and adds it waters to Bear Creek.

From Forest Road 2N11, Siberia Creek Trail passes the Champion Lodgepole, the largest known lodgepole pine in the world. It then travels alongside Siberia Creek through a wet tableland, detours around a ridge while Siberia Creek crashes down a precipitous gorge, then rejoins the creek at Siberia Creek Trail Camp.

This is an ''upside-down'' hike; the tough part is the trek uphill back to the trailhead. Pace yourself accordingly.

Directions to trailhead: From Highway 18 at the west end of Big Bear Lake Village, turn south on Tulip Lane. You'll pass Coldbrook Campground on the right, and one-half mile from the highway, turn right on Forest Road 2N11. Follow the ''Champion Lodgepole'' signs five miles to the signed trailhead. Parking is alongside the road.

The Hike: The trail follows a fern-lined little brook. You'll notice some tall cornstalk-like plants—corn lilies—and a generous number of red flowers—Indian paintbrush.

A half-mile's travel brings you to a signed junction. Go right 75 yards to the Champion Lodgepole, which towers above the east end of an emerald green meadow. You can't miss it. It's the only 110-foot tree around.

Lodgepole—also called tamarack—pines are usually found at higher elevations, but here at 7,500 feet, nurtured by the rich, well-watered soil, they not only thrive, but achieve mammoth proportions. The World Champion is 75 inches in diameter (the species usually measures 12 to 24 inches), and is estimated to be more than 400 years old. Lodgepoles are easily identified by their yellow-green paired needles. While hiking in Southern Cali-

fornia, these pines are probably the only ones you'll come across that have two needles per bundle. By way of comparison, you might notice that the pinon pine has one needle, the ponderosa three, and the limber pine five.

To The Gunsight: Return to the main trail and continue through open forest, skirting the meadowland. You cross and re-cross Siberia Creek. After the second crossing, the meadowland ends and the creek crashes down the gorge. The trail avoids the gorge and swings down and around the steep slopes of Lookout Mountain. About one mile from the Champion Lodgepole, an interesting rock formation called the Gunsight appears. Squint through the Gunsight, aim your anti-civilization gun at the haze below, and squeeze off a few shots.

To Siberia Creek Trail Camp: From the Gunsight, the trail descends the slopes of Lookout Mountain. A series of switchbacks brings you to a trail junction. Bear right (north) on the Seven Pines Trail and proceed three-quarters of a mile to Siberia Creek Trail Camp. For the day hiker, this oak- and alder-shaded camp makes a nice picnic spot or rest stop.

World-champion Lodgepole Pine.

80

Pine Knot Trail

Aspen Glen Picnic Area to Grand View Point
  6½ miles round trip; 1,200-foot gain

Season: April-November

Rim of the World Highway offers the traveler a fine view of Big Bear Lake. A better view, a hiker's view, is available from Pine Knot Trail, which climbs the handsome, pine-studded slopes above the lake and offers far-reaching panoramas of the San Bernardino Mountains. Big Bear Lake is a great place to escape the crowded metropolis, and Pine Knot Trail is a great way to escape sometimes-crowded Big Bear Lake.

The idea for Big Bear Lake came from Redlands citrus growers, who wanted to impound a dependable water source for their crops. Farmers and city founders formed Bear Valley Land and Water Co. and in 1884, at a cost of $75,000, built a stone-and-cement dam, thus forming Big Bear Lake. In 1910 a second, larger dam was built near the first one. This second dam is the one you see today.

Pine Knot Trail takes its name from the little community of cabins, stores and saloons that sprang up when Rim of the World Highway was completed. After World War II the town of Pine Knot changed its name to Big Bear Lake Village.

While Pine Knot Trail offers grand views of the lake, this hike's destination—Grand View Point—does not overlook the lake. The grand view is a breathtaking panorama of the San Gorgonio Wilderness and the deep canyon cut by the Santa Ana River.

Directions to trailhead: From California 18 in Big Bear Lake Village, turn southwest on Mill Creek Road and proceed about a half-mile to Aspen Glen Picnic Area on your left. The signed trail departs from the east end of the picnic area by Mill Creek Road.

The Hike: From Aspen Glen Picnic Area, Pine Knot Trail climbs a low, lupine-sprinkled ridge. The path follows a fence line for a short distance, then dips into and out of a willow-lined creekbed. You will get great over-the-shoulder views of the south shore of Big Bear Lake.

Ascending through Jeffrey pine and ponderosa pine forests, the trail meets and joins a fire road; after a short distance, it again becomes a footpath. Now your over-the-shoulder view is of the north shore of Big Bear Lake.

Pine Knot Trail passes near one of the runs of the Snow Forest Ski Area, then meanders through an enchanted area of castellated rocks. About 2 miles from the trailhead the trail intersects dirt Forest Service Road 2N17. Before you is a meadow, a rather amusing-looking landscape decorated with boulders, ponderosa pine, Indian paintbrush and skunk cabbage. Bear left on the dirt road for just 50 feet or so, then pick up the signed footpath again.

Passing black oak and willow, Pine Knot Trail skirts the moist meadow and soon arrives at Deer Group Camp. Benches and tables suggest a picnic or rest stop.

From the camp, continue on Pine Knot Trail, which crosses and then parallels another dirt Forest Service road. Ahead of you are tantalizing views of San Gorgonio Wilderness peaks—just a hint of things to come when you reach trail's end.

About a mile from Deer Group Camp, the trail intersects dirt Forest Service Road 2N11. Cross the road and follow the signed trail on a quarter-mile ascent to the top of a ridgeline.

From Grand View Point, enjoy the views of San Gorgonio Wilderness, a panorama of Southern California's highest peaks.

View of Santa Ana River country, San Gorgonio Wilderness, from Grand View Point.

81

Cougar Crest Trail

Highway 38 to Bertha Peak
  6 miles round trip; 1,100-foot gain

Season: April-November

Cougar Crest, the forested ridge between Big Bear Lake and Holcomb Valley is a treat for hikers. From the ridge, as well as from the ridge's two prominent peaks—Bertha and Delamar—you get great views of the lake, towering Mt. San Gorgonio and tranquil Holcomb Valley.

Holcomb Valley wasn't always so tranquil. In 1860, Billy Holcomb was out bear hunting and wandered over the ridge of hills that separates Bear Valley from the smaller, parallel valley to the north. He found gold. Prospectors swarmed into the valley from all over the West.

This day hike climbs the forested slopes above Big Bear Lake to a junction with the Pacific Crest Trail. From the PCT, you can ascend to Bertha Peak or to more distant Delamar Mountain for grand views of the middle of the San Bernardino Mountains.

Directions to trailhead: From Highway 18 in the town of Big Bear Lake, turn north on Stanfield cut off, crossing to the north shore of the lake and a junction with Highway 38. Turn left, drive a mile to the Big Bear Ranger Station, then a short distance beyond to the signed Cougar Crest trailhead and parking area off the north side of the highway.

If you're approaching from the east on Highway 38, the trailhead is a bit more than two miles beyond the hamlet of Fawnskin.

Billy Holcomb

The Hike: From the signed trailhead, join wide Cougar Crest Trail, a retiring dirt road. You climb through a pine and juniper woodland and pass a couple of old mining roads. After a mile, the trail narrows and begins ascending forested Cougar Crest via a series of well-constructed switchbacks.

Soon you'll begin enjoying over-the-shoulder views of Big Bear Lake and its dramatic backdrop—the two-mile-high peaks of the San Gorgonio Wilderness.

A bit more than two miles from the trailhead, Cougar Crest Trail reaches a signed junction with the Pacific Crest Trail. To reach Bertha Peak you'll bear right (east) and continue along the ridge crest for ½ mile to an intersection with an old dirt road. PCT continues straight at this junction, but you bear right on the dirt road and ascend a half-mile through pinyon pine and juniper woodland to the small relay station atop Bertha Peak. Best views are a bit below the peak.

Looking over an ocean of clouds on the Rim of the World Highway (to Lake Arrowhead and Big Bear Lake).

82

San Bernardino Peak Trail

Camp Angelus to Columbine Spring Camp
  9 miles round trip; 2,000-foot gain

To Limber Pine Bench Camp
  12 miles round trip; 3,200-foot gain

To San Bernardino Peak
  16 miles round trip; 4,700-foot gain

Season: May-November

Mount San Bernardino, together with its twin peak, Mount San Gorgonio, just five miles away and 900 feet higher, anchors the eastern end of the San Bernardino Mountains. At 11,499 feet, Mount San Gorgonio is the peak by which all other Southern California peaks are measured. Mount San Bernardino, too, is quite a landmark.

In 1852, Colonel Henry Washington and his Army survey party were directed to erect a monument atop Mount San Bernardino. The monument was to be an east-west reference point from which all future surveys of Southern California would be taken.

The colonel's crew took many readings, but heat waves from the San Bernardino Valley below befuddled their triangulations. The surveying party ingeniously solved this dilemma by lighting bonfires atop the peak in order to make their calculations at night.

This trail takes you from deep pine forest to exposed manzanita slopes and visits the old survey monument. The higher slopes of Mount San Bernardino are beautiful and rugged subalpine terrain. A number of trail camps along the way offer spring water and rest.

Camp Angelus trailhead is less visited than others at the edge of the San Gorgonio Wilderness, but it receives a lot of use, especially during summer weekends. A permit is required for entry into the wilderness. You can secure a permit by mail or in person from the Mill Creek Ranger Station in Mentone.

Directions to trailhead: Drive east on Interstate Highway 10 to Redlands, leaving the freeway at the Highway 30 exit. Follow Highway 38 twenty miles east to Camp Angelus. Turn right near the ranger station at a sign that reads "San Bernardino Peak Trail." Follow the dirt road a quarter-mile to the large parking area. The signed trailhead is at the north end of the lot.

The Hike: The trail begins ascending through a mixed forest of pine, fir and oak, switchbacking up the beautifully wooded slope. You mount a ridge, walk along its crest for a brief distance, then continue climbing. You're welcomed into the glories of the San Gorgonio Wilderness by a wooden sign, two miles from the trailhead. A little beyond the wilderness boundary, the grade grows less severe. As you climb above 8,000 feet, the Jeffrey pine become widely spaced. Shortly, the trail penetrates a manzanita-covered slope. You pass a side trail leading down to Manzanita Springs. Don't drink the water. The side trail continues on a quarter-mile to Columbine Springs Trail Camp, which usually has water later in the season than Manzanita.

To San Bernardino Peak: A short distance beyond Manzanita Springs Trail Junction, the trail begins climbing more earnestly. The trail ascends in fits and starts over slopes covered with manzanita and homely chinquapin; in 1½ more miles, it reaches Limber Pine Springs Camp. (Actually, all the shade in the area is provided by lodgepole pines.) Another quarter-mile up the trail is Limber Pine Springs, usually a dependable source of water.

The trail begins a long traverse south, switchbacking up to Camp Washington, a trail camp with plenty of view, but nothing to drink. One hundred yards from the trail is Colonel Washington's baseline monument, which looks like little more than a pile of stone rubble. The trail climbs another half-mile, where it intersects a brief side trail that takes you to the summit of Mount San Bernardino (10,624 feet).

Sign the summit register, enjoy the view, and return the way you came.

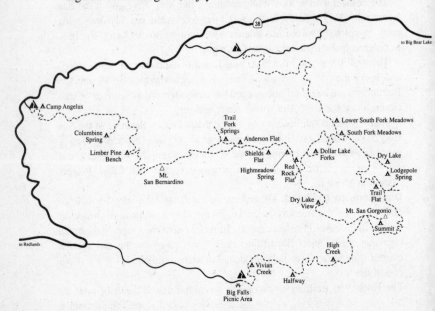

83

South Fork Trail

South Fork to South Fork Meadows
  8 miles round trip; 1,500-foot gain

To Dollar Lake
  12 miles round trip; 2,500-foot gain

To Mt. San Gorgonio
  21 miles round trip; 4,600-foot gain

Season: June-November

Most of us in the Southland have looked east and marveled at Mt. San Gorgonio, the highest peak in Southern California. The 11,499-foot mountain is most striking in winter when its snow-covered peak can be seen reaching far above the metropolis. In summer, the view is not so spectacular; the dull-gray granite summit is hard to find among the hydrocarbons.

But summer and early autumn are the best seasons in the alpine high country, allowing you to look down at what you left behind. Enjoy a 360-degree panoramic view from the Mexican border to the southern Sierra, from the Pacific Ocean to the far reaches of the Mojave Desert.

Mt. San Gorgonio's alpine vegetation includes carpets of buttercups, and that venerable survivor of inclement weather, the limber pine. Mountain lions, mule deer and bighorn sheep roam the high slopes, and golden eagles soar over the summit.

The mountain got its name from an obscure 4th-century Christian martyr, but irreverent Americans began calling the mountain "Grayback." Its bare, gravelly summit stretches laterally for some distance above the timberline, giving the appearance of a long, gray back.

Below the peak is some fine hiking on good trails that tour the heart of the San Gorgonio Wilderness. You'll pass through lovely meadows and visit two small lakes, Dry and Dollar. Ambitious hikers in top form will want to make the 21-mile round trip trek all the way to the top of Old Grayback for the best view of Southern California available to a hiker.

Directions to trailhead: From Interstate 10 in Redlands, exit on California 38. As you head up the highway into the San Bernardino National Forest, remember to stop at the Mill Creek Ranger Station just beyond the hamlet of Mentone and pick up your wilderness permit. At the station (open 8 A.M. to 4:30 P.M.), you can also pick up maps and the latest trail information. The ranger station has a self-service booth outside that dispenses permits. Permits are limited; alternative routes may be offered at the ranger station.

Follow the highway 19 miles past the ranger station to Jenks Lake Road. Turn right and proceed 3 miles to the new South Fork trailhead. The Forest Service closed the Poopout Hill trailhead and opened this one in 1988.

The Hike: From the parking area, you cross Jenks Lake Road and pick up the unsigned trail. The path ascends moderately through a mixed pine forest. Enjoy the occasional views of Sugarloaf Peak behind you and San Gorgonio ahead. About 1½ miles from the trailhead, you'll intersect Poopout Hill Road, now closed to vehicle traffic. Continue straight ahead and another ¾ mile of travel brings you to an intersection with the old Poopout Hill Trail. Bear right here.

Continue ascending through the woods. In a mile, South Fork Creek appears on your left, and you parallel it toward South Fork Meadows, also known as Slushy Meadows.

Dozens of tiny streams, which form the headwaters of the Santa Ana River, roam through the ferns and wispy waist-high grasses. Lower South Fork Meadows Trail Camp and Middle South Fork Meadows Trail Camp offer places to picnic.

You also can locate an idyllic picnic spot beneath the ponderosa pine and white fir. If you're not feeling especially energetic, you could spend a day in South Fork Meadows and be quite happy.

The more energetic will continue on the trail as it skirts the west edge of the meadow and reaches a junction. The left fork, Whitewater Trail, heads toward Dry Lake (another fine day hike destination) and the summit of Mt. San Gorgonio. You take the right fork, South Fork Trail, and begin switchbacking up wooded slopes.

After a mile of climbing, first through ponderosa pine and then through lodgepole pine, you'll begin a long contour around the wall of the basin that holds Dollar Lake. The trail passes a manzanita-covered slope and reaches a junction 1¾ miles from South Fork Meadows. Go left.

In a few hundred yards you reach another junction and turn left again. Follow the easy quarter-mile trail down the basin wall to the lake.

Dollar Lake, so named because it gleams like a silver dollar, is one of the most popular backcountry spots in the San Gorgonio Wilderness and is another ideal place to picnic or laze away a day. Return to the main trail the way you came.

If you're headed for the summit, resume climbing for another mile to Dollar Lake Saddle (approx. 10,000 feet) and a three-way junction. One-half mile beyond the junction, you pass another junction with the rocky side-trail that ascends Charlton Peak. In another ½ mile you pass Dry Lake View Camp, a waterless trail camp amidst great boulders. From here, you can look down into Dry Lake Basin, where you'll pass if you return from the peak via Sky High Trail. Soon you'll pass junctions with the Vivian Creek Trail and the Sky High Trail. Keep to your left at both junctions. Cross a last rise and climb to the summit of San Gorgonio.

No other Southern California mountain commands such an uninterrupted panoramic view. To the north are the deep green meadowlands of the upper valley of the Santa Ana River. To the west is the murky megalopolis. To the east is the Mojave. South is San Gorgonio Pass and just across from it, nearly level with your feet, is Mount San Jacinto.

Return the way you came or via the Sky High Trail, which descends the east slope of San Gorgonio to Mine Shaft Saddle and Dry Lake and deposits you in South Fork Meadows where you intersect the trail back to South Fork.

From the summit, retrace your steps on the main trail to its intersection with the Sky High Trail. Begin your descent from the clouds on the latter trail, circling first east, then north around the mountain's great shoulders. As you descend there are good views of the Whitewater drainage, gorges bearing snowmelt from San Gorgonio and carrying waters to the desert sands below.

As you round the east ridge, you'll pass the wreckage of a DC-3 squashed against the mountain. Three and a half miles from the summit you reach Mine Shaft Saddle on the divide between Dry Lake Basin and the Whitewater River.

Continue your descent, and in two more miles you'll reach Dry Lake at 9,200 feet. In dry years it is dry by midsummer, but some years the lake is filled to the brim, its water lapping against the trail that surrounds the lake.

From the Dry Lake basin, you switchback down through pine and fir 1¾ miles to South Fork Meadows, where you intersect the trail back to South Fork trailhead.

84

Sugarloaf National Recreation Trail

Green Canyon to Wildhorse Creek Trail Camp
  5 miles round trip; 700-foot gain

To Sugarloaf Mountain
  10 miles round trip; 2,000-foot gain

Season: May-November

Sugarloaf Mountain, highest peak in the San Bernardino Mountains outside the San Gorgonio Wilderness, is a particularly fine destination on a hot summer's day. The ridgeline leading to the summit is forested with pine, fir and cedar. A breeze cools the massive round shoulders of the mountain.

The first part of the trail—as far as Wildhorse Trail Camp—offers a family trip of moderate difficulty. Well-conditioned hikers will enjoy the challenge of the second part of the trail—a vigorous ascent to the summit of 9,952-foot Sugarloaf Mountain.

Directions to trailhead: From Big Bear City, head east on State Route 38. The highway turns south, and about 3 miles from town, turn right on Forest Road 2N84. The Forest Service has posted "passenger car not recommended" signs; those with low-slung cars should proceed with caution—or be prepared to walk part of the 1½ mile-distance to the trailhead if the

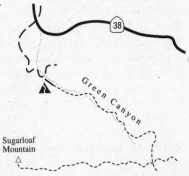

road is poor. When 2N84 veers left, proceed straight ahead on Forest Road 2N93, which climbs a mile to Green Creek crossing. On the other side of the creek, turn right (south) onto an unsigned dirt road and follow it a few hundred yards to a parking area at a locked gate.

The Hike: Ascend on the steep dirt jeep road which stays close to Green Creek. Two miles of hiking brings you to a saddle on the ridgeline and a trail junction. (Straight ahead, the trail continues a short distance to Wildhorse Creek Trail Camp—a fine picnic and rest stop.

Turn right (west) and ascend on the Sugarloaf Trail. Above 9,000 feet, the trail passes through stands of lodgepole pine. The trail contours around Peak 9775 and dips into a saddle. Gnarled and picturesque junipers hug the ridgeline. The trail then ascends to the forested summit of Sugarloaf Peak.

85

Santa Ana River Trail

South Fork Campground to Heart Bar Campground
9 miles round trip; 800-foot gain

Season: March-November

For most of its length, Southern California's largest river is not a thing of beauty. Concrete-lined and channelized, the Santa Ana River that crosses Orange County is a thoroughly domesticated watercourse. Its once-extensive riverbed has been covered with subdivisions, its natural course altered for human convenience. Glimpsing the river as it passes Costa Mesa backyards, Anaheim Stadium or the I-10/I-15 interchange does not in truth inspire further exploration.

Fortunately for hikers and nature lovers, there's another Santa Ana River, unfettered and unchanneled. At its headwaters high in the San Bernardino Mountains, the river waters a beautiful meadow and cuts through a deep canyon that separates the high peaks of the San Gorgonio Wilderness from the mountains of the Big Bear Lake area. The river, born of natural springs and snowmelt, is in its upper reaches an important wildlife habitat.

A 4½-mile length of the Santa Ana River Trail explores the river's headwaters. Ambitious plans are afoot for the trail, which one day may descend all the way from the San Bernardino Mountains to the sea. The idea is to connect the famed Pacific Crest Trail with Southern California's coastline.

Equestrians have been especially vocal in boosting a "crest to coast" route. The lower part of the trail, which follows the concrete channel from the river mouth inland to Yorba Linda at the base of the Chino Hills, is popular with cyclists and equestrians; it's not exactly a thrill a minute for walkers.

For hikers, the true Santa Ana River Trail begins in an area of the San Bernardino National Forest called Heart Bar, first settled by Mormon pioneers in the 1850s. During the latter part of the 19th Century and the first half of this one, cattlemen sent their herds to graze the lush Santa Ana River meadows. It was one cattleman's brand, a heart with a bar beneath it that gave the land its name about a century ago.

Santa Ana River Trail parallels the river as it winds from South Fork Campground to Heart Bar Campground. The path stays in piney woods for most of its length. A few side trails allow passage to the river.

Directions to trailhead: From Interstate 10 in Redlands, take the Highway 38 exit and proceed north 32 miles to South Fork Campground.

Almost opposite the entrance to the campground, on the north side of the highway, you'll find the Santa Ana River trailhead parking lot and the signed trail.

Santa Ana River Trail ends at Forest Road IN021, near Heart Bar Campground. If you want to make a one-way hike, you can arrange to have transportation waiting at the Forest Road IN021 trailhead. To reach this trailhead from the South Fork Campground trailhead, you would continue east on Highway 38 to the signed Heart Bar Campground turnoff, then drive a mile past the campground on the dirt Forest Road IN021 to the second signed Santa Ana River trailhead.

The Hike: From the parking area opposite South Fork Campground, Santa Ana River Trail meanders by its namesake, then veers under the Santa Ana River Bridge. Notice the rugged construction of the bridge and the wide bed of the river, two indications of the Santa Ana's size and strength after a storm.

The trail makes a short circle, reaches a second signed trailhead at the entrance to South Fork Campground and heads west. Switchbacking up a slope, the trail soon turns east—your direction for the rest of this hike.

During the first mile you will intersect a number of dirt roads, but strategically placed signs keep you on the path. Most of the climbing is in the first mile.

The trail travels through a mixed forest of ponderosa and Jeffrey pine, white fir and black oak. Ground squirrels are abundant, and deer are seen occasionally. Steller's jays, Western bluebirds, pygmy nuthatches, robins and juncoes are amond the birds you may see.

Above you to the southwest is the San Gorgonio Wilderness, dominated by its 11,499-foot signature peak, highest point in Southern California. To the north, above the forested canyon of the Santa Ana River, is Sugarloaf Mountain (9,952 feet), highest peak in the San Bernardinos outside the wilderness.

About the trail's midpoint you'll spot Heart Bar Station, headquarters for a Forest Service fire crew. Continuing east, the trail offers great views of well-named Big Meadow. Watering the meadow are Heart Bar Creek, Coon Creek, Cienega Seca Creek and the headwaters of the Santa Ana. Big Meadow is especially pretty when a breeze sways the willows and tall grasses. During late spring and summer the meadow is splashed with colorful Indian paintbrush, purple sage, columbine, monkeyflower and lupine.

The meadows where cattle once grazed are now a valuable habitat for rabbits, foxes, skunks and raccoons. California golden beaver were brought into the area, and several pairs of them maintain dams on the Santa Ana River.

About a mile from trail's end you will intersect an unsigned side trail leading left down to Big Meadow and over to Heart Bar Campground. Continue straight at this junction to the end of the trail at Forest Road 1N021.

86

Aspen Grove Trail

Forest Road 1N05 to Fish Creek Meadows
  5 miles round trip; 600-foot gain

Season: May-November

One of the prettiest sights of autumn is the fluttering of the aspen's golden-yellow leaves. From a distance, the trees stand apart from the surrounding dark forest. In the right light, the aspens seem to burn, like fire in the wind.

Botanists say the aspen is the most widely distributed tree on the North American continent. Even not-so-lyrical American fur trappers and mountain men of the last century were impressed by the tree's range and beauty.

The water-loving aspen is a rarity in Southern California, but there is a handsome little grove in the San Bernardino Mountains. Aspen Grove, reached by a trail with the same name, is an ideal autumn excursion.

The hike to Aspen Grove is particularly inviting after Jack Frost has touched the trees. After the first cold snap, the aspens display their fall finery, a display of color unrivaled in Southern California.

It's only a short quarter-mile saunter to the aspens that line Fish Creek, but the trail continues beyond the grove, traveling through a pine and fir forest and a lovely meadow.

Directions to trailhead: From Interstate 10 in Redlands, exit on Highway 38 and proceed 32 miles east to the signed turnoff for Heart Bar Campground. (As you head up 38 into the San Bernardino National Forest, remember to stop at Mill Creek Ranger Station just beyond the hamlet of Mentone and pick up a wilderness permit.) Turn south (right) on dirt Forest Road 1N02, and drive 1¼ miles to a fork in the road. Stay right at the fork and follow it on a 1½-mile climb to a small parking area and signed Aspen Grove Trail on your right.

The Hike: The trail, for its first quarter-mile an abandoned dirt road, descends toward Fish Creek. The very beginning of Aspen Grove Trail offers the best view of San Gorgonio Wilderness peaks—the highest in Southern California. To the west stands mighty Grinnell Mountain, named for turn-of-the-century University of California zoologist Joseph Grinnell, who studied the animals of the San Bernardino Mountains. To the south is Ten Thousand Foot Ridge, headwaters for Fish Creek, which you soon see and hear meandering below.

At Fish Creek, a sign marks the boundary of the San Gorgonio Wilderness. Cross the creek and enjoy the aspen grove that lines Fish Creek. It's a small grove, but a pretty one. No one will blame you if you picnic among the whitewashed trunks and quaking leaves and hike no farther.

The aspens have been suffering of late at the hands of—or more accurately, the jaws of—a creature that loves the trees even more than humans. The aspen-chomping California golden beaver is not a native of the San Bernardino Mountains, but since its introduction it has found the area—and the aspens to its liking. Forest Service wildlife experts are working on a plan to manage the native aspens and the beaver.

After admiring the aspens, continue on Aspen Grove Trail, which heads up-creek. The path soon wanders a bit away from Fish Creek and travels through a forest of ponderosa pine, Jeffrey pine and Douglas fir.

About a mile from Aspen Grove, the trail passes little Monkey Flower Flat. During late spring and early summer, columbine and lupine join the monkeyflowers in bedecking the flat.

Beyond Monkey Flower is a much larger flat—Fish Creek Meadow. Aspen Grove Trail skirts this meadow and ends at a signed junction with Fish Creek Trail. The left fork of Fish Creek Trails leads a bit more than half a mile to Forest Road 1N05. Take the right fork of the trail, which angles toward Upper Fish Creek. The path ascends above the creek, passes through a pine and fir forest and, a bit more than a mile from the junction with Aspen Grove Trail, reaches Fish Creek Camp. This fir-shaded camp is an ideal place to relax.

87

Vivian Creek Trail

Mill Creek Canyon to Vivian Creek Trail Camp
2½ miles round trip; 1,200-foot gain

To Halfway Trail Camp
5 miles round trip; 1,800-foot gain

To High Creek Trail Camp
8 miles round trip; 3,400-foot gain

To Mt. San Gorgonio Peak
14 miles round trip; 5,300-foot gain

Season: May-November

"The mountains"—he continued, with his eyes upon the distant heights —"are not seen by those who would visit them with a rattle and clatter and rush and roar—as one would visit the cities of men. They are to be seen only by those who have the grace to go quietly; who have the understanding to go thoughtfully; the heart to go lovingly; and the spirit to go worshipfully."

—Harold Bell Wright
The Eyes of the World, 1914

A half-dozen major trails lead through the San Gorgonio Wilderness to the top of Mt. San Gorgonio, Southern California's highest peak. Oldest, and often regarded as the best, is Vivian Creek Trail.

Not long after the formation of San Bernardino Forest Preserve in 1893, pioneer foresters built Government Trail to the top of San Gorgonio. This path was later renamed Vivian Creek Trail because it winds along for a few miles with its namesake watercourse before climbing the steep upper slopes of San Gorgonio.

Vivian Creek Trail begins in Mill Creek Canyon. The lower stretches of the canyon, traveled by Highway 38, displays many boulders, evidence of great floods in years past.

Upper Mill Creek Canyon is where Big Falls falls. Tumbling from the shoulder of San Bernardino Peak, snowmelt-swollen Falls Creek rushes headlong over a cliff near Mill Creek Road. (Unfortunately, too many foolish people were killed or injured by trying to climb Big Falls and the Forest Service has closed the ½-mile path leading to Big Falls Overlook.)

Mill Creek Canyon was the retreat for pastor-turned-novelist Harold Bell Wright (1872–1944). His wholesome, tremendously popular novels featured rugged individualists, as well as Southwest and Southland settings. One novel, *Eyes of the World*, uses the San Bernardino Mountains as a setting and explores the question of an artist's responsibility to society and to himself.

Leaving the head of Mill Creek Canyon, Vivian Creek Trail climbs into the valley cut by Vivian Creek, visits three inviting trail camps—Vivian Creek, Halfway and High Creek—and ascends rocky, lodgepole pine-dotted slopes to the top of Old Grayback.

Directions to trailhead: From Interstate 10 in Redlands, exit on Highway 38 and proceed 14 miles east to a junction with Forest Home Road. (Halfway to this junction, on Highway 38, is Mill Creek Ranger Station, where you must stop and obtain a wilderness permit.) Follow Forest Home Road 4½ miles to its end.

The Hike: The trail, an old dirt road, travels ¾ mile through (closed) Falls Campground to another (the former) Vivian Creek trailhead. The trail, a dirt path from this point, crosses boulder-strewn Mill Creek wash, then begins a steep ascent over an exposed, oak-dotted slope. Soon you'll reach Vivian Creek Trail Camp, where pine- and fir-shaded sites dot the creek banks.

Past the camp, Vivian Creek Trail follows its namesake, crossing from one side to the other and passing little lush meadows and stands of pine and cedar.

Halfway, a trail camp about halfway between Vivian Creek and High Creek Camps, is another welcome retreat. Another 1½ miles of steep climbing up forested slopes brings you to High Creek Camp.

Above High Creek, located at 9,000-foot elevation, you leave behind the Ponderosa pine and cedar and encounter that hearty, high altitude survivor, the lodgepole pine. Two miles high, you start getting some great views; at 11,000 feet, the trail ascends above the timberline.

When you reach a junction with the trail coming up from Dollar Lake you'll turn right. Soon you'll pass a junction with the Sky High Trail, cross a last rise and climb to the summit of San Gorgonio.

88

Kitching Creek Trail

Kitching Creek to Kitching Peak
  9½ miles round trip; 2,400-foot gain

Season: October-June

Kitching Peak, which lies atop the headwaters of the Whitewater River in the San Gorgonio Wilderness, has a wonderful air of remoteness. High on the dry southeast end of the San Bernardino Mountains, the 6,598-foot peak offers superb views of Mt. San Jacinto and Mt. San Gorgonio, as well as the Mojave and Colorado Deserts.

The Whitewater country, added to the wilderness in 1984, is mostly trailless and rarely traveled. No doubt this rugged country could be considered among the most wild, if not the most wild region in the Southland.

On the steep slopes of the awesome Whitewater country the bighorn sheep have their lambing grounds, and in its waters, the legendary San Gorgonio trout is making its last stand. Deer, mountain lions and even black bears live here.

The Whitewater River, swollen by snowmelt from the shoulders of Mt. San Gorgonio, rushes down the San Bernardino Mountains to meet the desert sands far below. Many pioneer water-seekers of the last century tried to capture this river and send its waters to the San Bernardino Valley and Palm Springs. Today, northbound Pacific Crest Trail hikers leave the desert behind and enter the San Bernardino Mountains through White-water Canyon.

This hike ascends the east branch of Millard Canyon to a divide, then travels a ridgeline to the summit of Kitching Peak. Clear-day winter views are unforgettable.

Directions to trailhead: From Interstate 10, 2 miles east of Banning, exit on Fields Road and drive north through the Morongo Indian Reservation. After 1¼ mile, turn right onto Morongo Road, where a sign indicates Millard Canyon. After ½ mile bear left on Forest Road 2S05, which soon turns to dirt. You bear sharply right (east) at a junction, then left at another, continuing a final mile to road's end. Park just before the creek crossing.

The Hike: The trail ascends northeast up the east branch of Millard Canyon. Oak and spruce shade the trail, which crosses and recrosses little Kitching Creek. After 2 miles, the path rises out of the shade of the canyon and switchbacks up the brushy ridge that divides Millard Canyon from the canyon cut by the Whitewater River.

Atop the ridge is a signed junction. Kitching Creek Trail (2E09) heads north another two miles to The Sink, a trail camp. You veer sharply right (south) on Trail 2E24 along the oak- and chaparral-covered ridgeline. Farther along you'll encounter a stand of white fir and a few sugar pine.

Sometimes this ridgetop trail is quite brushy, so you might have to push through the chaparral to get to the very top of Kitch-

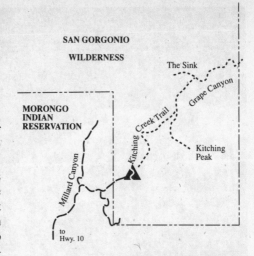

ing Peak. From the summit, almost due south, is mighty Mt. San Jacinto and just below that great gash between the San Jacinto and San Bernardino Mountains—San Gorgonio Pass. East are the Little San Bernardino Mountains of Joshua Tree National Monument. You can trace the course of Whitewater River into the Coachella Valley and off toward Palm Springs. Above you to the north is San Gorgonio, highest peak in Southern California.

Big Horn Sheep roam this end of the San Bernardino Mountains.

9. San Jacinto Mountains

MANY HIKERS in the San Jacinto Mountains can't resist comparing this range with the High Sierra. While comparisons often leave low chaparral-covered mountains on the short end, the alpine San Jacintos fare well because the range shares many geologic similarities with the Sierra Nevada.

Both ranges are bold uplifted masses of granite. Both are westward tilted blocks located near powerful earthquake faults. Both veer abruptly out of the desert without the geologic fanfare of foothills preceding them.

Author Carey McWilliams called Southern California an "island on the land." The San Jacintos could well be described the same way. The 10,000-foot peaks of the San Jacintos are completely separated from the rest of Southern California by low passes and desert valleys. The range is bounded by San Gorgonio Pass on the north, the San Jacinto Valley on the west, the Colorado Desert and the great Coachella Valley on the east, and Anza-Borrego Desert State Park to the south.

The San Jacintos seem an island in the sky because of their incredibly rapid rise from the desert floor. No other place in California do alpine and desert vegetation thrive in such close proximity. Six distinct life zones, from cactus-dotted desert and palm canyons to arctic alpine summits, can be encountered within five horizontal miles of travel. On the base is Lower Sonoran vegetation of creosote and ironwood. Above this is the Upper Sonoran or manzanita and scrub oak, soon giving way with rise in elevation to dense mountain forests of pine and cedar. In narrow belts around the high summits are those hearty survivors—the lodgepole pine and limber pine. Finally some stunted species, including alpine sorrel, grow on the peaks and are classified in the Arctic-Alpine Zone. Each life zone has a unique set of inhabitants. Shy and reclusive bighorn sheep patrol the desert-facing high country, mule deer browse the verdant meadows, golden eagles soar over the high peaks.

During the great logging boom of 1880–1910, timber barons sent their choppers farther and farther up the slopes of the San Jacintos. Ranchers grazed thousands of sheep and cattle in the alpine meadows. Even the most shortsighted could see the destruction of the mountain watershed, and with local settlers urging protection for the range, President Grover Cleveland established the San Jacinto Timberland Reserve in 1897. It was a huge chunk of land, extending from the San Gorgonio Pass to the Mexican border. The San Jacinto Reserve was later combined with a portion of the Santa Ana Mountains to create the Cleveland National Forest.

After several devastating fires in 1924, federal foresters decided the huge tract of land was too unwieldy for fire suppression purposes, and the San Jacintos were taken from the Cleveland National Forest and attached to the nearby San Bernardino National Forest, where they remain today.

In the mid-1930s, CCC workers camped in Round and Tahquitz Valleys and built an extensive, well-engineered trail system through the San Jacintos. Some years, as many as 15,000 hikers travel the backcountry on these trails.

The wild areas in the San Jacinto Mountains are now administered by both state park and national forest rangers. The middle of the region, including San Jacinto Peak, is included within Mount San Jacinto Wilderness State Park. On both sides of the peak, north and south, the wilderness is administered by the San Jacinto District of the San Bernardino National Forest.

Access to the San Jacintos was difficult until Highway 243, "The Banning to Idyllwild Panoramic Highway" was built. As late as World War II, it was a muffler-massacring, steep, narrow, unpaved route that forded streams. A new paved "high gear" road opened in 1948, with actress Jane Powell performing the ribbon-cutting duties as the Banning High School Band played.

Palm Springs Aerial Tramway makes it easy for hikers to enter Mount San Jacinto State Wilderness. Starting in Chino Canyon near Palm Springs, a tram takes passengers from 2,643-foot Lower Tramway Terminal (Valley Station) to 8,516-foot Upper Tramway Terminal (Mountain Station) at the edge of the Wilderness.

The Swiss-made gondola rapidly leaves terra firma behind. Too rapidly, you think. It carries you over one of the most abrupt mountain faces in the world, over cliffs only a bighorn sheep can scale, over several life zones, from palms to pines. The view is fantastic.

Construction of the Tramway was opposed by conservationists who pointed out that Mount San Jacinto slopes were totally unsuited to its stated purpose—skiing. First proposed in the 1930s, the project was finally completed in 1963 after approval and funding from the State of California.

Now, most nature-lovers enjoy witnessing flora and fauna changes equivalent to those viewed on a motor trip from the Mojave Desert to the Arctic Circle in just minutes. In pre-tramway days, John Muir found the view "the most sublime spectacle to be found anywhere on this earth!"

The range is one of those magical places that lures hikers back year after year. The seasons are more distinct here than anywhere else in Southern California. Hikers also enjoy the contrasts this range offers—the feeling of hiking in Switzerland while gazing down on the Sahara.

89

Ernie Maxwell Trail

Humber Park to Saunders Meadow
5 miles round trip; 300-foot gain

Season: May-November

The founder of the *Idyllwild Town Crier* is honored by the Ernie Maxwell Scenic Trail, a woodsy, 2½-mile path through the San Jacinto Mountains. Maxwell, longtime Idyllwild conservationist, has hiked his namesake trail many times.

As Maxwell explains it, his trail came into being as a result of his horse's inability to get along with automobiles. After riding through the San Jacinto Wilderness, Maxwell and his fellow equestrians were forced to follow paved roads back through town to the stables. Maxwell's barn-sour pack horses, so slow and sullen on the trail, would become suddenly frisky and unmanageable as they neared home. Equine-auto conflicts were frequent. Maxwell thought: Why not build a trail from Humber Park, at the edge of the San Jacinto Wilderness, through the forest to the stables, thus avoiding the horse-spooking congestion of downtown Idyllwild?

Maxwell got cooperation from the U.S. Forest Service and from Riverside County inmates, who provided the labor. Ernie Maxwell Trail was completed in 1959.

And a lovely trail it is. The path meanders through a mixed forest of pine and fir and offers fine views of the granite face of Marion Ridge.

Since founding the newspaper in 1946, Maxwell has often written about what he wryly calls "the urban-wildlands interface issue. That's the one that deals with more and more people moving into the hills."

People began moving into the hills with their axes and sheep more than a hundred years ago. Fortunately, the San Jacinto Mountains have had many conservation-minded friends, including Ernie Maxwell, who for many years served as president of the local chapter of the Izaak Walton League. Maxwell has seen the emphasis of the

surrounding national forest change from commodity production to recreation; seen isolated Idyllwild become a popular weekend getaway. Conservationists are aware that the future of the mountains depend to a large extent on the attitude of the millions of Southern Californians living 7,000 feet below and a 1½-hour drive away from Idyllwild.

"Walk the trails," urges Maxwell. "Enjoy the fresh air. And get to know these mountains. The mountains need more friends."

Directions to trailhead: From Interstate 10 in Banning, exit on California 243 (Banning-Idyllwild Highway) and proceed about 25 miles to Idyllwild County Park Visitor Center. A small museum interprets the history and natural history of the area.

From downtown Idyllwild, head up Fern Valley Road. Following the signs to Humber Park, drive two miles to the large parking area. Signed Ernie Maxwell Trail departs from the lower end of the parking lot.

The Hike: The trail begins at Humber Park, the main jumping-off point to the San Jacinto Wilderness for hikers and rock climbers. You'll get frequent over-the-shoulder views of the dramatic pinnacles popular with Southern California climbers.

The mostly level trail (the inmates did a great job!) contours gently around wooded slopes. Ponderosa, Jeffrey and Coulter pines, fir and incense cedar grace the mountainside and carpet the path with needles.

This hike's destination, Saunders Meadow, is named for Amasa Saunders, who in 1881 operated a huge sawmill not too far down slope in Strawberry Valley. Take a moment to be thankful that not all the pine and fir became grist for Saunders' mill, then scout the tree tops for the abundant bird life. Look for Steller's jays, the white-headed woodpecker, and the colorful orange-headed, yellow-breasted western tanager.

Ernie Maxwell Scenic Trail ends somewhat abruptly and ingloriously at dirt Tahquitz View Drive. Maxwell had envisioned that his trail would continue another few miles around Idyllwild and connect to the path leading to Suicide Rock, but this trail plan ended in a bureaucratic thicket.

Contemplating the notion that half a terrific trail is better than none, return the same way.

90

South Ridge Trail

South Ridge Road to Tahquitz Peak
  6 miles round trip; 2,000-foot gain

Season: May-October

Tahquitz Peak dominates the southern San Jacinto Mountains, lording over Strawberry Valley and Idyllwild on one side, and Tahquitz Valley on the other. A fire lookout tower is perched on the summit. The view from the peak is inspiring: clear-day vistas of the San Jacintos, the desert and the distant Santa Rosas.

You may notice what appear to be insect-like creatures high on the rock walls of the mountain. Southland rock climbers often come to practice their craft on the superb rock walls of Tahquitz. You may hear the distant shouts of "On belay," "climbing," or sometimes "Ohhhh nooo."

Lily Rock, named for a surveyor's daughter, is the official name of the great rock, though most climbers prefer the more rugged-sounding Tahquitz. After taking one of the hundred routes (some quite hazardous) up the several faces of the rock, you can't blame the climbers for preferring something more dramatic than Lily.

South Ridge Trail, true to its name, ascends the steep south ridge of Tahquitz Peak. The trail climbs through stands of pine and fir and offers great views of Strawberry Valley and the storybook hamlet of Idyllwild.

If you want a longer hike than the six-mile round trip to Tahquitz Peak, there are a number of ways to extend your trek. By arranging a car shuttle, you could descend Tahquitz Peak to Humber Park at the outskirts of Idyllwild. For a very long loop hike, you could even follow the Ernie Maxwell Trail from Humber Park down to the foot of South Ridge Road, then up the road to the South Ridge trailhead.

Directions to trailhead: From Interstate 10 in Banning, exit on Highway 243 (Banning-Idyllwild Highway) and proceed about 25 miles to Idyllwild. After you've obtained your wilderness permit from the Forest Service Station in Idyllwild, you'll double back a wee bit to the south edge of town and make a left turn on Saunders Meadow Road. Turn left on Pine Avenue, right on Tahquitz Drive, then right on South Ridge Road. (If the gate across this road is closed (it's usually open during good weather), you'll have to park at the base of South Ridge Road. Otherwise, passenger cars with good ground clearance may continue 1½ miles up part dirt/part paved, potholed South Ridge Road to its terminus at signed South Ridge trailhead.

The Hike: From the trailhead at the top of South Ridge Road, the well-constructed path zigzags through a forest of Jeffrey Pine and white fir. You'll get fine south views of Garner Valley and Lake Hemet, Thomas Mountain and Table Mountain. Far off to the west, on a clear day, you'll be able to pick out the Santa Ana and San Gabriel Mountains.

South Ridge Trail climbs to a boulder-strewn saddle, which marks the trail's halfway point. Here you'll find a rock window-on-the-world, a great place to rest or to frame a picture of your hiking mate.

From the saddle, the trail climbs in earnest past thickets of spiny chinquapin, and past scattered lodgepole pine. You'll sight the fire lookout tower atop Tahquitz Peak many a switchback above you, but the last mile of trail goes by faster than you might expect if you maintain a slow, steady pace.

Enjoy the summit views, then either return the same way or follow your heart and forest service map through the San Jacinto Wilderness down to Humber Park and Idyllwild.

Tahquitz Peak

91

Deer Springs Trail

Idyllwild to Suicide Rock
7 miles round trip; 2,000-feet gain

Season: May-November

Suicide Rock is a sheer granite outcropping that provides the romantic with a tale of star-crossed lovers, and rewards the hiker with splendid views of Strawberry Valley and a forest wonderland of pine and fir. Legend has it that the rock got its tragic name from an Indian princess and her lover who leaped to their deaths over the precipice rather than be separated, as their chief had commanded.

Suicide Rock is a splendid place to observe the ever-changing four seasons (though you'll have a hard time climbing the rock in winter). The seasons fade in and out with clarity and distinction in the San Jacintos. Fall colors tint the black oak and azalea, winter brings a white blanket, spring is heralded by a profusion of wildflowers, and the long, hot summers are tempered with thunder and lightning displays. Views like this bring hikers back again and again to sample the beauty of the San Jacinto Mountains.

Directions to trailhead: Deer Springs Trail begins across the highway from the Idyllwild County Park Visitor Center parking area, one mile west of town on the Banning-Idyllwild Highway 243. If you'd like to learn something about the history of the area, the nature museum at the county park is helpful.

The Forest Service's Idyllwild Ranger Station is on California 243 at Pine Crest Avenue; the Mount San Jacinto State Park Ranger Station in Idyllwild is at 25905 California 243.

The Hike: Signed Deer Springs Trail picks its way through an elfin manzanita forest, then ascends past spreading oaks and tall pines. You switchback up a ridge to Suicide Junction, 2.3 miles from the trailhead. Here you leave the Deer Springs Trail and bear east, contouring across Marion Ridge. You cross Marion Creek, whose performance is seasonal, and on wet years, inspiring. A long mile from Suicide Junction you reach the back side of Suicide Rock.

From the white granite rock you'll be able to look down and see tiny Idyllwild and Strawberry Valley. On the far horizon are Tahquitz Peak and Lily Rock.

92

Seven Pines Trail

Dark Canyon to Deer Springs
7½ miles round trip; 2,600-foot gain

To Little Round Valley Camp
10½ miles round trip; 3,600-foot gain

To San Jacinto Peak
13½ miles round trip; 4,400-foot gain

Seven Pines Trail ascends the cascading North Fork of San Jacinto River to its headwaters at Deer Springs. Energetic hikers will join the Deer Springs Trail for an ascent of Mount San Jacinto.

Remember to obtain a wilderness permit and map from park headquarters, off California 243 just before you get to the town of Idyllwild (if you reach the town's stop sign, you're about 100 yards past it).

Directions to trailhead: Take Highway 243 (Banning-Idyllwild Road) about 20 miles from Banning or 6 miles from Idyllwild. Just south of Alandale Forest Service Station, take the turnoff (4S02) toward Dark Canyon Campground. After a mile's travel on the dirt road, veer left at a junction. Pass through the camp and bear left at Azalea Trail junction to the trailhead.

The Hike: Seven Pines Trail ascends the ridge between Dark Canyon and the canyon cut by the North Fork. You hike out of the San Bernardino National Forest into Mount San Jacinto State Park. After a mile, the trail tops the ridge and descends eastward to the North Fork. In spring, when the river is swollen with snowmelt, the North Fork has quite a heady flow.

The trail climbs along a pine- and fir-covered slope, recrosses the river, and reaches a junction with Deer Springs Trail. (A right turn on the trail leads to Strawberry Junction, past Suicide Rock on Highway 243 (see Hike 60). Another possibility is to bear south on the Marion Mountain Trail which descends steeply a little more than two miles to Marion Mountain Camp. A three-mile car shuttle or three-mile walk leads back to Dark Canyon Campground and the trailhead.)

Follow Deer Springs Trail left (east) a quarter-mile to the former site of Deer Springs Trail Camp. The camp, overused in past years, has been abandoned by Mount San Jacinto State Park. However, its all-year water supply and pleasant locale makes it an ideal lunch or rest stop.

To Little Round Valley Camp: A short walk up Deer Springs Trail from the former camp brings you to another junction. The leftward fork is Fuller Ridge Trail, which leads northwest 5 miles to Black Mountain

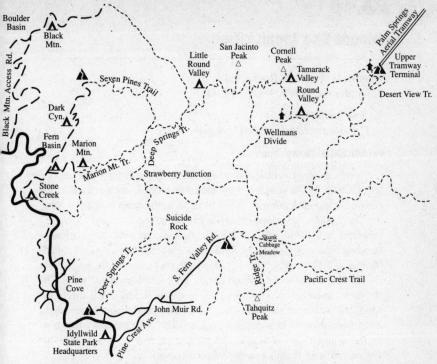

Camp. Bear right at this junction. The trail passes through some meadow-land on the way to Little Round Valley Trail Camp.

To Mount San Jacinto: From Little Round Valley, the trail climbs through stands of lodgepole pine, and in a little more than a mile arrives at a junction with San Jacinto Peak Trail. A left turn on this trail takes you a quarter-mile past a stone shelter cabin to the top of the 10,084-foot peak.

93

Mount San Jacinto Trail

Mountain Station to Round Valley
  4 miles round trip; 600-foot gain

To San Jacinto Peak
  11 miles round trip; 2,300-foot gain

Season: May-November

There's a strong geologic similarity between the High Sierra and the San Jacintos. While standing upon the summit of Mount San Jacinto, the perceptive mountaineer may notice a subtle atmospheric similarity—both the San Jacintos and Sierra Nevada can be called a "range of light." Powerful sunlight illuminates the San Jacintos, creating sharp contrasts between light and shadow, the kind of contrast found in an Ansel Adams photograph. There may be a six *f*-stop difference between the bright light shimmering on the rocky summit and the dark forest primeval below. The sun burns upon the lower slopes of Mount San Jacinto like a fire in the wind, but the upper elevations receive a more gentle incandescent light and a fraction of the heat dispersed below. Our civilization measures time by the sun, yet as you watch sunlight and shadow play tag across the slopes, you are left with a feeling of timelessness.

Directions to trailhead: From Interstate 10, exit on California 111 (the road to Palm Springs). Proceed nine miles to Tramway Road, turn right, and follow the road four miles to its end at Mountain Station. Contact the Tramway office for information about prices and schedules.

The Hike: From Mountain Station, walk down the cement walkway through the Long Valley Picnic Area. Soon you will arrive at the state park ranger station. Obtain a wilderness permit here.

Continue west on the trail, following the signs to Round Valley. The trail parallels Long Valley Creek through a mixed forest of pine and white fir, then climbs into lodgepole pine country. Lupine, monkeyflower, scarlet bugler and Indian paintbrush are some of the wildflowers that add seasonal splashes of color.

After passing a junction with a trail leading toward Willow Creek, another three-tenths of a mile of hiking brings you to Round Valley. There's a trail camp and a backcountry ranger station in the valley, and splendid places to picnic in the meadow or among the lodgepole pines. An alternative to returning the same way is to retrace your steps three-tenths of a mile back to the junction with the Willow Creek Trail, take this trail a mile through the pines to another signed trail north back to Long Valley

Mt. San Jacinto

Ranger Station. This alternative route adds only about a quarter-mile to your day hike, and allows you to make a loop.

To Mount San Jacinto Peak: From Round Valley, a sign indicates you may reach the peak by either Tamarack Valley or Wellman Divide Junction. Take the trail toward Wellman Divide Junction. From the Divide, a trail leads down to Humber Park. At the divide, you'll be treated to spectacular views of Tahquitz Peak and Red Tahquitz, as well as the more-distant Toro Peak and Santa Rosa Mountain. You continue toward the peak on some vigorous switchbacks. The lodgepole pines grow sparse among the crumbly granite. At another junction, a half-mile from the top, the trail continues to Little Round Valley but you take the summit trail to the peak. Soon you arrive at a stone shelter—an example of Civilian Conservation Corps handiwork during the 1930s—built for mountaineers who have the misfortune to be caught in winter storms. From the stone hut, you boulder-hop to the top of the peak.

The view from the summit—San Gorgonio Pass, the shimmering Pacific, the Colorado Desert, distant Mexico—has struck some visitors speechless, while other have been unable to controle their superlatives. Helen Hunt Jackson's heroine Ramona found "a remoteness from earth which comes only on mountain heights," and John Muir found the view "the most sublime spectacle to be found anywhere on this earth!"

249

94

Desert View Trail

Mountain Station to Desert View
 2 miles round trip

Mountain Station to Round Valley
 6 miles round trip; 500-foot gain

Season: May-November

For an introduction to the alpine environment of Mount San Jacinto State Park, take the short nature trail that begins at Mountain Station, then join Desert View Trail for a superb panorama of Palm Springs. You can extend your hike by looping through lush Round Valley.

Directions to trailhead: From Highway 111 at the northern outskirts of Palm Springs, turn southwest on Tramway Road and drive 3½ miles to the tramway terminal.

The Hike: From Mountain Station, walk down the paved pathway to the signed beginning of the trail to Desert View. You join the Nature Trail for a short distance, cross the path used by the "mule ride," and soon get the first of a couple great desert views. The view takes in Palm Springs, Tahquitz and other palm-lined canyons of the Agua Caliente Indian Reservation and the basin and hills of the Coachella Valley.

Continue on Desert View Trail, which makes a full circle and junctions with the path back up to Mountain Station. For a longer hike, walk through the Long Valley Picnic Area to the state park ranger station. Obtain a wilderness permit here.

Continue west on the trail, following the signs to Round Valley. The trail parallels Long Valley Creek through a mixed forest of pine and white fir, then climbs into lodgepole pine country. Lupine, monkeyflower, scarlet bugler and Indian paintbrush are some of the wildflowers that add seasonal splashes of color. After passing a junction with a trail leading toward Willow Creek, another ³/₁₀ mile of hiking brings you to Round Valley. There's a trail camp and a backcountry ranger station in the valley and splendid places to picnic in the meadow or among the lodgepole pines. The truly intrepid hiker will head for the summit of Mt. San Jacinto, a 3½ mile ascent from Round Valley.

An alternative to returning the same way is to retrace your steps ³/₁₀ of a mile back to the junction with Willow Creek Trail, take this trail a mile through the pines to another signed junction, and follow the signed trail north back to Long Valley Ranger Station. This alternative adds only about ¼ mile to your day hike and allows you to make a loop.

Palm Springs Aerial Tramway

95

Spitler Peak Trail

Apple Canyon to Desert Divide
  10 miles roundtrip; 2,000-foot gain

To Apache Peak
  12 miles round trip; 2,600-foot gain

To Antsell Rock
  14 miles round trip; 2,600-foot gain

Season: All year

Riding the Palm Springs Aerial Tramway or driving the Palms to Pines Highway are two ways to view the astonishing change in vegetation that occurs with a change in elevation in the San Jacinto Mountains. A third way to observe the startling contrast between desert and alpine environments is to hike up the back side of the San Jacinto Mountains to aptly named Desert Divide. The imposing granite divide, which reminds some mountaineers of the High Sierra, offers far-reaching views of the canyons back of Palm Springs and of the Coachella Valley.

Most visitors to the San Jacinto Mountains begin their explorations in Idyllwild or from the top of the tramway. Few hike—or even think about—Desert Divide. Too bad, because this land of pine forest, wide meadows and soaring granite peaks has much to offer.

The trail begins in Garner Valley, a long meadowland bordered by tall pine. Meandering across the valley floor is the South Fork of the San Jacinto River, whose waters are impounded at the lower end of the valley by Lake Hemet. Splashing spring color across the meadow are purple penstemon, golden yarrow, owl's clover and tidy tips. Autumn brings a showy "river" of rust-colored buckwheat winding through the valley.

Spitler Peak Trail offers a moderate-to-strenuous route up to Desert Divide. You can enjoy the great views from the divide and call it a day right there, or join Pacific Crest Trail and continue to the top of Apache Peak or Antsell Rock.

Directions to trailhead: The hamlet of Mountain Center is some 20 miles up Highway 74 from Hemet and a few miles up Highway 243 from Idyllwild. From the intersection of Highway 243 (Banning-Idyllwild Highway) and Highway 74 in Mountain Center, proceed southeast on the latter highway. After 3 miles, turn left at the signed junction for Hurkey Creek County Park. Instead of turning into the park, you'll continue 1¾ mile on Apple Canyon Road to signed Spitler Peak Trail on the right. Park in the turnout just south of the trailhead.

The Hike: Spitler Peak Trail begins among oak woodland and chaparral. The mellow, well-graded path contours quite some distance to the east before beginning a more earnest northerly ascent. Enjoy over-the-shoulder views of Lake Hemet and of Garner Valley. Actually, geologists say Garner Valley is not a valley at all but a graben, a long narrow area that downdropped between two bordering faults.

Garner Graben?

Nope, just doesn't have the right ring to it.

The trail climbs steadily into juniper-Jeffrey pine-Coulter pine forest. Most of the time your path is under conifers or the occasional oak. There always seem to be quite a number of deadfalls to climb over, climb under or walk around along this stretch of trail.

About a mile from the divide the going gets steeper and you rapidly gain elevation. Finally you gain the windblown divide just northwest of Spitler Peak and intersect signed Pacific Crest Trail. Enjoy the vistas of forest and desert. Picnic atop one of the divide's many rock outcroppings.

PCT, sometimes known as Desert Divide Trail in these parts, offers the energetic a range of options. PCT heads north and soon passes through a section of ghost forest—the charred result of the 1980 Palm Canyon Fire that roared up these slopes from Palm Springs. After a half-mile you'll pass a side trail that descends steeply another half-mile to Apache Springs. Another half-mile along the PCT brings you to a side trail leading up to bare 7,567-foot Apache Peak.

Another mile brings you to a point just below 7,720-foot Antsell Rock. Unless you're a very good rock climber, stay off the unstable slopes and avoid the urge to ascend to the very top of the rock.

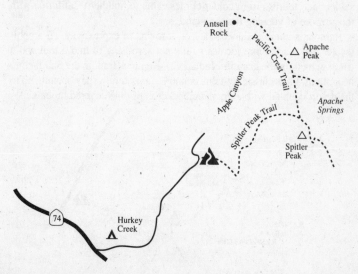

96

Ramona Trail

Highway 74 to Ramona Camp
  7 miles round trip; 1,400-foot gain

Highway 74 to Thomas Mountain
  11 miles round trip; 2,100-foot gain

Season: All year

For more than a century, the romantic novel *Ramona* has fascinated Southern Californians. Helen Hunt Jackson's 1884 saga of star-crossed Indian lovers and Spanish/Mission customs is the region's most enduring myth.

Señora Moreno's Southern California rancho is the setting for the story, which tells of the romance between half-Indian Ramona Ortega and her full-blooded Indian lover Alessandro. After Señora refuses Ramona permission to marry the Indian, the couple elopes, chased from place to place by evil, land-grabbing Americans. Poor shepherd Alessandro is killed, the rancho sold to American capitalists and Ramona is left broken-hearted.

Jackson had intended to write an *Uncle Tom's Cabin* of the Mission Indians. Some social critics thought she succeeded at this task while more conservative Southern Californians were appalled at her portrayal of race, religion and intolerance in the region. However, even dismayed members of the business community changed their point of view when hordes of settlers and tourists from colder climes came to Southern California with the purpose of viewing Ramona-land.

Ramona's name endures today on a town, an expressway, an amphitheater and many more locales so it's not surprising to find a trail and a camp named for the beautiful Indian girl. Ramona Trail, in the San Jacinto Mountains, tours classic Ramona country—a pastoral valley opening up to the desert coupled with a dramatic backdrop of pine covered mountains.

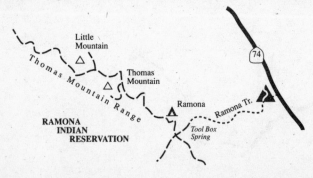

*Ramona is remembered
with a pageant in Hemet
and a scenic trail*

Ramona Trail climbs to a divide where Tool Box Spring offers water and Ramona Camp some welcome shade. Pack your copy of *Ramona* and read it under the pines.

Directions to trailhead: Drive to Mountain Center, some 20 miles up Highway 74 from Hemet, or a few miles from Idyllwild on Highway 243. From the junction of 243 and 74 proceed southeast on the latter highway 8 miles to the signed Ramona trailhead. Park in a safe manner along the highway.

The Hike: Begin at a gate across a dirt road. Pass through the gate and walk along the dirt road a hundred yards or so to the unsigned Ramona Trail departing from the left side of the dirt road.

The well-engineered path switchbacks gently up hillside of sage, manzanita and red shank. The latter plant, also called ribbonwood for the way its bark peels off in long strips, is the dominant plant on the lower slopes of Thomas Mountain. Enjoy good views of Garner Valley and the Desert Divide area of the San Jacintos.

About 2 miles along, Ramona Trail enters a cool Jeffrey pine forest. Just over 3 miles from the trailhead, the trail joins a dirt road and almost immediately arrives at Tool Box Spring. Fill your canteen from the water spigot and continue on the dirt road ¼ mile to Ramona Camp. Tables scattered amongst the pines suggest a picnic.

While the dirt fire road offers pleasant, pine-shaded walking, it's open to vehicles. (Traffic is rare.) Follow the road 1½ miles to a junction, then turn left another half-mile to the summit. The views of Ramona Country include a look down at Anza Valley.

Doane Valley, Palomar Mountain State Park

10. Palomar Mountains

THE PALOMAR MOUNTAINS, extending twenty-five miles along the northern boundary of San Diego County, are one of the few Southern California mountain ranges not bordering the desert. The range is an uplifted block with distinct fault lines on both the north and south sides. The north and south slopes are quite precipitous as a result of these faults.

Three major ridges make up the Palomars. A long ridge near the Observatory rises to the range's highest point, unimaginatively named "High Point" (6,126 feet). A western ridge, protected by a federal wilderness area, is called Agua Tibia and the rocky ridge east of high point is Aguanga Mountain.

Indians called the Palomars, "Pauuw," which means quite simply, "mountains." The Spanish noticed a large number of band-tailed pigeons in the area and named the mountains Palomar, "pigeon roost."

During the 1890s the Palomars were a popular vacation spot. Hotels and a tent city welcomed mountain lovers. When automania took hold in the teens and twenties, vacationers were lured to farther and more exotic locales. The Palomars reverted to semi-wilderness, undeveloped land thick with private property signs.

The Palomars were dubbed the "Mystery Moutains" because few people lived there when plans for Palomar Observatory were formulated. Access to the range was difficult. Cars had to climb up a steep, nerve-wracking grade. Motorists descending the grade tied trees to their car bumpers to slow their descent. Trees discarded at the bottom of the hill supplied local Indians with firewood for a long time. A new south-grade road, the "Highway to the Stars," was built to the observatory site and opened up the mountains to visitors.

The beauty of the Palomars is entrusted to Palomar Mountain State Park and the Cleveland National Forest. Considering the mountains' pristine beauty and popularity with visitors, it's surprising that there isn't an extensive trail network. However, the few trails take hikers through diverse ecosystems. Moist high-altitude environments, characteristic of coastal ranges much farther north, are found on upper Palomar slopes. Lower, sun-drenched slopes host a chaparral community typical of Southern California mountains. Whether you hike through blue lupine on sunny slopes or tiger lilies in the shade, manzanita on dry slopes or azalea in damp canyons, a hike in San Diego County's "Mystery Mountains" is a memorable event.

97

Dripping Springs Trail

Dripping Springs to Giant Chaparral
   7 miles round trip; 1,200-foot gain

To Palomar Divide Truck Trail
   13 miles round trip; 2,800-foot gain

Season: November-June

Agua Tibia, place of tepid waters, refers to a warm spring at the foot of the mountains used by the Indians for their health. Today, Agua Tibia is the name given to a mountain and a wilderness on the border of Riverside and San Diego counties in the Cleveland National Forest.

The Agua Tibia Wilderness Area is on the northwest crest of the Palomar Mountains. The rugged area, three by five miles, seems inhospitable at first or even second glance. The slopes are covered with thorny chaparral. Stream erosion has carved deep and precipitous canyons. Temperatures exceed 100 degrees in summer and as much as two feet of snow may fall on an open ridge in winter. Despite outward appearances, this land of radical temperatures and odd foliage has much to offer the hiker.

Dripping Springs Trail takes you to an area of giant chaparral. Huge manzanita have miraculously escaped the ravages of fire for more than 100 years. Following the Dripping Springs Trail all the way to the abandoned Palomar Divide Fire Road brings you to oak- and pine-dotted upper slopes that give you a panoramic view of the San Jacintos and San Bernardinos.

Directions to trailhead: From Interstate Highway 15, exit east on Highway 79. Proceed 10 miles to the Dripping Springs Campground on your right. Signed Dripping Springs Trail begins at the south end of the campground. Near the entrance to the campground is a Forest Service station, where you may obtain a wilderness permit.

The Hike: Dripping Springs Trail immediately crosses the only water en route, Arroyo Seco Creek. It climbs south and southwest, switchbacking forever and ever up one false summit after another on the north side of Agua Tibia Mountain (4,779 feet). Look over your shoulder and you'll see Vail Lake and the mighty San Jacintos. Only the buzzing of a multitude of bees breaks the silence. In this land of little shade, uninterrupted views are provided of San Jacinto Peak to the northeast, San Gorgonio Peak to the north, and Mount Baldy to the northwest.

You arrive at the Giant Chaparral 3½ miles from the trailhead. Twenty-foot manzanita reside in an area watered by a seasonal, undependable spring. Usually when you look at manzanita, you have difficulty deciding whether it's a tree or a shrub. Botanists say it's officially a shrub, but these specimens in the Agua Tibia Wilderness Area are tree-sized and shaped. In winter, white flowers tinged with pink decorate the red-brown bark. It's a tree . . . er, shrub that's particularly well-adapted to its environment. In hot weather, the simple oval leaves turn on their sides, pointing their edges at the sun. In this way, the manzanita keeps its water supply from evaporating.

Return the same way or continue on the Dripping Springs Trail to higher and greener Agua Tibia slopes.

To Palomar Divide Truck Trail: A half-mile beyond the Giant Chaparral, the trail descends and you get a view southeast over the Palomars. Crowning a far-off ridge, the silver dome of Palomar Observatory sparkles in the sun. You begin switchbacking again and rise above the chaparral to oak- and pine-dotted slopes. Three miles from the Giant Chaparral, the Dripping Springs Trail intersects the Palomar Divide Truck Trail. From the truck trail, you can look over distant peaks and valley and occasionally glimpse the Pacific Ocean, 40 miles away. If you turn left at the truck trail and walk yet another mile, you'll reach a primitive campsite, just as the truck trail begins to head west.

98

Observatory Trail

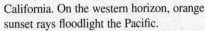

Observatory Campground to Palomar Observatory
  4 miles round trip; 800-foot gain

Season: All year

Astronomer George Hale will be remembered both for his scientific discoveries and his vision of constructing great observatories. His first vision materialized as the Yerkes Observatory with its 40-inch telescope, his second as Mount Wilson Observatory with its 60- and 100-inch telescopes, and finally Palomar Observatory with its 200-inch telescope. The Great Glass at Palomar is the most most powerful telescope in America and has done more to increase our knowledge of the heavens than any other instrument.

Most visitors traveling to Palomar drive their cars all the way to the top, visit the Observatory and drive back down. Too bad! They miss a nice hike. Observatory Trail roughly parallels the road, but is hidden by a dense forest from the sights and sounds of traffic.

Palomar Mountain doesn't have the distinct cone shape of a stereotypical mountain top. It soars abruptly up from the San Luis River Valley to the south, but flattens out on top. Atop and just below the long crest, are oak valleys, pine forests, spring-watered grasslands and lush canyons.

All the great views from the top do not come from the Hale telescope. Palomar Mountain provides a bird's-eye-view of much of Southern California. Miles and miles of mountains roll toward the north, dominated in the distance by the San Bernardino Mountain peaks. Southward, Mount Cuyamaca is visible, and even farther south, the mountains of Baja

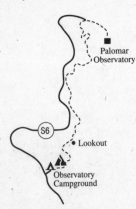

California. On the western horizon, orange sunset rays floodlight the Pacific.

Observatory Trail, designated a National Recreation Trail by the Forest Service, is a delightful introduction to the geography of the Palomar Mountains. It takes you from Observatory Campground to the peak, where you can learn about the geography of the heavens.

Directions to trailhead: From Interstate Highway 15, exit on Highway 76 east. Proceed to Rincon Springs. For a couple of miles, S6 joins with Highway 76. Continue on S6, forking to the left at South Grade

View from Palomar Observatory Trail

Road (Highway to the Stars). South Grade winds steeply to Observatory Campground and up to the Observatory. Turn right into Observatory Campground. The Forest Service charges a day use fee. The campground closes in mid-December for the winter. Follow the campground road until you spot the signed trailhead between campsites 19 and 20. The Forest Service booklet "Guide to the Observatory Trail," which highlights flora and fauna found along the trail, is available at the trailhead.

You could just as well hike the Observatory Trail from top to bottom and have a friend or family member pick you up at the bottom. To reach the upper trailhead, simply continue up the road to the Observatory parking area. The top of the trail is just outside the gates of the Observatory grounds.

The Hike: The signed trail begins at the edge of the campground. You begin climbing over wooded slopes and soon get a grand view of Mendenhall Valley. You continue ascending over slopes watered by the headwaters of the San Luis Rey River. As the legend goes, young Indian girls visited one of the trickling mountain springs whose waters rushed over beautiful slender stones. The maidens would reach into the water to gather these stones, the number found indicating the number of children she would bear.

The last part of the trail climbs more abruptly up manzanita-covered slopes. Soon you see the silvery dome of the Hale telescope. This obelisk of symmetry and precision dwarfs nearby trees. Ever-changing patterns of sunlight and shade play upon the top of the dome.

Visit the Observatory gallery to see the great telescope. And take a look at the nearby museum whose exhibits explain some of the mysteries unraveled by the 200-inch lens.

99

Scott's Cabin Trail

**Silver Crest Picnic Area to Scott's Cabin, Cedar Grove
Campground, Boucher Lookout**
  3½ mile-loop; 800-foot gain

Season: All year

Palomar Mountain is a state park for all seasons. Fall offers dramatic color changes, and blustery winter winds ensure far-reaching views from the peaks. In spring, the dogwood blooms, and during summer, when temperatures soar, the park offers a cool, green retreat.

A mixed forest of cedar, silver fir, spruce and black oak invites a leisurely exploration. Tall trees and mountain meadows make the park especially attractive to Southern California day hikers in search of a Sierra Nevada-like atmosphere.

The discovery of bedrock mortars and artifacts in Doane Valley indicate that Indians lived in this area of the Palomars for many hundreds of years. The mountains' pine and fir trees were cut for the construction of Mission San Luis Rey. Remote Palomar Mountain meadows were a favorite hiding place for cattle and horse thieves, who pastured their stolen animals in the high country until it was safe to sneak them across the border.

This day hike, a 3½-mile loop, is a *grande randonnée* of the park, a four-trail sampler that leads to a lookout atop 5,438-foot Boucher Hill.

Directions to trailhead: From Interstate 5 in Oceanside, drive northeast on State Highway 76 about 30 miles. Take County Road S6 north; at S7, head northwest to the park entrance. There is a day use fee. Park in the lot at Silver Crest Picnic Area just inside the park. Scott's Cabin Trail takes off from the right side of the road about 20 yards beyond the lot entrance.

The Hike: A trail sign points the way to Scott's Cabin, a half-mile away. Noisome Stellar's jays make their presence known along this stretch of trail. Scott's Cabin, built by a homesteader in the 1880s, is found on your left. The crumpled remains aren't much to look at.

You'll descend steeply through a white fir forest and reach the signed jucntion with the Cedar-Doane Trail, which heads right (east). This steep trail, formerly known as the Slide Trail because of its abruptness, takes the hiker down oak-covered slopes to Doane Pond. The pond is stocked with trout, and fishing is permitted. A pond-side picnic area welcomes the hiker.

Continue past the Cedar-Doane Trail junction a short distance to Cedar Grove Campground. Follow the trail signs and turn left on the campground road, and then right into the group campground. Look leftward for

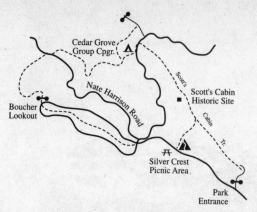

the signed Adams Trail, which cuts through a bracken fern-covered meadow. Once across the meadow, you'll encounter a small ravine where dogwood blooms during April and May. The trail winds uphill past some big cone spruce and reaches Nate Harrison Road.

The road is named in honor of Nathan Harrison, a Southern slave who followed his master to the California gold rush—and freedom—in 1849. Harrison laid claim to a homestead on the wild eastern edge of what is now state parkland, and had a successful hay-making and hog-raising operation, despite numerous run-ins with bears and mountain lions.

Across the road, your path becomes Boucher Trail, which ascends a north-facing slope through white fir, then through bracken ferns and black oaks, to the summit of Boucher Hill.

Atop the hill is a fire lookout and microwave facility. From the summit, you get a view of the surrounding lowlands, including Pauma Valley to the west.

Return to the parking area via Oak Ridge Trail, which descends one mile between the two sides of the loop road that encircles Boucher Hill. The trail heads down an open ridgeline to a junction of five roads, where it's a mere hop, skip and a jump back to the Silver Crest Picnic Area.

11. Cuyamaca Mountains

DIGUEÑO INDIANS called the range "Ah-ha Kwe-ah-mac," which meant "no rain behind." The ancients were accurate observers, for the Cuyamacas seem to gather all storm clouds around their summits and then ration the rain among themselves. Residents on the desert side of the mountains can only gaze forlornly up at the thunderheads; the Cuyamacas see to it that not one drop falls on the vast sandscape to the east.

Plentiful rain and the Cuyamacas' geographical location between coast and desert make these mountains a unique ecosystem. The 4,000 to 6,500-foot peaks host rich forests of ponderosa and Jeffrey pine, fir and incense cedar, as well as some wonderful specimens of live and black oak. In lower elevations, broad grasslands stretch toward the horizon. The Cuyamacas are a delight for bird-watchers because desert, coastal and mountain species are all found in the range.

In 1845, the Mexican government deeded Rancho Cuyamaca to Don Augustín Olvera (the same Spanish don of Olvera Street fame in Los Angeles). Olvera sold the rancho in 1869 for $1,000. Unfortunately for him, gold was discovered on the land a year later. Hundreds of Yankee and Chinese prospectors poured into the mountains. The Americans forced the Indians to move onto a reservation and give up their ancient ways. The Stonewall Mine near Cuyamaca Lake was one of the most successful hardrock mines. It produced over $2,000,000 worth of gold. The gold boom lasted only a decade; most prospectors moved on to Tombstone in 1888.

The rancho property passed through the hands of banks and businessmen before being purchased by the Dyar family. During the Depression, the Dyars generously sold their rancho to the state for half its appraised value, thus founding Cuyamaca Rancho State Park. A good portion of the Cuyamaca Mountains are protected by the state park and William Heise County Park.

More than 110 miles of hiking trails pass through the old rancho. The Cuyamacas offer four-season hiking at its colorful best: fall with its brown, yellow and crimson leaves; winter snows on the higher peaks; spring with its wildflowers; and sudden summer thunderstorms.

100

Kelly Ditch Trail

Cuyamaca Rancho State Park to William Heise Park
11 miles round trip; 1,200-foot gain

Season: All year

One of the Southland's most splendid autumn pathways is the Kelly Ditch Trail, which travels from Cuyamaca Reservoir at the north end of the state park to William Heise Park. Enroute, you'll cross mile-high slopes, which host rich forests of ponderosa and Jeffrey pine, fir and incense cedar, as well as some wonderful specimens of live and black oak.

Kelly Ditch Trail is so-named because it follows Kelly Ditch, a century-old waterworks project. Chinese laborers dug a ditch in order to channel runoff from the Cuyamaca Mountains into the then newly-formed Cuyamaca Reservoir.

Kelly Ditch Trail can be a one-way day hike. You can begin at the state park trailhead and arrange to be picked up a few hours later at William Heise Park, operated by San Diego County. Most hikers will prefer beginning at the state park end of the trail because the route will be mostly downhill.

Directions to trailhead: From Julian, drive eight miles south on State Highway 79. As you reach Cuyamaca Reservoir, just past the point where Engineers Road crosses the highway, you'll see a state park boundary sign and another sign that reads "Trail." Park in a safe manner on the shoulder of the highway.

If you're planning a one-way hike, here's how to get to William Heise Park: Drive one mile west of Julian on State Highway 78/79. Turn south on Pine Hills Road and proceed four miles, following signs to the park. Kelly Ditch Trail departs from the picnic area near the park entry kiosk.

The Hike: The trail crests a low rise and promptly descends into the historic ditch. Oaks and tall brush overhang the ditch and for a mile you feel as if you're walking in a tunnel. Sometimes you parallel the ditch and sometimes you walk in the ditch itself. Through gaps in the oak canopy, you get glimpses of nearby canyons aflame with fall color and when the light is just right—the blue Pacific.

After a mile, the ditch continues, but the trail turns north and ascends over a manzanita-covered slope. Soon you'll cross paved Engineers Road and pick up the trail again on the other side near a horse trough.

At an unsigned junction, the trail meets an old dirt road. Bear right on the dirt road, which curves up and around a forested slope of North Peak. You hike through a pastoral Southern California that you thought had

disappeared a hundred years ago. Gnarled old oaks stand above a blanket of ferns and dry grasses, autumn-colored in soft shades of yellow and brown. After a few more bends in the road, you pass through a handsome stand of sugar pine.

About 2½ miles from the trailhead, you'll encounter another unsigned junction. Stay left and continue on the more well-traveled road, which soon becomes a trail and descends to a grassy area.

Your descent to William Heise Park begins on an acorn- and pine needle-covered trail that travels through a forest of black oaks, ponderosa and Coulter pine, and cedar. Two miles of steep switchbacks and a thousand-foot elevation loss brings you to Cedar Creek. The trail climbs out of the creek bed, descends ½ mile on a dirt road, then climbs another ½ mile to the picnic area in William Heise Park.

Round trip hikers will gather their strength for the return to Cuyamaca Rancho State Park, while those employing a car shuttle will relax in pretty William Heise Park.

101

Middle Peak Trail

Middle Peak Trail
5¾-mile loop through Cuyamaca Rancho State Park

Season: All year

Middle Peak, in the middle of the Cuyamaca Mountains in the middle of San Diego County, is the place for a summer saunter if you like tall trees. Encircling the peak are big specimens of silver fir and cedar, plus Coulter, sugar, ponderosa and Jeffrey pine.

Centerpiece of the park—and of the Cuyamaca Mountains —is a chain of three forested peaks: North, Middle and Cuyamaca. Cuyamaca Peak, at 6,512 feet high, is the highest summit in the range and offers the best views. Most of North Peak (5,993 feet) is on private property. Middle Peak (5,883 feet) has the best trail network, the tallest trees.

The hike around Middle Peak uses several different trails. One good path that ascends the north side of the peak is Sugar Pine Trail. Utilizing this trail and a couple of others, it's possible to make several loops of varying distances around Middle Peak.

Directions to trailhead: This hike begins at a parking area off Highway 79 in Cuyamaca Rancho State Park. The parking area is opposite the Boy Scouts' Camp Hual-Cu-Cuisi. If you're traveling Highway 79 south to the state park, the trailhead is some ten miles from Julian. If you're heading north on Highway 79, the trailhead is located 5 miles north of park head-quarters and 1½ miles north of the entrance to Paso Pichacho Camp/Picnic Area. Parking is located at a nearly right-angle bend in the highway.

The end of the trail is easy to spot; it's the road across from the parking area that leads through the Boy Scout camp. The unsigned beginning of the trail is more difficult to find. Look on the left (west) side of Highway 79 for a path that parallels the highway. Can't find it? Walk 75 yards or so north up the highway, then head left, dip in and out of a roadside drainage ditch, and you'll pick up the trail heading north.

The Hike: Minshall is the name of the unsigned trail that parallels Highway 79. Looking east, the most obvious geographical feature is Cuyamaca Reservoir. Before the dam was built creating the reservoir, Cuyamaca Lake, as it was called, was a sometimes affair. Indians never trusted it as a dependable water source and the Spanish referred to it as *la laguna que de seco*, "the lake that dries up." During dry years, there's more meadow than reservoir.

After a half mile, the trail skirts Lakeland Resort and turns west. Signs inform you that you're now on the way to Middle Peak and that you're

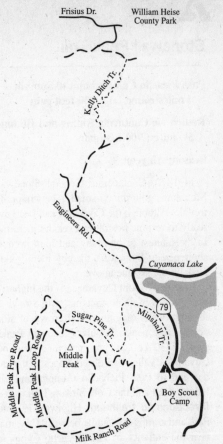

entering a state park wilderness area. Your path, a retiring dirt road now known as Sugar Pine Trail, begins ascending into the pines. At lower elevation, the pines mix it up with oak woodland.

A short mile's ascent on Sugar Pine Trail brings you a a junction with Middle Peak Fire Road. If a three-mile loop is plenty for you this day, turn left on the fire road and follow it down to the Boy Scout Camp and the trailhead.

Otherwise continue on Sugar Pine Trail past some fine specimens of Southern California's largest native pine. The bark of these trees is reddish brown and deeply furrowed into scaly plates. Sugar pines have larger branches and cones than their somewhat similar-looking Middle Peak neighbors—the ponderosa pines.

Nearing the halfway point of the hike, the trail passes the stone foundation ruins of an old cabin, turns southwest and comes to a signed junction. You join Middle Peak Loop Road, which at first curves west then heads south. Middle Peak itself is possible to ascend, but trees and shrubs prevent any kind of view of Cuyamaca country.

Middle Peak Loop Road descends out of the pines to Milk Ranch Road. Bear left on this dirt fire road which crosses oak-dotted meadowland. You'll get a feeling for the "rancho" part of the state park. The dirt road becomes gravel, skirts the Boy Scout Camp and brings you back to Highway 79 and the trailhead.

102

Stonewall Peak Trail

Paso Picacho Campground to Summit
  4 miles round trip; 900-foot gain

Return via California Riding and Hiking Trail, Cold Stream Trail
  5½ miles; 900-foot gain

Season: All year

In 1870, Confederate General Stonewall Jackson had a Cuyamaca Mountains gold mine named in his honor. The name immediately caused trouble. Although the Civil War had been over for five years, miners were ready to resume hostilities over the mere mention of the general's name. In the interest of harmony and high productivity, the mine's name was shortened to Stonewall, thereby identifying it with the prominent stony peak on the skyline above.

Rounded Mount Cuyamaca is the highest peak in the range, but Stonewall Peak is more prominent. "Old Stony" is about 1,000 feet lower, but its huge walls of granite and crown of stone make it stand out among neighboring peaks. Popular Stonewall Peak Trail leads to the top of the peak (5,730 feet) and presents grand views of the old Stonewall Mine Site, Cuyamaca Valley and desert slopes to the east. An optional route lets you descend to Paso Pichacho Campground via the California Riding and Hiking Trail and the Cold Stream Trail.

Directions to trailhead: Highway 79 enters Cuyamaca Rancho State Park and climbs to a saddle between Cuyamaca and Stonewall peaks. Park near the entrance of Paso Picacho Campground. The trail to Stonewall Peak begins just across the highway from the campground.

The Hike: From Paso Picacho Campground, the trail ascends moderately, then steeply through oak and boulder country. The black oaks display vivid fall colors.

The trail switchbacks up the west side of the mountain. Hike through a thick cluster of incense cedar and when you emerge from the spicy-smelling trees, views from the north unfold. Cuyamaca Reservoir is the most obvious geographical feature. Before a dam was built to create the reservoir Cuyamaca Lake, as it was called, was a sometime affair. The Indians never trusted it as a dependable water source and the Spanish referred to it as *la laguna que de seco*, or "the lake that dries up." During dry years, the cows enjoy more meadow than reservoir and during wet years, have more reservoir than meadow.

Vegetation grows more sparse and granite outcroppings dominate the high slopes as the trail nears the top of Old Stony. A hundred feet from the summit, a guardrail with steps hacked into the granite helps you reach the top. Far-reaching views to the east and west are not possible because a number of close-in mountains block your view. You can, however, orient yourself to Cuyamaca geography from atop Stonewall Peak. Major Cuyamaca peaks, from north to south, are North Peak, Middle Peak and Cuyamaca Peak.

It's exciting to be atop Stonewall Peak when a storm is brewing over the Cuyamacas, but use utmost caution. The peak has been known to catch a strike or two. Black clouds hurtle at high speed toward the peak. Just as they are about to collide with the summit, an updraft catches them and they zoom up and over your head.

To return via California Riding and Hiking Trail: Backtrack 100 yards on Stonewall Peak Trail to an unsigned junction. From here, bear right (north). The trail descends steeply at first, then levels off near Little Stonewall Peak (5,250 feet). It then descends moderately to the California Riding and Hiking Trail, a long trail that runs through San Diego and Riverside Counties. This trail traverses the west side of the park. You travel for one mile on the California Riding and Hiking Trail, which is actually part of the Stonewall Peak Trail. It forks to the right and crosses Highway 79. Don't take the fork, but continue a half-mile down the Cold Stream Trail, paralleling the highway, back to Paso Picacho Campground.

103

Cuyamaca Peak Trail

Paso Picacho Campground to Summit
  6 miles round trip; 1,600-foot gain

Season: All year

Of the more than 100 miles of trails in Cuyamaca Rancho State Park, the route offering the most spectacular views is surely the three-mile-long Cuyamaca Peak Trail, which climbs through a forest of oak, pine and fir past Deer Spring to the summit. From the 6,512-foot peak, the hiker has an open view from the Pacific to the Salton Sea.

Most day hikers are surprised to find such a densely forested mountain in Southern California. Encircling Mount Cuyamaca are silver fir and cedar, plus Coulter, sugar, ponderosa and Jeffrey pine.

Indian legend has it that many more high peaks were once in the Cuyamaca Range, but the peaks took to quarreling amongst themselves. One troublemaking peak, Hilsh-ki-e (Pine Tree) battled the rest, who belched rocks upon his head. In the heat of battle, Hilsh-ki-e twisted the neck of Pook-k-sqwee, which acquired the name of Crooked Neck during this battle and is now known as Mount Cuyamaca. Hilsh-ki-e retreated and was exiled to lower elevation.

The trail, Cuyamaca Peak Fire Road, is a paved one-lane road (closed to public vehicle traffic) that winds slowly to the summit. While this guide and its author generally avoid pavement like the plague, an exception has been made for this road; it offers a most enjoyable hike and view.

Directions to trailhead: You may begin this hike from two places, neither of which has good parking. The Cuyamaca Peak Fire Road intersects Highway 79 just south of the park interpretive center. Look for a legal place to park along Highway 79. Or you can pick up the trail at the southernmost campsites in Paso Picacho Campground. There's a state park day use fee.

The Hike: The ascent, shaded by oaks, is moderate at first. Look over your shoulder for a fine view of Stonewall Peak. After passing the junction with the California Riding and Hiking Trail, the route grows steeper. Pine and fir predominate high on the mountain's shoulders.

Just about at the halfway point, the road levels out for a short distance and you'll spot Deer Spring on the left (south) side of the road. Cool and delicious water gushes from a pipe.

As you near the top, better and better views of Cuyamaca Reservoir and the desert are yours. The road veers suddenly south, passes junctions with Conejos Trail and Burnt Pine Fire Road, and arrives at the summit.

The peak, located nearly in the exact center of San Diego County, provides quite a panorama. Because of the fire lookout, antennae and trees on top, you'll have to walk around the peak a bit and get your panoramic view in pieces. Some of the highlights include the Santa Rosa and Laguna mountains. You can look across the desert into Mexico and westward over to Point Loma, the Silver Strand and the wide Pacific. Atop Mount Palomar, the white observatory can be seen sparkling in the distance.

Return the same way, or perhaps improvise a return route back to Paso Picacho Campground via the California Riding and Hiking Trail and the Azalea Glen Trail.

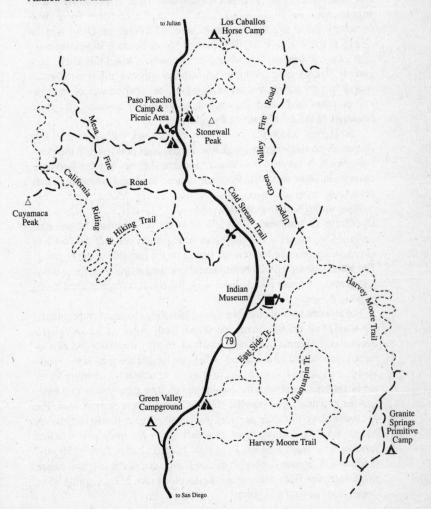

104

Harvey Moore Loop Trail

Loop through Cuyamaca Rancho State Park
  12 miles round trip; 1,000-foot gain

Season: All year

Harvey Moore Trail honors a 20th-Century cowboy who became the first superintendent of Cuyamaca Rancho State Park. Moore cowboyed all over the West before becoming ranch foreman for the Ralph Dyars, who owned the Cuyamaca Ranch from 1923 to 1933. When the Dyars sold the rancho to the state in 1933, they insisted Moore be made superintendent.

It's easy to see why Moore and other cowboys loved this idyllic cow country. The Cuyamacas differ from other Southern California mountain ranges in one aspect: instead of being an elevated tumble of boulder-strewn peaks and steep canyons, they are grassy rolling hills where boulders are the exception, not the rule.

The Harvey Moore Trail is a tour of the park's life zones; rolling chaparral, manzanita groves, oak woodlands, grass prairies, lush meadow-land. Not only are the zones readily apparent, but the way the landscape changes in response to sunlight and shade, wind and water, is clearly observable from the trail. Traveling the Harvey Moore Trail is like walking through a living ecology guide.

Directions to trailhead: The trailhead is just off Highway 79, one mile south of Cuyamaca Rancho State Park headquarters or a half-mile north of Green Valley near the Sweetwater Bridge on the east side of the highway.

The Hike: The signed trail begins just above the parking area. Since this is a loop trail, you may hike it either way; the climb is more gradual if you begin to the right (south).

The trail heads south, then west through rolling chaparral and continues a gradual climb through an oak woodland. Keep an eye out for the colorful deciduous California black oak. In winter, its very dark bark and almost-barren branches stand in majestic silhouette against the gray sky. In early spring, the young shoots are pink or crimson. In summer, the mature leaves are bright green, and with the coming of fall, they glow yellow and red.

After two miles, you pass the junction with the Dyar Springs Trail. The junctions along this hike are very well marked with handsome Harvey Moore Trail signs emblazoned in split logs. A half-mile past this first junction, you reach another. Bear right toward Granite Spring. Shortly, you arrive at Granite Springs Primitive Camp, one of the two trail camps in the state park. This shady spot is perfect for a picnic. Tasty spring water comes from an old hand pump.

Beyond Granite Spring, you rejoin the main trail, actually the East Mesa Fire Road. The East Mesa country that you'll be walking in for the next several miles is well-watered upland hosting wild oats, mustard and in spring, splashes of wildflowers. In the morning and late afternoon, deer move silently through the tall waving grasses. Several Indian villages were once in the East Mesa area.

The Harvey Moore Trail leaves behind the East Mesa Fire Road, continues north through lush meadowland, then begins to climb up mixed pine and oak slopes. The trail zigzags steeply down to Harper Creek, crosses the creek, and heads down-canyon. It then drops down the canyons and in a mile, joins the creek, where there's a junction. The Harvey Moore Trail goes to the right and soon arrives at a main road just north of park headquarters. Bear left on the East Side Trail, cross the creek, and begin hiking through the grassy Sweetwater River basin. The grassland is cut with numerous minor trails, but you really can't get lost if you remember to keep the river on your right. It's easy, nearly level hiking back to the trailhead.

12. Southern California Coast

FOR THE DAY HIKER, the Southern California Coast offers not only those white sand beaches depicted on postcards, but a wide variety of shoreline features—the palms of La Jolla and Santa Monica, the cliffs of Torrey Pines and Palos Verdes.

The air and water temperatures are Mediterranean, the place names Spanish. Southland beaches are an attraction for visitors (foreign and domestic) who come for the sun, the fun and depending on age and orientation, the historical romance or the cutting-edge trendiness of the coast.

Each of the Southland's five coastal counties—San Diego, Orange, Los Angeles, Ventura and Santa Barbara—has its own character. And each beach seems to have its own personality as well—best surfing, clearest water, panoramic view, most bird life, etc.

It is said that California began in San Diego, when Portuguese navigator Juan Rodríguez Cabrillo landed on Pt. Loma in 1542. The beaches near the Mexican border are wide sandy stretches. From Point Loma to La Jolla, rocks and reefs carve the oceanfront into a series of pocket beaches, dramatically altering waves and currents so that a few feet of movement can transport a hiker from a safe swimming area to a paradise for surfers to a frothy, wave-swept cauldron.

Although it shares a single coastal plain with neighboring Los Angeles County, Orange County retains a distinct shoreline identity as a boating community (Newport Harbor), a surfing community (Huntington Beach), and as place much sought-after for recreation and residence.

When the summer sun beats down on the metropolis and smog thickens, it seems half the Basin and San Fernando Valley flee to Los Angeles County's seventy-four miles of coastline. Perhaps a hundred million visits a year are made to county beaches, although, as hikers soon discover, most cluster blanket to blanket on the same beaches, leaving less accessible areas to those willing to hike. Among the hike-able locales are Palos Verdes Peninsula and the rugged bluffs north of Malibu.

Ventura County's 43 miles of shoreline offers several fine sandy beaches. The best ones are in state parks: Point Mugu, McGrath, San Buenaventura and Emma Wood.

From Carpinteria west, the Santa Barbara County shoreline extends to Point Conception, one sandy and mellow beach after another. The coastline's southern exposure results in clearer water, smoother sand, warmer sun. In the northern part of the county some hidden beach treasures await those willing to venture off the beaten track.

105

Point Sal Trail

Point Sal State Beach to Point Sal
  5 miles round trip

Season: All year

When your eye travels down a map of Central California coast, you pause on old and familiar friends—the state beaches at San Simeon, Morro Bay, and Pismo Beach. Usually overlooked is another state beach—remote Point Sal, a nub of land north of Vandenberg Air Force Base and south of the Guadalupe Dunes.

Windy Point Sal is a wall of bluffs rising 50 to 100 feet above the rocky shore. The water is crystal-clear, and the blufftops provide a fine spot to watch the boisterous seals and sea lions.

Point Sal was named by explorer Vancouver in 1792 for Hermenegildo Sal, at that time commandante of San Francisco, The state purchased the land in the 1940s. There are no facilities whatsoever at the beach, so remember, if you pack it in, pack it out.

This hike travels Point Sal State Beach, then takes to the bluffs above rocky reefs. At low tide, you can pass around or over the reefs; at high tide the only passage is along the bluff trail. Both marine life and land life can be observed from the bluff trail. You'll pass a seal haul-out, tidepools, sight gulls, cormorants and pelicans, and perhaps see deer, bobcat and coyote on the ocean-facing slopes of the Casmalia Hills.

The trail system in the Point Sal area is in rough condition. The narrow bluff trails should not be undertaken by novice hikers, the weak-kneed or those afraid of heights. Families with small children and less experienced trekkers will enjoy beachcombing and tidepool-watching opportunities at Point Sal and the pleasure of discovering this out-of-the-way beach.

Directions to trailhead: From Highway 101 in Santa Maria, exit on Betteravia Road. Proceed west past a commercial strip and then out into the sugar beet fields. Betteravia Road twists north. About eight miles from Highway 101, turn left on Brown Road. Five miles of driving on Brown Road (watch for cows wandering along the road) brings you to a signed junction; leftward is a ranch road, but you bear right on Point Sal Road, partly paved, partly dirt washboard (impassable in wet weather). Follow this road 5 miles to its end at the parking area above Point Sal State Beach.

Be advised that Point Sal Road is sometimes closed during the rainy season. The Air Force sometimes closes the road for short periods during its missile launches.

The Hike: From the parking area, follow one of the short steep trails down to the beautiful crescent-shaped beach. Hike up-coast along the windswept beach. In ¹/₃ mile, you'll reach the end of the beach at a rocky reef, difficult to negotiate at high tide. A second reef, encountered shortly after the first, is equally difficult. Atop this reef, there's a rope secured to an iron stake to aid your descent to the beach below. The rope is also helpful in ascending the reef on your return.

Unless it's very low tide, you'll want to begin following the narrow bluff trail above the reefs. The trail arcs westward with the coast, occasionally dipping down to rocky and romantic pocket beaches sequestered between reefs.

About 1½ miles from the trailhead, you'll descend close to shore and begin boulder-hopping. After a few hundred yards of boulder-hopping, you'll begin to hear the bark of sea lions and get an aviator's view of Lion Rock, where the gregarious animals bask in the sun. Also be on the lookout for harbor seals, often called leopard seals because of their silver, white, or even yellow spots.

Your trek continues on a pretty decent bluff trail, which dips down near a sea lion haul-out. (Please don't approach or disturb these creatures.) You'll then ascend rocky Point Sal. From the point, you'll view the Guadalupe Dunes complex to the north and the sandy beaches of Vandenberg Air Force Base to the south. Before returning the same way, look for red-tailed hawks riding the updrafts and admire the ocean boiling up over the reefs.

Energetic hikers can follow a trail which passes behind Point Sal, joins a sandy road, and descends to a splendid beach north of the point. Here you'll find a two-mile-long sandy beach to explore. This unnamed beach is almost always deserted except for a few fishermen and lots of pelicans.

106

Sea Rocket Trail

Ocean Beach County Park to Pt. Pedernales
  7 miles round trip

Season: All year

Pssst! Want to know a secret? A military secret? There's a five-mile long beach in the middle of Vandenberg Air Force Base no one knows, where no one goes.

Vandenberg Air Force Base in Santa Barbara County occupies more Southern California coastline than any other private landholder or government agency. The base encompasses some 35 miles of coastline—about the same amount of shore that belongs to Orange County—and public access is severely restricted.

Happily, Ocean Beach County Park puts a small part of Vandenberg's beach within reach. The park's facilities and picnic ground have recently been upgraded, though the beach itself is as windswept and wild as ever.

Next to the county park is a large, shallow lagoon at the mouth of the Santa Ynez River. There's enough freshwater, mixed with some Pacific saltwater, to form a 400-acre marsh. Near the sandbar at the river mouth, birders will spot gulls and sandpipers and perhaps even a nesting colony of the endangered least tern.

After you've visited the estuary, it's time to hit the beach. This day hike heads south along windswept Ocean Beach toward Pt. Arguello. However, before you reach the point, you'll be stopped by another—Pt. Pedernales—named by the 1769 Portolá expedition when flints, or *pedernales*, were found here. Pt. Pedernales is about the end of the public beach; besides, the surf crashing against the point is nature's way of telling you to turn around.

Directions to trailhead: North of Santa Barbara, just past the Gaviota Pass tunnel, you'll exit Highway 101 onto Highway 1 and proceed toward Lompoc. Join Highway 246 heading west toward Vandenberg and drive about 8 miles out of Lompoc to signed Ocean Park Road on your right. Another sign reads: Ocean Park/Coastal Access. Turn right onto Ocean Park Road and drive a mile (don't be discouraged by the ugly approach) past some railroad sidings and freight cars to Ocean Beach County Parks' parking lot. Ocean Beach is often very windy, so dress accordingly.

The beach is wide and passable at either high or low tide; it's easier at low tide, however, so consult a tide table.

The Hike: Walk over the low dunes, dotted with clumps of European beach grass, ice plant and hottentot fig, toward the ocean. You'll pass a

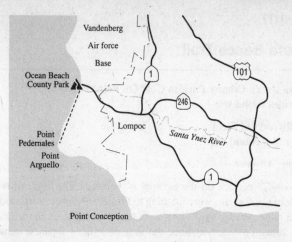

couple of pilings sticking out of the sand—the remains of an old fishing pier. Continue over the sands, sprinkled with sea rocket and sand verbena, to the shore. You could walk a mile north on public beach (though sometimes the Santa Ynez River Mouth is difficult to ford), but this day hike heads south.

After a mile of walking down-coast, the cliffs rise above you and add to a splendid feeling of isolation. Vandenberg Air Force Base, occupying the cliffs above, used to be the Army's Camp Cooke until the Army turned it over to the Air Force in 1957 and it was renamed for Air Force General Hoyt S. Vandenberg. Atlas ICBMs, Discoverer I, the first polar-orbited satellite, and missiles of all kinds have been launched from the base during the last three decades. Because this stretch of coast bends so far westward, it's ideal for launches into a polar orbit. Look on the world map and you can see there's nothing but empty ocean between here and the South Pole; if a launch fails, the debris will fall on water not land.

You can see some of the launch pads and towers as you continue down-coast. You'll also sight dramatic Pt. Arguello, overlooking the treacherous waters that have doomed many a ship. One of the worst accidents in U.S. Naval history occurred in 1923 when seven destroyers ran aground just north of the point. In the dense fog of the Santa Barbara Channel, the ships got off course. Officers refused to heed the new-fangled radio equipment or Radio Directional Finder (RDF) stations onshore and instead plotted their course by "dead reckoning" which proved to be dead wrong.

One of the minor reefs of Pt. Pedernales will no doubt stop your forward progress. If you have a pair of binoculars, you might be able to spot some harbor seals sunning themselves on the rocks below the point.

281

107

Goleta Beach Trail

Goleta Beach County Park to Coal Oil Point Preserve
  7 miles round trip

To Ellwood Oil Field
  12 miles round trip

Season: All year

Around 7 o'clock on the evening of February 23, 1942, while most Southern Californians were listening to President Roosevelt's fireside chat on the radio, strange explosions were heard near Goleta. In the first (and only) attack on U.S. soil since the War of 1812, a Japanese submarine surfaced off the rich oil field on Ellwood Beach, twelve miles north of Santa Barbara, and lobbed sixteen shells into the tidewater field.

"Their marksmanship was poor," asserted Lawrence Wheeler, proprietor of a roadside inn near the oil fields. Most observers agreed with Wheeler, who added there was no panic among his dinner patrons, "We immediately blacked out the place," he said. "One shell landed about a quarter-mile from here and the concussion shook the building, but nobody was scared much."

The unmolested, unhurried Japanese gunners were presumably aiming at the oil installations and the Coast Highway bridge over the Southern Pacific tracks. Tokyo claimed the raid "a great military success" though the incredibly bad marksmen managed to inflict only $500 worth of damage. The submarine disappeared into the night, leaving behind air raid sirens, a jumpy population and lower real estate values.

The walk along Goleta Beach to Ellwood Oil Field is interesting for more than historical reasons. On the way to the Oil Field/Battlefield, you'll pass tidepools, shifting sand dunes, and the Devereaux Slough. The slough is a unique intertidal ecosystem and is protected for teaching and research purposes by Coal Oil Point Preserve.

Directions to trailhead: From Highway 101 in Goleta, head south on Ward Memorial Drive (Route 217) for two miles to Goleta Beach County Park. Park in the large beach lot.

The Hike: Proceed up-coast (west—remember, you're in confusing Santa Barbara County where the coast stretches east to west). In a quarter-mile you'll reach a stretch of coast called the Main Campus Reserve Area, where you'll find the Goleta Slough. The same month the Japanese bombed Ellwood Beach, Santa Barbara voters approved a bond issue to buy land around the Goleta Slough and a modern airport was constructed

282

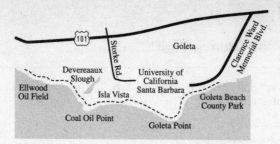

on the site of the old cow pasture/airfield. The slough, host to native and migratory waterfowl, is a remnant of a wetland that was once much more extensive.

Continue up the beach past handsome sandstone cliffs. Occasionally, a high tide may force you to detour atop the bluffs through the UC Santa Barbara campus to avoid getting wet. A mile and a half from the county park, you'll round Goleta Point and head due west. You pass a nice tidepool area; judging from the number of college students, it is well studied.

Two more miles of beachcombing brings you to Coal Oil Point. You'll want to explore the nature reserve here. (Please observe all posted warnings; this is a very fragile area.) The dunes are the first component of the reserve encountered on the seaward side. Sandy hillocks are stabilized with grasses and rushes. Salty sand provides little nourishment, yet the hardy seaside flora manages to survive, settling as close to the water as the restless Pacific will permit. The dunes keep the plants from blowing away and the plants return the favor for the dunes.

Pick up the trail over the dunes on the east side of the reserve. The fennel-lined trail passes under cypress trees and climbs a bluff above the slough to a road on the reserve's perimeter. It's a good place to get ''the big picture'' of the slough, a unique ecosystem. Something like an estuary, a slough has a mixture of fresh and salt water, but an estuary has a more stable mixture. The water gets quite salty at Devereaux Slough, with little fresh water flushing. At the slough, bird-watchers rhapsodize over snowy egrets and great blue herons, black bellied plovers and western sandpipers. Bird watchers flock to the slough for bird-a-thons—marathon bird-sighting competitions.

In addition to the scores of native and migratory species, birds affectionately known by their watchers as ''vagrants''—lost birds who have no business in the area—often visit the slough.

Return to the beach and continue walking up the coast. Sometimes horses gallop over the dunes, suggesting Peter O'Toole and Omar Sharif's meeting in *Lawrence of Arabia* . . . except there's oil on the beach, as you'll readily notice when you look at your feet. In two miles you'll pass under an old barnacle-covered oil drilling platform and enter Ellwood Oil Field. Here the Japanese fired shots heard 'round the world . . . and missed.

108

McGrath Beach Trail

McGrath State Beach to McGrath Lake
  4 miles round trip

To Oxnard Shores
  8 miles round trip

To Channel Islands Harbor
  12 miles round trip

Season: All year

McGrath State Beach and McGrath Lake were named for the McGrath family which had extensive coastal land holdings in the Ventura coastal area dating from 1874. Located on the western city limits of Oxnard, the 2-mile-long state beach extends south from the Santa Clara River.

A small lake in the southern portion of the park helps to attract more than two hundred species of birds, including white-tailed kites, marsh hawks, owls, and herons. Such rare birds as ospreys, white wagtails and black skimmers have been sighted here. The Santa Clara Estuary Natural Preserve on the northern boundary of the park also offers a haven for birds and habitat for weasels, skunks, jackrabbits, opossum, squirrels and mice, plus tortoises and gopher snakes.

Near the state beach entry kiosk, a small visitors center has exhibits about the area's plants and wildlife.

This walk takes you on a nature trail through the Santa Clara River Estuary, visits McGrath Lake and travels miles of sandy beach to Channel Islands Harbor.

Directions to trailhead: To reach McGrath State Beach, visitors southbound on U.S. 101 should take the Seaward Avenue offramp to Harbor Boulevard, turn south on Harbor and travel ¾ mile to the park. Northbound visitors should exit Highway 101 on Victoria Avenue, turn left at the light, Olivas Park Drive, then right to Harbor Boulevard. Turn left on Harbor and proceed ¾ mile to the park. The signed nature trail leaves from the day use parking lot. Signposts along the nature trail are keyed to a pamphlet, available from the entry kiosk.

The Hike: From the parking lot, follow the nature trail through the estuary. The river bank is a mass of lush vegetation: willow, silverweed and yerba mansa. In 1980, the Santa Clara River area was declared a natural preserve, primarily to protect the habitat of two endangered birds—the California least tern and Belding's Savannah Sparrow. When you reach nature trail signpost 11, join a nearby trail that leads atop an old levee, first along the river, then down coast along the periphery of the state beach campground. This trail joins a dirt road and continues down coast, but the far more aesthetic route is along water's edge, so trudge over the low dunes and walk along the shoreline.

Along the beach, visitors enjoy sunbathing or surf fishing for bass, corbina, or perch. In two miles you'll spot McGrath Lake, tucked away behind some dunes.

Extending south are more sandy beach and dunes. You pass a huge old Edison power plant, and arrive at Oxnard Shores, a development famous for getting clobbered by heavy surf at high tide. The beach is flat and at one time was eroding at the phenomenal rate of 10 feet a year. Homes were built right on the shoreline and many were heavily damaged.

Past Oxnard Shores, a mile of beach walking brings you to historic Hollywood Beach. *The Sheik,* starring that great silent movie idol Rudolph Valentino, was filmed on the desert-like sands here. Real estate promoters of the time attempted to capitalize on Oxnard Beach's instant fame and renamed it Hollywood Beach. They laid out subdivisions called Hollywood-by-the-Sea and Silver Strand, suggesting to their customers that the area was really a movie colony and might become a future Hollywood.

This hike ends another mile down-coast at the entrance to Channel Islands Harbor.

109

Zuma-Dume Trail

Zuma Beach to Point Dume
  1 mile round trip

To Paradise Cove
  3 miles round trip

Season: All year

Zuma Beach is one of Los Angeles County's largest sand beaches and one of the finest white sand strands in California. Zuma lies on the open coast beyond Santa Monica Bay and thus receives heavy breakers crashing in from the north. From sunrise to sunset, board and body surfers try to catch a big one. Every month the color of the ocean and the Santa Monica Mountains seem to take on different shades of green depending on the season and sunlight, providing the Zuma Beach hiker with yet another attraction.

During the whale-watching season (approximately mid-December through March), hikers ascending to the lookout atop Point Dume have a good chance of spotting a migrating California gray whale.

This walk travels along that part of Zuma Beach known as Westward Beach, climbs over the geologically fascinating Point Dume Headlands

for sweeping views of the coast, then descends to Paradise Cove, site of a romantic little beach and a fishing pier.

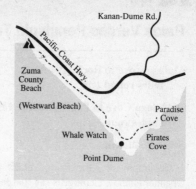

Directions to trailhead: From Pacific Coast Highway, about 25 miles up-coast from Santa Monica and just down coast from Zuma Beach County Park, turn oceanward on Westward Beach Road and follow it to its end at a parking lot. There is a an entrance fee.

Consult a tide table. Passage is easier at low tide.

The Hike: Proceed down-coast along sandy Westward Beach. You'll soon see a distinct path leading up the point. The trail ascends through a plant community of sea fig and sage, coreopsis and prickly pear cactus to a lookout point.

During the winter months, the possibility of spotting a migrating gray whale swimming south toward Baja is good. The migration route brings them quite close to shore.

From atop Point Dume, you can look down at Pirate's Cove, two hundred yards of beach tucked away between two rocky outcroppings. In past years, this beach was the scene of much dispute between nude-beach advocates, residents and the county sheriff.

As you stand atop the rocky triangle projecting into the Pacific, observe the dense black Zuma volcanics and the much softer white sedimentary beds of the sea cliffs extending both east and west. The volcanics have resisted the crashing sea far better than the sedimentary rock and have protected the land behind from further erosion, thus forming the triangle shape of the point.

From the lookout, retrace your steps a short distance and continue on the main trail over the point, which has been set aside as a preserve under the protection of the California Department of Fish and Game. A staircase lets you descend to the beach.

A mile of beach-walking brings you to Paradise Cove, sometimes called Dume Cove. It's a secluded spot, and the scene of much television and motion picture filming. The Sand Castle restaurant and a private pier are located at the cove.

110

Palos Verdes Peninsula Trail

Malaga Cove to Rocky Point
5 miles round trip

Malaga Cove to Point Vincente Lighthouse
10 miles round trip

Season: All year

Geographically, the Palos Verdes bluffs and beaches resemble the Channel Islands. Geologists say that long ago, before the Ice Age began, the Peninsula was an island, separated from the rest of Los Angeles basin by the sea. However, toward the end of the last glacial period, the eighteen-mile-long Peninsula was connected to the mainland by masses of sediment discharged from the mountains to the north.

The Peninsula is famous for its rocky cliffs, which rise from 50 to 300 feet above the ocean and for its thirteen wave-cut terraces. These terraces, or platforms, resulted from a combination of uplift and sea-level fluctuations caused by the formation and melting of glaciers. Today the waves, as they have for so many thousands of years, are actively eroding the shoreline, cutting yet another terrace onto the land.

While enjoying this walk, you'll pass many beautiful coves, where whaling ships once anchored and delivered their cargo of whale oil. Large iron kettles, used to boil whale blubber, have been found in sea cliff caves. Indians, Spanish rancheros and Yankee smugglers have all added to the Peninsula's romantic history. Modern times have brought white-stuccoed, red-tiled mansions to the Peninsula bluffs, but the beach remains almost pristine. Offshore, divers explore the rocky bottoms for abalone and shellfish. Onshore, hikers enjoy the wave-scalloped bluffs and splendid tidepools.

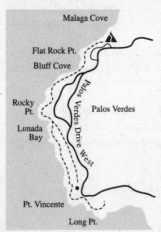

Wear sturdy shoes on this hike. Hiking this beach is like walking over a surface of broken bowling balls. The route is rocky and progress slow, but that gives you more time to look down at the tidepools and up at the magnificent bluffs.

Check the tide table in your newspaper and walk only at low tide.

Pt. Vincente Lighthouse

Directions to trailhead: The narrow, rocky Palos Verdes beaches can be reached by a number of unofficial access points along Paseo Del Mar. To reach Malaga Cove trailhead, take Pacific Coast Highway to Palos Verdes Boulevard. Bear right on Palos Verdes Drive. As you near Malaga Cove Plaza, turn right at the first stop sign (Via Corta). Make a right on Via Arroyo, then another right into the parking lot behind the Malaga Cove School. The trailhead is on the ocean side of the parking area where a wide path descends the bluffs above the Flatrock Point tidepools. A footpath leaves from Paseo del Mar, ¹/₁₀ mile past Via Horcada, where the street curves east to join Palos Verdes Drive West.

The Hike: From the Malaga Cove School parking lot, descend the wide path to the beach. A sign indicates you're entering a seashore reserve and asks you to treat tidepool residents with respect. To the north are sandy beaches for sedentary sun worshipers. Active rock-hoppers clamber to the south. At several places along this walk you'll notice that the great terraces are cut by steep-walled canyons. The first of these canyon incisions can be observed at Malaga Cove, where Malaga Canyon slices through the north slopes of Palos Verdes Hills, then cuts west to empty at the cove.

The coastline curves out to sea in a southwesterly direction and Flatrock Point comes into view. The jade-colored waters swirl around this anvil-shaped point, creating the best tidepool area along this section of coast. Above the point, the cliffs soar to 300 feet. Cloaked in morning fog, the rocky seascape here is reminiscent of Big Sur.

Rounding Flatrock Point, you pick your way among the rocks, seaweed and the flotsam and jetsam of civilization to Bluff Cove, where sparkling combers explode against the rocks and douse the unwary with their tangy spray. A glance over your right shoulder brings a view of Santa Moncia Bay, the Santa Monica Mountains in gray silhouette and on the far horizon, the Channel Islands.

A mile beyond Bluff Cove, Rocky (also called Palos Verdes) Point juts out like a ship's prow. Caught fast on the rocks at the base of the point is the rusting exoskeleton of the Greek freighter *Dominator,* an early 1960s victim of the treacherous reef surrounding the Peninsula.

Trek around Rocky Point to Lunada Bay, a good place to observe the terrace surfaces. From here you'll walk under almost perpendicular cliffs that follow horseshoe-shaped Lunada Bay. Shortly you'll round Resort Point, where fishermen try their luck. As the coastline turns south, Catalina can often be seen glowing on the horizon. Along this stretch of shoreline, numerous stacks, remnants of former cliffs not yet dissolved by he surf, can be seen.

The stretch of coast before the lighthouse has been vigorously scalloped by thousands of years of relentless surf. You'll have to boulder-hop the last mile to Point Vincente. The lighthouse has worked its beacon over the dark waters since 1926. Guided tours of the lighthouse are available by appointment.

Passage is sometimes impossible around the lighthouse at high tide; if passable, another ½ mile of walking brings you to an official beach access (or departure) route at Long Point.

111

Crown of the Sea Trail

Corona Del Mar Beach to Arch Rock
  2 miles round trip

To Crystal Cove
  4 miles round trip

To Abalone Point
  7 miles round trip

Season: All year

In 1904, George Hart purchased 700 acres of land on the cliffs east of the entrance to Newport Bay and laid out a subdivision he called Corona Del Mar ("Crown of the Sea"). The only way to reach the townsite was by way of a long muddy road that circled around the head of Upper Newport Bay. Later a ferry carried tourists and residents from Balboa to Corona Del Mar. Little civic improvement occurred until Highway 101 bridged the bay and the community was annexed to Newport Beach.

This hike explores the beaches and marine refuges of "Big" and Little Corona Del Mar Beaches and continues to the beaches of Crystal Cove State Park.

Consult a tide table. Best beach-walking is at low tide.

Directions to trailhead: From Pacific Coast Highway in Corona Del Mar, turn oceanward on Marguerite Avenue and travel a few blocks to Corona Del Mar State Beach. There is a fee for parking in the lot.

The Hike: Begin at the east jetty of Newport Beach, where you'll see sailboats tacking in and out of the harbor. Snorkelers and surfers frequent the waters near the jetty. Proceed down-coast along wide sandy Corona Del Mar State Beach.

The beach narrows as you approach the cove that encloses Little Corona Del Mar Beach. Snorkeling is good beneath the cliffs of "Big" and Little Corona beaches. Both areas are protected from boat traffic by kelp beds and marine refuge status.

A mile from the jetty, you'll pass well-named Arch Rock, which is just offshore and can be reached at low tide. The beach from Arch Rock to Irvine Cove, 2½ miles to the south was purchased by the state from the Irvine Corporation and is now part of Crystal Cove State Park. Trails lead up the bluffs. From December to about March, the blufftops offer a good vantage point from which to observe the California gray whale migration.

Continuing your stroll down the undeveloped beach and past some tidepools brings you to the tiny resort community of Crystal Cove, site of

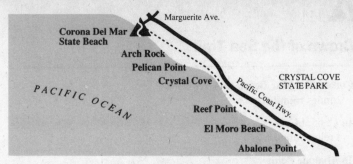

Corona Del Mar
State Beach

Marguerite Ave.

Arch Rock

Pelican Point

Crystal Cove

CRYSTAL COVE
STATE PARK

Pacific Coast Hwy.

Reef Point

El Moro Beach

Abalone Point

PACIFIC OCEAN

a few dozen beach cottages. The wood frame cottages have been little altered since their construction in the 1920s and were recently collectively named to the National Register of Historic Places. "Cove" is something of a misnomer; the beach here shows almost no coastal indentation.

Rounding Reef Point, you'll continue along El Moro Beach. The sandy beach is sometimes beautifully cusped. El Moro is a misspelling of the Spanish word *morro*, meaning round, and describes the round dome of Abalone Point which lies dead ahead. The point, a rocky promontory located just outside Laguna Beach city limits, is made of eroded lava and other volcanic material distributed in the San Joaquin Hills. It's capped by a grass-covered dome rising two hundred feet above the water.

Return the same way or ascend one of the coastal accessways to the blufftops of Crystal Cove State Park. You can use blufftop trails for a portion of your return route.

Catching a wave at Little Corona

112

Trestles Trail

San Clemente State Beach to San Mateo Point
  3 miles round trip

Season: All year

"Our beach shall always be free from hurdy-gurdies and defilement. We believe beauty to be an asset as well as gold and silver, or cabbage and potatoes."

This was the pledge of Norwegian immigrant Ole Hanson, who began the town of San Clemente in 1925. It was quite a promise from a real estate developer, quite a promise in those days of shameless boosterism a half-century before the California Coastal Commission was established.

Thanks is part to Hanson's vision, some of the peaceful ambiance of San Clemente, which he regarded as "a painting five miles long and a mile wide" has been preserved. And some of it's isolation, too. Most everyone in the real estate community thought Hanson crazy for building in a locale 66 miles from San Diego, 66 miles from Los Angeles, but today this isolation attracts rather than repels. This isolation was one of the reasons President Richard Nixon (1969–74) established his Western White House on the bluffs above San Clemente Beach.

San Clemente Beach is a great place for a walk. The beach is mercifully walled off from the din of the San Diego Freeway and the confusion of the modern world by a handsome line of tan-colored bluffs. Only the occasional train passing over Santa Fe Railroad tracks, located near the shore interrupt the cry of the gull, the roar of the breakers. The trestles located at the south end of San Clemente Beach at San Mateo Point gave Trestles Beach its name.

Trestles Beach is one of the finest surfing areas on the west coast. When the surf is up, the waves peel rapidly across San Mateo Point, creating a great ride. Before the area became part of the state beach, it was restricted government property belonging to Camp Pendleton Marine Base. For well over 25 years, surfers carried on guerrilla warfare with U.S. Marines. Trespassing surfers were chased, arrested and fined, and on many occasions had their boards confiscated and broken in two. Veteran surfers tell you about escapes from jeep patrols and guard dogs. Many times, however, the cool Marines would charitably give surfers rides while out on maneuvers.

This day hike's destination, San Mateo Point, is the northernmost boundary of San Diego County, the beginning of Orange County. When the original counties of Los Angeles and San Diego were set up in 1850,

the line that separated them began on the coast at San Mateo Point. When Orange County was formed from southern Los Angeles County in 1889, San Mateo Point was established as the southern point of the new county. You can have the fun of sunning in one county, swimming in another.

Hikers with the time and inclination can easily extend this beachwalk several miles south to San Onofre State Beach. Another option worth considering is to take the train to San Clemente and walk south from the Amtrak station.

Directions to trailhead: From the San Diego Freeway (I-5) in San Clemente, exit on Avenida Calafia and head west a half mile to Calafia Beach Park, where there is metered parking. You can also park (for a fee) at San Clemente State Beach. A limited amount of free parking is available in the residential area near the state beach.

The hike: From Calafia Beach Park, cross the railroad tracks, make your way down an embankment and head south. As you'll soon see, San Clemente State Beach is frequented by plenty of shorebirds, as well as plenty of surfers, body surfers, and swimmers.

At distinct San Mateo Point, which marks the border of Orange and San Diego counties, you'll find San Mateo Creek. The headwaters of the creek rise way up in the Santa Ana Mountains above Camp Pendleton. A portion of the creek is protected by the Cleveland National Forest's San Mateo Canyon Wilderness. Rushes, salt grass and cattails line the creek mouth, where sand pipers, herons and egrets gather.

You can ford the creek mouth (rarely a problem except after winter storms) and continue south toward San Onofre State Beach and the giant domes of San Onofre Nuclear Power Plant. Or you can return the same way.

Or here's a third alternative, an inland return route: Walk under the train trestles and join the park service road, which is usually filled with surfers carrying their boards. The service road takes you up the bluffs, where you'll join the San Clemente Coastal Bike Trail, then wind through a residential area to an entrance to San Clemente State Beach Campground. Improvise a route through the campground to the park's entry station and join a footpath next to the station. The path descends through a prickly pear- and lemonade berry-filled draw to Calafia Beach Park and the trailhead. The wind and water-sculpted marine terraces just south of the trailhead resemble Bryce Canyon in miniature and are fun to photograph.

113

Del Mar Beach Trail

Train Station to Torrey Pines State Reserve
  6 miles round trip

Season: All year

Along Del Mar Beach, the power of the surf is awesome and cliff collapse unpredictable. Permeable layers of rock tilt toward the sea and lie atop other more impermeable layers. Water percolates down through the permeable rock, settles on the impermeable rock and "greases the skids" —an ideal condition for collapsing cliffs.

On New Year's Day in 1941 a freight train suddenly found itself in midair. Erosion had undermined the tracks. A full passenger train had been delayed and the freight train's crew of three were the only casualties.

This hike takes you along the beach, visits the superb Flat Rock tidepool, and detours up the bluffs to Torrey Pines State Reserve. At the Reserve, you'll see those relics from the Ice Age, Torrey Pines, which grow only atop the Del Mar bluffs and on Santa Barbara Island; no other place in the world.

Consult a tide table and schedule your hike at low tide when there's more beach to walk and tide pool life is easier to observe.

Most visitors come to view the 3,000 or so *Pinus torreyana,* but the reserve also offers the walker a striking variety of native plants. If you enjoy interpretive nature trails, the reserve has some nice ones. Protect the fragile ecology of the area by staying on established trails.

Be sure to check out the interpretive displays at the park museum and the native plant garden near the head of the Parry Grove Trail. Plant and bird lists, as well as wildflower maps (February-June) are available for a small fee.

Directions to trailhead: By train: Board a southbound train at Los Angeles' Union Station or another station along the line, and get off in Del Mar. Reservations are usually not necessary. Call Amtrak for fares and schedules.

By car: From Interstate 5 in Del Mar, exit on Via de la Valle. Continue west to Highway S21 and turn left (south) along the ocean past the race tracks and fairgrounds to reach the train station. If you can't find a place to park at the train station, park in town.

The Hike: From the train station, cross the tracks to the beach and begin hiking south. With the high cliffs on your left and the pounding breakers on your right, you'll feel you're entering another world. Follow the sometimes wide, sometimes narrow beach over sparkling sand and soft green limestone rock. Holes in the limestone are evidence of marine life that once made its home there.

You'll hike past a couple of numbered lifeguard towers. When you reach Tower 5, turn left and make a brief detour through the Highway S21 underpass to Los Penasquitos Lagoon, a saltwater marsh patrolled by native and migratory waterfowl. After observing the least terns and light-footed clapper rails, return to the beach trail.

After three miles of beachcombing, you'll see a distinct rock outcropping, named appropriately enough, Flat Rock. Legend has it that this gouged-out rock, also known as Bathtub Rock, was the site of a luckless Scottish miner's search for coal. Common tidepool residents housed in the rocks at the base of the bluff include barnacles, mussels, crabs and sea anemones.

Just north of Flat Rock, a stairwell ascends the bluffs to Torrey Pines State Reserve. Torrey pines occupy the bold headlands atop the yellow sandstone; these rare and graceful trees seem to thrive on the foggy atmosphere and precarious footing. The reserve features superb nature trails, native plant gardens and interpretive exhibits.

Among the reserve trails:

Parry Grove Trail, named in honor of Dr. C.C. Parry, takes you through a handsome grove of Torrey pines. Parry was a botanist assigned to the

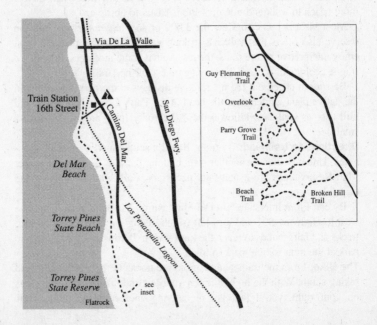

Torrey Pines

boundary commission that surveyed the Mexican-American border in 1850. While waiting for the expedition to start, Parry explored the San Diego area. He investigated a tree that had been called the Soledad pine for the nearby Soledad Valley. Parry sent samples to his teacher and friend, Dr. John Torrey of Princeton and asked that if it proved to be a new species, it be named for Torrey. The Soledad pine became *Pinus torreyana,* or Torrey pine, in honor of the famous botanist and taxonomist.

The 4/10-mile loop trail also leads past many kinds of plants in the reserve: toyon, yucca, and other coastal shrubs.

Broken Hill Trail visits a drier, chaparral dominated landscape, full of sage and buckwheat, ceanothus and manzanita. From Broken Hill Overlook, there's a view of a few Torrey pines clinging to life in an environment that resembles a desert badlands.

Beach Trail leads to Yucca Point and Razor Point and offers precipitous views of the beach below. The trail descends the bluffs to Flat Rock, a fine tidepool area.

Guy Fleming Trail is a 6/10-mile loop that travels through stands of Torrey pine and takes you to South Overlook, where you might glimpse a migrating California gray whale.

114

Bayside Trail

Old Point Loma Lighthouse to Cabrillo National Monument Boundary
  2 miles round trip

Season: All year

Cabrillo National Monument on the tip of Point Loma marks the point where Portuguese navigator Juan Rodríguez Cabrillo became the first European to set foot on California soil. He landed near Ballast Point in 1542 and claimed San Diego Bay for Spain. Cabrillo liked this "closed and very good port" and said so in his report to the King of Spain.

One highlight of a visit to the national monument is the old Point Loma Lighthouse. This lighthouse, built by the federal government, first shined its beacon in 1855. Because fog often obscured the light, the station was abandoned in 1891 and a new one built on lower ground at the tip of Point Loma. The 1891 lighthouse is still in operation today, operated by the Coast Guard. The 1855 lighthouse has been wonderfully restored to the way it looked when Captain Israel and his family lived there in the 1880s.

Bayside Trail begins at the old lighthouse and winds past yucca and prickly pear, sage and buckwheat. The monument protects one the last patches of native flora in southernmost California, a hint at how San Diego Bay may have looked when Cabrillo's two small ships anchored here.

Directions to trailhead: Exit Interstate 5 on Rosecrans Street (Highway 209 south) and follow the signs to Cabrillo National Monument. There is a small entry fee.

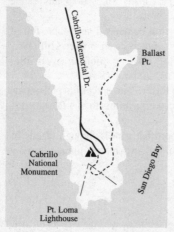

Cabrillo National Monument opens daily at 9:00 A.M. Before embarking on this easy family hike, you may want to obtain a trail guide at the visitors center. The guide describes the coastal sage and chaparral communities, as well as local history.

The Hike: The first part of the Bayside Trail winding down from the old lighthouse is a paved road. At a barrier, you bear left on a gravel road, once a military patrol road. During World War II, the Navy secreted bunkers and searchlights along these coastal bluffs.

Old Point Loma Lighthouse

Bayside Trail provides fine views of the San Diego Harbor shipping lanes. Sometimes when Navy ships pass, park rangers broadcast descriptions of the vessels. Also along the trail is one of Southern California's most popular panoramic views: miles of seashore, 6,000-foot mountains to the east and Mexico to the south.

The trail dead-ends at the park boundary.

115

Border Field Trail

Border Field State Park to Tijuana River
  3 miles round trip

To Imperial Beach
  6 miles round trip

Season: All year

Border Field Trail begins at the very southwest corner of America, at the monument marking the border between Mexico and California. When California became a territory at the end of the Mexican-American War, an international border became a necessity. American and Mexican survey crews determined the boundary and the monument of Italian marble was placed in 1851 to mark the original survey site. Today the monument stands in the shadow of the Tijuana Bull Ring and still delineates the border between the United States and Estados Unidos Mexicanos.

During World War II the Navy used Border Field as an air field. Combat pilots received gunnery training, learning to hit steam-driven targets that raced over the dunes on rails called Rabbit Tracks. Despite multifarious real estate schemers, the Navy retained control of Border Field until the land was given to the state in the early 1970s.

Before you walk down the bluffs to the beach, take in the panoramic view: the Otay Mountains and the San Miguel Mountains to the east, Mexico's Coronado Islands out to sea, and to the north—the Tijuana River flood plain, the Silver Strand, Coronado.

Much of the Tijuana River Estuary, one of the few salt marshes left in Southern California and one of the region's most important bird habitats, is within Border Field's boundaries.

This hike explores the dune and estuary ecosystems of the state park and takes you to wide sandy Imperial Beach. Wear an old pair of shoes and be prepared for the soft mud of the marsh.

Directions to the trailhead: Border Field State Park is located in the extreme southwestern corner of California, with Mexico and the Pacific Ocean as its southern and western boundaries. From Interstate 5 (San Diego Freeway) south, exit on Hollister Street, proceed to a T-intersection, bear west (right) 2 miles on Monument Road to the state park. The park closes at sunset.

The Hike: Follow the short bluff trail down to the beach, which is under strict 24-hour surveillance by the U.S. Border Patrol. The beach is usually deserted, quite a contrast to crowded Tijuana Beach a few hundred yards

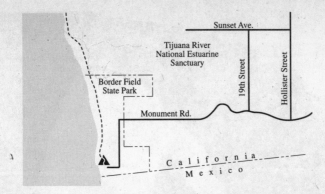

to the south. As you walk north on Border Field State Park's 1½-mile-long beach, you'll pass sand dunes anchored by salt grass, pickleweed and sand verbena. On the other side of the dunes is the Tijuana River Estuary, an essential breeding ground, feeding and nesting spot for more than 170 species of native and migratory birds.

Take time to explore the marsh. You may spot a marsh hawk, brown pelican, California gull, black-necked stilt, snowy egret, western sandpiper and American kestrel—to name a few of the more common birds. Fishing is good for perch, corbina and halibut, both in the surf along Border Field Beach and in the estuary.

A mile-and-a-half from the border you'll reach the mouth of the Tijuana River. Only after heavy storms is the Tijuana River the wide swath pictured on some maps. Most of the time it's fordable at low tide, but use your best judgement.

Continue north along wide, sandy Imperial Beach, past some houses and low bluffs. Imperial Beach was named by the South San Diego Investment Company to lure Imperial Valley residents to build summer cottages on the beach. Waterfront lots could be purchased for $25 down, $25 monthly and developers promised the balmy climate would "cure rheumatic proclivities, catarrhal trouble, lesions of the lungs," and a wide assortment of other ailments.

In more recent times, what was once a narrow beach protected by a seawall has been widened considerably by sand dredged from San Diego Bay. There's good swimming and surfing along Imperial Beach and the waves can get huge. The beach route reaches Imperial Pier, built in 1912 and the oldest in the county.

Anacapa Island: Arch at Land's End

Anacapa Island: Picnic ground and lighthouse

13. Channel Islands

CONGRESS, in establishing Channel Islands National Park, did not intend it as a vaction spot for the comfort-loving, but rather as a preserve for what some scientists have called the "American Galapagos." Top priority was given to the protection of sea lions and seals, endemic plants like the Santa Cruz pine, rich archaelogical digs, and what may be the final resting place of Portuguese navigator Juan Rodríguez Cabrillo, who explored the California coast for the Spanish Crown in the 16th century.

Would-be adventurers enjoy the visitors center in Ventura Harbor as an exciting sneak preview of the splendid park out there in the Pacific, 12 to 60 miles away, a series of blue-tinged mountains floating on the horizon. The visitors center not only has island history and ecology exhibits, but provides up-to-the minute boat transportation information.

The Channel Islands parallel the Southern California coast, which at this point is running in a more or less east-west direction. In 1980, five of the eight Channel Islands—Anacapa, San Miguel, Santa Barbara, Santa Cruz and Santa Rosa—became America's fortieth national park. The U.S. Navy practices maneuvers on San Nicholas and San Clemente. Farther south, Santa Catalina, has pursued a destiny apart.(See Chapter 14) The waters surrounding the national park islands are protected as the Channel Islands National Marine Sanctuary.

Scientists theorize that the islands rose out of the Pacific through volcanic action 14 million years ago, later sinking and rising many times as glaciation alternated with massive melting. The four northern islands were linked, until about twenty thousand years ago, into a super-island called *Santaroasae*, only to part company during the final glacial melt into the wave-sculpted islands we see today.

The islands' even sea-tempered climate has preserved plants that either were altered through evolution on the mainland, or perished altogether at man's hand. What you see on the islands is Southern California of a millenium ago.

Because of the fragile islands ecology, hiking on the islands is more regulated than it is in most places. You must always stay on the trail, and on some islands be accompanied by a national park ranger or Nature Conservancy employee.

116

Anacapa Island

Loop Trail
  2 miles round trip

Season: All year

Anacapa Island, closest to the mainland, was called *Las Mesitas* (Little Tables) by Spanish explorer Gaspar de Portolá in 1769. Ventura sheep ranchers once owned the island, which has no water. It's hard to imagine how the sheep survived. The popular belief is that night fog was so dense that the sheep's coats became soaked, each sheep becoming a woolly sponge by morning. Or so the story goes . . .

Anacapa, 12 miles southwest of Port Hueneme, is the most accessible Channel Island. It offers the hiker a sampling of the charms of the larger islands to the west. Below the tall wind-and-wave-cut cliffs, sea lions bark at crashing breakers. Gulls, owls, herons and pelicans call the cliffs home.

Anacapa is really three islands chained together with reefs that rise above the surface during low tide. West Anacapa is the largest segment, featuring great caves where the Chumash Indians are said to have collected water dripping from the ceiling. The middle isle hosts a wind-battered eucalyptus grove.

It's a romantic approach to East Anacapa as you sail past Arch Rock. As you come closer, however, the island looks forsaken; not a tree in sight. But as you near the mooring at the east end of the isle, the honeycomb of caves and coves is intriguing. A skiff brings you to the foot of an iron stairway. You climb 150 stairs, ascending steep igneous rocks to the cliff tops.

What you find on top depends on the time of year. In February and March, you may enjoy the sight of 30-ton gray whales passing south on their way to calving and mating waters off Baja California. In early spring, the giant coreopsis, the island's featured attraction, is something to behold. It is called the tree sunflower, an awkward thick-trunked perennial that grows as tall as 10 feet.

The east isle, where the National Park has a visitors center, is the light of the Channel Islands; a Coast Guard lighthouse and foghorn warn ships of the dangerous channel. This hike tours East Anacapa Island. The island is barely a mile long and a quarter-mile wide, so even though you tour the whole island, it's a short hike.

Directions to trailhead: For the most up-to-date information about boat departures, contact Channel Islands National Park or the park concessionaire, Island Packers in Ventura Harbor.

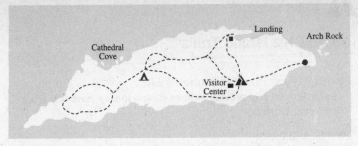

Most commercial tour operators leave from the Ventura and Oxnard marinas. A number of whale-watching tours are offered during winter when the gray whales migrate. Some of these tour boats land on Anacapa and some don't.

The Hike: The nature trail leaves from the visitors center, where you can learn about island life, past and present. A helpful pamphlet is available describing the island's features. Remember to stay on the trail; the island's ground cover is easily damaged.

Along the trail, a campground and several inspiring cliff-edge nooks invite you to picnic. The trail loops in a figure-eight through the coreopsis and returns to the visitors center.

117

Santa Cruz Island Trails

Pelican Bay and Prisoners Harbor Trails
 3 miles round trip around Pelican Bay; 6 miles round trip from Prisoners Harbor

Season: All year

Santa Cruz Island was, until recent years, a working cattle ranch. It's now managed by the Nature Conservancy and part of the national park

Santa Cruz Island is tantalizingly close to the mainland, dominating the horizon of Santa Barbara. California's largest offshore island, it boasts the most varied coastline and topography, the highest peak, (2,434 feet) and safest harbors.

Island anchorages hint at its history: Smugglers Cove, Prisoners Harbor (the island was once a Mexican penal colony), Coches Prietos ("Black Pigs," for the Mexican-introduced hogs). Chumash Indians had both permanent and summer villages on Santa Cruz until the early 1800s when they were brought to mainland missions.

In the 1800s, a colony of French and Italian immigrants led by Justinian Caire began a Mediterranean-style ranch, raising sheep and cattle, growing olives and almonds, even making wine. In 1937, Edwin Stanton of Los Angeles bought the western nine-tenths of the island from the Caire family. Edwin's son, Dr. Carey Stanton, ran the Santa Cruz Island Co. from 1957 until his death in 1987, when the era of family ownership of the island ended and the Nature Conservancy assumed management. The other one-tenth of the island—the east end—is partly privately owned and partly owned by the National Park Service.

The two most popular and easily booked trips to Santa Cruz Island depart from Ventura Harbor at 8 a.m and return to the mainland between 5 and 6 P.M. Sometimes the boats pause to observe dolphins, whales, sealions and seals. Figure about a two-hour boat ride each way and about five hours on the island. You and three dozen others make up a good boatload. The Main Ranch's main emphasis is on human history, while the Pelican Bay Trip stresses natural history.

Main Ranch Day Trip: From the landing at Prisoners Harbor, it's a three-mile hike under old oaks and through eucalyptus groves along an old fennel-lined ranch road. Your party will be accompanied by a Nature Conservancy employee who will point out some of the botanical and historical highlights encountered en route.

Upon arrival at the ranch, visitors eat lunch around a pool. (Bring a swim-

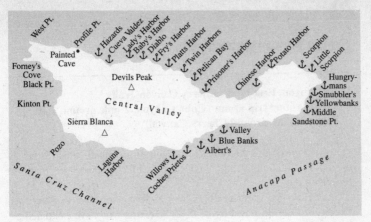

West Pt. Profile Pt. Hazards Cueva Valdez Lady's Harbor Baby's Harbor Diablo Fry's Harbor Platts Harbor Twin Harbors Prisoner's Harbor Pelican Bay Chinese Harbor Potato Harbor Scorpion Little Scorpion

Painted Cave

Forney's Cove Black Pt. Devils Peak △ Hungry-mans Smubbler's Yellowbanks Middle Sandstone Pt.

Kinton Pt. *Central Valley*

Sierra Blanca △

Valley Blue Banks Albert's

Pozo

Santa Cruz Channel Laguna Harbor Willows Coches Prietos *Anacapa Passage*

suit so you can take a dip.) After lunch you can take a tour of the ranch buildings, including a tiny cabin converted into an anthropology museum, the main ranch house and some dilapidated winery buildings. A recently restored stone Catholic church celebrated its 100th anniversary in 1991 with a visit by Archbishop (now Cardinal) Roger Mahony. Next to the old church is a cemetery where both humans and ranch dogs rest in peace.

Pelican Bay Day Trip: After arrival at Pelican Bay, landing is by a small skiff ont a rocky ledge. You'll have to climb up a somewhat precipitous cliff trail to reach the picnic spot overlooking the bay.

A Nature Conservancy naturalist leads your group on an educational hike along the north shore. Two special botanical delights are a bishop pine forest and a grove of Santa Cruz Island ironwood.

Ranch house

118

Santa Rosa Island Trails

Lobo Canyon, East Point, Cherry Canyon Trails
5 miles round trip around Lobo Canyon; 1 mile around East
Point; 4 miles around Cherry Canyon.

Rolling grasslands cover much of Santa Rosa Island, which is cut by rugged oak and ironwood filled canyons. Torrey pines are found at Beecher's Bay.

Santa Rosa had a considerable Chumash population when explorer Juan Rodríguez Cabrillo sailed by in 1542. Scientists who have examined the island's extensive archaeological record believe the island was inhabited at least 8,000 years ago; quite possibly, early man lived on Santa Rosa 40,000 years ago.

After the Chumash era, the island was land granted to Don Carlos and Don José Carrillo. For many years their families raised sheep on the island and were known on the mainland for hosting grand fiestas at shearing time. In 1902, Walter Vail and J.W. Vickers bought the island and raised what many considered some of the finest cattle in California. The island became part of Channel Islands National Park in 1986.

The National Park Service offers a couple of ranger-guided walking tours of the island. Hikers are transported to the more remote trailheads by four-wheel drive vehicles.

(See Anacapa Island hike for visitor information)

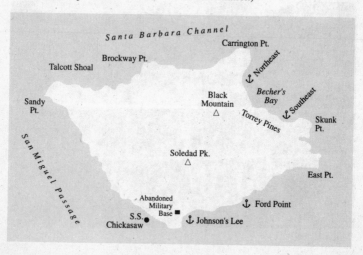

Lobo Canyon (5 miles round trip): Hikers descend the sandstone walled Canada Lobos, pausing to admire such native flora as island monkey flower, dudleya and coreopsis. At the mouth of the canyon, near the ocean, is a Chumash village site. The hike continues, as the trail ascends the east wall of the canyon, then drops into Cow Canyon. At the mouth of Cow Canyon is an excellent tidepool area.

East Point Trail (1 mile round trip): Visit a rare stand of Torrey pines, and a large freshwater marsh where bird-watchers will enjoy viewing shorebirds and waterfowl. Trail's end is one of Santa Rosa's beautiful beaches.

Cherry Canyon Trail (4 miles round trip) offers the opportunity to see plants and animals that are found nowhere else. Two miles up the canyon is an oak grove. On the return trip, the trail offers far-reaching views of the interior, roaming deer and Roosevelt elk, and the dramatic sweep of Beechers Bay. Trail's end is the island's historic ranch complex.

The westernmost Channel Islands, Santa Rosa and San Miguel (shown above), offer terrific hiking.

119

San Miguel Island Trail

Cuyler Harbor to Lester Ranch
3 miles round trip; 700-foot gain

Season: All year

San Miguel is the westernmost of the Channel Islands. Eight miles long, four miles wide, it rises as a plateau, 400 to 500 feet above the sea. Wind-driven sands cover many of the hills which were severely overgrazed by sheep during the island's ranching days. Owned by the U.S. Navy, which once used it as a bombing site and missile tracking station, San Miguel is now managed by the National Park Service.

San Miguel is home to six pinniped species: California sea lion, northern elephant seal, steller sea lion, harbor seal, northern fur seal and Guadalupe fur seal. The island may host the largest elephant seal population on earth. As many as 15,000 seals and sea lions can be seen basking on the rocks during mating season.

A trail runs most of the way from Cuyler Harbor to the west end of the island at Point Bennett, where the pinniped population is centered. The trail passes two round peaks, San Miguel and Green Mountain, and drops in and out of steep canyons to view the lunar landscape of the caliche forest. You must hike with the resident ranger and stay on established trails because the island's vegetation is fragile.

Directions to trailhead: Plan a very long day—or better yet, an overnight trip to San Miguel. It's at least a five-hour boat trip from Ventura. (See Anacapa Island hike for more visitor information).

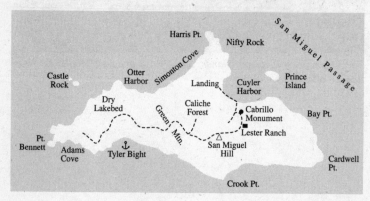

The Hike: Follow the beach at Cuyler Harbor to the east. The beach around the anchorage was formed by a bight of volcanic cliffs that extend to bold and precipitous Harris Point, the most prominent landmark on San Miguel's coast.

At the east end of the beach, about ¾ of a mile from anchoring waters, a small footpath winds its way up the bluffs. It's a relatively steep trail following along the edge of a stream-cut canyon. At the top of the canyon, the trail veers east and forks. The left fork leads a short distance to Cabrillo Monument.

Juan Rodríguez Cabrillo, Portuguese explorer, visited and wrote about San Miguel in October 1542. While on the island he fell and broke either an arm or a leg (historians are unsure about this). As a result of this injury he contracted gangrene and died on the island in January 1543 and it's believed (historians disagree about this, too) he was buried here. In honor of Cabrillo, a monument was erected in 1937.

The right fork continues to the remains of a ranch house. Of the various ranchers and ranch managers to live on the island, the most well-known were the Lesters. They spent 12 years on the island and their adventures were occasionally chronicled by the local press. When the Navy evicted the Lesters from the island in 1942, Mr. Lester went to a hill overlooking Harris Point, in his view the prettiest part of the island, and shot himself. Not much is left of the ranch now. The buildings burned down in the 1960s and only a rubble of brick and scattered household items remain.

For a longer 8-mile round trip the hiker can continue on the trail past the ranch to the top of San Miguel Peak (916 feet), down, and then up again to the top of Green Mountain (850 feet). Ask rangers to tell you about the caliche forest, composed of calcified sheaths of plants that died thousands of years ago. Calcium carbonate has reacted with ancient plants' organic acid, creating a ghostly forest.

120

Signal Peak Loop Trail

Around Santa Barbara Island
  2 to 5 miles round trip; 500-foot gain

Only one square mile in area, Santa Barbara is the smallest Channel Island. It's located some 38 miles west of San Pedro—or quite a bit south of the other islands in the national park.

Geologically speaking, Santa Barbara arose a bit differently from the other isles. The island is a volcano, leftover from Miocene times, some 25 million years ago, and shares characteristics with Mexico's Guadalupe Islands.

From a distance, the triangular-shaped island looks barren—not a tree in sight. The tallest plant is the coreopsis, the giant sunflowers that can grow ten-feet hight.

To bird-watchers, Santa Barbara means seabirds, lots of them—gulls, cormorants, pelicans and black-oyster catchers. And the island boasts some rare birds, too: the black storm-petrel and the Xantus murrelet. Land

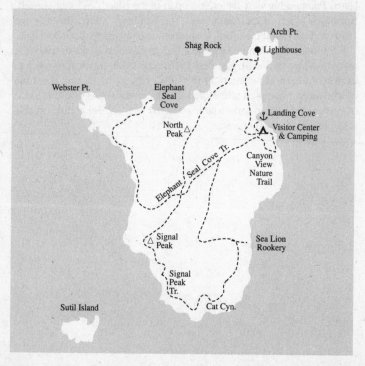

birds commonly sighted include burrowing and barn owls, hummingbirds, horned larks and finches.

Besides the birds, another reason to bring binoculars to the island is to view sea lions and elephant seals. Webster Point on the western end of the isle is a favorite haul-out area for the pinnipeds.

Explorer Sebastián Vizcaíno sailed by on December 4, 1602. That day happened to be the day of remembrance for Saint Barbara, so the island was named for her. During the 1700s, the Spanish used the isle as a kind of navy base, from which they could set sail after the pirates plaguing their galleons.

Early in this century, the isle's native flora was all-but destroyed by burning, clearing, and planting nonnative grasses, followed by sheep grazing. Besides the grasses, iceplant, a South African import, began to spread over the island. Even when the hardy iceplant dies, it hurts the native plant community because it releases its salt-laden tissues into the soil, thus worsening the odds for the natives. Park service policy is to re-introduce native plants and eliminate non-natives.

Six miles of trail crisscross the island. A good place to start your exploration is Canyon View Nature Trail. Request an interpretive brochure from the resident ranger and enjoy learning about island ecology.

Directions to trailhead: Santa Barbara Island is infrequently serviced by boat, but it is possible to join a trip. Contact park headquarters.

Avalon Harbor, Catalina Island

14. Catalina Island

THE ISLOPHILE expecting a lush landscape is often surprised by Catalina Island's backcountry. Catalina's vegetation is sparse, spartan. Catalina resembles a Greek island—one of Cyclades, perhaps—far more than a tropical South Seas paradise.

Catalina shares the semi-arid conditions of Southern California, but hosts a surprising amount of plant life. About 600 species, 400 or so of them native plants, grow on the island.

Each year about a million people travel to Catalina, but few of these visitors are hikers. The adventurer who strides out of Avalon will leave the crowds behind and be treated to superb island, ocean and mainland views.

Among the island's owners was James Lick, founder of Lick Observatory from 1867 to 1887; he was followed by the Banning family, who founded the Santa Catalina Island Company in order to develop Catalina into a resort. Chewing-gum magnate and Chicago Cubs-owner William Wrigley took over in 1919, with the intention of putting Avalon on the map as a world-class destination while at the same time conserving the island's special natural resources. Avalon's landmark Casino, built in 1929, featured a grand ballroom from which Big Band music was broadcast, gaining the island national attention.

The non-profit Santa Catalina Island Conservancy, established in 1972, and dedicated to preserving the island environment, now holds 86 percent of Catalina. The Conservancy has an active interpretive program and coordinates wildlife managment and plant rehabilitation efforts.

For the hiker, Catalina offers its famous coast and its less-well-known backcountry. A mountain range extends northwest-southeast over the 21-mile length of the island.

An extensive network of dirt roads plus some footpaths help you explore the island's flora—grasslands, oak woodland, coastal scrub, stands of ironwood trees and Catalina cherry—and recreation spots—camps, picnic sites, and beaches.

121

Avalon Canyon Loop Trail

Avalon to Botanical Garden
  3 miles round trip; 200-foot gain
Return via Hermit Gulch Trail
  6½ miles round trip; 1,000-foot gain

Season: All year

The route out of Avalon, which I have dubbed, "Avalon Canyon Loop Trail" leads to the Botanical Garden, a showcase for plants native to Catalina and the Channel Islands. At the head of the canyon is the imposing Wrigley Memorial, a huge monument honoring chewing gum magnate William Wrigley, who purchased most of the island in 1919.

Families with children, and those visitors looking more for a walk than a hike will enjoy the trip as far as the Botanical Garden. More adventurous hikers will undertake the second, much more strenuous part of this loop trip; it utilizes fire roads and Hermit Gulch Trail and offers a sampling of Catalina's rugged and bold terrain.

Directions to trailhead: Several boat companies offer ferry service to Catalina, with departures from San Diego, Newport Beach, Long Beach and San Pedro. Usually, least expensive round trip fare is offered by Catalina Cruises, which operates out of San Pedro and Long Beach. The 22-mile crossing to Catalina takes about 2 hours. Catalina Express, which offers the fastest boats (90 minutes to Avalon), also operates out of both Long Beach and San Pedro. For more information about ferryboat schedules, island services and accomodations, call the Catalina Island Chamber of Commerce.

If you intend to hike into the Catalina backcountry (anywhere past the Botanical Garden) you must secure a free hiking permit from the Los Angeles County Department of Parks and Recreation. The department operates an information center in the Island Plaza, located at 213 Catalina Street. You can pick up a trails map here and secure your permit at the office.

The Hike: Head uphill along Catalina Street, which soon joins Avalon Canyon Road, passes a few residences, and begins a 1½ mile ascent toward the Botanical Garden. On your right, watch for one of William Wrigley's many contributions to the island, Bird Park, which once held thousands of unusual birds in the "largest bird cage in the world." Bird Park is now a campground. On the left side of the road, bleacher bums will stop and pay homage to the one-time spring training camp of Wrigley's beloved Chicago Cubs.

At the end of the road is the Botanical Garden. Enter the Garden (an admission fee is charged). The garden began in the 1920s, when Wrigley's wife, Ada, began planting native and exotic plants in Avalon Canyon. More recently, the garden has greatly expanded, emphasizing native Southern California flora. Particularly interesting are plants endemic to Catalina, including Catalina mahogany, Catalina manzanita, Catalina live-forever, and Catalina ironwood.

Proceed up the dirt path to the Wrigley Memorial. At one time, Wrigley's body was entombed here. If you wish, climb up the many stairs to the 232-foot-wide, 130-foot-high monument, and enjoy the great view of Avalon Harbor.

At this point, intrepid hikers will pass through an unlocked gate below and to the right of the memorial and stride up Memorial Road. Scrub oak, manzanita and lemonade berry—and many more of the same plants, sans identification plaques, that you studied at the Botanical Garden—line the fire road.

The vigorous ascent on Memorial Road offers better and better views of Avalon Harbor. It's likely your approach will flush a covey or two of quail from the brush. Practiced birders might recognize the Catalina quail, a slightly larger and slightly darker subspecies than its mainland relatives.

Memorial Road reaches a divide, where appropriately enough, you'll intersect Divide Road. Bear right. From the 1,000-foot high divide, you'll have commanding views of both sides of the island and of the mainland. The mainland sometimes has an interesting look from this vantage point: You see the major topographical features of the Southern California area—the Santa Monica and San Gabriel Mountains—but not a trace of civilization.

Continue along the divide, which bristles with prickly pear cactus. The slopes below are crisscrossed with trails made by the island's many wild goats. After about ¾ of a mile of walking atop the divide, you'll bear right on unsigned Hermit Gulch Trail. This trail is difficult to spot and the early going steep. The trail descends 2.4 miles along a waterless canyon back to Avalon Canyon Road. You'll intersect Avalon Canyon Road a few hundred yards below the Botanical Garden. Turn left and saunter downhill to the comforts of Avalon.

122

Black Jack Trail

Black Jack Trail
  8 miles one way; 1,500-foot loss

Season: All year

Catalina Island's terrain is rugged and bold, characterized by abrupt ridges and V-shaped canyons. Many of the mountaintops are rounded, however, and the western end of the island is grassland and brush, dotted with cactus and seasonal wildflowers. Bison, deer, boar, and rabbits roam the savannas.

This walk is a good introduction to the island; it samples a variety of terrain on the island, inland and coastal. Transportation logistics are a bit complex, but the trail is easy to follow.

Directions to trailhead: Several boat companies offer ferry services to Catalina from Long Beach and San Pedro. For information about boat schedules and island services and accomodations, contact the Catalina Island Chamber of Commerce.

If you intend to hike into the Catalina backcountry, you must secure a (free) hiking permit from the Los Angeles County Department of Parks and Recreation. The Parks Department operates an information center in the Island Plaza, located at 213 Catalina Avenue (the island's "Main Street"). You can pick up a trails map here and secure your permit.

From Avalon, you'll be traveling to the trailhead via the Catalina Island Interior Shuttle Bus, which departs from the information center. The shuttle bus (fee) will drop passengers off at Black Jack Junction.

The Hike: At signed Black Jack Junction, there's a fire phone and good views of the precipitous west ridges. The trail, a rough fire road, ascends for one mile over brush- and cactus-covered slopes. You'll pass the fenced, but open shaft of the old Black Jack Mine (lead, zinc and silver). On your left a road appears that leads up to Black Jack Mountain, at 2,006 feet the second highest peak on Catalina. Continue past this junction.

Ahead is a picnic ramada with a large sunshade and a nearby signed junction. You may descend to Black Jack Camp, which is operated by Los Angeles County. Here you'll find tables, shade, and water. Set in a stand of pine, the camp offers fine channel views.

Bear right on the signed Cottonwood/Black Jack Trail. A second junction soon appears. Continue straight downhill. The other trail ascends to Mount Orizaba (2,097 feet), the island's highest peak.

The trail drops through a canyon, whose steep walls are a mixture of chaparral and grassland and are favored by a large herd of wild goats. At

318

the bottom of the canyon pass through three gates of a private ranch. (Close all gates; don't let the horses out.) The trail reaches the main road connecting Little Harbor with Airport-in-the-Sky. You may bear left at this junction and follow the winding road 3½ miles to Little Harbor. For a more scenic route of about the same distance, turn right on the road. Hike about 200 yards to the end of the ranch fence line, then bear left, struggling cross-country briefly through spiny brush and intersect a ranch road. This dirt road follows the periphery of the fence line on the east side of the ranch to the top of a canyon. You bear left again, still along the fence line. You ascend and then descend, staying atop this sharp shadeless ridge above pretty Big Springs Canyon. When you begin descending toward the sea, you'll spot Little Harbor.

Little Harbor is the primary campground and anchorage on the Pacific side of the island. It's a good place to relax while you're waiting for the shuttle bus, or to refresh yourself for the hike through buffalo country to Two Harbors.

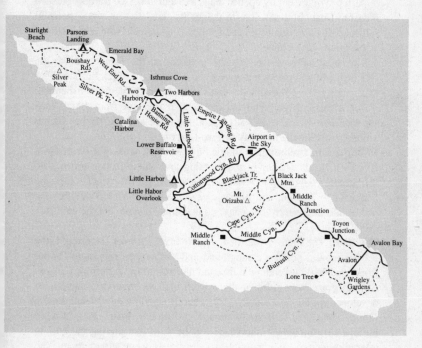

123

Little Harbor Trail

Little Harbor to Two Harbors
   7 miles one way

Season: All year

   In 1602, when Vizcaíno's ship sailed toward the mountains of Catalina, the explorer was certain he had reached two islands. From a distance, the mountainous land on the east end appears to be separated from a smaller portion on the west end; in fact, it's an optical illusion. The eye is tricked by a low-lying isthmus, the narrowest section of Catalina. Catalina Harbor lies on the ocean side of this isthmus, Isthmus Cove on the channel side, and together this area is called Two Harbors.

   As the Wrigley family opened the isle to tourism, Two Harbors pursued a destiny apart from Avalon. In the 1920s and 1930s, it was a peaceful sanctuary for film celebrities and the Los Angeles elite who could indulge in the luxury of yachting.

   This hike takes you across the island from the Pacific side to the Channel side and offers fine views and a chance to watch buffalo. Your destination is Two Harbors, popular with campers, boaters and fishermen.

   For a relaxing weekend backpack, take the trail from Black Jack Junction (see Black Jack Trail), spend the night at Little Harbor Campground, and hike the next day to Two Harbors.

Directions to trailhead: A shuttle bus takes you across the island from Avalon to Little Harbor in the morning and will pick you up in Two Harbors for your return to Avalon. If you purchased a ferry ticket from the mainland to Avalon, and plan to leave the island from Two Harbors, please inform the ferry company; no additional charge, but the company needs to know.

The Hike: The route, a fire road, departs from a former stagestop, Little Harbor, now a popular campground and anchorage. Join Little Harbor Road, and begin ascending higher and higher into Little Springs Canyon. Buffalo graze both sides of the canyon and two reservoirs have been developed for the animals. In 1924, when Hollywood moviemakers were filming Zane Grey's classic Western, *The Vanishing American,* 14 head of buffalo were brought to the island for the film. Recapturing the buffalo after filming proved impossible so the beasts were left to roam. The animals adapted well to life on Catalina and quickly multiplied. Today's population is held at 400 to 500, the ideal number for available pasturage.

   At an unsigned junction a mile past Lower Buffalo Reservoir, bear left on Banning House Road, which will take you 3¼ miles to Two Harbors.

(Little Harbor Road continues north, then west to Two Harbors if you prefer to stick to this road.) Rough Banning House Road ascends very steeply up a canyon roamed by wild boar. At the windswept head of the canyon you are rewarded with superb views of the twin harbors of Catalina Harbor and Isthmus Cove and can see both the eastern and western fringes of the island.

A steep northeasterly descent brings you to the outskirts of Two Harbors. You'll have no trouble improvising a route past ranchettes and private clubs to the ferry building.

Buffalo have a home and a place to roam on Catalina.

124

West End Trail

Two Harbors to Cherry Cove
3½ miles round trip; 300-foot gain

To Parsons Landing Campground
14 miles round trip; 800-foot gain

Season: All year

Even the names sound intriguing: Cherry Cove and Parsons Landing, Arrow Point and Emerald Bay. Catalina's west end is a very special place—a series of bold headlands and crescent-shaped coves.

The coastal hills and canyons extending between Two Harbors and Parsons Landing is more botanically intact (ie. less eaten by feral goats and pigs) than other parts of the island. The windswept oak and chaparral ecoystems are thriving.

One floral highlight is a grove of the native Catalina cherry. Depending on your point of view, it's either a tree or a shrub; its profile is shrub-like, but its height (specimens reach 40 to 50 feet) is more tree-like.

The lovely, waxy-leaved native celebrates spring with spiky clusters of white flowers. It produces a dark red, cherry-like fruit. Though the cherries are more pit and pulp than juicy fruit, the Gabrielino people harvested them in days gone by, and they are eaten today by birds and foxes.

West End Trail, a mellow dirt road, begins at Two Harbors, Catalina's "Second City," which isn't a city at all but a drowsy hamlet with a small lodge, cabins and campsites.

Two Harbors' history is colorful, checkered and seems to have revolved around smuggling. During Spanish days, *contrabandistas* stashed cargo here in order to avoid mainland customs collectors. And during Prohibition, bootleggers' boats hid out at remote west end coves.

A pleasant family outing on fairly level trail is the walk from Two Harbors to Cherry Cove. A long, but not particularly rugged hike is the jaunt to Parsons Campground, seven miles west.

Directions to trailhead: Two Harbors is accessible via ferries departing from San Pedro, as well as ferries from Avalon (summer only). If you can work out the logistics with the ferry schedule, you might be able to arrange transportation to or from Parsons Landing and make this a one-way hike.

The Hike: From Isthmus Cove Beach, look for the trail ascending 50 yards to an intersection with West End Road. Go west. Looking oceanward, you'll spy Bird Rock, a white rock that's a landmark for sailors. Western gull guano gives it its distinctive white color.

Geology minded hikers will pause to look down at the Catalina schist, the fine-grained metamorphic rock that forms the shoreline.

You'll pass Fourth of July Cove, a mooring named for the Independence Day celebrations held here by the Banning family when they owned the island.

After 1¼ miles of walking, you'll reach Cherry Cove named, obviously, for the Catalina cherry that thrive in the mouth of a wide, V-shaped valley. Through the valley you go, passing, over the next few miles a number of scout and group camps, as well as private moorings. Particularly beautiful is aptly named Emerald Bay.

Six miles from Two Harbors, you'll pass an intersection with Boushay Trail (a dirt road) on your left. Staying right, you walk another half-mile, leaving West End Road as it bends left and joining a trail leading through grassland to Parsons Landing Campground.

The eagle has returned to Catalina.

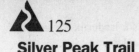 125

Silver Peak Trail

Parsons Landing to Silver Peak
  7 miles round trip; 1,700-foot gain

To Starlight Beach
  11 miles round trip; 1,700-foot gain

Season: All year

Like the Wild West on the mainland, Catalina's west end attracted its share of gold-seekers. Twin brothers Nathaniel and Theophiles Parsons (for whom Parsons Landing is named) were two such gold-seekers.

Optimistic (are there any other kind?) miners began construction of "Queen City" on the coast in 1863. The ambitious argonauts were halted, however, by the Union Army. While surveying the island, (with the idea of putting an Indian reservation here), the Army booted the miners off Catalina.

Wild animals roam the wild west end of the isle, particularly wild goats, which have denuded the hillsides and created quite an erosion/management problem. A more welcome sight for the wildlife lover may be found soaring over the rocky cliffs near Land's End: an American bald eagle. The Catalina Island Conservancy is reintroducing the big birds to the island.

This hike ascends Silver Peak, highest promontory on the west end of Catalina, visits Starlight Beach, and returns via a coastal trail that overlooks a number of coves and sand strands.

Directions to trailhead: To get to Parsons Landing, you can walk seven miles along West End Road or take a shoreboat from Two Harbors. It's a great boat ride with superb coastal views. Schedule is seasonal.

The Hike: From the camp at Parsons Landing, join the trail east, soon junctioning with West End Road. Go east (toward Two Harbors). Half-a-mile of hiking and you'll meet Boushay Trail, a dirt road, ascending to the right (south).

Climbing the brushy hills, the road winds two miles to a ridgeline and a meeting with Silver Peak Trail. The trail, a dirt road, extends along the backbone of the mountain range. You could head southeast down to Two Harbors, but this day hike turns right (northwest) and begins ascending toward Silver Peak. You'll climb past some red, barren badlands, prickly pear cactus and wild goats are the flora and fauna you'll spy en route.

A mile's climb will bring you to a point some 50 yards below the spartan summit of Silver Peak. Clamber past scattered ironwood trees to the top. If it's a clear day, enjoy mainland and ocean views; if it's particularly clear, you might spot Santa Barbara and San Nicholas Islands.

Now Silver Peak Trail descends, deteriorating as it does so into a steep bulldozer-cut path. Your abrupt descent brings you to a junction with the coastal road that will return you (right) to Parsons Landing. Beach connoisseurs will, however, turn left and hike a mile down to Starlight Beach, one of the most remote on the Catalina—in fact, on the Southern California—coast.

The dirt coastal road dips in and out of oak-shaded canyons and serves up great coastal views as it meanders east back toward Parsons Landing.

Antelope Valley views from Saddleback Peak

15. Antelope Valley

SITUATED SOUTH OF THE Tehachapi Mountains and northwest of the San Gabriel Mountains, the Antelope Valley makes up the western frontier of the Mojave Desert. The rapidly expanding cities of Palmdale, Lancaster and Victorville are located here.

Topographically, the East and West Mojave are quite different. The West presents great sandscapes, with many flat areas and some isolated ridges and buttes. The East Mojave is more mountainous.

The Antelope Valley's natural attractions include a reserve for the state's official flower—the California poppy—and another reserve for the endangered desert tortoise. Other parks preserve a Joshua tree woodland (Saddleback Butte State Park) and display the remarkable earthquake-fractured geology of this desert (Devil's Punchbowl County Park).

Joshua trees thrive in the valley. Palmdale, established in 1886 was named for the Joshuas; settlers mistakenly figured the spiky trees were palms. Saddleback Butte was originally named Joshua Tree State Park when it was created in 1960. The name was changed to avoid confusion with Joshua Tree National Monument.

When the Los Angeles to San Francisco rail line was constructed through the valley in the 1870s, it completely changed the ecology of the West Mojave. Because the Antelope Valley, a natural reservoir, had extensive ground water, farmers grew alfalfa. Hay was supplied to dairy farmers in Los Angeles until well into the 1920s.

The spartan-looking valley once supported thousands of proghorn antelope—hence the name Antelope Valley—and the numerous Indian tribes who hunted them. The railroad tracks interrupted the antelope's migration, thus dooming the animals. The antelope could easily cross the tracks, but instinct prevented them from doing this; they soon perished from exposure to harsh winters and the shrinkage of their habitat.

The California poppy blooms on many a grassy slope in the Southland, but only in the Antelope Valley does the showy flower blanket whole hillsides in such brilliant orange sheets. Surely the finest concentration of California's state flower (during a good wildflower year) is preserved at the California State Poppy Reserve in the Mojave Desert west of Lancaster.

Valley residents are proud of their spring wildflower show and look forward to showing visitors the beauties of the West Mojave.

Antelope Loop Trail

Visitors Center to Antelope Butte Vista Point
2½ miles round trip; 300-foot gain

Season: March-June

At the California State Poppy Reserve in the Mojave Desert west of Lancaster, the poppy is the star of the flower show, which includes a supporting cast of fiddlenecks, cream cups, tidy tips and gold fields. March through Memorial Day is the time to saunter through this wondrous display of desert wildflowers.

The poppy has always been recognized as something special. Early Spanish Californians called it Dormidera, "the drowsy one," because the petals curl up at night. They fashioned a hair tonic/restorer by frying the blossoms in olive oil and adding perfume.

At the reserve, you can pick up a map at the Jane S. Pineiro Interpretive Center, named for the painter who was instrumental in setting aside an area where California's state flower could be preserved for future generations to admire. Some of Pineiro's watercolors area on display in the center, which also has wildflower interpretive displays and a slide show.

Built into the side of a hill, the center includes award-winning solar design, windmill power and "natural" air conditioning.

Antelope Loop Trail—and all trails in the reserve—are easy walking and suitable for the whole family. Seven miles of gentle trails crisscross the 1,760-acre reserve; many hikers take every trail in the park without getting too tired.

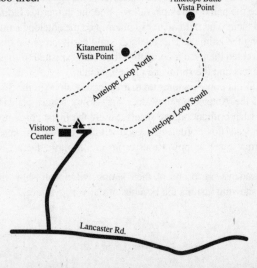

Directions to trailhead: From the Antelope Valley Freeway (California 14) in Lancaster, exit on Avenue I and drive west 15 miles. Avenue I becomes Lancaster Road a few miles before the Poppy Reserve. The reserve is open 9 A.M. to 4 P.M. daily. There is a state park day use fee. Spring wildflower displays are always unpredictable. To check on what's blooming where, call the park at (805) 724-1180 before making the trip.

The Hike: Begin on the signed Antelope Loop Trail to the left of the Visitors Center. The trail passes through an orange sea of poppies and fiddlenecks, then climbs briefly to Kitanemuk Vista Point, ¾ mile from the Visitors Center. Atop Vista Point are those flowery symbols of faithfulness and friendship, forget-me-nots, and an unforgettable view of the Mojave Desert and the snow-covered Tehachapis.

After enjoying the view, continue on to Antelope Butte Vista Point, where another lookout offers fine desert panoramas. From here, join the south loop of the Antelope Loop Trail and return to the visitors center.

After you've circled the "upper west side" of the Poppy Reserve, you may wish to extend your hike by joining the Poppy Loop Trail and exploring the "lower east side."

Punchbowl Trail

South Fork Campground to Devil's Chair
  6 miles round trip; 1,000-foot gain

South Fork Campground to County Park Headquarters
  12 miles round trip; 1,000-foot gain

Season: All year, but very hot in summer

Southern California has many faults, and the mightiest of these is the San Andreas. Nowhere is the presence of this fault more obvious than in Devil's Punchbowl County Park. The dun-colored rocks have been tilted every which way and weathered by wind and rain. They are a bizarre sight to behold.

Punchbowl Trail takes you into the Devil's domain, a satanically landscaped rock garden on the desert side of the San Gabriel Mountains. The trip offers views of the Punchbowl Fault and the San Jacinto Fault— part of what seismologists call the San Andreas Rift Zone. If you're superstitious, you'll want to carry a good-luck charm in your day pack when you hike to the monstrous mass of white rock known as the Devil's Chair.

Winter is a fine time to visit the Punchbowl. Winds scour the desert clean and from the Devil's Chair, you can get superb views of this land, as well as the seemingly infinite sandscape of the Mojave.

Note that six-mile-long Punchbowl Trail may be hiked from two directions. For aesthetic and logistical reasons, I prefer the route from the Forest Service's South Fork Campground to Devil's Chair.

The leg-weary or families with small children may wish to proceed directly to Devil's Punchbowl County Park. A ¹/₃-mile nature trail, Pinyon Pathway, introduces visitors to park geology and plant life, and a one-mile loop trail offers grand views of the Punchbowl. A picnic area is perched on the rim of the Punchbowl.

Directions to trailhead: From Pearblossom Highway in Pearblossom (Highway 138), turn south onto Longview Road, then briefly left on Fort Tejon Road and right on Valyermo Road. Follow Valyermo 3 miles to Big Rock Creek Road. Two-and-a-half miles past this junction, turn right on a signed dirt road to South Fork Campground and proceed one mile to the special day use/hiker's parking lot below the campground. The road is suitable for passenger cars, but on occasion, Big Rock Creek may be too high for a low-slung car to ford; you may have to walk an extra mile to the trailhead. The signed trail departs from the parking area.

If you want to go directly to Devil's Punchbowl County Park, turn south on County Road N6 from Highway 138 in Pearblossom and follow it to Devil's Punchbowl County Park. Punchbowl Trail begins near the picnic area.

The Hike: From the parking area below South Fork Campground, join the signed trail. Almost immediately you'll reach a trail junction. (The steep South Fork Trail follows the canyon cut by the South Fork of Big Rock Creek up to the Angeles Crest Highway at Islip Saddle. Save this fine trail, which ascends from cactus to pine, from desert to alpine environments, for another day.)

Stay on the Punchbowl Trail and boulder-hop across the creek. If your imagination has already run away with you, perhaps the mythological Charon the Ferryman (who conveyed the dead to Hades over the River Styx) will carry you across this watercourse.

The trail climbs through manzanita- and heat-stunted pinyon pine to a saddle where there's a view of the park and its faults. Descend from the

saddle, down chaparral-covered slopes and over to Holcomb Canyon. Along the way, notice the strange dovetailing of three plant communities: yucca-covered hills, oak woodland, and juniper and piney woods.

You may wish to take a break near Holcomb Creek crossing. Oaks and big cone spruce shade the creek.

From Holcomb Creek, the trail ascends steeply up another ridge through a pinyon pine forest to the Devil's Chair. From a distance, those with fanciful imaginations can picture the devil himself ruling over this kingdom of fractured rock. Below the chair, there's an awesome panorama of the Punchbowl and its jumbled sedimentary strata. The somersaulted sandstone formation resembles pulled taffy. If you look west to the canyon wall, you can see the vertical crush zone of the fault, marked by white rocks.

The Punchbowl itself may have been the work of the devil, or more likely, it was a deep canyon cut by streams running out of the San Gabriel Mountains. Over millions of years, the streams tore at the sedimentary rock and eroded the steep and cockeyed rock layers of the Punchbowl formation. Originally horizontal, these layers of siltstone and sandstone were folded into a syncline (U-shaped fold), by the pinching action of earthly forces.

While visiting the Devil's Chair, stay behind the protective fence; people have taken a plunge into the Punchbowl. Return to the trailhead the way you came or continue on the Punchbowl Trail to county park headquarters.

Above Devil's Chair, the trail contours west and offers good close-up views of the Punchbowl. A mile-and-a-half from the Chair, your route crosses Punchbowl Creek, briefly joins a dirt road, then bears right on the trail leading to the Punchbowl parking area.

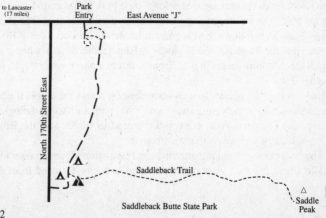

128

Saddleback Butte Trail

Campground to Saddleback Peak
  4 miles round trip; 1,000-foot gain

Season: October-May

Rarely visited Saddleback Butte State Park, located on the eastern fringe of Antelope Valley, offers an easily reached, but out-of-the-way destination for a day hike.

This is high-desert country, a land of creosote bush and Joshua trees. The park, located 75 miles north of Los Angeles, takes the name of its most prominent feature—3,651-foot Saddleback Butte, a granite mountaintop that stands head and shoulders above Antelope Valley.

Visitors may glimpse animals native to Antelope Valley, including coyote, jackrabbits lizards and the Antelope Valley ground squirrel. Some fortunate hikers may even spot a desert tortoise.

Before you hike to the top of the butte, you may wish to hike the short nature trail located near the park entrance. It's a good introduction to the Joshua tree and other plant life found in this corner of the desert.

The trail to the boulder-strewn summit of Saddleback Peak takes a straight-line course, with most of the elevation gain occuring in the last half-mile. From atop the peak, enjoy far-reaching desert views.

Directions to trailhead: From Highway 14 (Antelope Valley Freeway) in Lancaster, take the 20th Street exit. Head north on 20th and turn east (right) on Avenue J. Drive about 18 miles, past barren land and farmland, to Saddleback Butte State Park. Follow the dirt park road to the campground, where the trail begins. Park near the trail sign.

The Hike: The signed trail heads straight for the saddle. The soft, sandy track, marked with yellow posts (this may be the best-marked trail in the state park system), leads through an impressive Joshua tree woodland.

After 1½ miles, the trail begins to switchback steeply up the rocky slope of the butte. An invigorating climb brings you to the saddle of Saddleback Butte. To reach Saddleback Peak, follow the steep leftward trail to the summit.

From the top, you can look south to the San Gabriel Mountains. You may be able to spot Mount Baldy, lording over the eastern end of the range. At the base of the mountains, keen eyes will discern the California Aqueduct, which carries water to the Southland from the Sacramento Delta. To the east is the vast Mojave Desert, to the north is Edwards Air Force Base. To the west are the cities of Lancaster and Palmdale and farther west, the Tehachapis.

16. Joshua Tree Nat'l. Monument

WELL-KNOWN FOR ITS incredible granite boulders that attract rock-climbers and its forests of Joshua trees, the 870-square mile national monument attracts visitors from around the world. It's a year-around destination for a variety of outdoor activities including hiking and camping.

During the 1920s, a worldwide fascination with the desert emerged, and cactus gardens were very much in vogue. Entrepreneurs hauled truckloads of desert plants into Los Angeles for quick sale or export. The Mojave was in danger of being picked clean of its cacti, yucca and ocotillo. A wealthy socialite, Minerva Hoyt, organized the International Desert Conservation League to halt this destructive practice. Through her lobbying efforts, Joshua Tree National Monument was established in 1936.

The Joshua tree is said to have been given its name by early Mormon settlers traveling West. The tree's upraised limbs and bearded appearance reminded them of the prophet Joshua leading them to the promised land.

Despite its harsh appearance, the Joshua tree belongs to the lily family. Like lilies and other flowers, it must be pollinated in order to reproduce. The Tegeticula moth does the job for the Joshua tree, which in turn provides seeds for the newly hatched larvae of the moth. Long ago, during the evolutionary history of the Mojave Desert, the Joshua tree and the moth joined together to produce more Joshua trees and more moths, a partnership that continues to this day.

Joshuas are found almost exclusively in the Mojave Desert (2,500 to 5,000 feet). The higher elevations, (relatively) cooler temperatures and more northerly latititude of the Mojave suits the Joshua better than the lower, dryer, hotter Colorado Desert. They grow at the foot of mountain slopes and capture the surface and groundwater draining from higher elevations. Once in a while you'll see a Joshua tree clumsily embrace one of its fellows but, generally, its water requirement keeps it distant from other trees.

The Joshua tree is a small world unto itself and gives life to a number of creatures. A multitude of insects swarm in and on the tree. Birds nest in its limbs and feed on the insects. Lizards take shelter under the fallen trees and limbs. Termites break down dead Joshuas to dust and the tree returns to the earth from which it sprung.

Another wonder of the national monument is the Wonderland of Rocks, 12 square miles of massive jumbled granite. This curious maze of stone hides groves of Joshua trees, trackless washes and several small pools of water.

The national monument also holds several of California's loveliest palm oases—several of which are accessible to the hiker.

129

Ryan Mountain Trail

Sheep Pass to Ryan Mountain
  4 miles round trip; 700-foot gain

Season: October-May

This day hike tours some Joshua trees, visits Indian Cave and ascends Ryan Mountain for a nice view of the rocky wonderland in this part of the National Monument. Ryan Mountain is named for the Ryan brothers, Thomas and Jep, who had a homestead at the base of the mountain.

Despite its harsh appearance, the Joshua tree, *yucca brevifolia,* belongs to the lily family. Like lilies and other flowers, it must be pollinated to reproduce. The Tegeticula moth does the job for the Joshua tree, which in turn, provides seeds for the newly hatched larvae of the moth. Long, long ago, during the evolutionary history of the Mojave Desert, the Joshua tree and the moth joined together to produce more Joshua trees and more moths, a partnership that continues to this day.

The Joshua tree is a small world unto itself; it gives life to a number of creatures. A multitude of insects swarm in and on the tree; birds nest in its limbs and feed on the insects. Lizards take shelter under the fallen trees and limbs; termites break dead Joshuas down to dust, allowing the tree to return to the earth from which it sprang.

Joshua trees are found almost exclusively in the Mojave Desert at elevations ranging from 2,500 to 5,000 feet. The higher elevations, rela-

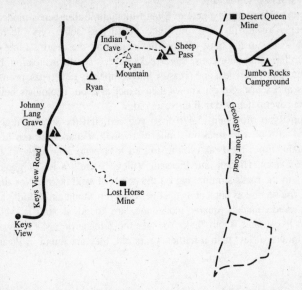

tively cooler temperatures and more northerly latitude of the Mojave suit the Joshua better than the lower, drier, hotter Colorado Desert. The trees grow at the foot of mountain slopes and capture the surface and ground-water draining from higher elevations. Once in a while, you'll see a Joshua tree clumsily embrace one of its fellows, but generally, its water requirement keeps it distant from other trees.

The view from atop Ryan Mountain is to be savored, and is one of the finest in the National Monument.

Directions to trailhead: From the Joshua Tree National Monument Visitor Center at Twentynine Palms, drive 3 miles south on Utah Trail Road (the main park road), keeping right at Pinto Y junction and continuing another 8 miles to Sheep Pass Campground on your left. Park in the campground, but don't take a camping space. You may also begin this hike from the Indian Cave Turnout just up the road. Be sure to visit Indian Cave; a number of bedrock mortars found in the cave suggests its use as a work site by its aboriginal inhabitants.

The Hike: From Sheep Pass Campground, the trail skirts the base of Ryan Mountain and passes through a lunar landscape of rocks and Joshua trees. The Joshua is categorized as an evergreen, though each year much of its foliage withers, dies and falls off. The ones near the trail would be better described as ''everlasting'' rather than evergreen.

Soon you intersect a well-worn side trail coming up from your right. If you like, follow this brief trail down to Indian Cave, typical of the kind of shelter sought by the nomadic Cahuilla and Serrano Indian clans that traveled this desert land.

Continuing past the junction, Ryan Mountain Trail ascends moderate-to-steeply toward the peak. En route, you'll pass some very old rocks which make up the core off this mountain and the nearby Little San Bernardino range. For eons, these rocks have, since their creation, been metamorphosed by heat and pressure into completely new types, primarily gneiss and schist. No on knows their exact age, but geologists believe they're several hundred million years old.

Atop Ryan Mountain (5,470 feet) you can sign the summit register, located in a tin can stuck in a pile of rocks that marks the top of the mountain. From the peak, you're treated to a panoramic view of Lost Horse, Queen, Hidden and Pleasant Valley. There's a lot of geologic history in the rocks shimmering on the ocean of sand below. Not all the rocks you see are as ancient as the ones on Ryan Mountain. Middle-aged rocks, predominately quartz monzonite, are found at Hidden Valley, Jumbo Rocks and White Tank. Younger rocks made of basaltic lava are mere infants at less than a million years old; they are found in Pleasant Valley.

130

Lost Horse Mine Trail

Parking Area to Lost Horse Mine
 3½ miles round trip; 400-foot gain

Season: October-May

Lost Horse Mine was the most successful gold mining operation in this part of the Mojave. More than 9,000 ounces of gold were processed from ore dug here in the late 1890s. The mine's 10-stamp mill still stands, along with a couple of large cyanide settling tanks and a huge winch used on the main shaft. The trail to the mine offers a close-up look back into a colorful era and some fine views into the heart of the national monument.

Many are the legends that swirl like the desert winds around the Lost Horse Mine. As the story goes, Johnny Lang in 1893 was camping in Pleasant Valley when his horse got loose. He tracked it out to the ranch belonging to Jim McHaney, who told Lang his horse was "no longer lost" and threatened Lang's health and future.

Lang wandered over to the camp of fellow prospector Dutch Diebold, who told him that he, too, had been threatened by McHaney and his cowboys. A pity too, because Diebold had discovered a promising gold prospect, but had been unable to mark his claim's boundaries. After sneaking in to inspect the claim, Johnny Lang and his father, George, purchased all rights from Diebold for $1,000.

At first it looked like a bad investment, because the Langs were prevented by McHaney's thugs from reaching their claim. Partners came and went, and by 1895, Johnny Lang owned the mine with the Ryan brothers, Thomas and Jep.

Peak production years for the mine were 1896 through 1899. Gold ingots were hidden in a freight wagon and transported to Indio. The ruse fooled any would-be highwaymen.

But thievery of another sort plagued the Lost Horse Mine. The theft was of amalgam, lumps of quicksilver from which gold could later be separated. Seems in this matter of amalgam, the mill's day shift, supervised by Jep Ryan, far out-produced the night shift, supervised by Lang. One of Ryan's men espied Lang stealing part of the amalgam. When Ryan gave Lang a choice—sell his share of the mine for $12,000 or go to the penitentiary—Lang sold out.

Alas, Johnny Lang came to a sad end. Apparently, his stolen and buried amalgams supported him for quite some time, but by the end of 1924, he was old, weak and living in an isolated cabin. And hungry. He had shot and eaten his four burros and was forced to walk into town for food. He

Lost Horse Mine

never made it. His partially mummified body wrapped in a canvas sleeping bag was found by prospectors alongside present-day Keys View Road. He was buried where he fell.

Directions to trailhead: From the central part of Joshua Tree National Monument, turn south from Caprock Junction on Keys Road and drive 2½ miles. Turn left on a short dirt road. Here you'll find a Park Service interpretive display about Johnny Lang's checkered career. (You can also visit Lang's grave, located a hundred feet north of the Lost Horse Mine turnoff on Keys Road.) The trail, a continuation of Lost Horse Mine Road, begins at a road barrier.

The Hike: The trail, the old mine road, climbs above the left side of a wash.

An alternative route, for the first (or last) mile of this day hike, is to hike from the parking area directly up the wash. Pinyon pine and the nolina (often mistaken for a yucca) dot the wash. Nolina leaves are more flexible than those of yucca, and its flowers smaller. The wash widens in about ¾ of a mile and forks; bear left and a short ascent will take you to the mine road. Turn right on the road and follow it to the mine.

A few open shafts remain near the Lost Horse, so be careful when you explore the mine ruins. Note the stone foundations opposite the mill site. A little village for the mine workers was built here in the late 1890s. Scramble up to the top of the hill above the mine for a panoramic view of Queen Valley, Pleasant Valley and the desert ranges beyond.

131

Lost Palms Oasis Trail

Cottonwood Springs Campground to Lost Palms Oasis
8 miles round trip; 300-foot elevation gain

Season: October-May

Lost Palms Oasis Trail passes through a cactus garden, crosses a number of desert washes, and takes you to the two southern oases in the National Monument: Cottonwood and Lost Palms. Largely man-made Cottonwood Spring Oasis was once a popular overnight stop for freight-haulers and prospectors during the mining years of 1870 to 1910. Travelers and teamsters journeying from Banning to the Dale Goldfield east of Twentynine Palms, rested at the oasis. Teamsters planted the trees that gave this oasis its name.

Lost Palms Oasis is a hidden gem. More than 100 palms are found in the deep canyon whose steep igneous walls sparkle in the desert sun.

Directions to trailhead: Joshua Tree National Monument is reached off Interstate Highway 10 east of Indio. Enter the south end of the monument, follow the park road 8 miles to Cottonwood Spring Campground, and park your car at the campground. The trailhead is at the end of the campground.

The Hike: Leaving Cottonwood Spring Campground, the trail ambles through a low desert environment of green-trunked palo verde, ironwood and cottonwood trees, spindly ocotillo plants and cholla cactus. Park Service identification plaques describe the area's flora and fauna.

The trail, a bit difficult to follow through the sandy wash, brings you to Cottonwood Spring Oasis in a half-mile. Cottonwood Spring is home to a wide variety of birds and a large number of bees.

From Cottonwood Spring, the trail marches over sandy hills, past heaps of huge rocks and along sandy draws and washes. A number of Park Service signs point the way at possibly confusing junctions. Finally, you rise above the washes and climb to a rocky outcropping overlooking the canyon harboring Lost Palms Oasis. From the overlook, descend the steep path around the boulders to the palms.

Little surface water is present at Lost Palms Oasis, but enough is underground for the palms to remain healthy. Lost Palms remained relatively untouched throughout the mining years, through some of its water was pumped to settlements eight miles to the south at Chiriaco

Summit. Adjacent to Lost Palms Canyon is a handsome upper canyon called Dike Springs.

Shy and reclusive desert bighorn sheep are often seen around this oasis—particularly in hot weather when they need water more often.

132

Barker Dam Loop Trail

Wonderland of Rocks to Barker Dam
1¼-mile round trip

Season: October-May

One of the many wonders of Joshua Tree National Monument is the Wonderland of Rocks, 12 square miles of massive jumbled granite. This curious maze of stone hides groves of Joshua trees, trackless washes and several small pools of water.

Perhaps the easiest, and certainly the safest way to explore the Wonderland is to follow the Barker Dam Loop Trail. The first part of the journey is on a nature trail that interprets the botanical highlights of the area. The last part of the loop trail visits some Indian petroglyphs.

This hike's main destination is the small lake created by Barker Dam. A century ago, cowboys took advantage of the water catchment of this natural basin and brought their cattle to this corner of the Wonderland of Rocks. C.O. Barker and his cowboys constructed the dam, which was later raised to its present height by Bill Keys and his family in the 1950s.

The trail to Barker Dam, while interesting, is not likely to occupy much of a day for the intrepid day hiker. One way to explore a little more of the Wonderland of Rocks is to pick up the Wonderland Wash Ranch Trail to the Astrodomes. Departing from the next spur road and parking area past the Barker Dam trailhead, this path leads to the ruins of a pink house known as Olsen house. From the back corner of the house, you'll pick up a wash and follow an intermittent trail through boulder clusters. The trail is popular with rock climbers, who use this trail to reach the Astrodomes—steep, 300-foot tall rocks that tower above the wash.

A myriad of narrow canyons and washes lead into the Wonderland, but route-finding is extremely complex and recommended only for the very experienced with map-and-compass skills.

Common sense dictates that you exit the Wonderland of Rocks by nightfall; it's also a Park Service regulation, designed to allow the shy bighorn sheep a chance to reach water without human interference.

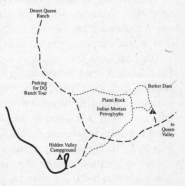

Barker Dam

Directions to trailhead: From I-10, a little east past the Highway 111 turnoff to Palm Springs, take Highway 62 northeast to the town of Joshua Tree. Continue 4 miles south to the park entrance, then another 10 miles to Hidden Valley Campground. A dirt road leads 2 miles from Hidden Valley Campground to Barker Dam parking area.

The Hike: From the north end of the parking area, join the signed trail that enters the Wonderland of Rocks. You'll pass a special kind of oak, the turbinella, which has adjusted to the harsh conditions of desert life.

For the first half-mile, interpretive signs point out the unique botany of this desert land. The path then squeezes through a narrow rock passageway and leads directly to the edge of the lake. Bird-watching is excellent here because many migratory species not normally associated with the desert are attracted to the lake.

The trail is a bit indistinct near Barker Dam, but resumes again in fine form near a strange-looking circular water trough, a holdover from the area's cattle ranching days. A toilet-like float mechanism controlled the flow of water to the thirsty livestock.

The path turns southerly and soon passes a huge boulder known as Piano Rock. When this land was in private ownership, a piano was hauled atop this rock and played for the amusement of visitors and locals.

Beyond Piano Rock the trail enters a rock-rimmed valley. A brief leftward detour at a junction brings you to the Movie Petroglyphs, so named because in less-enlightened times, the native rock art was painted over by a film crew in order to make it more visible to the camera's eye.

Back on the main trail, you'll parallel some cliffs, perhaps get a glimpse of some Indian bedrock mortars, and loop back to the parking area.

133

Fortynine Palms Trail

Parking Area to Fortynine Palms Oasis
  3 miles round trip; 400-foot gain

Season: October-May

Fortynine Palms Oasis, reached only by trail, has retained a wonderful air of remoteness. From the parking area, an old Indian trail climbs a steep ridge and offers the hiker expansive views of the Sheephole and Bullion mountain ranges.

On the exposed ridge, barrel cacti, creosote, yucca, and brittlebush brave the heat. As the trail winds up and over a rocky crest, the restful green of the oasis comes into view. At the oasis, nature's personality abruptly changes and the dry, sunbaked ridges give way to dripping springs, pools, and the blessed shade of palms and cottonwoods.

Unlike some oases, which are strung out for miles along a stream, Fortynine Palms is a close-knit palm family centered around a generous supply of surface water. Seeps and springs fill numerous basins set among the rocks at different levels. Other basins are supplied by "rain" dripping from the upper levels. Mesquite and willow thrive alongside the palms. Singing house finches and croaking frogs provide a musical interlude.

Perched on a steep canyon wall, Fortynine Palms Oasis overlooks the town of Twentynine Palms, but its untouched beauty makes it seem a lot farther removed from civilization.

Directions to trailhead: From Interstate 10, a few miles east of the Highway 111 turnoff going to Palm Springs, bear north on Highway 62. After passing the town of Yucca Valley, but before reaching the outskirts of Twentynine Palms, turn right on Canyon Road. (Hint: Look for an animal hospital at the corner of Highway 62 and Canyon Road) Follow Canyon Road 1¾ miles to its end at a National Park Service parking area and the trailhead.

The Hike: The trail rises through a spartan rockscape dotted with cacti and jojoba. After a brisk climb, catch your breath atop a ridgetop and enjoy the view of Twentynine Palms and the surrounding desert.

You may notice colorful patches of lichen adhering to the rocks. Lichen, which conducts the business of life as a limited partnership of algae and fungi, is very sensitive to air pollution; the health of this tiny plant is considered by some botanists to be related to air quality. Contemplate the abstract impressionist patterns of the lichen, inhale great draughts of fresh air, then follow the trail as it descends from the ridgetop.

Fortynine Palms

The trail leads down slopes dotted with barrel cactus and mesquite. Soon the oasis comes into view. Lucky hikers may get a fleeting glimpse of bighorn sheep drinking from oasis pools or gamboling over nearby steep slopes.

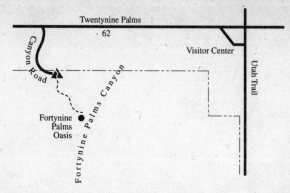

As the path leads you to the palms, you'll notice many fire-blackened tree trunks. The grove has burned several times since this land was set aside a half century ago and placed under the protection of the National Park Service.

Fortunately, palms are among the most fireproof trees in existence, and fire—whether caused by man or lightning—seldom kills them. Fire may actually be beneficial for the palms because it serves to temporarily eliminate the competition of such trees as mesquite and cottonwood and bushes like arrowweed, all of them thirsty fellows and able to push their roots much deeper in search of water than palms. Burning also opens the oasis floor to sunlight, which seedling palms need.

Fortynine Palms Oasis celebrates life. Our native California fan palm clusters near handsome boulder-lined pools. Fuzzy cattails, ferns and grasses sway in the breeze. An oasis like this one gives the hiker a chance to view the desert in terms that are the exact opposite of its stereotypical dry hostility. If the desert is the land God forgot, then the Creator must have had a sudden afterthought and decided to sprinkle this parched land with oases, reminders of His lush handiwork.

17. Anza-Borrego Desert State Park

ANZA-BORREGO DESERT State Park includes virtually every feature visitors associate with a desert: washes, badlands, mesas, palm oases and much more. This diverse desert park boasts more than 20 palm groves and year-around creeks, great stands of cholla and elephant trees, slot canyons and badland formations.

Anza-Borrego is diverse, and it is huge; more than three times the size of Zion National Park. The 600,000-acre park stretches almost the whole length of San Diego County's eastern border between Riverside County and Mexico. Its elevation ranges from 100 feet below sea level near the Salton Sea to 6,000 feet above sea level atop San Ysidro Mountain.

California's largest state park (in fact, the nation's largest state park) preserves a 60-mile long, 30-mile wide stretch of Colorado Desert from the Santa Rosa Mountains to the Mexican border. Lower in elevation than the Mojave Desert, the Colorado Desert is also hotter and drier. (The Colorado Desert in the extreme southeastern portion of California is only a small part of the larger Sonoran Desert, which covers about 120,000 acres of the American Southwest.)

The park, set aside in 1933, is named for the Mexican explorer (Juan Bautista de Anza) and the Spanish word for bighorn sheep *(borrego)*. De Anza traveled through the area in 1774, and the bighorn sheep still roam this land.

Travelers are welcomed to Anza-Borrego by what is probably the best visitors center in the state park system. Numerous self-guided nature trails and automobile tours allow visitors to set their own pace. An active natural history association and foundation sponsors many regularly scheduled ranger- and naturalist-led activities.

While the park is oriented to exploration by vehicle, a number of fine hikes await the desert trekker. A note to the uninitiated: Hiking in this section of the Colorado Desert is guaranteed to make a desert rat out of anyone.

Among the sights are Calcite Canyon, where nature's cutting tools, wind and water, have shaped the ageless sandstone into steep, bizarre formations. The elephant tree grove is another strange sight. Its surreal color scheme, parchment-like bark and stout elephant-like trunk is something to behold.

134

Borrego Palm Canyon Trail

Borrego Campground to Falls
   3 miles round trip; 600-foot gain

To South Fork
   6½ miles round trip; 1,400-foot gain

Season: October-May

Borrego Palm Canyon is the third-largest palm oasis in California, and was the first site sought for a desert state park back in the 1920s. It's a beautiful, well-watered oasis, tucked away in a rocky V-shaped gorge.

The trail visits the first palm grove and a waterfall. A longer option takes you exploring farther up-canyon. In winter, the trail to the falls is one of the most popular in the park. In summer, you'll have the oasis all to yourself. Watch for bighorn sheep, which frequently visit the canyon.

Directions to trailhead: The trail begins at Borrego Palm Canyon Campground, located one mile north of park headquarters. Trailhead parking is available at the west end of the campground near the campfire circle.

The Hike: Beginning at the pupfish pond, you walk up-canyon past many desert plants used by the Indians for food and shelter. Willow was used for home-building and bow-making; brittle bush and creosote were used for their healing qualities; honey, along with mesquite and beavertail cactus, was a food staple. You might also notice shallow Indian grinding holes in the granite.

The broad alluvial fan at the mouth of the canyon narrows and the sheer rock walls of the canyon soon enclose you as the trail continues along the healthy, but seasonal stream. Already surprised to learn how an apparently lifeless canyon could provide all the Indians' necessary survival ingredients, you're surprised once more when Borrego Palm Oasis comes into view. Just beyond the first group of palms is a damp grotto, where a waterfall cascades over huge boulders. The grotto is a popular picnic area and rest stop.

From the falls, you may take an alternate trail back to the campground. This trail takes you along the south side of the creek, past some magnificent ocotillos, and gives you a different perspective on this unique desert environment. By following the optional route, you can continue hiking up the canyon. Hiking is more difficult up-canyon after the falls, with lots of dense undergrowth and boulders to navigate around.

To South Fork: From the "tourist turnaround" continue up the canyon.

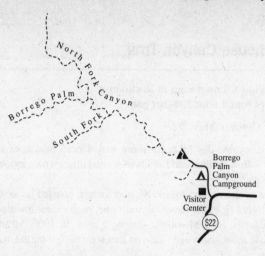

The creek is a fairly dependable water supply and is usually running late in the fall. The canyon is wet, so watch your footing on the slippery, fallen palm fronds. The canyon narrows even further and the trail dwindles to nothing. Parallel the streambed and boulder-hop back and forth across the water. The canyon zigs and zags quite a bit, so you can never see much more than a few hundred yards ahead. The hike is well-worth the effort though, because most of the 800 or so palms in the canyon are found in its upper reaches. Sometimes you'll spot rock-climbers practicing their holds on the steep red-rock cliffs above you.

The canyon splits 1¾ miles from the falls. Straight ahead, to the southwest, is South Fork. The rocky gorge of South Fork, smothered with bamboo, is in possession of all the canyon's water. It's quite difficult to negotiate. South Fork ascends to the upper slopes of San Ysidro Mountain (6,417 feet). The Middle Fork (the way you came) of Borrego Pam Canyon is dry and more passable. It's possible to hike quite a distance first up Middle Fork, then North Fork of Borrego Palm Canyon, but check with park rangers first. It's extremely rugged terrain.

135

Rockhouse Canyon Trail

Bow Willow Campground to Rockhouse
 7 miles round trip; 700-foot gain

Season: October-May

This enjoyable day hike, for more experienced hikers, explores two canyons—Bow Willow and Rockhouse—and offers a nice introduction to the state park.

A turn-of-the-century miner, Nicolas Swartz, boasted he took $18,000 worth of gold from his remote desert mine. In the great tradition of Lost Mine Legends, he died without leaving a map. In 1906, Swartz built a rock house in an anonymous canyon that soon picked up the name of his structure.

History is a muddled affair. There are two rock houses in the state park and there's some question as to which actually belonged to Swartz. Some local historians believe that Swartz located his house in another canyon on the other side of the park and say that the Darrel McCain family built the rock house in Rockhouse Canyon as a line shack for a cattle operation.

This looping day hike takes you climbing through a single palm canyon, visits the rock house and its canyon and returns via the wash on the bottom of Bow Willow Canyon. Spring scatters color in the wash. Monkeyflowers, desert stars and a host of wildflowers brighten the sands and gravel bars. Even ocotillo changes its fit-only-for-firewood appearance and displays its new green leaves and flaming red flowers.

Directions to trailhead: From Interstate 8 in Ocotillo, take County Road S-2 sixteen miles to the turnoff for Bow Willow Canyon and Campground. Follow the good hardpack sand road 1½ miles to the campground. Park in the campground, but don't take a campsite someone could use.

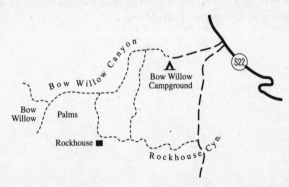

Rockhouse Canyon

The Hike: Walk up Bow Willow Canyon on the signed jeep trail. Before you get much past the campground, make a 90-degree left turn (south) across a few hundred yards of wash to pick up the foot trail. One-quarter mile up the trail is a beleaguered young palm tree. You begin climbing steadily through a desert garden of granite boulders, agave and cholla.

As you near Rockhouse Canyon, the trail descends briefly and intersects Rockhouse Canyon Jeep Trail. Follow the Jeep Trail west for one mile to Swartz's abandoned rock house. We can only pray that Swartz was a better prospector than architect. However, it's the only shade around, so this is no time to quibble over aesthetics.

From the rock house, you follow a tentative foot trail that drops down into Bow Willow Canyon. The wash on the canyon floor makes a unique hiking experience. In the wash, there's less of that relentless creosote that gives so much of the desert its monotonous look. Water, scarce as it is, is the dominant force working here. Flash floods carry great chunks of rock down to the canyon bottom. Water sculpts the cliffs and has carved the great V you're hiking in.

Coyote melon, bitter-tasting to humans and to the coyotes as well, dots the wash. The melons dry in the sun and the gourds blow around the wash. I'm often seized with the urge to bat them around and play some kind of prehistoric ballgame.

Before long you'll come to a barrier across the wash preventing off road vehicles from ascending into the upper reaches of the canyon. Past the barrier, the canyon widens and it's an easy 2-mile hike over soft sand back to Bow Willow Campground.

136

Calcite Canyon Trail

County Road S-22 to Calcite Mine
  4 miles round trip; 500-foot gain

Season: October-May

Nature's cutting tools, wind and water, have shaped the ageless sandstone in Calcite Canyon into steep, bizarre formations. The cutting and polishing of the uplifted rock mass has exposed calcite crystals. Calcite is a common enough carbonate and found in many rocks, but only in a few places are the crystals so pure.

It was the existence of these crystals, with their unique refractive properties that brought man to this part of the desert. The jeep trail was built in the mid-1930s for miners to gain access to Calcite Canyon, as it came to be called. Because of their excellent double refraction properties, calcite crystals were useful in the making of bomb sights. Mining activity increased during World War II.

The calcite was taken from the canyon in long trenches, which look as if they were made yesterday. The desert takes a long time to heal.

The day hike takes the jeep road to its dead end at the mine. You'll see the Calcite Mine Area up-close and get a good overlook of the many washes snaking toward the Salton Sea. A return trip through Palm Wash and its tributaries lets you squeeze between perpendicular walls and gives

a unique perspective on the forces that shape the desert sands. The awesome effects of flash flooding are easily discerned by the hiker and suggest a narrow wash is the last place in the world you want to be in a rainstorm.

Directions to trailhead: Follow County Road S-22 west from Highway 86, or 20 miles from the Christmas Circle to Calcite Jeep Road. The jeep road is just west of a microwave tower.

The Hike: Follow the jeep road, which first drops into the south fork of Palm Wash, then begins to climb northwest. Along the road you'll see long, man-made slots cut into the hillsides for the removal of calcite. Calcite Jeep Road dips a final time, then climbs a last half-mile toward the mine. Two miles from the trailhead, the road ends at the mining area.

Calcite crystal fragments embedded in the canyon walls and scattered on the desert floor glitter in the sun. Behind the mining area, to the northeast, is a gargantuan hunk of white sandstone dubbed "Locomotive Rock." The imaginative can picture a great Baldwin locomotive chugging up a steep grade. If you look carefully, you'll be able to see Seventeen Palms and some of the palms tucked away in Palm Wash in a bird's-eye-view of the east side of the state park.

You can return the same way or descend through tributaries of the middle fork of Palm Wash. Take a last look at the steep ravines and washes to get your bearings. Middle Fork is but a hop, skip and a jump from the mine, but the jump's a killer—a 50-foot plunge to a deep intersecting wash. To get into the wash, you need to descend a half-mile down Calcite Road to a small tributary wash. Descend this wash, which is fairly steep at first. The sandstone walls close in on you. One place, "Fat Man's Misery," allows only one fat man (or two skinny day hikers) to squeeze through at a time. When you reach the middle fork, a prominent canyon, follow it about a quarter-mile to the brief jeep trail connecting the wash to Calcite Road. Hike back up Calcite Road one-tenth of a mile to the parking area.

Calcite Canyon

137

Elephant Trees Discovery Trail

Elephant Trees Discovery Trail
1½ miles round trip; 100-foot gain

A rarity in California deserts, the odd elephant tree is much admired by visitors to Anza-Borrego Desert State Park. Its surreal color scheme (was this tree designed by committee?) of green foliage, red-tan twigs, yellow-green peeling parchment-like bark, white flowers and blue berries, is something to behold. The stout trunk and the way the branches taper, vaguely suggests an elephant, but lots of imagination is required.

The tree's red sap is aromatic and related to frankincense and myrrh. Mayans and Aztecs burned the resin as incense and used the sap to dye their clothes.

Enjoy this hike by following the 1½ mile nature trail and/or by trekking along an alluvial fan to some elephant trees.

A herd estimated at five hundred elephant trees grow at this end of the state park. *Birsera microphylla* is more common in Baja California and in the Gila Range of Arizona. (The elephant tree, along with all other park vegetation, is protected by state law.) The park has three populations of elephant trees, but the one off Split Mountain Road is the most significant.

Elephant Trees Discovery Trail, besides examining this botanical oddity, also interprets various desert flora and geological features of this part of the Colorado Desert. An interpretive brochure, keyed to numbered posts along the trail, is available at the trailhead, from park rangers, and from the visitors center.

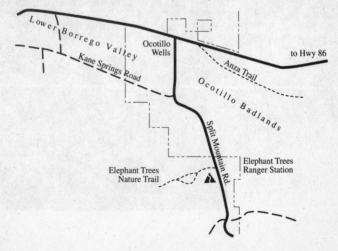

Directions to trailhead: From Ocotillo Wells (located about 40 miles west of Brawley and 78 miles east of Escondido on Highway 78), turn south on Split Mountain Road and proceed 6 miles to the signed turnoff for the Elephant Trees Area. Follow a dirt road 1 mile to the trailhead.

The Hike: Follow the nature trail until signpost #10, where you'll see the first elephant tree on the hike.

Those experienced hikers who wish to see more elephant trees will leave the trail here and hike west up the broad alluvial fan. You'll encounter bits of trail, but really the route is cross-country. Keep the mountains on the western horizon in your sight. A mile's walk brings you to some elephant trees.

Return the way you came back to the nature trail, which follows the numbered posts through a dry streambed and loops back to the trailhead.

The unusual Elephant Tree

18. Palm Springs

IN THE EARLY YEARS of this century, it was called a "Desert Eden," "Our Araby" and "A Garden in the Sun." Now it's called a "Desert Hollywood," "Fairway Living" and "Rodeo Drive East."

Palm Springs today means different things to different people, but one thing is for certain—the golf courses, condos and country clubs of the resort are a far cry from what the first residents of Agua Caliente intended.

What most Palm Springs pioneers intended was to leave this desert land more or less alone. Turn-of-the-century health-seekers and nature-lovers recognized their discovery for what it was—a true oasis. Here was a palm-dotted retreat where an ancient hot springs gushed forth. Here was nature, simple and unadorned.

Joseph Smeaton Chase, in his 1920 guidebook *Our Araby*, insisted that he and his 300 fellow Palm Springs residents were "well content to remain far down the list in census returns. We decline to take part in the Race for Improvements, and are (so we feel, anyway) wise enough to know when we are well off."

Chase championed the creation of Palm Canyon National Monument, in order to preserve the canyons on the outskirts of Palm Springs known collectively as the Indian Canyons—Palm, Murray and Andreas. The national monument was approved by Congress in 1922 but no funds were ever allocated and the palm canyons never did win National Park Service protection.

Finally, however, in 1990, a sizeable portion of the palm canyons, as well as the surrounding mountains came under federal protection with the establishment of the Santa Rosa Mountains National Scenic Area, administered by the U.S. Bureau of Land Management.

Fortunately, for the modern visitor, there yet remains a wild side of Palm Springs—parks, preserves and special places that offer opportunities to see the desert of old. Palm Springs wildlife, not to be confused with the Palm Springs wild life enjoyed by thousands of college students who come here during spring break, can be viewed in a number of quiet and picturesque locales.

"Essentially, the desert is Nature in her simplest expression," wrote Chase. The Living Desert Preserve, Palm Canyon, Big Morongo Canyon and the Coachella Valley Preserve are places for the hiker to commune with this simple nature.

138

Big Morongo Canyon Trail

Parking Lot to Waterfall
2½ miles round trip

To Canyon Mouth
12 miles round trip; 1,900-foot gain

Season: October-June

For many centuries native peoples used Big Morongo Canyon as a passageway between the high and low deserts. The last of these nomads to inhabit the canyon were a group of Serrano Indians known as the Morongo, for whom the canyon is named. When white settlers entered the area in the mid-Nineteenth Century, the Morongos were forced onto a reservation and the canyon became the property of ranchers. Today, Big Morongo Canyon is managed and protected by the Nature Conservancy and the U.S. Bureau of Land Management.

The relative abundance of water is the key to both Big Morongo's long human history and its botanical uniqueness. Several springs bubble up in the reserve and one of the California desert's very few year-around creeks flows through the canyon. Dense thickets of cottonwood and willow, as well as numerous water-loving shrubs line Big Morongo Creek. This lush, crowded riparian vegetation sharply contrasts with the well-spaced creosote community typical of the high and dry slopes of the reserve and of the open desert beyond.

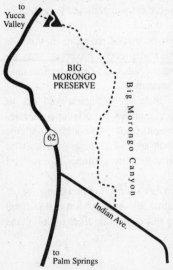

The oasis at Big Morongo is a crucial water supply for the fox, bobcat, raccoon, coyote and bighorn sheep. Gopher snakes, rosy boas, chuckawallas and California tree frogs are among the amphibians and reptiles in residence.

Big Morongo Canyon is best known for its wide variety of birds, which are numerous because the canyon is not only at the intersection of two deserts, but also at the merging of two climate zones—arid and coastal. These climates, coupled with the wet world of the oasis, means the preserve is an attractive stopover for birds on their spring and fall migrations.

For the hiker, the preserve offers several short loop-trails ranging from a quarter to one mile long. Some of the wetter canyon bottom sections of trail are crossed by wooden boardwalks, which keep hikers dry and fragile creekside flora from being trampled. Desert Wash, Cottonwood, Willow, Yucca Ridge and Mesquite Trails explore the environments suggested by their names.

A longer path, Canyon Trail, travels the 6-mile length of Big Morongo Canyon. You could make this a one-way, all downhill journey by arranging a car shuttle or by having someone pick you up on Indian Ave. Families with small children or the leg-weary will enjoy a 2½ mile round trip canyon walk to a small waterfall.

Directions to trailhead: From Interstate 10, 15 miles east of Banning and a bit past the Highway 111 turnoff to Palm Springs, exit on Highway 62. Drive 10 miles north to the signed turnoff on your right for Big Morongo Wildlife Preserve. Turn east and after ¹/₁₀ mile you'll see the preserve's service road leading to a parking area.

To reach the end of the trail at the mouth of Big Morongo Canyon, you'll exit on Highway 62 on Indian Avenue and drive exactly a mile to a dirt road on your left. A "Dip" sign precedes the turnoff and a pump enclosed by a chain link fence suggests your parking space.

The Hike: From the parking lot, you may pick up the trail by the Preserve's interpretive displays or join the dirt road that leads past the caretaker's residence.

Off to the right of the old ranch road, you'll see a pasture lined with cottonwood and a barn built in the 1880s. Often the road is muddy, so detour with the signed and aptly named Mesquite Trail which utilizes a wooden boardwalk to get over the wet spots. Take a moment to listen to the sound of running water, the many chirping birds and croaking frogs.

Canyon Trail meanders with the creek for a gentle mile or so and arrives at a corrugated metal check dam that has created a small waterfall. For the less energetic, this is a good turnaround point. The trail continues descending through the canyon with Big Morongo Creek until a bit over three miles from the trailhead, the creek suddenly disappears. Actually, the water continues flowing underground through layers of sand.

The canyon widens and so does the trail. About 5 miles from the trailhead is the south gate of the preserve. The canyon mouth and every inanimate object in the vicinity have been shot to hell by off-the-mark marksmen. Compensating for Big Morongo's somewhat inglorious end is a stirring view of snow-capped Mt. San Jacinto, which lies straight ahead. Stick to your right at every opportunity as you exit the canyon and a dirt road will soon deliver you to Indian Avenue.

139

McCallum Trail

1- to 5-mile loop through Coachella Valley Preserve

Season: October-May

If it looks like a movie set, don't be surprised. Thousand Palms Oasis was the setting for Cecil B. DeMille's 1924 silent film epic, *King of Kings* and the 1969 movie *Tell Them Willie Boy is Here* starring Robert Redford, Robert Blake and Katherine Ross.

The oasis is something special, and deserving of protection, but that's not why Coachella Valley Preserve was established. The reserve's *raison d'être* is habitat for the threatened Coachella Valley fringe-toed lizard.

For the most part, *Uma inornata* goes about the business of being a lizard beneath the surface of sand dunes, but scientists have been able to discover some of the peculiar habits of this creature, which manages to survive in places where a summer's day surface temperature may reach 160 degrees.

The eight-inch reptile is also known as the "sand swimmer" for its ability to dive through sand dunes. Its entrenching tool-shaped skull rams through the sand, while round scales on its skin reduce friction as it "swims." Fringes (large scales) on its toes give the lizard traction—as well as its name.

Alas, all is not fun in the sun for the fringe-toed lizard. The creature must avoid becoming dinner for such predators as roadrunners, snakes and loggerhead shrikes. But the biggest threat to the lizards was/is real estate development and consequent loss of habitat.

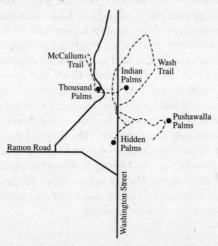

Fortunately for the fringe-toed lizard, real estate developers, the U.S. Bureau of Land Management, Congress, the California Department of Fish and Game, the U.S. Wildlife Service and the Nature Conservancy were able to find a common ground and establish a 13,000 acre preserve in 1986. Some conservationists believe the $25 million price tag may be the most expensive single species preservation effort of all time.

Still, the reserve would be something special even without its namesake lizard. It protects flora and fauna once common in the Coachella Valley before it grew grapefruit, golf courses and subdivisions.

Thousand Palms Oasis is California's second-largest collection of native California fan palms. Thousand Palms, along with Indian Palms, Horsehoe Palms and a couple of other oases in the reserve came into existence as the result of earthquake faults which brought water to the surface.

Before the reserve was set aside, the Thousand Palms area was purchased by turn of the century rancher Louis Wilhelm and his family. The Wilhelms built "Palm House" (now the reserve's visitors center) and by the 1930s were using it as a commissary for campers, scientists, scout troops and anyone else who wanted to enjoy a weekend in one of their palm-shaded cottages.

Hikers can explore Coachella Valley Reserve on a half-dozen trails. Three of these trails depart from Thousand Palms Oasis. Shortest (a fifteen minute walk) is Smoke Tree Ranch Trail, which encircles the palms oasis. Good bird-watching in the mesquite thickets and among the smoke trees. Watch for the smoke tree's bright blue/purple flowers in May or June.

Don't miss McCallum Trail, a 1½ mile round trip nature trail. It meanders by a jungle of willows, palms, cottonwoods and mesquite. At the trailhead, pick up an interpretive pamphlet that's keyed to numbered posts along the path.

Indian Palms Trail leads a half-mile to small Indian Palm Oasis.

More ambitious hikers will head for Wash Trail which, true to its name, winds through washes in the northern portion of the reserve. You can also visit Bee Rock Mesa, where Malpais Indians camped 5,000 years ago, hike into adjoining Indio Hills County Park, and visit more oases— Horsehoe Palms and Pushawalla Palms.

Directions to trailhead: From Interstate 10, about ten miles east of where Highway 111 leads off to Palm Springs, exit on Washington Street/ Ramon Road. Head north on Washington Street, which bends west and continues as Ramon Road. Soon after the bend, turn right (north again) onto Thousand Palms Canyon Road. Continue to the entrance to Coachella Valley Preserve and park in the dirt lot.

140

Lykken Trail

Palm Springs Desert Museum to Desert Riders Overlook
   2 miles round trip; 800-foot gain

To Ramon Drive
   4 miles round trip; 800-foot gain

Season: October-June

Palm Springs today is a curious sight—a chain of sparkling green islands on the desert sand. For a good overview of the resort hikers can join Museum and Lykken Trails.

This hike in the hills begins at Palm Springs Desert Museum, where natural science exhibits recreate the unique ecology of Palm Springs and the surrounding Colorado Desert. Displays interpret the astonishing variety of plant and animal life as well as the powerful geological forces that shaped this desert land. The museum also has exhibits portraying the original inhabitants of the Coachella Valley. Steep Museum Trail ascends the western base of Mt. San Jacinto. Letters painted on the rocks suggest that Museum was once a nature trail. After a mile's climb, Museum Trail junctions with Lykken Trail. This trail, formerly known as Skyline Trail, winds through the Palm Springs hills north to Tramway Road and south to Ramon Road.

Skyline Trail was renamed Lykken Trail in 1972 in honor of Carl Lykken, Palms Springs pioneer and the town's first postmaster. Lykken,

Desert Riders Overlook

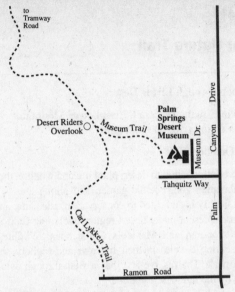

who arrived in 1913, owned a general merchandise store, and later a department/hardware store. Early Palm Springs social life consisted of stopping at the Desert Inn to check if any new and interesting guests had arrived, then dropping by Carl Lykken's store to pick up the mail, make a phone call (Lykken had the first telephone) and catch up on all the gossip.

Directions to trailhead: From Highway 111 (Palm Canyon Drive) in the middle of downtown Palm Springs, turn west on Tahquitz Drive, then a right on Museum Drive. Park in Palm Springs Desert Museum's north lot.

The trail begins back of the museum, between the museum and an administration building, by a plaque honoring Carl Lykken. The trail is closed during the summer months for health reasons (yours).

The Hike: The trail ascends the rocky slope above the museum. Soon you'll intersect a private road, jog left, then resume trail walking up the mountainside. As you rapidly gain elevation, the view widens from the Desert Fashion Plaza to the outskirts of Palm Springs to the wide-open spaces of the Coachella Valley.

A mile's ascent brings you to a picnic area, built by the Desert Riders, local equestrians whose membership included Carl Lykken. One Desert Rider, former Palm Springs Mayor Frank Bogart's efforts contributed much to the state's trail system.

Bear left (south) on Lykken Trail, which travels the hills above town before descending to Ramon Road near the mouth of Tahquitz Canyon. You can follow Ramon Road to downtown Palm Springs or return the way you came.

141

Jaeger Nature Trail

2-mile loop through Living Desert

**Return via Eisenhower Trail, Eisenhower Mountain
    5 miles round trip; 500-foot gain**

Season: October-May

A superb introduction to desert plant life and wildlife, the Living Desert is a combination zoo, botanic garden and hiking area. The 1,200-acre, nonprofit facility is dedicated to conservation, education and research.

Gardens represent major desert regions including California's Mojave, Arizona's Sonoran and Mexico's Chihuahuan. Wildlife-watchers will enjoy observing coyotes in their burrows and bighorn sheep atop their mountain peak. The reserve also has a walk-through aviary and a pond inhabited by the rare desert pupfish.

Nature and hiking trails provide an opportunity to form an even closer acquaintance with an uncrowded, undeveloped sandscape. Easy trails lead past the Arabian Oryx and bighorn sheep, past desert flora with name tags and eco-systems with interpretive displays, and over to areas that resemble the open desert of yesteryear.

Presidents Eisenhower, Nixon, Ford and Reagan relaxed in Palm Springs. Eisenhower spent many winters at the El Dorado Country Club at the base of the mountain that now bears his name. Palm Desert boosters petitioned the Federal Board of Geographic Names to name the 1,952 (coincidentally, 1952 was the year of his election)-foot peak for part-time Palm Springs resident Dwight D. Eisenhower.

The first part of the walk through The Living Desert uses a nature trail named after the great naturalist Edmund Jaeger. It's keyed to a booklet available from the entrance station. An inner loop of ²/₃ mile and an outer

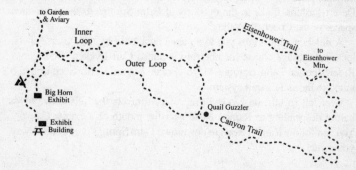

loop of 1½ miles lead past a wide array of desert flora and 60 interpretive stops. A longer loop can be made using Canyon Trail and Eisenhower Trail. The hike to Ike's peak ascends about halfway up the bald mountain and offers great views of the Coachella Valley.

Directions to trailhead: From Highway 111 in Palm Desert, turn south on Portola Avenue and drive 1½ miles south to the park. Hours: 9-5; closed mid-June to the end of August.

The Hike: The trail begins at the exhibit buildings. Follow either the numbered nature trail, beginning at number one, or make a short rightward detour to the bighorn sheep enclosure. The trail junctions once more and you begin heading up the alluvial plain of Deep Canyon. Walking up the wash, you'll observe the many moisture-loving plants that thrive in such environments, including smoke trees, desert willows and palo verde.

Stay right at the next junction and begin the outer loop of the Jaeger Nature Trail. You'll pass plenty of that common desert dweller; the creosote bush, and wind along the base of some sand dunes.

The trail climbs out of the wash and into a kind of plain that true desert rats call a "bajada." Here you'll find a quail guzzler which stores rainwater to aid California's state bird in the hot summer months. And here you'll find a junction with Canyon Trail (the south loop of the Eisenhower Trail).

Canyon Trail heads up the bajada. After climbing through a little canyon, the trail winds up the south slope of Eisenhower Mountain to a picnic area and a plaque describing the region's date industry.

From the picnic area, you'll descend Eisenhower Mountain, getting good views of the mountains and the Coachella Valley. After passing the signed Eisenhower trailhead, you'll reach the north loop of the Nature Trail and begin heading west down the brittlebush-dotted floodplain back to the exhibit buildings and the central part of the preserve.

Kit Fox

142

Murray Canyon Trail

Andreas Canyon to Murray Canyon
2 miles round trip; 200-foot gain

Season: October-May

In the foothills above Palm Springs are two lovely palm-lined canyons—Andreas and Murray. Both have hundreds of palms, crystalline streams and dramatic rock walls. Andreas, with about 700 native California fan palms and Murray with about 1,000 palms, are among the most populous palm groves in the state. Both canyons are tributaries of nearby Palm Canyon, undisputed king of California's palm oases.

Both canyons honor Palm Springs pioneers. Andreas is named after a Cahuilla Indian chieftan of the late 1800s, while Murray honors irascible Scotsman and dedicated botanist Dr. Welwood Murray, who built a hotel/health resort in the very early days of Palm Springs. Many of those making their way to the Murray Hotel came for the curative climate and the rejuvenation of their health, but a number of literary figures also visited and these scribes soon spread the word that Palm Springs was a very special place indeed.

Andreas Canyon was once a summer retreat for the Agua Caliente band of the Cahuilla. The Indians spent the winter months in the warm Coachella Valley then sought the relative coolness of Andreas and other palm canyons during the warmer months.

Unlike most palm oases, which are fed by underground springs or sluggish seeps, Andreas is watered by a running stream. Fortunately for the palms and other canyon life, white settlers were legally prevented from diverting this stream to the emerging village of Palm Springs. Ranchers and townspeople had to turn to the larger, but notoriously undependable Whitewater River.

Meandering through the tall *Washingtonias*, hikers can travel a ways upstream through Andreas Canyon. Adding to the lush scene are alders and willows, cottonwoods and sycamores.

The trail between Andreas Canyon and Murray Canyon is only a mile long, but you can travel a few more miles up the canyons themselves.

Directions to trailhead: From the junction of State Highway 111 and South Palm Canyon Drive in Palm Springs, proceed south on the latter road for 1½ miles, bearing right at a signed fork. After another mile you'll reach the Agua Caliente Indians Reservation tollgate.

Just after the tollgate, bear right at a signed fork and travel ¾ mile to Andreas Canyon picnic ground. The trail begins at the east end of the splendid picnic area. A sign suggests that Murray Canyon is ''20 min'' away.

The Hike: Notice the soaring, reddish-brown rocks near the trailhead. At the base of these rocks are grinding holes once used by the Cahuilla.

The trail runs south along the base of the mountains. A dramatic backdrop to the path is the desert-facing side of the San Jacinto Mountains.

It's an easy walk, occasionally following a dry streambed. Here, away from water, you encounter more typical desert flora: cholla, hedgehog cacti, burrobush.

When you reach Murray Canyon, you can follow the palms and stream quite a ways up-canyon. Joining the palms are willows, cottonwoods, mesquite, arrowweed and desert lavender. Mistletoe is sometimes draped atop the mesquite and attracts lots of birds.

As you take the trail back to Andreas Canyon you can't help noticing the luxury housing and resort life reaching toward the palm canyons. And you can't help being thankful that these tranquil palm oases are still ours to enjoy.

Murray Canyon

143

Palm Canyon Trail

Hermit's Bench to turnaround
 4 miles round trip; 200-foot gain

Season: October-May

"During the last few years much has been written in newspapers and magazine articles about Palm Canyon. Briefly stated, its charm consists in the startling combination of rocky gorges and canyons, essentially savage and desert-like, with the arboreal grace of tall, tropic-seeming palms growing in native loveliness beside a snow-fed, gushing stream. If the effect of the whole were to be summed up in one word, I think the word would be, not grandeur, nor even beauty, but strangeness to a notable degree."

—Joseph Smeaton Chase, 1922
Our Araby: Palm Springs and the Garden of the Sun

Long forgotten trail rider/nature writer Joseph Smeaton Chase lived the last few years of his life in Palm Springs. He championed the creation of Palm Canyon National Monument, in order to preserve the canyons located on the outskirts of Palm Springs, known collectively as the Indian Canyons—Palm, Murray, and Andreas.

The palm canyons never did achieve National Park Service protection, but are under the jurisdiction of the Agua Caliente Indians and the U.S. Bureau of Land Management's Santa Rosa Mountains National Scenic Area.

The hills and canyons bordering Palms Springs have the greatest concentration of palm trees in the U.S., and in number of trees, Palm Canyon is the uncrowned king of America's desert oases. A meandering stream and lush undergrowth complement over three thousand palms, creating a jungle-like atmosphere in some places.

Palm fans will enjoy viewing the largest concentration of California fan palms, located on the Agua Caliente Indian Reservation. Washingtonia filifera, the palm's botanical name honors our first president, who is more commonly associated with chopping down cherry trees. Some palms are estimated to be 2,000 years old.

Directions to trailhead: From Interstate 10, exit on Highway 111 and proceed to downtown Palm Springs. Highway 111 is also known as Palm Canyon Drive.

Continue through town on Palm Canyon Drive. At a fork, Highway 111 veers east and becomes known as East Palm Canyon Drive. You head straight ahead, south, on South Palm Canyon Drive, following the signs to "Indian Canyons." You'll reach the Aqua Caliente Indians tollgate, where you must pay a fee to enter tribal lands. The reservation is open daily 8:30 A.M. to 5:00 P.M. Parking is a short distance beyond the tollgate at the head of Palm Canyon at Hermit's Bench, where there is a trading post and a good view north into Palm Springs. Many signs remind visitors that they must be off the reservation before 5:00 P.M.

The Hike: From the trading post, the trail descends into the canyon. Some of the palms stand 60 feet tall, with three-foot trunk diameters. In 1980, a fire burned some of the palms just below Hermit's Bench. The trees lived, but today their trunks are black and their skirts short.

The trail follows the canyon for two miles to a tiny grotto that seems an ideal place to turn around.

Hearty adventurers will relish the challenge of proceeding up Palm Canyon seven more miles, gaining 3,000 feet, to a junction with Highway 74, the Palms-to-Pines Highway. Note: This extremely strenuous hike is best done by beginning at the Highway 74 trailhead, hiking down Palm Canyon, and convincing a friend to pick you up at Hermit's Bench.

In 1990, the palm canyons of Palm Springs were placed within a National Scenic Area, administered by the U.S. Bureau of Land Management.

144

Cactus Springs Trail

Pinyon Flat to Horsethief Creek
  5 miles round trip; 900-foot loss

To Cactus Spring
  9 miles round trip; 300-foot gain

Season: All year (best Oct-May)

The Santa Rosas are primarily a desert range and a unique blend of high and low desert environments. Desert-facing slopes of these mountains are treeless—scorched and sparse as the desert itself. Throughout the foothills and canyons, lower Sonoran vegetation—chamise, barrel cactus, ocotillo and waxy creosote—predominate. In some of the canyons with water on or near the surface, oases of native California fan palms form verdant islands on the sand. With an increase in elevation, the wrinkled canyons and dry arroyos give way to mountain crests bristling with pine and juniper.

The Santa Rosa Wilderness, set aside in 1984, lies within the boundaries of the San Bernardino National Forest. Another part of the Santa Rosa Mountains is under state stewardship; it provides protected habitat for the bighorn sheep. A third section, the Santa Rosa Mountains National Scenic Area, under U.S. Bureau of Land Management administration, was established in 1990.

When visiting the Santa Rosas, early California botanist/travel writer Charles Francis Saunders was so overwhelmed by the contrast between the harshness of the lower desert slopes and relative gentleness of the higher slopes that he called it "a botanic version of the millenial day when lion and lamb shall lie down together." Saunders may have massacred a metaphor, but the hiker who dodges cholla and yucca, then takes a snooze upon a soft bed of pinyon pine needles, will find it easy to tell lion from lamb, botanically speaking.

Trails are few in the Santa Rosas; most are faint traces of Cahuilla Indian pathways. The ancients climbed the mountains to hunt deer, gather

pinyon pine nuts, and escape the desert heat. When the snows began, they descended from the high country to the gentle, wintering areas below.

Cactus Spring Trail, an old Indian path overhauled by the Forest Service, gives the hiker a wonderful introduction to the delights of the Santa Rosas.

The trail first takes you to Horsethief Creek, a perennial waterway that traverses high desert country. A hundred years ago, horse thieves pastured their stolen animals in this region before driving them to San Bernardino to sell. The cottonwood-shaded creek invites a picnic. Continuing on the Cactus Spring Trail, you'll arrive at Cactus Spring. Along the trail is some wild country, as undisturbed as it was in 1774 when early Spanish trailblazer Juan Bautista de Anza first saw it.

Two hiking tips: No dependable water source exists along the Cactus Springs Trail, so bring your own. (2) Although the trail traverses a wilderness area, it also crosses private land; please respect private property.

Directions to trailhead: From Highway 111 in Palm Desert, drive 16 miles up Highway 74 to the Pinyon Flat Campground. (From Hemet, it's a 40-mile drive along Highway 74 to Pinyon Flat Campground.) Opposite the campground is Pinyon Flat Transfer Station Road, also signed "Elks Mountain Retreat." You'll follow this road about ¾ miles. Just before reaching the (trash) Transfer Station. a rough dirt road veers to the left. Follow this road 200 yards to road's end.

The Hike: Follow the dirt road east a short distance to Fire Road 7S01, then head south for ¼ mile. You'll then take the first road on your left. A sign reassures you that you are indeed on the way to Cactus Spring, and you'll soon pass the abandoned Dolomite Mine, where limestone was once quarried. Approximately ¼ mile past the mine site, the dirt road peters out and the trail begins. Here you'll find a sign and a trail register.

The trail bears east to the east and dips in and out of several (usually) dry gullies. A half-mile past the sign-in register, a sign welcomes you to the Santa Rosa Wilderness. Cactus Spring Trail does not contour over the hills, but zigs and zags, apparently without rhyme or reason. The bewitching, but easy-to-follow trail finally drops down to Horsethief Creek. At the creek crossing, Horsethief Camp welcomes the weary with flowing water and shade.

Return the same way, explore up and down the handsome canyon cut by Horsethief Creek, or continue to Cactus Spring.

To Cactus Spring: Crossing the creek, you climb east out of the canyon on a rough and steep trail past sentinel yuccas guarding the dry slopes. The trail stays with a wash for a spell (the route through the wash is unmarked except for occasional rock piles), then gently ascends over pinyon pine-covered slopes. It's rolling wild country, a good place to hide out. Alas, Cactus Spring, a few hundred yards north of the trail is almost always dry.

The Hiker's Index

Celebrating the Scenic, the Sublime, and the Ridiculous Points of Interest Visited by this Guide.

Only spot on the U.S. mainland attacked by the Japanese Navy during World War II:
Goleta Beach, February 23, 1942

Spiritual Journeys:
Mt. Zion (San Gabriel Mountains), Solstice Canyon (Santa Monica Mountains), Holy Jim Trail (Santa Ana Mountains)

First federally funded Wilderness Area set aside by Wilderness Act of 1964:
San Rafael Wilderness (Los Padres National Forest)

Southwesternmost point in the contiguous forty-eight states:
Border Field State Park

Largest national forest in California:
Los Padres National Forest

Second-largest national forest in California:
San Bernardino National Forest

Best swimmin' hole:
Santa Ynez River (Los Padres National Forest)

Best historical hike:
Mt. Lowe Railway Trail (San Gabriel Mountains)

California's most expensive state park:
Chino Hills State Park ($47 million spent by the time it opened in 1986)

Least-inspirational name:
(Four-way tie:) Inspiration Point (San Gabriels), Inspiration Point (Santa Ynez Mountains), Inspiration Point (Cuyamaca Mountains), and Inspiration Point (Santa Monica Mountains)

Southland's smallest island:
Santa Barbara Island

Southland's largest island:
Santa Cruz Island

Best Autumn Color:
Sycamore Canyon (Pt. Mugu State Park), Aspen Grove (San Bernardino Mountains), and the black oaks in Cuyamaca Rancho State Park

Most inappropriate place name:
Sandstone Peak—it's granite (Santa Monica Mountains)

Second-most inappropriate place name:
Crystal Cove—nothing is crystalline and there's neither a cove nor coastal indentation of any kind (Orange County)

Best close-up view of the San Andreas Fault:
Devil's Punchbowl County Park

We'll Be Dead Before It's Done Award:
To the Santa Monica Mountains' Backbone Trail—after more than 25 years only two-thirds of this 65-mile trail has been completed

Best wildflower-watching:
Antelope Valley Poppy Reserve, Charmlee County Park (Santa Monica Mountains), and Torrey Pines State Reserve (Del Mar)

Tallest Lodgepole Pine:
World champion Lodgepole in San Bernardino Mountains

Remembering Republican Presidents:
Eisenhower Peak (outside Palm Springs), Reagan Ranch (Santa Monica Mountains), (Grover) Cleveland National Forest, Richard M. Nixon's San Clemente Beach Trail

Most Palms in a Palm Oasis:
Palm Canyon (Palm Springs)

Second-most Palms in a Palm Oasis:
Thousand Palms (Coachella Valley)

Third-most Palms in a Palm Oasis:
Borrego Palm Canyon (Anza-Borrego Desert State Park)

Pardon the obvious:
Ocean Beach (Santa Barbara Co.), High Point (Palomar Mountains)

Devil of a time:
Devil's Punchbowl County Park, Devil's Backbone Trail (to Mt. Baldy), Devil's Slide Trail (San Jacinto Mountains), Devil's Canyon (San Gabriel Mountains), and Devil's Gateway (Los Padres National Forest)

Honoring Southland naturalists:
Edmund Jaeger Trail (living Desert Reserve), and Dick Smith Wilderness Area (Los Padres)

But seriously, they're fun places:
Rattlesnake Canyon (Santa Ynez Mountains), Suicide Rock (San Jacinto Mountains), and Prisoners Bay (Santa Cruz Island)

Least lyrical place name:
Peak 9775 (San Bernardino Mountains); runner-up: Peak 7114 (Los Padres National Forest)

They Must Know We're Coming Award:
Group award to the many national forest and state park ranger stations and visitor information centers that are closed on the weekends—the time when 95 percent of us go for a hike

Information Sources

Angeles National Forest
Headquarters:
701 N. Santa Anita Ave.
Arcadia, CA 91006
(818) 574-5200
Chilao Visitors Center:
Star Route, La Canada 91111
(818) 796-5541
Arroyo Seco Ranger District:
Oak Grove Park
Flintridge, CA 91011

Antelope Valley Calif. Poppy Reserve
15101 Lancaster Road
Lancaster, CA 93536
(805) 724-1180

Anza-Borrego Desert State Park
200 Palm Canyon Dr.
Borrego Springs, CA 92004
(619) 767-5311/767-4205

Avalon Visitors Center
Santa Catalina Island Company
P.O. Box 737
(800) 428-2566

Big Morongo Preserve
P.O. Box 780
Morongo Valley, CA 92256
(619) 363 7190

Border Field State Park
(Frontera District)
Suite 3990 Old Town Avenue
Suite 300-C
San Diego, CA 92110
(619) 238-3195

Cabrillo National Monument
1800 Cabrillo Memorial Drive
P.O. Box 6670
Tip of Point Loma
End of Catalina Boulevard
San Diego, CA 92106
(619) 557-5450

Carbon Canyon Regional Park
4442 Carbon Canyon Road
Brea, CA 92621
(714) 996-5252

Caspers Wilderness Park
33401 Ortega Highway
San Juan Capistrano, CA 92675
(714) 728-0235 / 831-2174

Channel Islands National Park
1901 Spinnaker Drive
Ventura, CA 93001
(805) 658-5700

Cleveland National Forest
(Trabuco District)
1147 E. 6th Street
Corona, CA 91720
(714) 736-1811

Crystal Cove State Park
8471 Pacific Coast Highway
Laguna Beach, CA 92651
(714) 494-3539

Cuyamaca Rancho State Park
12551 Hwy. 79
Descanso, CA 91916
(619) 765-3020

Devil's Punchbowl Co. Reg. Park
28000 Devil's Punchbowl Road
Pearblossom, CA 93553
(805) 944-2743

Joshua Tree National Monument
74485 National Monument Drive
Twentynine Palms, CA 92777
(619) 367-7511

Leo Carrillo State Beach
Santa Monica Mountains Dist. Office
35000 Pacific Coast Highway
Malibu, CA 90265
(310) 706-1310

The Living Desert
47900 Portola Avenue
Palm Desert, CA 92260
(619) 346-5694

Los Padres National Forest
6144 Calle Real
Goleta, CA 93117
(805) 683-6711

Ojai District Office:
1190 E. Ojai Avenue
Ojai, CA 93023
(805) 646-4348

McGrath State Beach
%Channel Coast District
24 E. Main Street
Ventura, CA 93001
(805) 654-4632 / 654-4611

Mt. San Jacinto State Park
P.O. Box 308
Idyllwild, CA 92549
(714) 659-2607

O'Neill Regional Park
30892 Trabuco Canyon Road
Trabuco Canyon, CA 92678
(714) 858-9366

Palm Springs Desert Museum
101 Museum Dr.
Palm Springs, CA 92262
(619) 325-7186

Palomar Mountain State Park
Highway S7, S6
Palomar Mountain, CA 92060
(619) 765-0755

Point Sal State Beach
%La Purisma Mission SHP
2295 Purisima Road
Lompoc, CA 93436
(805) 733-3713

Saddleback Butte State Park
17102 E. Ave. J
Lancaster, CA 93535
(805) 942-0662

San Bernardino National Forest
Big Bear District:
P.O. Box 290
Fawnskin, CA 92333
(909) 866-3437

San Gorgonio District:
34701 Mill Creek Road
Mentone, CA 92359
San Jacinto District:
P.O. Box 518
Idyllwild, CA 92349
(909) 659-2117

Santa Monica Mts. Conservancy
3700 Solstice Canyon road
Malibu, CA 90265
(310) 456-5046

Santa Monica Mts. Dist. Hqts.
Calif. Dept. of Parks and Recreation
2860-A Camino Dos Rios
Newbury Park, CA 91320
(818) 706-1310

Santa Monica Mts. Nat'l. Rec. Area
30401 Agoura Road
Suite 100
Agoura Hills, CA 91301
(818) 888-597 9192

Santiago Oaks Regional Park
2145 North Windes Drive
Orange, CA 92669
(714) 538-4400

Topanga State Park
20829 Entrada Road
Topanga, CA 90290
(213) 455-2465

Torrey Pines State Reserve
12000 N. Torrey Pines Park Road
San Diego, CA 92008
(619) 755-2063

Tucker Wildlife Sanctuary
29322 Modjeska Canyon road
Modjeska Canyon
Orange, CA 92667
(714) 649-2760

Index